Cowboy Hamlets
and zombie Romeos

Manchester University Press

Cowboy Hamlets and zombie Romeos
Shakespeare in genre film

Kinga Földváry

Manchester University Press

Copyright © Kinga Földváry 2020

The right of Kinga Földváry to be identified as the author of this work has been asserted by her in accordance with the Copyright, Designs and Patents Act 1988.

Published by Manchester University Press
Oxford Road, Manchester M13 9PL
www.manchesteruniversitypress.co.uk

British Library Cataloguing-in-Publication Data
A catalogue record for this book is available from the British Library

ISBN 978 1 5261 4209 2 hardback
ISBN 978 1 5261 6713 2 paperback

First published 2020
Paperback published 2022

The publisher has no responsibility for the persistence or accuracy of URLs for any external or third-party internet websites referred to in this book, and does not guarantee that any content on such websites is, or will remain, accurate or appropriate.

Typeset by Servis Filmsetting Ltd, Stockport, Cheshire

To my friends, who taught me to love the cinema

Contents

List of figures	viii
Acknowledgements	xi
Introduction: Shakespeare meets genre film	1

Part I: Classical Hollywood cinema

Introduction	19
1 Will in the Wild West: western adaptations of Shakespeare	34
2 Shakespeare the tear-jerker: from woman's film to global melodrama	72
3 Dark-minded Othellos, mobster Macbeths: *film noir*, gangster, gangster *noir*	104

Part II: Contemporary blockbusters

Introduction	147
4 Back to school, Will: Shakespeare the teen idol	170
5 Shakespeare the undead: a renaissance of vampires and zombies	210
6 Will, Bill and the Earl: versions of the author in contemporary biopics	247
Conclusion	285
Bibliography	290
Filmography	310
Index	316

Figures

1.1 Anne Baxter in *Yellow Sky*. Directed by William A. Wellman, 1948. Twentieth Century Fox. 39
1.2 Robert Wagner and Jean Peters in *Broken Lance*. Directed by Edward Dmytryk, 1954. Twentieth Century Fox. 45
1.3 Felicia Farr and Glenn Ford in *Jubal*. Directed by Delmer Daves, 1956. Columbia Pictures. 51
1.4 Stefanie Powers, Patrick Wayne, Maureen O'Hara and John Wayne in *McLintock!* Directed by Andrew V. McLaglen, 1963. Batjac Productions. 55
1.5 Andrea Giordana and Gilbert Roland in *Johnny Hamlet* or *Quella sporca storia nel West*. Directed by Enzo G. Castellari, 1968. Daiano Film/Leone Film. 61
1.6 Tonto, Art Carney and Barbara Rhoades in *Harry and Tonto*. Directed by Paul Mazursky, 1974. Twentieth Century Fox. 67
2.1 Miriam Hopkins and Gertrude Lawrence in *Men Are Not Gods*. Directed by Walter Reisch, 1936. London Film Productions. 75
2.2 Paul Harris and Marti Stevens in *All Night Long*. Directed by Basil Dearden, 1962. The Rank Organisation. 84
2.3 Michelle Williams, Jessica Lange and Elisabeth Moss in *A Thousand Acres*. Directed by Jocelyn Moorhouse, 1997. Touchstone Pictures/Propaganda Films/Prairie Films/Beacon Pictures/Via Rosa Productions. 92
2.4 Sharmila Tagore in *Life Goes On*. Directed by Sangeeta Datta, 2009. SD Films/Stormglass Productions. 94

List of figures

3.1	James Lydon in *Strange Illusion*. Directed by Edgar G. Ulmer, 1945. Producers Releasing Corporation.	110
3.2	Ronald Colman and Shelley Winters in *A Double Life*. Directed by George Cukor, 1947. Kanin Productions/Universal.	118
3.3	Ruth Roman and Paul Douglas in *Joe Macbeth*. Directed by Ken Hughes, 1955. Columbia Pictures/Film Locations.	125
3.4	Mark Wahlberg and Joaquin Phoenix in *We Own the Night*. Directed by James Gray, 2007. Columbia Pictures/2929 Productions/Industry Entertainment.	139
4.1	Heath Ledger and Julia Stiles in *10 Things I Hate About You*. Directed by Gil Junger, 1999. Touchstone Pictures/Mad Chance/Jaret Entertainment.	174
4.2	Jordan Ladd, Drew Barrymore, Michael Vartan and Martha Hackett in *Never Been Kissed*. Directed by Raja Gosnell, 1999. Fox 2000 Pictures/Flower Films/Bushwood Pictures/Twentieth Century Fox.	179
4.3	Channing Tatum and Amanda Bynes in *She's the Man*. Directed by Andy Fickman, 2006. DreamWorks/Lakeshore Entertainment/Donners' Company.	185
4.4	Josh Hartnett in *O*. Directed by Tim Blake Nelson, 2001. Chickie the Cop/Daniel Fried Productions/Dimension Films/FilmEngine/Rhulen Entertainment.	193
4.5	Piper Perabo in *Lost and Delirious*. Directed by Léa Pool, 2001. Cité-Amérique/Dummett Films.	199
4.6	Tanner Cohen in *Were the World Mine*. Directed by Tom Gustafson, 2008. SPEAKproductions/The Group Entertainment.	203
5.1	Kate Beckinsale in *Underworld*. Directed by Len Wiseman, 2003. Lakeshore Entertainment/Subterranean Productions/Underworld Produktions GmbH/Laurinfilm.	217
5.2	Mike Landry and John Ventimiglia in *Rosencrantz and Guildenstern are Undead*. Directed by Jordan Galland, 2009. C Plus Pictures/Off Hollywood Pictures/Offhollywood Digital.	220
5.3	Chloë Grace Moretz and Kodi Smit-McPhee in *Let Me In*. Directed by Matt Reeves, 2010. Overture Films/Exclusive Media Group/Hammer Films/EFTI.	225
5.4	Hulk Hogan in *Zombie Hamlet*. Directed by John Murlowski, 2012. Three Girls Running/Maple Island Films/Zombie Hamlet.	231

5.5	Nicholas Hoult and Teresa Palmer in *Warm Bodies*. Directed by Jonathan Levine, 2013. Summit Entertainment/Make Movies/Mandeville Pictures/Quebec Film and Television Tax Credit.	240
6.1	Gwyneth Paltrow in *Shakespeare in Love*. Directed by John Madden, 1998. Universal Pictures/Miramax/The Bedford Falls Company.	253
6.2	Indira Varma and Rupert Graves in *A Waste of Shame*. Directed by John McKay, 2005. British Broadcasting Corporation.	258
6.3	Sebastian Armesto and Rhys Ifans in *Anonymous*. Directed by Roland Emmerich, 2011. Columbia Pictures/Relativity Media/Centropolis Entertainment/Studio Babelsberg.	265
6.4	Helen McCrory in *Bill*. Directed by Richard Bracewell, 2015. BBC Films/Cowboy Films/Punk Cinema.	273
6.5	Kenneth Branagh in *All is True*. Directed by Kenneth Branagh, 2018. TKBC.	277

Acknowledgements

A book that has been in the making for nearly a decade will inevitably be indebted to many people and institutions that have in one way or another contributed to its creation along the way. Looking back on these years, I have to confess that probably the best thing about such a long journey was this accumulation of friends and companions, who have helped me and this project by providing support in various ways, giving feedback and criticism, sharing their ideas and materials with me, or simply standing by patiently while I kept dragging my writing feet.

First and foremost, I wish to express my gratitude to my workplace, Pázmány Péter Catholic University, and all the institutional and departmental heads that I have had the honour to work with, for allowing me precious research time when I most needed it, and most of all, for their encouragement throughout these years. The warm and friendly atmosphere of our constantly changing venues testifies to both the strength of our community and the leadership. The Renaissance Research Group – aka the Renaisséance – has given invaluable feedback on several earlier fragments of this manuscript, and I continue to be inspired by the research conducted by my friends and colleagues, Zsolt Almási, Gabriella Reuss, Veronika Schandl, Erzsébet Stróbl, Katalin Tabi, and our founding father, Tibor Fabiny. Pázmány Péter Catholic University also provided me with generous grants from the Központi Alapok Program budget, which allowed me to gain access to books and journals, research and conference trips, and even a semester on leave. During that semester I had the opportunity to work in the Shakespeare Research Library of Ludwig-Maximilians-Universität in Munich, where I could always count on Bettina Boecker's expert advice whenever I needed it. That semester-long trip was funded by the

Katholischer Akademischer Ausländer-Dienst, whose support allowed me to concentrate all my energies on the task at hand, for which I am extremely grateful. Earlier research trips took me to the University of Notre Dame, thanks to the generosity of the Nanovic Institute for European Studies, and to the Shakespeare Institute of the University of Birmingham in Stratford-upon-Avon, on a research grant from the European Society for the Study of English.

Beyond the immediate circle of my colleagues and friends, however, I have been fortunate to meet many others whose feedback on my conference papers, essays, and ideas has been equally fundamental for this project. Mariangela Tempera, who is sorely missed by everyone who had the good fortune to know her, was always a generous provider of otherwise inaccessible films and sharp-sighted critical advice. Victoria Bladen, Sarah Hatchuel, Diana Henderson, Peter Holland, Douglas Lanier, Nathalie Vienne-Guerrin and countless others have welcomed me into their discussions with a warmth and openness that was the best motivation for pursuing research on screen adaptations of Shakespeare's work. I am grateful for John Jowett's advice on the first version of my book proposal, and I am also heavily indebted to the Hungarian Shakespeare Committee and all its members, particularly Natália Pikli, our President, and Péter Dávidházi, my former supervisor, whose continued support for my work always reminds me of the sizeable shoes I am trying to fill. Equally heartfelt thanks must go to the Jágónak conference, in itself an institution of Shakespeare research in Hungary, which shows that it is possible to combine the highest professional ideals with the friendliest of atmospheres – living proof that Shakespeare can and should continue to be a vital force in our lives.

I also have to acknowledge my debt to my students, whose questions, comments, interest (and sometimes lack thereof) provided me with much needed feedback and inspiration even when I was not directly engaged in the writing of this volume. Nikkie Whan and her family, and Ursula Sauer, have provided me with homes away from home, but, more importantly, they have offered me their friendship. Last but not least, my deepest gratitude must go to my family and friends, first and foremost to Béla Polyák, who did not spare either himself or the text when I asked for his advice, and to countless others, who may or may not have shared my concerns with obscure genre films or grand Shakespearean ideas, but who have never failed to encourage me to keep working on what seemed at times a never-ending story, and who were always there for me, waiting patiently until I would re-emerge from this project and once again join their company.

Acknowledgements

Earlier versions of some of my film analyses appeared in several essays, although the text, its interpretive context, and often the conclusions have undergone considerable revision since the previous versions. Minor passages in the Introduction have been taken from my '"Brush Up Your Shakespeare": Genre-Shift from Shakespeare to the Screen', published in S. A. Brown, R. I. Lublin, and L. McCulloch (eds), *Reinventing the Renaissance: Shakespeare and his Contemporaries in Adaptation and Performance* (Basingstoke: Palgrave Macmillan, 2013). An earlier version of my interpretation of *Life Goes On* was published as 'Postcolonial Hybridity: The Making of a Bollywood *Lear* in London', in *Shakespeare: Journal of the British Shakespeare Association*, 9:3 (2013). Finally, some passages on *A Double Life* appeared in S. Hatchuel and N. Vienne-Guerrin (eds), *Shakespeare on Screen: Othello* (Cambridge: Cambridge University Press, 2015), and parts of my reading of *Yellow Sky* appeared in 'Ghost Towns and Alien Planets: Variations on Prospero's Island in Screen Versions of *The Tempest*', in S. Hatchuel and N. Vienne-Guerrin (eds), *Shakespeare on Screen: The Tempest and Late Romances* (Cambridge: Cambridge University Press, 2017). My gratitude must also extend to all colleagues and editors involved in the making of these publications; even more importantly, I am extremely grateful to the anonymous reviewers for their helpful comments on all versions of the manuscript, and the unfailing support of Matthew Frost and all his colleagues at Manchester University Press.

Introduction:
Shakespeare meets genre film

Romeo as a love-struck zombie, Hamlet as a cowboy riding off into the sunset, Katherine the Shrew leading Her Majesty's Opposition and King Lear heading a dynasty of circus acrobats – you name it, we have it! By the twenty-first century, one can hardly think of popular genre themes or settings that have not been tried and tested in screen adaptations of Shakespearean drama. The other side of the coin is equally remarkable: it is not simply adaptors of Shakespeare who rely on popular visual formats, but creators of popular visual culture also mine his work for inspiration, and as a result, Shakespeare is practically everywhere in our contemporary mediascape. Cinema and television audiences have been familiar with his name since the birth of these media, and not only does he appear as author of canonical, highbrow texts, but also as the best source of plots and ideas for writers and directors of new (or newly minted) popular works. Naturally, the quality and diversity of the resulting adaptations show a broad range between the extremes of visionary works of creative art and shamelessly derivative commercial products. And yet we may be surprised when we realise the sheer quantity of films that have been inspired by Shakespeare's *oeuvre* in some way or another, and particularly the fact that the eagerness of scriptwriters and adaptors to turn to his work for inspiration has not noticeably dwindled, even in the twenty-first century amid the proliferation of new media forms. The vast number of films based on, or associating themselves with Shakespeare's *oeuvre* speaks volumes for his continued presence in visual culture, which in turn testifies to the – possibly diminishing and clearly changed, but still undeniable – significance of the 'Shakespeare film' as a phenomenon and to the vitality of the Shakespeare cult as a whole.

Nonetheless, the concept of the 'Shakespeare film' needs careful (re)consideration, as it seems no longer a viable category that could mark out a distinct group of films, although the phrase still carries some meaning not only for scholars but for general audiences as well. The notions of both 'Shakespeare' and 'film' have recently come under attack on several fronts, but even if we disregard for a moment the uncertainties surrounding them and attempt to mark out the territory of the Shakespeare film based on generally accepted principles, we have to realise that it is practically impossible to reach a consensus.

The problem is, on the one hand, that in a number of scholarly accounts the term tends to include only the straightforward, textually faithful, visually often conservative adaptations, disregarding the less respectful derivatives whose connections to Shakespeare may not even be recognised by most viewers. On the other hand, if we take the more flexible approach and open up the category of Shakespeare films to allow practically every Shakespeare-related moving picture to find a place in this class, then the category will be useless by virtue of its indiscriminate inclusivity. While I believe that this inclusive approach is still the lesser of two evils, and the more instructive one by far when it comes to understanding the ways Shakespeare is present in contemporary culture, the scope of examples comprised in such a category also creates more problems than solutions. Consequently, it becomes necessary to lay down some organising principles, to bring at least a semblance of order to this chaos, if we wish to have an overview of Shakespeare-inspired moving images, since the appropriate taxonomy is often crucial for understanding the nature of the work itself and therefore providing a sound basis for interpretation.

This is where I believe film genre as a category may prove to be the key, as producers, critics and audiences equally rely on generic identification when they define or describe moving pictures. Consequently, this volume argues that the most efficient approach to the understanding of film adaptations must be based on the adapting genre, that is, the *type* of film created as the end product of the adaptation process. I intend to point out that the very same genres that we encounter and recognise in the world of global cinema are relevant not simply for the classification and interpretation of films based on original screenplays, but for adaptations as well, including those inspired by Shakespearean drama. Naturally, any genre-based study needs to be aware of the dangers inherent in such an approach, as John G. Cawelti summarises the limitations of genre criticism: 'It tends to lose sight of the genius of individual works and creators. It can encourage the kind of proliferating pigeonholing of the arts which Shakespeare satirized in Polonius' speech on the varieties of drama.'[1] In a sense, therefore, Shakespeare's reputation as a genius, and the tradition of appreciating his dramas for their merits, rather than as generic products, may be safeguards against the trap genre criticism could unwittingly create.

After all, Shakespeare is particularly suitable for such synthesising and generalising overviews by virtue of the number of existing variants, whether called appropriations, derivatives, offshoots or simply adaptations, since all forms of reworkings are examples of his continuing cultural influence. This sheer quantity allows us to draw broader conclusions, and achieve more far-reaching, statistically more convincing results than a smaller *oeuvre* – a more limited dataset – would make possible. While the adaptation industry uses and abuses the work of Jane Austen and Charles Dickens with equal vigour, it is indubitable that Shakespeare's plays have inspired cinematic adaptations on an unparalleled scale, in practically all known cinematic genres. Examples range from science fiction to the western, the gangster film and *film noir*, animations and teen flicks, romantic comedies and melodramas, epic costume dramas, fantasy films and musicals, to name but a few of the long and rapidly growing list. We may thus safely claim that Shakespeare-inspired movies perfectly exemplify the colourful palette of the practically endless variety of genre adaptation.

This variety of genres is all the more interesting as these clearly have had greater influence on the adaptation process than the limited number of Aristotelian or early modern English dramatic genres of the source texts. (The Folio editors only distinguished comedy, tragedy and history, after all.) Sometimes, with the help of very simple modifications of plot or characterisation, originally tragic plots are adapted into romantic comedies, transforming *Othello* into *Stage Beauty* (2004, dir. Richard Eyre) or retelling *King Lear* with slightly more optimism in *A Bunch of Amateurs* (2008, dir. Andy Cadiff). *Romeo and Juliet* has also been 're-animated' in the happily ending *Gnomeo & Juliet* (2011, dir. Kelly Asbury), where no less an authority than the statue of William Shakespeare makes a cynical-sounding, but essentially metadramatic remark on the tyranny of authorial control over a comic or tragic *denouement*. This stone-hearted Bard admits to a love-stricken Gnomeo how simple it would be to avert the imminent tragic ending, but for the fact that he likes 'the whole death part better'.[2] Adaptations that undermine or fully reverse an originally comic ending can also be found, for example in *The Merchant of Venice* (2004, dir. Michael Radford) or in Christine Edzard's *As You Like It* (1992), where not even the formally intact romantic ending is able to express real optimism about the future. An even more straightforward example is 'Léa Pool's subversive indie tragedy *Lost and Delirious* (2001)',[3] discussed in Chapter 4, which is loosely based on Shakespeare's *Twelfth Night*, but has no trace of comedy in its conclusion.

The importance of film genres in the interpretation of adaptations is not a completely new discovery, of course, and in order to understand the state of affairs today, it is crucial to look back on how film genre studies gained acceptance in academic research. Taking its cue from literary genre analyses, the systematic theoretical study of cinematic genres became widespread in the 1970s, in response to the *auteur* theory that dominated post-war criticism. Genre studies then found popular support for its thorough and enlightening readings of a number of classical Hollywood genres, particularly the western, *film noir* or the musical. Edward Buscombe, Steve Neale, Rick Altman, and others pointed out how a common set of conventions dominate – and conversely, even retrospectively define – the production and interpretation of films and popular culture in general.[4] Later, however, some of the very same critics raised their doubts concerning the existence of genres themselves – put simply: whether genres only exist because we talk about them, or if they can truly be found in an abstract and ideal form as well. Altman's *Film/Genre* investigated the issue with an uncompromising critical thoroughness, yet his provocative conclusions – that it is indeed criticism that creates and upholds generic concepts – did not result in a complete dismissal of genre study.[5] Even if partly out of habit, reference to genres is still commonplace practice in all three pillars of film study (production, reception and criticism), and whether this means that genres have always been here, or that they are here to stay – or possibly neither – it makes them eminently useful in general descriptions and classifications of films.

At the same time, it is also important to acknowledge that twenty-first-century film and media theory has moved beyond traditional descriptive uses of genre theory, and using some of the conclusions, and even more of the burning questions of earlier research, investigates the constantly changing fields of digital media and previously unexplored relationships between consumers of popular culture.[6] The very same explorations have also been taken up by Shakespeare studies, as discussed below in this Introduction, making a genre-based reading of Shakespeare adaptations a seemingly dated enterprise, but one which nonetheless needs to be completed, I would argue, to fill a gap that should by rights have been filled decades ago. This is what I have undertaken to accomplish in this volume, in the hope that my findings will prove useful even in a considerably changed media environment compared to the one that produced most of the films discussed here.

Naturally, I would not wish to claim that genre-centred studies of Shakespeare films have never been written before, as there have been many individual essays, even monographs, dedicated to comparing various adaptations, including genre films, based on the same dramatic source text, or conversely, examining several Shakespeare texts adapted into the same commercial film genre. And yet this aspect of films rarely merits a central role in analyses, let alone becomes an organising principle in book-length studies. Yvonne Griggs goes as far as claiming that 'there remains a critical resistance to genre readings of screen Shakespeare and an academic disregard for film adaptations that openly identify their genre roots',[7] although her own volume on *Screen Adaptations: Shakespeare's King Lear* takes a giant step in the direction of including genre films as equal participants in the discourse. (Not all volumes in the *Screen Adaptations* series are as inclusive, however.) Another important essay, Harry Keyishian's analysis of *Hamlet* and movie genre, anticipates at the dawn of the new millennium that 'as more Shakespeare comes to the screen, it will not develop towards some standard, self-contained genre, but will instead be more fully dispersed among existing genres'.[8] Keyishian has been proved right in the growing proportion of genre-inflected films, as opposed to traditional *auteur* versions, but genre-based interpretations have not followed suit, at least certainly not to the same extent. Yet I believe that it is not only in the twenty-first century that we have been able to find Shakespeare fitting into popular movie genres, but the very same generic dispersion has characterised Shakespeare adaptations from the earliest days of film history. That is why, in my view, it is worth revisiting the cornucopia of adaptations produced throughout cinema history, and look at them with a more consistently genre-based approach.

Although the concentration on genre and the organisation of the volume may suggest that film genre is a clear and straightforward concept in itself, unfortunately, this is very far from the case. Quite the contrary: the difficulty of finding any generally acceptable definition for the notion of genre reveals the complexity of forces at work behind audience choices and marketing decisions, which all find expression in generic labels. Cinematic genre, in the broadest and most popular usage of the term, is based on the system of audience expectations targeted (and shaped) by industrial decisions. In the words of Sarah Berry-Flint: 'Genres offer prospective customers a way to choose between films and help indicate the kind of audience for whom a particular movie was made.'[9] Along these lines, we can find genres based on the age or gender of the target audience (e.g. teen film, woman's film or chick-flick, family entertainment or children's film); the theme, a favoured location or certain properties of the plot (e.g. horror, western, thriller); typical characters (e.g. gangster or superhero films); material qualities or cinematic technique (e.g. animation, *film noir*, expressionist film); or even the dominance of diegetic music, song or dance (musical, opera or ballet film). In other cases, genre may reflect a cinematic era; that is how we recognise a typical 1930s melodrama, can point out French or Czech New Wave films, or New Hollywood blockbusters, since all these groups usually share stylistic or technical features as well as the dates of their production. The role of production studios can be no less significant in defining certain genres, as MGM musicals, Gainsborough melodramas or Hammer horror became known on both sides of the Atlantic, and even today, Disney animations, Marvel superhero films and plenty of other works are associated with their production background.

What further complicates the theoretical background of genre-based studies is the fact that despite its many branches and several outstanding authors, genre theory does not offer an easily generalisable overview of the basic criteria that could be used in the characterisation of all genres. There is a similar uncertainty regarding the acceptance of certain genres as genres per se, as opposed to seeing them as stylistic features, thematic elements or other descriptive criteria (melodrama and *film noir* being two such problematic, though commonly used, terms). At the same time, the fact that genres as labels are recognised and employed by producers and critics as well as consumers in a more or less consistent manner, makes it clear that genre as a term (and its application to a set of commonly agreed concepts) is perfectly apt in describing production and consumption patterns of commercial cinema. Marcia Landy expresses the insights of a theoretical approach to genre texts:

> Genre study has called attention to the reciprocal function of texts, that they are a contract between the audience and the film, thus challenging the notion that audiences are totally passive victims manipulated by the culture industry. Moreover, genres are not static. They make concessions to their changing audiences through the renewal and transformation of their filmic conventions.[10]

The way changing societies leave their marks on generic conventions is illustrated particularly nicely by the genres with the longest cinematic history. As the first group of genres examined in this volume testifies, traditional genres of Hollywood cinema have mutated throughout their history to accommodate new social demands, while retaining a consistent core of their elements, and these transformed generic conventions are also reflected in the Shakespeare adaptations that make use of them.

This approach, though, does not mean that each and every (or indeed any) film could or should be put into a single genre category, particularly as the purity of genres has long been debated (and refuted) by genre theory as well as commonplace viewing experience.[11] Investigating genre in an altogether different context, Jacques Derrida's 1979 lecture entitled 'The Law of Genre' may be consulted for an apt illustration of how an acceptance of generic hybridity is not inimical to a genre-based approach. In his philosophical account, Derrida describes the law of genre as 'a principle of contamination, a law of impurity, a parasitical economy', speaking 'of a sort of participation without belonging – a taking part in without being part of, without having membership in a set'.[12] This 'sort of participation' is an ideally tentative description of what the average viewer often experiences when encountering commercial cinema: seeing a product that gives the impression of unity and relative originality, while it also displays a number of elements familiar from previous works. Moreover, this familiarity, although it creates expectations which may or may not be fulfilled by the product, also allows consumers to acquire a set of interpretational tools that accumulate, but do not expire or lose their relevance even if tested on further products. The seemingly disorganised, but intricately associated, network of both interpretive frameworks and the works they are abstracted from may in turn recall another theory, Gilles Deleuze and Félix Guattari's concept of the rhizome, brought to bear on Shakespeare criticism by Douglas Lanier.[13] As Lanier argues, 'a rhizomatic conception of Shakespeare stresses the power of those ever-differentiating particulars – specific adaptations, allusions, performances – to transform and restructure the aggregated Shakespearean field into something forever new'.[14]

Subscribing to this understanding of Shakespeare-related moving images as equally participating in and contributing to an infinite and endlessly changing field, what this volume intends to show is how certain elements of genres, some of them central, others marginal, may be present even in films that are primarily known as adaptations based on Shakespeare's work. As a result, we may only do justice to a teen adaptation such as *10 Things I Hate About You* (1999, dir. Gil Junger) if we realise that the reason why it has discarded the Shakespearean dialogue lies precisely in its participation in the genre of the teen film. In the same way, an alternative ending to an originally tragic plot may be explained by the need to create a convincing *denouement* for a western, where the hero is obliged to ride off into the sunset, as happens in *Johnny Hamlet* (1968, dir. Enzo G. Castellari).

Similarly, the distinctive camerawork of a romantic comedy, maximising the star appeal of celebrity actors, will override critical concerns for more subtle character development or narrative tension present in the source text.

While Lanier introduces his concept of rhizomatic criticism as an alternative for 'post-fidelity' Shakespeare,[15] we may still need to look back briefly on how film adaptations of literary works have traditionally been examined and classified: on the basis of their supposed proximity or loyalty to the original. Even today, audiences tend to compare their viewing experiences with textual sources – if they are aware of those – and filmmakers continue to make generous use of terms such as 'fidelity' and 'authenticity' as part of their marketing strategies, employing the Shakespearean label as the authority that may help to sell the product on the high-culture market.[16] Nonetheless, the mainstream critical tendency of the 2010s shows that by now, it is not only the Shakespearean text and its centrality in adaptation studies that have been destabilised, but also film and traditional media have been replaced by new media forms in research questions, expanding the field to include video games, computer animations, vlogs, interactive websites and other computer-based forms of media distribution. Shakespeare as an icon and a household name is still present in contemporary culture, but in a considerably different manner than even at the end of the millennium, a few decades ago. This altered consciousness of what constitutes Shakespeare therefore needs examination. Before we dismiss contemporary popular culture's knowledge of Shakespeare as minimal or even non-existent, it may be worthwhile to ponder on the implications of the altered cultural context in which short quotations, randomly poached snatches of text, fake quotations authenticated with an image and a name find a natural place.[17] This fragmented textual presence is one of the common features of the three genres examined in Part II of the volume, the teen film, undead horror and the biopic. These genres have come to new prominence since the 1990s, and they consequently display postmodern tendencies, especially in their 'disrespectful' attitude to the original text and in the absence of a desire to recreate the source work in any manner other than parody or pastiche.

Alongside its engagement with digital media, contemporary adaptation studies also appears to strive for more applicable – and more flexible – definitions of what adaptation itself means. As scholars are no longer satisfied with the definitions offered by Linda Hutcheon and Julie Sanders in their ground-breaking works, today the questioning of even the possibility of such clear-cut definitions as theirs is the norm rather than the exception.[18] For instance, Kate Newell argues in her *Expanding*

Adaptation Networks: From Illustration to Novelization that 'Linda Hutcheon's often-cited definition [that] defines adaptation-the-product as "an extended, deliberate, announced revisitation of a particular work of art"' is no longer tenable.[19] As Newell points out, adaptations often exist in what appear to be networks, rather than one-to-one relationships, between one particular source work and a derivative product. In such networks (which may remind us of Lanier's rhizomes), new products may revisit a group of earlier works, such as a previous film, an illustrated book or even a well-known musical adaptation of a text, in ways that are possibly neither announced, nor extended, and sometimes not even entirely deliberate – but most certainly not referencing a single and particular source work. Another volume dedicated to the ways such inspirations can be meaningful and significant even when not announced is Eric S. Mallin's 2019 *Reading Shakespeare in the Movies: Non-Adaptations and Their Meaning*. Mallin describes his volume 'as a study about movies that do not know they are Shakespeare plays', and yet elements of Shakespeare's plays are embedded in these films in 'fortuitous, often uncanny, sometimes inevitable ways'.[20] This in turn confirms what Newell suggested: that it is not only works with announced and deliberate connections to their source work that are worth discussing within the framework of adaptation studies.

Other twenty-first-century volumes' research questions are directed against the definitions and the definability of seemingly clear-cut terms, such as adaptation, original or source work, product and process, even the notions of producer and consumer, and the relationship between the two. Instead of – or beside – audiences, we can now talk about users, as it appears in the title of *The Shakespeare User*, which 'specifically attends to Shakespeare use in the digital age and principally turns its critical attention to user agency and authority in the face of shifting cultural practices that take place in both offline and online contexts'.[21] The authors emphasise how the notion of the network is apparent not only in connection with the various creative products, but on the human side as well: contemporary society is a networked society, in which technology is a prime enabler of changing social relations. Another volume in Palgrave Macmillan's Reproducing Shakespeare series (edited by Thomas Cartelli and Katherine Rowe), *Shakespeare/Not Shakespeare*, edited by Christy Desmet, Natalie Loper and Jim Casey, broadens the field in similar directions, asking the probing question: 'What is at stake in confronting the binary opposition between what is and what is "not" Shakespeare?'[22]

Questions such as these then quickly take us to the examination of new forms of production and performance, as in Stephen O'Neill's *Shakespeare and YouTube*, or his edited collection on the role of new technologies in our understanding of what 'Shakespeare' is.[23] Equally vital theoretical concerns are addressed by volumes which approach the recent phenomenon of the so-called 'live' (or 'as-live') theatre broadcast from a variety of viewpoints, emphasising the necessity of a complete theoretical revision of what performance and adaptation mean today. As the editors of *Shakespeare and the 'Live' Theatre Broadcast Experience* discuss Phyllida Lloyd's *Julius Caesar* in 2017, their 'engagement with this production during and after the screening spoke to the important and ongoing shift in how audiences participate in an event, are present in the theatre and interact with one another and with stage performances of Shakespeare'.[24]

The list could – and even should – go on, since I am fully aware that more and more ground-breaking new research is being published as we speak, and most critical works in the late 2010s address much more topical issues than this present volume has set out to do. As new media formats keep bombarding us with ever more innovative media content, vying for our attention, it is indeed vital that we try to follow their novelties with our critical methodologies, and remind ourselves of the mercurial nature of contemporary culture, constantly changing in invisible yet unstoppable ways, at such a speed that neither our research nor our publishing practices can keep up with. And yet, however paradoxical it seems, I believe that it is precisely because the world is moving ahead so fast that there is still a need to fill the gaps which we have left in the foundations of our research. That is why I propose in this volume a traditional, even conservative, reading of an increasingly outdated – although still lively and eminently adaptable – format: a genre-based reading of Shakespeare-inspired films.

Since I believe that it is their genre frameworks that define the most important qualities of film adaptations, the volume is organised around genres, rather than literary texts, in order to enable us to see the common features and make the connections between various cinematic products. What I wish to offer is a new perspective, which may help us to find the systematic features among the daunting number of Shakespeare adaptations. I hope that by collecting and combining my own understanding of the films with what others have written before, I can give the reader the impression that pieces of a puzzle are finally falling into place. Some of what follows might therefore appear self-evident, and even seem like the natural way of looking at the world of the cinema, since my claim is based on the strong conviction that genres are natural categories, used by all and sundry, whether by general cinemagoers or Shakespeare scholars (or both).

Although I have repeatedly claimed that the study of genres is old-fashioned, I still believe that the discussion does have continued relevance, even in this most advanced and technologically inclined world we inhabit in the twenty-first century. One way of justifying this attention to genre is the observation of algorithms, whether employed by social media sites, online marketplaces or digital archives, which constantly apply generic criteria when organising their big data into meaningful categories. They try to induce us to consume more based on our earlier search and purchase histories, or other measurements of our digital footprint. Looking at Amazon, the Internet Movie Database or any online marketplace – advertising their new offerings with the catchphrase: 'if you liked this product, you may like that one as well' – it becomes clear that the relationship between these items is a similarity of kind, which may be supported by thematic, stylistic or technical connections, in a system strikingly reminiscent of genres.

Much has been said thus far in this Introduction about the vast number of films that are in one way or another associated with Shakespeare's work, but since this volume does not aspire to encyclopaedic breadths, I am only too well aware of the multitude of screen products that had to be left out of the discussion, and therefore of the need for some justification of my selection. Although the best-known and most famous Shakespeare adaptations – the *auteur* films – are the ones that are systematically absent from the volume, I also specified further criteria for inclusion. My focus here lies on films that are typically not known (or have not been marketed) as Shakespeare films, although they contain a Shakespearean plotline or conflict, or even a set of recognisably Shakespearean characters. These are often films that scholars describe as appropriations, derivatives or offshoots, but in this volume the term 'adaptation' is employed for all adapted works throughout, since I do not believe that the usual distinctions between the various other terms used in the literature are particularly helpful or reliable. Adaptations that have used a literary work for their inspiration could be arranged on a continuous scale, representing various types and stages of fidelity, but the dividing lines between these stages are nowhere near as precise as the proliferation of terminology would suggest.

The films discussed in the volume are works typically described as genre films: popular or commercial products first and Shakespeare adaptations only second. Their script is primarily in English, yet all of them abandon the original early modern language of the dramatic dialogues and keep no more than selected fragments of it; nonetheless, the Shakespearean elements in their plotlines are either explicit or easily recognisable for viewers with some knowledge of the source material. My primary reason for this choice is rooted in the belief that these films might play a more fundamental and more democratic role in the Shakespeare cult, as they do not wish to uphold the elitist and respectful status of their canonical source. On the contrary, they intend to disseminate Shakespeare's *oeuvre* to a broader range of consumers, and since these films tend to gain less attention than the more lauded *auteur* adaptations, they still have the power to surprise us with their ingenuity. In brief: they are more often appreciated for the kind of film they are than for the prestige of their literary source.

As a result of the choice of films and method of investigation, this study cannot and should not be expected to provide an overview of all Shakespeare film adaptations. What it intends to be is rather an alternative, or possibly a complementary, volume to other accounts, either those investigating the screen versions of a single source text, like the excellent Shakespeare on Screen series edited by Sarah Hatchuel and Nathalie Vienne-Guerrin, or discussions of individual genres or *auteurs*. In this way, it hopes to open up the field of Shakespeare on screen studies to areas where only the rare enthusiast has ventured so far. At the same time, I believe that the approach illustrated here could be enlightening and useful for the broader field of adaptation studies as well, employed to examine either adaptations of other English classics, such as those by Jane Austen or Charles Dickens, or contemporary bestsellers, or even practically unknown source texts. I like to believe that the colourful diversity and wide applicability of Shakespeare to popular culture that the volume exemplifies will also add to our appreciation of the Shakespeare cult and show the continuing presence of the Bard in our times.

After so many disclaimers, I fear yet another one is in order, for leaving out so many films that are no doubt several readers' favourites. Being spoilt for choice, I have eventually narrowed my focus to two groups of three genres each, one from the classical Hollywood period, and another one that came into prominence around the 1990s. The first part of the volume deals with the western, the melodrama and the gangster *noir* (the latter group combining features that are often treated as distinct genres). Taking examples of Shakespeare-inspired films from various stages within the development of each of these genres, we can observe not only the ways various individual films comply with the requirements set by their generic contexts, but also how subsequent periods of filmmaking have left their mark on the genres themselves. The films discussed have been shaped by the historical periods of their creation, following and confirming social changes and new artistic expectations. As a result, these chapters also offer a quasi-historical overview, not primarily of Shakespeare adaptations, but of the life cycle of the genres themselves.

A major omission in Part I of the volume is, of course, the musical, one of the signature genres of the classical Hollywood era, and one which has produced a number of extremely successful Shakespeare variants as well. Nevertheless, I believe the musical is one of those genres that have been treated extensively, both within the sphere of genre criticism and Shakespeare adaptation studies. Apart from two recent monographs, Frances Teague's *Shakespeare and the American Popular Stage* and Irene G. Dash's *Shakespeare and the American Musical*, Shakespeare-inspired musical films are regularly discussed in journals and essay collections, therefore they do not seem to suffer from the critical neglect I wanted to remedy in connection with other genre products.[25] Yet the previous – if not abundant, at least sufficient – scholarly attention to the musical is also connected to another issue, inherent in the birth of most film musicals. They tend to be created as stage productions, before the best of them get a second chance at fame through being recorded and then reworked into a musical film proper, therefore their cinematic analysis is often problematic.

Leaving classical Hollywood behind, Part II of the volume examines genres that have come (or returned) to prominence and gained significant popularity since the 1990s. None of these genres is an entirely new invention, but as the introduction to Part II will discuss in more detail, they have lately been revitalised, and their new-found popularity has brought them into creative alliances with Shakespeare's work as well. The first genre included here is the teen film, which has spawned a number of blockbusters during and since the 1990s; the second is the subgenre of horror featuring undead or supernatural characters, including zombies and vampires. It is true that there is a considerable overlap between the target audiences of undead horror and teen films, but as Chapter 4 focuses exclusively on the high school subgenre of the teen flick, and Chapter 5 places the emphasis on the horror context of the latter group, I believe their separate treatment is justified. The last genre discussed in the volume is in some ways an odd one out: the biopic, the genre that presents the author as character, offering a fictionalised account of Shakespeare's life and times. Fictional biographies are typically not based on any individual play, as they are most interested in the making of the genius itself, the everydays of the mortal person who became known as the immortal author of the great *oeuvre*. These films could therefore be disputed as adaptations, but a close attention to the specific and recognisable conventions of the genre allows us to observe how they also participate in the contemporary Shakespeare cult.

One methodological – or structural – decision that may need a few words of explanation is the organisation of the volume into individual film analyses, even if these are grouped according to their generic background. Another possible method would have been the discussion of examples in an arrangement based on the generic features they illustrate, that is, in chapters that discuss the genres first and foremost, and make references to cinematic manifestations of certain generic features whenever relevant. While I believe that such a structure would have strengthened the emphasis on the common – and indeed genre-associated – features of individual films, I am also convinced that it would have made the volume somewhat impractical for everyday use. After much deliberation, and even more discussion with colleagues, I have come to the conclusion that readers are much more likely to search for specific films, whether in aid of their research or teaching, than for overarching theoretical arguments. These purposes are better served by a volume where discussions of individual films can easily be found, presented in separate units within the chapters, but with these analyses clearly bridged by pointing out thematic connections between them.

When inviting the reader to set out on this journey through the complex but spectacular labyrinth of screen genres and their intersections with Shakespeare's work, I sincerely hope that the enterprise can offer them enjoyment, and possibly even a challenge to watch or re-watch films that they have either never seen before, or saw in a different light. I also invite anyone with a shared interest in adaptations to try out this method of approaching non-Shakespearean adaptations through the context of cinematic genres and see if they arrive at a more balanced interpretation of the films. If there is one thing I have learned during the many years while this volume has been in the making, it is that working with adaptations combines the joys of literary appreciation with the excitement of the cinema, and I could not in all sincerity wish the reader more fun than I have experienced along the way.

Notes

1 J. G. Cawelti, 'The Question of Popular Genres', *Journal of Popular Film and Television*, 13:2 (1985), 55–61, 55.
2 Because of the technical uncertainties involved in defining precise timing in visual files, most films being available in a number of different formats, quotations from film dialogues are only referenced if they are taken from a published script.
3 E. Klett, 'Reviving Viola: Comic and Tragic Teen Film Adaptations of *Twelfth Night*', *Shakespeare Bulletin*, 26:2 (2008), 69–87, 69.

4 Esp. E. Buscombe, 'The Idea of Genre in the American Cinema', *Screen*, 11:2 (1970), 33–45; S. Neale, *Genre* (London: British Film Institute, 1980); S. Neale, *Genre and Hollywood* (London and New York: Routledge, 2000); R. Altman, 'A Semantic/Syntactic Approach to Film Genre', *Cinema Journal*, 23:3 (1984), 6–18.
5 R. Altman, *Film/Genre* (London: British Film Institute, 1999).
6 E.g. P. Young, 'Film Genre Theory and Contemporary Media: Description, Interpretation, Intermediality', in R. Kolker (ed.), *The Oxford Handbook of Film and Media Studies* (New York: Oxford University Press, 2008), pp. 224–59.
7 Y. Griggs, '*King Lear* as Western Elegy', *Literature/Film Quarterly*, 35:2 (2007), 92–100, 92.
8 H. Keyishian, 'Shakespeare and Movie Genre: The Case of *Hamlet*', in R. Jackson (ed.), *The Cambridge Companion to Shakespeare on Film* (Cambridge: Cambridge University Press, 2nd edn, 2007), pp. 72–84, p. 83.
9 S. Berry-Flint, 'Genre', in T. Miller and R. Stam (eds), *A Companion to Film Theory* (Oxford: Blackwell, 2004), pp. 25–44, p. 25.
10 M. Landy, 'Introduction', in M. Landy (ed.), *Imitations of Life: A Reader on Film and Television Melodrama* (Detroit, MI: Wayne State University Press, 1991), pp. 13–30, p. 20.
11 Cf. J. Steiger, 'Hybrid or Inbred: The Purity Hypothesis and Hollywood Genre History', in B. K. Grant (ed.), *Film Genre Reader IV* (Austin: University of Texas Press, 2012), pp. 203–17.
12 J. Derrida, 'The Law of Genre', trans. A. Ronell, *Critical Inquiry*, 7:1, Special Issue: *On Narrative* (1980), 55–81, 59.
13 G. Deleuze and F. Guattari, *A Thousand Plateaus: Capitalism and Schizophrenia*, trans. Brian Massumi (Minneapolis: University of Minnesota Press, 1987).
14 D. Lanier, 'Shakespearean Rhizomatics: Adaptation, Ethics, Value', in A. Huang and E. Rivlin (eds), *Shakespeare and the Ethics of Appropriation* (New York: Palgrave Macmillan, 2014), pp. 21–40, p. 31.
15 Ibid., p. 27.
16 E. Walker, 'Getting Back to Shakespeare: Whose Film is it Anyway?', in D. E. Henderson (ed.), *A Concise Companion to Shakespeare on Screen* (Oxford: Blackwell, 2006), pp. 8–30, pp. 9–10.
17 Douglas Lanier uses Michel de Certeau's term 'textual poaching' to describe the phenomenon in D. Lanier, *Shakespeare and Modern Popular Culture* (Oxford: Oxford University Press, 2002), p. 52. Another important use of the term is provided by Henry Jenkins in *Textual Poachers: Television Fans and Participatory Culture* (London and New York: Routledge, 1992).
18 L. Hutcheon, *A Theory of Adaptation* (Abingdon and New York: Routledge, 2006). J. Sanders, *Adaptation and Appropriation* (Abingdon and New York: Routledge, 2006).
19 K. Newell, *Expanding Adaptation Networks: From Illustration to Novelization* (London: Palgrave Macmillan, 2017), p. 3.

20 E. S. Mallin, *Reading Shakespeare in the Movies: Non-Adaptations and Their Meaning* (Cham: Palgrave Macmillan, 2019), p. 1.
21 V. M. Fazel and L. Geddes, 'Introduction: The Shakespeare User', in V. M. Fazel and L. Geddes (eds), *The Shakespeare User: Critical and Creative Appropriations in a Networked Culture* (Cham: Palgrave Macmillan, 2017), pp. 1–22, p. 2.
22 C. Desmet, N. Loper and J. Casey, 'Introduction', in C. Desmet, N. Loper and J. Casey (eds), *Shakespeare/Not Shakespeare* (Cham: Palgrave Macmillan, 2017), pp. 1–22, p. 3.
23 S. O'Neill, *Shakespeare and YouTube: New Media Forms of the Bard* (London and New York: Bloomsbury Publishing, 2014); S. O'Neill (ed.), *Broadcast Your Shakespeare: Continuity and Change Across Media* (London and New York: The Arden Shakespeare, 2018).
24 P. Aebischer and S. Greenhalgh, 'Introduction: Shakespeare and the "Live" Theatre Broadcast Experience', in P. Aebischer, S. Greenhalgh and L. Osborne (eds), *Shakespeare and the 'Live' Theatre Broadcast Experience* (London: The Arden Shakespeare, 2018), pp. 1–16, p. 2.
25 F. Teague, *Shakespeare and the American Popular Stage* (Cambridge: Cambridge University Press, 2006). I. G. Dash, *Shakespeare and the American Musical* (Bloomington and Indianapolis: Indiana University Press, 2010). I have also discussed one of the genre's classics, *Kiss Me Kate*, elsewhere; cf. K. Földváry, '"Brush Up Your Shakespeare": Genre-Shift from Shakespeare to the Screen', in S. A. Brown, R. I. Lublin and L. McCulloch (eds), *Reinventing the Renaissance: Shakespeare and His Contemporaries in Adaptation and Performance* (Basingstoke: Palgrave Macmillan, 2013), pp. 47–62.

Part I
Classical Hollywood cinema

Introduction

The first part of our investigation into the ways Shakespeare has inspired commercial cinema takes us back to the earliest popular film genres, focusing on three classical types that defined Hollywood film production in the first half of the twentieth century, even though their conventions have remained recognisable until today. But before delving into the detailed interpretation of Shakespeare-inspired Hollywood films in the following chapters, a brief summary of the most significant features of the sociohistorical backdrop of their production may be necessary. Naturally, within the scope of this introduction it would be impossible to offer a comprehensive introduction to all industrial, economic, demographic or otherwise relevant contexts, but a few key points might still prove useful before the individual film analyses.

As is commonly known, between the 1930s and the 1960s, the studio system had a direct impact on the production, distribution and exhibition of films, and since it was in each studio's best interests to maintain successful formulas, or imitate other studios' recipes for success, this system also paved the way for the cyclical production of genre films. These recipes typically included not only a narrative, often associated with a specific setting, or a conflict between certain recognisable character types, but also relied on the attraction provided by contracted stars in roles with which audiences were familiar. In this way, studios were able to repeat the lucrative investment as often and as long as it was profitable, in turn reinforcing audience recognition of film types, which often employed returning stars, recurring conflicts, settings, themes, as closely imitating previous successes as possible.

Even with the end of the Hollywood studio era, the significance of studios did not disappear entirely, although today they no longer have a monopoly over the production and distribution cycle; nonetheless, their inclination to repeat certain formulaic patterns is unchanged. But genres, formulas, conventions were never confined to a single studio even at the height of their popularity: they became part of the vocabulary of meaning-making applied by general audiences. This ability to recognise familiar patterns allows audiences even now, often many decades after the appearance of such successful patterns, to interpret new productions as descendants of a long line of earlier works.

It is true that the choice of the genres included in the volume – the western, the melodrama and the gangster-*noir* hybrid – may seem arbitrary, as these were clearly not the only genre patterns used in the studio era. Thomas Schatz discusses six classical genres: the western, the gangster film, the hard-boiled detective film, including *film noir*, followed by the screwball comedy, the musical and the family melodrama.[1] Out of these six, I will endeavour to summarise the most important features of three selected classic genre formulas; however, it must be remembered that the significance of genres for understanding the wherefores and whys of film production could equally be relevant in association with films that belong to the genres absent from the volume.

The western

The western is the most appropriate starting point in any genre-based study, since in its prime, which coincided with the heyday of the Hollywood studio system, it was probably the single most popular genre of mainstream cinema, making up as much as the quarter of all films produced in Hollywood.[2] Contributing to its popularity were the long-held myth of the frontier, widely discussed since Frederick Jackson Turner's 1893 lecture on 'The Significance of the Frontier in American History',[3] and a number of central issues that found their most perfect embodiment in the conventions of the western. In Colin McArthur's summary,

> the particular historical debates which underpin the Western [are]: whether the West is garden or desert; whether industrialization or agrarianism carries the greater moral cachet; whether the Indian is a cruel savage or a noble primitive; whether Western energy is to be preferred to Eastern refinement; and how the traditional West (and Western) copes with the onset of modernity.[4]

But naturally, the success of the western as a genre of popular culture was based not only on its ability to ask probing questions, but even more on its simple and easy-to-recognise iconography and a limited set of narrative patterns, which could nonetheless resonate with fundamental American values, from a Puritan work ethic to a belief in American exceptionalism. At the same time, despite this deceptive simplicity, the western created an extremely rich cultural tradition, which is testified by the sometimes controversial terminology and theoretical approaches that characterise its century-long critical evaluation. As Steve Neale quotes Edward Buscombe, '"the consistency and rigour" of the western's world is "remarkable"'; however, 'the visual conventions of the western are both highly distinctive and highly coded', making it more the 'generic exception than the rule'.[5]

The most defining feature that dominates western iconography is naturally the setting, known as the Wild West, which, as John G. Cawelti emphasises, is 'not so much ... a particular geographic setting like the Rocky Mountains or the Great Plains, but ... a symbolic setting representing the boundary between order and chaos, between tradition and newness'.[6] In other words, it is the frontier experience where the clash between nature and culture, savagery and civilisation, or in more abstract terms, the Norm and the Other, takes place. These binary concepts were first introduced by Henry Nash Smith in his seminal work *Virgin Land: The American West as Symbol and Myth*,[7] and they 'have shaped all subsequent writings on the West as myth'.[8] Throughout the history of the genre, however, these binaries have acquired different meanings, as the western has naturally adapted to its socio-historical context, responding to contemporary concerns in various ways.

In the era of silent films, westerns tended to be 'positive expressions of nationalistic sentiments, celebrating the West as a place of personal regeneration, egalitarian democracy, and the superiority of Anglo-Saxon culture', and this attitude carried over to the post-war decades as well.[9] The 1930s and 1940s western often presented the outlaw as a glorified, heroic figure, 'who resists the evil influences of greedy industrialists or bankers' – as if in response to the common belief that the latter social group could be held directly responsible for the great Depression of the interwar years.[10] This attitude is tangible in *Yellow Sky* (1948, dir. William A. Wellman) and even in *Broken Lance* (1954, dir. Edward Dmytryk), discussed in Chapter 1. From the post-war decades onward, however, the representation of the western lifestyle took on increasingly dark overtones, emphasising the solitary, socially marginalised position resulting from the western hero's engagement in violence, and the isolation of the hero could also reflect deeper social and psychological anxieties, as in *Jubal* (1956, dir. Delmer Daves).

At the same time, the post-war years brought about more and more positive representations of the Other in the western imaginary. Leaving behind the stereotypical image of the bloodthirsty savage or the comical crazy Indian, which still informs *McLintock!* (1963, dir. Andrew V. McLaglen) to a certain extent, post-war films began to ascribe individual features to Native Americans, while also showing how, in the glorious story of westward expansion, their role was that of the victim, a vanishing race that was swept away as collateral damage by industrialisation, which forged the future of a prosperous America. This idea of the 'Vanishing American' (the phrase became commonly used after the title of a 1925 silent film, directed by George B. Seitz), disappearing together with his landscape, became solidified into a cinematic myth, described with nostalgia, but with a resignation felt for a dying race that must be sacrificed for the sake of progress.

André Bazin wrote in 1953 that 'the western does not age',[11] but, as it turned out, the decades of popularity were followed by an inevitable decline. After the 1960s, the western tended to emphasise the moral ambiguity and violence inherent in the archetypal clash between wilderness and civilisation, which is particularly tangible in the European westerns made in the period, the so-called spaghetti westerns, among them such films as *Johnny Hamlet* (1968, dir. Enzo G. Castellari). At the same time, as American society felt increasingly like 'a nation buffeted by a rapidly changing social order and war in Vietnam', the earlier, straightforward value system of the American western was no longer acceptable, and thus the so-called revisionist western was born, characterised by violence and bitterness and a generally grim moral landscape.[12] Following this moral decline, from the 1970s the shattered remnants of a belief in former values tended to be represented nostalgically, as in the melancholy road movie *Harry and Tonto* (1974, dir. Paul Mazursky). Yet even if many scholars saw a final fading away of the genre in the late 1990s, the twenty-first century proved that there is still life in the old warrior. One reason for its continued, if uneven, popularity, may be connected to America's unchanging belief in its own sacred mission, justifying its expansionist imperialism, and the way the image of the frontier lives on in the popular imagination and political rhetoric as well. As Gavin Jacobson summarises the longevity of the frontier myth in a book review: 'From the Wild West to Trump's border wall, the image of the frontier has enabled American imperialism', and as a consequence, it explains 'the racism, nativism and violent masculinity ... that defines America's political landscape' to this day.[13]

This is the rough framework in which Shakespearean dramas were embedded when they were transformed into western narratives, although it is hard to say which of the two may have enhanced the popularity of the other. As Robert F. Willson suggests: 'Shakespeare provides an appealing intertext that offers ready-made situations, characters, and speeches capable of being plugged into the appropriate scene or sequence.'[14] What the more detailed analyses will show is how natural such a combination can feel when handled by masters of the genre, which in turn explains why – although neither Shakespeare, nor the western in itself, offers a fool-proof recipe for success – filmmakers continue to find the challenge irresistible even in the twenty-first century.

From woman's film to melodrama

Not unlike the western, the melodrama, although a frequently used term both in everyday conversation and theoretical discussions of literature and cinema, proves to be a surprisingly challenging concept to define. Some scholars claim that it is the perfect complement to the western; for one, Geoffrey Nowell-Smith emphasises the parallel structures of western and melodrama when he argues that 'in the American movie the active hero becomes protagonist of the Western, the passive or impotent hero or heroine becomes protagonist of what has come to be known as melodrama'.[15] Others, however, suggest that the melodrama is rather the opposite of the western: the latter might be accused of being too straightforward and formulaic to be of much use for genre theories, whereas the melodrama is sometimes denied the status of a genre because it simply lacks recognisable semantic elements, as according to Rick Altman.[16] Linda Williams also argues for melodrama being a mode, rather than a genre,[17] and this seems to be the most commonly accepted consensus today, emphasising that 'Rather than defining content, *mode* shapes different materials to a given end.'[18] This end is the most distinctive feature of melodrama: the effect it strives to achieve, rather than any specific structural or narrative elements. Most theoreticians agree, moreover, that the melodramatic mode is not a marginal one, but one of the most universal organising structures behind the majority of Hollywood productions even in the early twenty-first century.

This diversity of definitions is tangible in how critics and audiences of Shakespeare film adaptations define what they experience as examples of melodrama. This comes as no surprise, considering that throughout the history of melodrama the term has been employed to denote a variety of styles and media, and also because the meaning the word has acquired in everyday use is often no more than a value judgement. Melodrama's etymology (a combination of Greek 'melos', 'music', as in melody, and drama) can be helpful when explaining the role of music in melodramatic works, where its application can range from atmospheric background element to central theme, as in *All Night Long* (1962, dir. Basil Dearden). Nonetheless, the word rarely refers to a musical element today; as James L. Smith shows, by the twentieth century '*melodrama* has in popular use become a blanket term of abuse and contempt',[19] and even in critical commentary the term 'melodramatic' is often applied in this general and negative way, rather than referring to any generic group.

Examining both the uses of the term within the film industry and looking at the dramatic antecedents of the genre, Neale also shows that 'by the turn of the [twentieth] century … melodrama had become … a cluster form, a form marked by a number of distinct aesthetic features and traditions, all of which found their way into the cinema and many of which continue to be drawn on today'.[20] But the most stereotypical interpretation of the genre has always equated the melodrama with the 'woman's film', a popular genre in the 1930s, exemplified here by *Men Are Not Gods* (1936, dir. Walter Reisch). The concerns of this formula were taken up by Douglas Sirk and Vincente Minnelli, great masters of the post-war family melodrama, who remade many of the woman's films of the silent or early sound era. It comes as no surprise therefore that most theoreticians, among them Williams, argue for a narrower definition of the melodrama. In her seminal essay on the so-called 'body genres', instead of including under the term 'melodrama' all that is sensational, Williams focuses solely on the woman's film. As she claims, 'These are films addressed to women in their traditional status under patriarchy – as wives, mothers, abandoned lovers – or in their traditional status as bodily hysteria or excess, as in the frequent case of the woman "afflicted" with a deadly or debilitating disease.'[21] Women are thus granted central roles in most melodramas (although post-war British social melodrama would point out male anxieties as well), and they typically appear in the role of victim, whose moral sense forces her to sacrifice what is most precious to her, in order to restore the moral balance of the universe.

As Cawelti argues, this sacrificial act is meaningful within the formula because melodrama represents 'a fantasy of a world that operates according to our heart's desires', which 'shows how the complex ambiguities and tragedies of the world ultimately reveal the operation of a benevolent, humanly oriented world order'.[22] This does not mean that the world seems benevolent throughout, or that there is no suffering depicted in melodrama – quite the opposite, in fact: melodrama may appear very similar to tragedy, but whereas in tragedy, the protagonist's catastrophe reveals the great gap between human desires and the limitations of the world; in melodrama this gap is bricked over. Melodramatic suffering and violence are means of testing and ultimately demonstrating the 'rightness' of the world order. If the melodramatic hero meets a catastrophic end, it is either as a noble sacrifice to some good purpose or because he has become deserving of destruction.[23]

To emphasise the heroic scope of the sacrifice, even if it is represented within the domestic sphere of women, and often within the petty confines of bourgeois society, melodrama relies on frequent representations of bodily excess, mostly shown in the form of weeping, or even in hysterical reactions, portraying characters 'in the grips of ... overpowering sadness'.[24] But, as in the case of all 'low body genres' (Williams follows the definition of Carol J. Clover, enlisting here horror and pornography along with melodrama, as the genres with the lowest cultural prestige), melodrama also incites a bodily response in its audiences.[25] While watching the – predominantly female – body in distress, 'the body of the spectator is caught up in an almost involuntary mimicry of the emotion or sensation of the body on the screen',[26] and consequently we also reach for our handkerchiefs and cry – hence the popular names of 'weepie' or 'tear-jerker' applied (derogatively) to the melodrama even in its heyday.

Based on this, it comes as little surprise that from Shakespeare's *oeuvre*, the tragedies are most likely to be adapted to melodramatic cinema. At the same time, as some of the melodramas examined in Chapter 2 will illustrate, the move towards the melodramatic mode is regularly enabled by giving a (previously marginalised) female character the opportunity to tell the story from her point of view, as in *A Thousand Acres* (1997, dir. Jocelyn Moorhouse, based on the eponymous novel by Jane Smiley). Interestingly, it is not only the general atmosphere of the films discussed here that earns them the label of melodrama, but even the most significant elements of the plot can be overwritten by the melodramatic, including the original tragic ending, proving the theory that it is not the source narrative that determines the outcome but the adapting genre. In this way, while the suffering of the protagonist, caused by his or her struggles against a seemingly antagonistic universe, might make us cry as much as when viewing a tragedy, the melodrama's *denouement* does not need to include death (or as many deaths as in Shakespeare's source texts), as long as the heroic sacrifice has succeeded in setting the world aright. This might simply be manifested by the way characters resign themselves to their fates, accepting their victimhood within a claustrophobic middle-class social structure. As Williams summarises in a later essay on the melodrama: 'In cinema the mode of melodrama defines a broad category of moving pictures that move us to pathos for protagonists beset by forces more powerful than they are and who are perceived as victims.'[27] This flexibility and adaptability to other genres in turn explains why contemporary visual narratives ranging from teen television series to dystopian science-fiction films continue to display melodramatic elements. The characteristic cinematography of the melodrama includes an often excessive focus on the representation of emotions, through the use of close-ups, slow-motion photography, blurred images implying a nostalgic recollection of the past and the preponderance of musical accompaniment, many of which can be traced back to the visuality already characterising the woman's film as far back as the 1930s.

To illustrate how the universality of the melodramatic mode has never been confined to the Hollywood studio system, or even the Anglo-American cultural sphere, the discussion of the melodrama ends with a brief investigation of a comparable mode employed within the other global cinema giant, Bollywood.[28] Despite being rooted in different literary and theatrical traditions, Indian cinema displays a similar love of spectacle, song and dance, and turbulent emotions, not to mention an overall openness towards a hybridity of generic features. Some scholars even claim that the melodramatic element in Indian cinema is Western in origin; Rachel Dwyer explicitly argues that 'cinema's hybrid nature combined Western technologies and modes such as melodrama with indigenous visual and performative traditions'.[29] As a result, by the beginning of the twenty-first century, in the globalised world of film production and consumption, we can observe significant similarities between the cinematic vocabularies of Hollywood and Bollywood filmmakers.

This proximity in cinematic styles is particularly noticeable in the films created for the diaspora market, and the increasingly popular subgroup of British-Asian films in the United Kingdom has garnered a huge following, even beyond their primary audiences, especially in the twenty-first century. As Dwyer emphasises the mixed cultural upbringing of the younger generation of British-Asian audiences who 'have mainly been socialised in Britain' and 'have grown up with Hollywood and British cinema and British television and other British media',[30] we may begin to understand why recent British-Asian cinema appears to be more successful at combining Bollywood and Hollywood elements into a natural whole. To illustrate these processes, Chapter 2 ends with the analysis of a recent British-Asian work, *Life Goes On* (2009, dir. Sangeeta Datta). In this film, the melodramatic mode functions as a signal of familiarity both to diasporic and global audiences that may no longer associate the melodrama with exotic and sensationalist Bollywood musicals, but see it as a universally recognisable genre of popular visual culture.

Film noir, gangster, gangster *noir*

If the melodrama was challenging for theoreticians to define, and incited debates as regards its very nature and status, *film noir* has received a no less controversial treatment throughout its history. The term has long entered the public vocabulary and is widely used by general audiences and critics alike, and the idea of *film noir* being a genre has also proved surprisingly resistant to critical attempts to deny its right to existence. On the one hand, the visual style and characteristic camera technique of *film noir* are easily recognisable, particularly when it comes to the so-called classic, or historical, *noirs* (the latter term used by James Naremore to distinguish the extinct genre from present-day films).[31] The stylistic influence of *noir* on later periods of filmmaking is equally undeniable, as testified by a number of neo-*noir* productions, some of them created with a parodic intent, others simply with the desire to revisit the atmosphere and cinematographic style of the classics. On the other hand, there seems to be no agreement regarding the exact characterisation or definition of the term, even while the significance of the label and the phenomenon is undisputed. Curiously, it is also common knowledge that the name itself was never used by the industry at the time of the films' creation but was retrospectively applied, by a French critic,[32] to a group of American films that shocked post-war Parisian audiences with their characteristically dark atmosphere, 'tinged with a unique kind of sexuality'.[33]

Neale, while describing the difficulties associated with *film noir* as a label, lists the most typical features that characterise the admittedly rather heterogeneous group of films usually listed under the heading. These features include 'the importance of crime, violence and death';[34] the casting of female characters into one of 'two basic types: alluring – and dangerous – *femmes fatales* on the one hand, and dependable, respectable, safe and undemanding partners, wives and girlfriends on the other'.[35] Typical *noir* narratives represent 'failed or doomed romances, and absent or distorted families and family relations', dramatising a 'crisis in male identity';[36] and the films also feature 'an obsession with male figures who are both internally divided and alienated from the culturally permissible (or ideal) parameters of masculine identity, desire and achievement'.[37] The importance of crime, however, is not simply a thematic element, but also confirms the mutual influence of *film noir* and gangster films, in terms of visual style, iconography and narrative. As Alain Silver summarises: 'Much as the gangster films of the 1930s influenced film noir, the classic period of that movement in turn influenced the filmmakers who helped revive the gangster genre in the late 1960s and early 1970s.'[38] This is why I feel justified in combining my discussion of *noir* and gangster Shakespeare films in Chapter 3, since a clear connection between the two genres, even a sense of continuity, are noticeable when looking at the films in this arrangement. Even though the classic gangster genre preceded the peak of *film noir*, the Shakespeare-inspired gangster films only appeared after the classic *noir* period, therefore the latter are discussed in the second half of Chapter 3, following the *noir* adaptations.

One of the stereotypical elements that never fails to appear in *film noir* – and is also characteristic of gangster films – is the setting. The *noir* is set in the city, most often an American metropolis, featuring dark skyscrapers and alienated crowds, and providing stark contrasts between the dilapidated tenements of the urban poor and the flashy villas or townhouses of the shady upper classes. *Noir* plots tend to unfold at night, and the streets where the lonely private eye or the psychopathic killer finds himself are rainswept, the neon lights only deepening the darkness by casting shadows everywhere. The *chiaroscuro* cinematography of *film noir* was partly made possible by various technical innovations of the 1940s that, among other things, 'permitted better location filming', as a consequence of which 'film noir found a world in the dark'.[39] The dark city is, however, not only a decorative or experimental element inspired by the new exposure meters and photoflood bulbs;[40] it is not even a disturbing reminder of the war and its leftover traumas and anxieties (although several early *noirs* made use of the blacked-out cities during the Second World War for their location shooting), but, most importantly, a metaphor. In Fran Mason's words, 'The *noir* city is a trap, not a place of freedom and mobility, and the image most often associated with the *noir* city is the labyrinth.'[41] The Shakespeare adaptations that engage the *noir* conventions for their psychologically motivated exploration of male anxieties are *Strange Illusion* (1945, dir. Edgar G. Elmer) and *A Double Life* (1947, dir. George Cukor), and both confirm these expectations.

The films discussed in the second half of this chapter, while visually and in their cinematography displaying a number of obvious connections to *film noir*, are distinguished from the first two examples by one significant thematic element: they all have a gangster as their protagonist. These films are sometimes labelled as *noir* (the later ones as neo-*noir*), at other times as gangster films, sometimes even as gangster *noir*, and these uneven classifications hint at the connections between the two categories, as well as the difficulties of providing clear-cut definitions for both. As Mason's study of American gangster cinema convincingly argues, the more we look at the genre, the more problematic its precise definition gets. Yet, whether we take the exclusionary approach and focus on a few paradigmatic examples, or take the broader view and are then forced to establish a number of sub-genres within the group, it seems clear that the *film noir* and the gangster film are members of the same family. The shared concerns between the two groups, both stylistic and thematic, are visible throughout all cinematic periods; it is no accident that accounts of *film noir* regularly include gangster films as a subgenre,[42] or, the other way around, they regard *noir* as a branch of the classical gangster genre.[43] As quoted above, Silver also argues for a historical dialogue between the two, and points our their joint influence on later filmmaking as well, claiming that 'neo-noir is itself a genre which easily uses elements of both noir movement and gangster genre'.[44]

Some of these shared features are highlighted in Robert Warshow's seminal essay in which he argues that the gangster film '*as an experience of art* is universal to Americans'.[45] In his discussion of the notions embodied by the figure of the gangster, together with the stereotypical cinematic contexts in which the character appears, Warshow also points out the common setting of the two genres. In his view, the American metropolis is not simply the real and familiar everyday environment of the genre's primary audiences (an increasingly suburban lifestyle characterising America by the 1950s, with little exposure to actual gangsters in the lives of the average citizen), but the 'dangerous and sad city of the imagination ... which is the modern world'.[46] This latter aspect is vital, as it lures its audiences into a psychological identification with the gangster as character, even hero, since 'the gangster ... is also, and primarily, a creature of the imagination'.[47] But even more importantly, this type of interiority or inner fiction is again something *film noir* focused on, by showing the psychological anxieties of its protagonist, which in turn were often shared by contemporary audiences, working through traumas of the Second World War and its consequences for the whole of American society. The psychological identification with protagonists in gangster films is manifested in cinematography familiar from *film noir*; the nocturnal, rainswept, labyrinthine metropolitan settings, brought to the viewer in close-ups and with canted camera angles, give an insight into the troubled psyche of the protagonist. All these elements are showcased in the two Shakespeare-associated gangster adaptations examined in Chapter 3: *Joe Macbeth* (1955, dir. Ken Hughes) and *Men of Respect* (1990, dir. William Reilly).

Another way to emphasise the continuity between the visual aspects of *film noir* and the gangster film can be found in the arguments that focus on the associations of darkness with criminality. The association goes back to the earliest examples of western films, but the theme is reworked in *noir* and gangster cinema as well. As Anita Lam argues:

> When taken as an example of *film noir* ..., gangster films additionally adopt blackness as a visual style, transforming the world into a nightmarish place of shadows and night scenes ... Light and darkness in film noir are also used to visualize moral and psychological Otherness, such that people become 'black' because of their criminal or immoral behaviour ... However, a slippage often occurs when the metaphor of blackness is made visible on film, weaving together concerns about criminality, morality, style and race ...[48]

This concern with Otherness tightly linked with blackness (particularly a metaphorical blackness) is exemplified in George Cukor's *A Double Life*, where the role of Othello that the protagonist plays on stage is clearly blamed for his own moral and psychological downfall. According to Eric Lott, Cukor's film is a particularly plain example of 'the raced double lives of noir protagonists';[49] as he argues, 'the troping of white darkness in noir has a racial source that is all the more insistent for seeming off to the side'.[50]

Following this *noir* heritage, in the gangster films examined in the second half of the chapter, Otherness is represented not as black, but merely as 'off-white', and blackness as a racial concept is replaced by the ethnic stereotyping of the Italian-American gang.[51] These films, like their non-Shakespearean contemporaries, address issues of heritage and assimilation, alienation and marginalisation, as well as generational conflicts between first-, second- and even third-generation immigrants. The last film examined in the chapter, *We Own the Night* (2007, dir. James Gray) also defines its criminals by their ethnic background, but they are no longer Italians: here the Russian mafia gets the blame for threatening the unity of American society. The film also shows how the thematic and visual features of gangster and *noir* films continue to be employed by subsequent generations of filmmakers, even indie *auteurs* working outside the dream factory.

We Own the Night, like all the films discussed in Part I of the volume, demonstrates the vitality of classical Hollywood formulas, challenging the assumption that the demise of the studio era brought about the end of its formulaic products as well. Moreover, this generic productivity is confirmed in the way Shakespearean narratives have been embedded in the long-established frameworks of genre conventions, providing evidence that mainstream cinema is a long-lasting form of cultural expression, whose creative energies can be deployed in the most surprising combinations of high and low, textual and visual, and canonical and innovative cultural elements.

Notes

1 T. Schatz, *Hollywood Genres: Formulas, Filmmaking, and the Studio System* (New York: Random House, 1981).
2 Cf. *Ibid.*, p. 6 in reference to the year 1950.
3 Subsequently published in F. J. Turner, *The Frontier in American History* (New York: Henry Holt & Company, 1920), pp. 1–38.
4 Quoted in J. G. Cawelti, *The Six-Gun Mystique Sequel* (Bowling Green, OH: Bowling Green State University Popular Press, 1999), p. 200.
5 Neale, *Genre and Hollywood*, p. 125.
6 Cawelti, *The Six-Gun Mystique Sequel*, p. 9.
7 H. N. Smith, *Virgin Land: The American West and Symbol and Myth* (Cambridge, MA: Harvard University Press, 1950), see esp. ch. 16: 'The Garden and the Desert', pp. 174–83.
8 R. P. Loy, 'The Frontier and the West', in P. C. Rollins (ed.), *The Columbia Companion to American History on Film: How the Movies Have Portrayed the American Past* (New York: Columbia University Press, 2003), pp. 578–82, p. 578.
9 *Ibid.*, p. 579.
10 *Ibid.*, p. 580.
11 A. Bazin, 'The Western: Or the American Film Par Excellence', in A. Bazin, *What is Cinema? Essays Selected and Translated by Hugh Gray*, vol. 2 (1971; Berkeley, Los Angeles and London: University of California Press, 2005), pp. 140–8, p. 141.
12 Loy, 'The Frontier and the West', p. 581.
13 G. Jacobson, 'The Myth of the American Frontier', *New Statesman* (26 June 2019), www.newstatesman.com/end-myth-frontier-america-greg-grandin-empire-greater-united-states (accessed 10 January 2020).
14 R. F. Willson, Jr, *Shakespeare in Hollywood, 1929–1956* (Cranbury, NJ, and London: Associated University Presses, 2002), p. 110.
15 G. Nowell-Smith, 'Minnelli and Melodrama', *Screen*, 18:2 (1977), 113–18, 115.
16 R. Altman, 'Cinema and Genre', in G. Nowell-Smith (ed.), *The Oxford History of World Cinema* (Oxford: Oxford University Press, 1996), pp. 276–85, p. 282.
17 L. Williams, 'Melodrama Revised', in N. Browne (ed.), *Refiguring American Film Genres* (Berkeley, Los Angeles and London: University of California Press, 1998), pp. 42–88, p. 42.
18 C. Gledhill, 'Prologue: The Reach of Melodrama', in C. Gledhill and L. Williams (eds), *Melodrama Unbound: Across History, Media and National Cultures*

(New York: Columbia University Press, 2018), pp. ix–xxv, p. xiii (italics in original).
19 J. L. Smith, *Melodrama*, The Critical Idiom 28 (London: Methuen, 1973), pp. 6–7 (italics in original).
20 Neale, *Genre and Hollywood*, p. 201.
21 L. Williams, 'Film Bodies: Gender, Genre, and Excess', in Grant (ed.), *Film Genre Reader IV*, pp. 159–77, p. 161.
22 J. G. Cawelti, *Adventure, Mystery, and Romance: Formula Stories as Art and Popular Culture* (Chicago and London: University of Chicago Press, 1976), p. 45.
23 *Ibid.*, p. 46.
24 Williams, 'Film Bodies', p. 162.
25 C. J. Clover, 'Her Body, Himself: Gender in the Slasher Film', *Representations*, 20 (1987), 187–228.
26 Williams, 'Film Bodies', p. 162.
27 Williams, 'Melodrama Revised', p. 42.
28 Even though the etymology of the word Bollywood and the history of its use make it rather controversial, for the sake of simplicity I employ it here in the most commonly used sense, to refer to popular Indian cinema as a whole, whether based in Bombay or elsewhere, using whichever vernacular.
29 R. Dwyer, 'Planet Bollywood', in N. Ali, V. Kalra and S. Sayyid (eds), *A Postcolonial People: South Asians in Britain* (London: Hurst & Company, 2006), pp. 361–9, p. 361.
30 *Ibid.*, p. 366.
31 J. Naremore, *More than Night: Film Noir in Its Contexts* (Berkeley, Los Angeles and London: University of California Press, 2008), pp. 3–4.
32 N. Frank, 'Un nouveau genre "policier": L'aventure criminelle', *L'Ecran français*, 61 (28 August 1946), 8–9, 14.
33 R. Borde and É. Chaumeton, 'Towards a Definition of *Film Noir*', in A. Silver and J. Ursini (eds), *Film Noir Reader* (New York: Limelight, 1996), pp. 17–26, p. 17.
34 Neale, *Genre and Hollywood*, p. 146.
35 *Ibid.*, p. 151.
36 *Ibid.*, p. 146.
37 *Ibid.*, p. 152.
38 A. Silver, 'The Gangster and Film Noir: Themes and Style', in A. Silver and J. Ursini (eds), *Gangster Film Reader* (Pompton Plains, NJ: Limelight, 2007), pp. 290–322, p. 322.
39 E. Lott, 'The Whiteness of Film Noir', *American Literary History*, 9:3 (1997), 542–66, 548.
40 *Ibid.*
41 F. Mason, *American Gangster Cinema from* Little Caesar *to* Pulp Fiction (Basingstoke and New York: Palgrave Macmillan, 2002), p. 77.

42 E.g. J. S. Whitney, 'A Filmography of Film Noir', *Journal of Popular Film*, 5:3–4 (1976), 321–71, 322.
43 Mason, *American Gangster Cinema*; J. Shadoian, *Dreams and Dead Ends: The American Gangster Film* (Oxford and New York: Oxford University Press, 2003).
44 Silver, 'The Gangster and Film Noir', p. 322.
45 R. Warshow, 'The Gangster as Tragic Hero', in J. Gross (ed.), *The Oxford Book of Essays* (Oxford: Oxford University Press, 2008), pp. 581–6, p. 583 (italics in original).
46 Ibid., pp. 583–4.
47 Ibid., p. 584.
48 A. Lam, 'Gangsters and Genre', in *Oxford Research Encyclopedia of Criminology*, 22 November 2016, www.dx.doi.org/10.1093/acrefore/9780190264079.013.149 (accessed 26 January 2020).
49 Lott, 'The Whiteness of Film Noir', 552.
50 Ibid., 545.
51 L. Mizejewski, 'Movies and the Off-White Gangster', in C. Holmlund (ed.), *American Cinema of the 1990s: Themes and Variations* (New Brunswick, NJ, and London: Rutgers University Press, 2008), pp. 24–44, referring to D. Negra's term, cf. *Off-White Hollywood: American Culture and Ethnic Female Stardom* (London and New York: Routledge, 2001).

1

Will in the Wild West: western adaptations of Shakespeare

The western, while its position as the most prototypical genre of classical Hollywood cinema is unquestioned, may still appear somewhat unusual, or at first sight rather untypical, as a Shakespearean genre; but, as this chapter illustrates, there are ample examples of films that include a recognisable Shakespearean element within their western narratives. Although hints and reminders of the iconography of the western have always been frequent in Hollywood cinema, it is not isolated images of cinematic self-referentiality that I wish to discuss here, such as the arrival of the seven riders at the beginning of Kenneth Branagh's *Much Ado About Nothing*, a clear reference to *The Magnificent Seven*, or the 'spaghetti-western leitmotif' Alfredo Michel Modenessi finds at the beginning of Baz Luhrmann's *William Shakespeare's Romeo + Juliet*,[1] or the battle scenes in Laurence Olivier's *Henry V* which also take their cue from the western,[2] or even the way 'the tradition of Indo-Westerns, popularly referred to as "curry westerns"' is invoked by Vishal Bhardwaj's *Omkara*.[3]

Neither will I deal with western films that only include brief textual quotations from one or more of Shakespeare's plays, unless the connection between the plays and the western's main themes or general plotline seem more than accidental. That is the reason why I do not discuss John Ford's *My Darling Clementine* (1946), which presents Hamlet's 'To be or not to be' soliloquy, and where the Shakespearean connections appear to be resonating from that single, although not insignificant, passage; nor *The Man Who Shot Liberty Valance* (1962, dir. John Ford), where Henry V's words from before the battle of Agincourt are heard, along with another passing reference to *Troilus and Cressida*.[4]

What I wish to show instead is that the transatlantic crossbreeding between Shakespeare's text and the narrative elements and iconography of this most distinctly American genre seems to have been extremely prolific on a variety of levels, and has resulted in several outstanding, even award-winning, cinematic productions. The group includes classical manifestations of the form, but also comic, even parodic variants, together with an example of the low-budget European version known as the spaghetti western, and a late, revisionist western as well. The discussion is arranged chronologically, to illustrate the internal, but socio-historically embedded, development of the genre itself, and to show how the Shakespearean source material was transformed by the various iterations of the formula.

The Shakespeare western, not surprisingly, illustrates both the straightforward generic features described in the Introduction, and at the same time allows us to ponder on the history, development and self-reflexivity of the genre, particularly if we do not regard the various examples as isolated cases, but see them as forming a tradition in themselves. Furthermore, the diversity of the western can also be easily observed in Shakespeare westerns, as they are always rooted in their generic contexts. As the cinematic western is defined by its distinctive iconography that takes precedence over the narrative, let alone textual elements, and as its brooding heroes are mostly men of few words, the cinematic features stemming from the western tradition easily override the influence of the Shakespearean source texts.

To illustrate this point, the chapter discusses altogether six films, made in consecutive historical periods, whose plotlines and casts comprise recognisable elements of Shakespearean origins. *Yellow Sky* (1948, dir. William A. Wellman), a loose adaptation of *The Tempest*, is followed by two films from the 1950s: *Broken Lance* (1954, dir. Edward Dmytryk), a reworking of *King Lear*, and *Jubal* (1956, dir. Delmer Daves), revisiting the *Othello* story. Then comes a more light-hearted version from the 1960s: *McLintock!* (1963, dir. Andrew V. McLaglen), a shrew-taming western comedy; and a brutal Italian spaghetti western, *Johnny Hamlet* (1968, dir. Enzo G. Castellari). The final section of the chapter discusses *Harry and Tonto* (1974, dir. Paul Mazursky), a bittersweet and somewhat tragicomic road movie spiced up with a few elements of the western.

What I hope to show is that these films indeed form a distinct group within the Shakespearean canon through the way they incorporate the cinematic and narrative features of their common generic framework. As we will see, any examination on the basis of faithfulness to the text is not simply difficult to achieve, but indeed rather futile, since the ways, styles and proportions in which these films rework the Shakespearean texts are extremely diverse. Textual references are rare – the cowboy is a characteristically silent figure, after all – as the films' conflict is typically rooted in the setting itself, the frontier, where the antagonistic forces of savagery and civilisation clash. Moreover, it is often nearly impossible to identify a single text as the source for the films' scripts and visual worlds. The Shakespearean text is clearly one of the roots that need to be taken into account, with each individual play functioning as the narrative source in particular, but it always needs the complementary generic context of western films to allow us to explain the most significant features of the final product.

Post-war optimism – *Yellow Sky*

It has been repeatedly stated that the western is characterised by its setting more than anything, but it is also important to note that its favoured (though not strictly geographically defined) location, the Wild West, is always imbued with nostalgia on the screen, since it survived only in cultural memory by the middle of the twentieth century when the western film as a genre enjoyed the peak of its popularity. It is therefore fitting that the first film to be examined here is one which takes this inherently paradoxical setting to the extreme: the 1948 western *Yellow Sky*, starring Gregory Peck, Anne Baxter and Richard Widmark. Although André Bazin labelled the film as one of 'many current westerns of honourable standing',[5] it has received little critical attention, and its Shakespearean elements even less, with the exception of Eric C. Brown's 2013 analysis.[6]

The film offers a rather loose reinterpretation of some motifs from *The Tempest*, but the symbolic significance of the Shakespearean island remains central to its vision, in the form of a distant, isolated place, accessible only by accident or disaster, or the cruel joke of the gods. The island here becomes an abandoned mining town, surrounded by vast salt flats through which only the desperate and the outcast venture, in this case a group of outlaws who no longer have anything to lose. The significance of the salt flats as remnants of a dried-out, dead sea hardly needs to be spelled out – in Tony Howard's words, 'The elemental metaphors are reversed. Shakespeare's sea gives way to thirst'[7] – and the dead old world through which the path to recovery and revival must necessarily cross seems particularly relevant in the post-war period. But even more significant is the way this landscape visualises one of the central binaries at work in the western: the contrast between garden and desert. The West is at once a Paradise-like land of plenty 'that held out the hope of a New Eden, of fresh beginnings, of the promise of the regenerative power of bountiful, natural terrain'[8] for settlers, yet it often turns out to be a harsh, punishing landscape that separates the real man from the weakling. The salt flats are a lifeless and life-threatening place indeed, and the little ghost town where the outlaws arrive seems barely more welcoming. However, it will prove to have the force of regeneration that is central to the classic western, allowing a romantic happy ending untainted by the moral ambiguities inherent in the plot. In this way, although Howard refers to *Yellow Sky* as 'a harsh post-war Western',[9] the film appears rather conservative in its resolution, even if its gender politics imply the changing attitudes to women's role in society characteristic of the post-war era.

Yellow Sky was made in the middle of the period described as the Golden Age of the western, spanning roughly from *Stagecoach* (1939, dir. John Ford) to the end of the 1950s, possibly even to the 1960s.[10] The film's temporal and spatial setting – '1867, The West' – is therefore meaningful to its audiences in more ways than one: it specifies an era that evokes nostalgia for heroic greatness in American history, but the untamed countryside of the West also identifies the genre enjoying considerable popularity in the present of its creation. In the film, the dilapidated, dead town, bearing the uncanny name of Yellow Sky, bodes ill for the protagonists who are in various kinds of trouble anyway.[11] After a successful bank robbery, a group of gangsters in need of a hideout and a place of rest escape their pursuers by crossing the salt flats, a journey that nearly kills them, making their arrival at Yellow Sky not simply unexpected but indeed miraculous. Like the uninhabited island of *The Tempest*, which turns out to be rather crowded by the time the plot begins, Yellow Sky is equally deceptive as a ghost town, since there are two residents living on its outskirts, both of whom provide diverse attractions to the newcomers. The young tomboy Constance Mae (Anne Baxter), or 'Mike' for short (a Miranda character with a similarly naive innocence concerning her own femininity), wreaks havoc with her widely swinging hips among the exhausted bank robbers who are hungry and thirsty for food and female company alike. Her grandfather (James Barton), however, possesses knowledge that is even more attractive: as the treacherous robber Dude (Richard Widmark) soon sniffs out, the old man has put aside a considerable amount of gold from the seemingly deserted mines.

However comic and superficial some of the *Tempest* allusions may be, from the pot-bellied drunkard through to the lovelorn young kid, and the blossoming romance between not-such-a-bad-guy-after-all James 'Stretch' Dawson (Gregory Peck) and Mike, the desolation of the place tells us yet another story that haunted American society in the post-war years. The film is set in 1867, only two years after the end of the Civil War, a period also referred to as the Reconstruction era – no wonder therefore that a member of Stretch's gang is still wearing a threadbare uniform. The place is defined as 'The West', the latter being not much more specific than the Shakespearean location of the 'uninhabited island', and equally and noticeably allegorical. *Yellow Sky* was made in 1948, shortly after another upheaval that shook the world in its foundations, making it easy to look for connections between the socio-historical context of the film's creation and the time and place specified in the narrative. Like the problems caused by Civil War gunmen, who needed to be disbanded and persuaded to go back to a civilian life, late 1940s America was haunted by anxieties of poverty and unemployment, but also by a need to return to a peaceful and civilised existence within a human community. It is no accident that in the film we learn about each character in turn that they come from good families, and that it was only fate and the war that has driven them out of society, to which they long to return now that the war is over.

The ghost town, still bearing the sign 'Yellow Sky – Fastest Growing Town in the Territory', is no more than a couple of dilapidated wooden shacks, where the only source of life – water – can be found outside the settlement. This is obviously no earthly paradise, no utopian island, but rather a place at the far edge of the universe, on the frontier of human civilisation. The inclination to stay put and brood on the greatness of the past, however, turns out to be self-destructive, and the conclusion makes it clear that both domestic happiness and socially acceptable citizenship are available only if one turns towards the future. Mike, whom we have long suspected of cherishing feminine traits under her tomboyish appearance (the camera has repeatedly observed her curvaceous body in moonlit scenes), is offered a way to find her real feminine self, symbolically represented by the hat that Stretch buys her when he returns the money to the bank they robbed in the opening scene (see figure 1.1).

The simple and somewhat naive optimism of this scene fits perfectly the gender politics of the classical western, in which the (white) woman's place is by the side of her husband, preferably within a domestic environment, and certainly dressed in feminine, rather than masculine, attire. Mike, however, seems a slightly more complex character than the simple and naive 'pure young woman – the good and strong virgin' that Bazin describes as the stereotypical female in the classical western.[12] Even the motif of rape that both Howard and Brown emphasise in their analyses as 'the most influential

Figure 1.1 Mae in her new hat – Anne Baxter in *Yellow Sky*. Directed by William A. Wellman, 1948. Twentieth Century Fox.

element of *The Tempest*,[13] arguing that it connects the gang of outlaws, rather than the Indians, with Shakespeare's Caliban, plays out somewhat differently than in the drama, more in line with western conventions in the era. I do not believe that the moment when the outlaw called Lengthy (John Russell) presses Mike against a tree displays 'the kind of Sycoraxian violence once smote upon Ariel';[14] all three scenes in which we see Mike grapple with her attackers function rather as a series of tests, primarily for Stretch. Since he proves capable of shedding the violence of his earlier life, and becomes a decent man who can help the damsel in distress, he also proves worthy of her attention. In turn, this makes him worthy of redemption in the film's universe, as opposed to the more immoral members of the gang, Dude and Lengthy in particular, who never leave the town alive. In this sense, the film also illustrates how 'frontier existence provides a testing ground for exploring how human society develops in a "state of nature", prior to the "corrupting" influence of civilization' – the more time they spend in Yellow Sky, the more we can observe the innermost characteristics of each individual.[15] At the same time, the classic western still believes in the benefits of civilisation, and laments, but also accepts society's inevitable progress towards a more organised social structure.

Concerning the seemingly paradoxical final image of Mike in her new floral hat, clearly suggesting her desire to be associated with a more civilised type of femininity than her previous conduct implied, it is vital to remember again the socio-historical context of the film's release. As Mark E. Wildermuth points out, late 1940s westerns often reflect on the confusion over public and domestic female roles created by the transformed employment structure of the war years. In this sense, Mike's continued joy at riding her horse in male company (and in trousers), while basking in the men's admiration for her beauty, emphasised by her new hat, can be a sign of a natural compromise. Such compromises were becoming more and more common within 'the divisive culture of the 1940s where many people still insisted that women must conform to traditional roles when the social and economic realities clearly showed that women had already proven their ability to move out of those roles'.[16] The message to the 1948 audience could not be clearer: after the war, there is law and order, peace and prosperity ahead, with an opportunity to start afresh, with a clean slate for anyone willing to work for it – but men should not be surprised to find that in their absence their women have also learned to stand their ground.

The issues of ethnicity that are often at the heart of the western may again play an interesting role in the background of *Yellow Sky*, explaining the presence of the Apache Indians, who appear as a distinct threat in a crucial moment of the narrative. Native Americans are presented as the Other, in contrast to the white population, even in the very first scene of the film, when the riders stop to look at a skull of a former prospector, pierced through by an Apache arrow, and comment on how all they need is to 'run into some crazy Indians'. I am not convinced that the skull should be seen as a Yorick reference here, as Brown suggests, as nothing else associates the scene with *Hamlet*, and the bodily remains of less fortunate travellers are regular features in a western *mise-en-scène*.[17] Here the Native Americans are represented as a nearly invisible power, although they are still a considerable threat in their numbers, so much so that they could easily thwart the outlaws' plans to get Grandpa's gold. However, the Indians end up only passing through the ruined town, as a ghostly memory rather than a defining presence, and the sides of good and evil are no longer defined in support or in opposition to them. What is more, the comic Prospero figure of Grandpa turns out to be in actual control of the Apaches, able to convince them to go back to the reservation and promising to sort out their troubles with the

Indian agent. In this sense, the film also conforms to what Bazin described as one of the fundamental myths of the western: 'The Indian, who lived in this world, was incapable of imposing on it man's order. He mastered it only by identifying himself with its pagan savagery. The white Christian on the contrary is truly the conqueror of a new world.'[18] Yet we can already see the reason why the concept of the Vanishing American was born: 'the notion that Indians were doomed to disappear, either through assimilation into white society, or ... through the attrition of warfare and disease'.[19] These Indians have been robbed of their land and liberty, and they are given no voice to tell their story: whenever they appear in the film, they either utter unintelligible noises, or are shown at a distance, through a window, impersonal, unheard.

This appearance of the Other in an adaptation of *The Tempest*, however loose an offshoot *Yellow Sky* is, presents another element where the film's sources of inspiration can be distinguished from each other. Both Ariel and Caliban are truly out-of-place characters who are doomed to remain either on the island, or in captivity, but certainly not looking forward to the cast's departure at the end of the play. In *Yellow Sky* there is no single character cast in the roles of either the airy spirit (although Brown argues that Mike shares some of Ariel's qualities, 'and even something of the wild, witchy Sycorax',[20] but this idea seems to me rather far-fetched). The Native Americans as a group may be associated with the 'savage and deformed slave', as Caliban is described in *The Tempest*, particularly if we take their stereotypical wisdom and natural knowledge into account. This wisdom is not only necessary but also vital to the white protagonists (as it was the Apaches who helped Grandpa dig for gold), but the Indians' associations with the location and their reluctance to leave their own natural setting still makes it impossible for them to progress (or even to survive) in the wider world.

The film also makes it clear that Mike's masculine savagery comes from her upbringing with the Apache, which is another reason why this association must be left behind in order for her to achieve true romantic happiness at the side of Stretch. The Other as an ethnic group in this sense is not a Shakespearean theme but an element introduced into the film by the genre of the western, as necessary for the western setting as the 'thousand twangling instruments' (3.2.134) are for Prospero's magical island.[21] (It is true that Shakespeare's play includes a famous reference to the dead Indian having a more profitable occupation than the lame beggar (2.2.32), but as Virginia Mason Vaughan and Alden T. Vaughan emphasise in their 'Introduction', the drunken butler's words should be read more as 'a comment on tightfisted English folk and their attraction to exotic exhibits rather than a description of the gaberdine-covered creature'.[22]) As regards the future fates of the Native Americans, though, the historical moment the film chooses for its temporal setting bodes no good for the Apache; the following year, 1868, brought President Ulysses S. Grant's Peace Policy, which launched the era of forced relocation and assimilation for Native Americans. Wellman's film thus manages to combine the optimistic resolution of the plot with the darker undertones that we also find in Shakespeare's play: a romance on the surface, but hiding deep down a farewell to all that is dear.

Crisis in the family, crisis in society – *Broken Lance*

The two 1950s westerns discussed in this section, although based on different Shakespeare plays, are connected by their shared thematic interests: both are concerned with traditional roles and relationships within the family, and a general sense of uncertainty and distrust that characterised American culture in the decade. As Steven Mintz summarises the significance of this theme in the period: 'During the late 1940s and 1950s, the heyday of the western talkie, the family often occupied an important place in such films. But the family patterns displayed differed fundamentally from those portrayed in romantic melodramas. Instead of focusing on spousal relations, many expressed a deep nostalgia for strong rural families.'[23] Whether the plot concerns parent–child or sibling relationships, or temptations within a conjugal bond, 'Metaphorically, these films reinforced the primacy of the family in postwar culture', embedded in broader social issues, as discussed later in this section.[24]

In terms of their Shakespearean roots, *Jubal*'s close resemblances to *Othello* make it easier to identify as an adaptation, while *Broken Lance* is a reimagining of the *Lear* plot, with Spencer Tracy in the lead role. However, tracing the authorial credits of the latter only to Shakespeare may be misleading, and indeed, to find the so-called origins of the film's script could be a rather daunting task. Douglas Lanier mentions *Broken Lance* among 'second-order adaptations – that is, works based upon novels or plays themselves often loosely based upon Shakespeare's play'.[25] Its screenplay was written by Philip Yordan in 1954 (and it earned him an Academy Award), but in actual fact it was a reworking of the material of an earlier *film noir* script, *House of Strangers* (1949, dir. Joseph L. Mankiewicz), also written by Yordan, together with the director (the latter also known for his 1953 *Julius Caesar* adaptation). *House of Strangers*, however, was not based on an original screenplay either, but was an adaptation of Jerome Weidman's novel *I'll Never Go There Anymore* (1941).

Yet nowhere in this chain of adaptations and re-adaptations is the *Lear* story mentioned, and indeed, hardly any secondary source dealing with the western genre has remarked on the Shakespearean connection to *Broken Lance* or its predecessors until the twenty-first century. The December 1977 issue of *Shakespeare on Film Newsletter* even takes a firm stand against identifying the film as an adaptation of Shakespeare: 'It's time to lay to rest the notion that *Broken Lance* (1954, directed by George [*sic*] Dmytryk) is an adaptation of *Lear*. Nowhere in the publicity releases, credits, or contemporary reviews is Lear mentioned. Indeed, one would be hard put to find any resemblances.'[26] While the lack of references may indeed be true (as opposed to plenty of references, clear similarities and even direct quotations from the script of *House of Strangers*), I would suggest that for readers of Shakespeare there is much that will strike them about the story. When an elderly, rather tyrannical father divides his property among his children, only the youngest of whom has any desire to be loyal to him, and is willing to undergo suffering in order to protect the father from shame and humiliation, Lear immediately and inevitably comes to mind.

True, here we have sons rather than daughters, and three, rather than two, evil brothers set against the one faithful child, but the abused father, dying alone in nature, driven from his home by his own scheming offspring while he was trying to remedy his wrongs, is an obvious Lear figure in *Broken Lance* as well. He is endowed with all the contradictions of the stubbornly powerful old man, both 'sinned against' and 'sinning' (3.2.60), with whom we can increasingly sympathise as we are following him on the road to ruination and death.[27] Lanier is naturally also right in claiming that the film's 'protagonist is not the Lear-figure but rather the Cordelia-figure, the faithful son who takes a fall for his father only to learn years later that his siblings have, out of greed, betrayed him and his father'.[28] The frame narrative indeed focuses on Joe (Robert Wagner), the youngest son who has just returned from prison, and whose reflections on the past conflict take up most of the screen time, but the story's key figure is still old Matt Devereaux (Spencer Tracy). Moreover, it is not simply the folktale elements that connect *Broken Lance* and *Lear*, but the story of filial ingratitude is set against a symbolic landscape that can easily be identified with the heath. The image of solitary man – symbolised in the film by the lone wolf that appears in every significant moment – finding solace in the harshness of nature from human predators is a Shakespearean addition that the archetypal sources or Yordan's other scripts rarely reflect on, but it is at the heart of *Broken Lance* as well as *King Lear*. The breathtaking vista of the western setting is naturally a central element of the genre, and as Yvonne Griggs argues, 'what is staged through ceremonious division of the land at the start of the play is presented cinematically in *Broken Lance* via the lingering shots of the frontier landscape that will be contested throughout the narrative'.[29] At the same time, the camerawork, characteristic of Edward Dmytryk's *oeuvre*, also adds emphasis to the significance of space:

> Dmytryk also practiced another form of economy: full use of the frame, as if it were a canvas to be filled with images of such diversity that the eye does not lose interest in them. Even when he leaves part of the frame empty – as he does in *Broken Lance* (1954), his first encounter with CinemaScope, in which a shot at one end of the frame is not balanced by a corresponding shot at the other – that spatial void is still functional; in *Broken Lance* it has less to do with the wide screen than with the dramatic effect of family disunity.[30]

In true western fashion, the setting is not simply a backdrop, but contributes to the conflict, and it also becomes a participant in the protagonist's mental and physical disintegration. The imbalance displayed by Matt Devereaux, who refuses to behave in a rational manner, is easy to associate with Lear's madness as well, and his Native American wife and his servant, who remain at his side, are socially just as marginalised as Lear's Shakespearean companions.

It is, however, important to look at the change of gender in the patriarch's children from the viewpoint of the western, to see how the gender policies of the era are reflected by the cast. The western is a masculine genre, but the few roles it assigns to females are always crucial, even if limited in detail. Nonetheless, by the 1950s Hollywood cinema appeared to no longer believe in simplistic characterisations of women as confined to the domestic sphere, as post-war American society had to face radical changes in social and family structure. The female figures in *Broken Lance* cannot exert real control over the narrative, but both are vital for the resolution of the conflict. The youngest son's mother, Devereaux's Comanche wife (Katy Jurado), is forced by her natural wisdom as well as her ethnicity into the position of the outsider. The other significant female in the cast is Barbara (Jean Peters), young Joe's sweetheart (and eventually wife), daughter of the governor, who fits the bill for the strongminded and morally immaculate virgin that is a staple element of the western. In a sense, both females play characters who should be absent from a *Lear* narrative, but the roles both Senora Devereaux and young Barbara take on themselves in *Broken Lance*, in particular that of the trusted companion, are vital for the narrative development. Cawelti shows how a common solution for the threat that 'the presence of women usually [means for] the primacy of the masculine group' is that 'The woman in effect takes over the role of the masculine comrades and becomes the hero's true companion.'[31] Barbara, who at first appears to be a superficial character in frilly dresses, with an education in the East that must have turned her away from the appreciation of the essential values of life, in the end wins over even Joe's Comanche mother, and proves herself worthy by patiently waiting out Joe's prison sentence.

The gender roles in *Broken Lance*, surprisingly different from the Shakespearean source, are therefore once more explained by the western genre, in a way even more clearly than in *Yellow Sky*. Quoting Bazin again: 'The myth of the western illustrates, and both initiates and confirms woman in her role as vestal of the social virtues, of which this chaotic world is so greatly in need. Within her is concealed the physical future, and, by way of the institution of the family to which she aspires as the root is drawn to the earth, its moral foundation.'[32] This moral foundation was all the more important in the 1950s as the decade was plagued by mounting divorce rates in the USA, and it is no wonder that popular and high culture equally sought to address (or at least represent) the problem in their own ways. The hostility between the sons of the two mothers may be one reminder of this; however, the film's ending nevertheless sides with the females and confirms that their roles are in no way simplistic within the narrative, let alone the genre. As Sue Matheson argues, 'Whether or not the cowboy rides off alone into the sunset at his movie's end, intense caring and affectionate interpersonal relations are found at the heart of this genre'.[33] This is particularly noticeable in *Broken Lance*, where young Joe is markedly lacking in male

Figure 1.2 Riding away from the past – Robert Wagner and Jean Peters in *Broken Lance*. Directed by Edward Dmytryk, 1954. Twentieth Century Fox.

comrades – he is always on his own, even if he is generally liked, whether in jail or in town. As his mixed-race origins prevent him from being fully acknowledged as an equal member of the bourgeois community, the elevation of Barbara to a fully supportive companion is indeed significant.

With the help of the strong and loyal females, but also with the unshakeable loyalty of the Native Americans, *Broken Lance* shows a sensitivity to the broader social concerns of the time of its release, 'offering a commentary on the hypocrisy, racism, and opportunism at the core of a post-war America in the guise of the historically removed frontier western'.[34] One particularly painful aspect of post-war American society may also be felt in the film's references to the world of politics, elections bought and sold, and a general lack of trust. As Griggs argues,

> Through his exploration of the corruption and prejudice at the core of this newly established, superficially more cultured and civilized society, Dmytryk challenges its stability both within its historical cinematic context and that of his contemporary America – an America which, in the fifties, blacklisted him, hauling him before the House of Un-American Activities Committee.[35]

These motifs can also be found at the heart of *Jubal*, the *Othello* adaptation made only two years later, reinforcing the connection between the two works, as we shall see in the following section.

Broken Lance gives a nod to several contemporary popular westerns, among others *High Noon* (1952, dir. Fred Zinnemann), a film labelled as 'an unquestioned masterpiece, possibly the number one western of all time'.[36] The connection is actress Katy Jurado, who plays the Mexican Helen Ramírez in *High Noon* and Senora Devereaux in *Broken Lance*, her two roles sharing a number of features. More importantly, the film's title can be seen as a reflection on *Broken Arrow*, a 1950 film directed by Delmer Daves and starring James Stewart, much praised for its sympathetic portrayal of Native Americans, and 'regularly cited as a milestone on Hollywood's road towards a more liberal view of Indian–white relations'.[37] The connection between the two films is partly the participle in the title, signifying a desire to lay down weapons and end the devastating cycle of revenge between locals and newcomers. More important, however, is the motif of sacrifice: the price to be paid for the reluctant acceptance of peace between the white man and the Indians in *Broken Arrow* is the death of the protagonist's young Chiricahua Apache wife. In *Broken Lance* it is the protagonist, the Lear figure himself, who has to be sacrificed, since he was the main obstacle blocking the future of the young generation who was unable to acknowledge that social progress had left him behind.

The real opposition represented in the film, however, is no longer between savages and civilised pioneers, as in many classic westerns dealing with the era of westward expansion. Here the clash is between East and West, the corrupt and ruthless industrialists from the East Coast, who only see the potential for investment in the land, never having worked for it, and whose exploitation of natural resources effectively destroys the land itself, standing in opposition to the real man of the West. The copper mine established by the Eastern industrialists on the Devereaux ranch ends up poisoning the river and killing cattle, and thus becomes directly responsible for the old rancher taking the law into his own hands. This, however, is no longer the age of heroic cowboys who would fight it out with each other, face to face, which is still the ideal form of conflict resolution for the old patriarch. As a result, his attack on the mine lands him in court, and eventually leads to his youngest son's imprisonment, but, more importantly, to the complete disintegration of the world old Devereaux has spent his whole life building up. At the same time, the film does not fully take his side, as we are aware of the interests of the state in the mine and the potential prosperity held by new forms of industry. While it is undeniable that industrialisation is a threat to nature, it is also an inevitable part of life, and this contradiction is another central notion in many westerns. As John C. Tibbets points out, 'The "Machine in the Garden" myth defines an essentially American ambivalence toward the contradictory conditions of pastoral promise and material experience.'[38] The fight against the forces of progress is, of course, a losing battle, as civilisation and industrialisation are the foundations of the promise of the New World; nonetheless, the western is allowed to reflect on the times of innocence and heroism with nostalgia.

This nostalgia is best observed in the visual imagery of the west, not only in the spectacular landscape, the herds of cattle, the ten-gallon hats and western costumes, but in the general, rather melancholy atmosphere that seems to lament the demise of a world in which men and nature still lived in harmony. The most powerful image that reinforces the vision of the decay of the noble old world is the dilapidated ranch, the house that is falling apart not only in the physical sense but which also represents the downfall of the Devereaux family itself by the time Joe returns from prison. Nature and the Comanche are still alive, though their days are already on the wane, and the film's depiction of the gradual disintegration of the world of the western and the protection provided for Native Americans by the old-fashioned heroes leaves us with the impression of a melancholy nostalgic lament of the western, rather than a Shakespearean tragedy. In the final scenes, we can see Joe and Barbara already dressed in urban elegance as newlyweds, saying their farewells to the old man's grave (see figure 1.2), before they ride off in their carriage – not into the sunset, but presumably to a more settled, even bourgeois form of social existence, away from the toxic atmosphere of the past.

Anxieties of the male psyche – *Jubal*

The other 1950s western includes a more easily recognisable reference to Shakespeare's *Othello*: the plot of *Jubal* focuses on a story of jealousy, in which an easily duped husband is led to believe that his wife has been unfaithful to him, and his rage eventually leads to the death of both. The details, however, run in somewhat different directions, making the parallels at times problematic to maintain. The plot is simple: a weak and lonely horseless man, Jubal Troop (Glenn Ford), is taken in by prosperous Shep Horgan (Ernest Borgnine) to work on his ranch, where Jubal easily rises to the position of foreman, making an enemy in Pinky (Rod Steiger), a spiteful ranch hand, who has had an affair with Shep's bored wife, Mae (Valerie French). She sets her eyes on Jubal, but he stays away, drawn instead to a young girl, Naomi (Felicia Farr), a member of a Puritan community passing through the ranch, much to the annoyance of Pinky and his gang. Pinky's machinations and lies eventually incite Shep's anger, who is led to believe that Mae betrayed him with Jubal, but when provoked to a shootout in the town, Jubal proves to have a faster hand, killing Shep. A dying Mae, however, tells the truth, thus at the end Pinky is brought to justice and Jubal is free to ride away with Naomi and her family.

Even though the assignment of functions and themes to members of the cast shows significant differences from Shakespeare's tragedy, the similarities are clear enough to identify, as Mary Lea Bandy and Kevin Stoehr also discuss the film under the label 'Othello on the Range'.[39] Again, as with the previous films, the western conventions demand a radical reimagining of gender roles, therefore the victim brutally murdered is no Desdemona, but a flirtatious woman who is dissatisfied with her lot and brings her tragedy upon herself. By the end she confesses her sins and tries to redeem herself, but she has no place in the world of the western. In contrast to her immoral behaviour, the cast also includes an innocent and virtuous maiden in the shape of Naomi, whom we will find at the side of Jubal at the end. (It may be no accident that only these two characters have Biblical names, even if their resemblance to their Old Testament counterparts is marginal.) Robert F. Willson summarises the changes in the female roles: 'Woman, unlike man in this genre, is denied complexity as well as the right to act on her own; she must be true to type, whether that be villain or angel.'[40] And Willson's conclusion suggests an understanding of the socio-cultural context that brought this vision of *Othello* to life:

> The transformation of Cassio-Jubal into hero rather than accused seducer of his mentor's wife shifts the story's perspective as well, transforming a tale about an alienated Moor to one of a wandering loner whose life as a nomad ends when he finds the right woman and family. Such an upbeat resolution reflects the practice of studios in the Golden Age and the conventions of the western, where the hero's actions lead to victory over evil and where women are assigned more typical, subordinate roles.[41]

The (often deceptive) simplicity of female roles, however, supports the main intention of the western: the woman is what the hero fights for in the first place, as she 'represents the domestic virtues of civilization – and so the man who fights for her struggles for the sake of a future society where violence has been tamed'.[42] The other type of female character, the loose woman, is seen as a threat to this civilised domestic world and has therefore no place in it – the most positive outcome of a life of sins is her chance to redeem herself by making a final sacrifice in order to aid the hero in saving the world.

The ethnic setup of the cast of *Jubal* is again clearly defined by the cinematic context, which in turn is based on the socio-historical realities of 1950s America: the cast includes no actor of colour, least of all in the title role. Although historically it was not uncommon for African-Americans to work as cowherds in the west,[43] a black-skinned Othello character would have severely restricted the film's distribution opportunities in the 1950s, therefore the Otherness of the Othello figure had to be shown in strictly non-ethnic ways.[44] This in turn modifies the film's focus and betrays that, for all its heroic simplicity, the film belongs to 'the more psychologically and existentially charged Westerns of the 1950s';[45] *Jubal* does not offer a contemplation of race, but it does discuss jealousy, loyalty to family and community, duty and hard work, poverty and wealth, opportunities gained and lost – all of which are familiar from the Shakespearean source narrative. And while Willson argues that Jubal is more of a Cassio figure,[46] I believe that he is also the outsider, the one who gains advantages and a position of leadership over the locals, but never entirely fits into the local society, and this marginalised status endows him with sufficient Othello-like characteristics as well. At the same time, the owner of the ranch and proud husband of the only wife around, Shep is even more easily associated with the Moor, particularly as he is the one who falls victim to the plotting of Pinky, his evil subordinate. But several minor elements, like the handkerchief, are also used in an altered way: here Naomi gives it to Jubal as a farewell gift, and asks for a kiss in return, since she has never been kissed before, but she is aware that her fate has been laid down by her people and she may have no choice in it herself.

The conclusion of the narrative is again defined by the genre of the western. Because of the shifting perspective that Willson also observes in the quote just mentioned, *Jubal* is not a tragedy, and the *denouement* offers merely a somewhat melancholy consideration of the waste of life and power, that is, the death of Shep and his flirtatious wife, Mae. At the same time, it also provides reassurance of the justice served to the main plotter (Pinky, the Iago figure), and the hope of a new beginning, where Jubal can be happy with his innocent and loyal Naomi, and the two of them can put right what Jubal's parents and their broken family nearly destroyed. The emphasis on the family comes to the foreground several times, in particular when Jubal talks about his childhood made miserable by an unloving (and unmarried) mother, who never wanted the child and even wished he had died. All this childhood suffering cast him into the role of the homeless wanderer until Naomi came along, to help him find domestic happiness after all. This interest in popular psychology is, of course, never too far from Hollywood filmmaking, but 'The idea of the past shaping the future in psychological terms plays a key role ... especially in the "neurotic" and "Freudian" Westerns of the 1950s.'[47]

Young Naomi, however, stands for more than simply traditional domesticity – she also wishes to break free of her people's unsettled lifestyle, from being constantly on the road, in search of the Promised Land. (This wide-eyed naiveté is slightly mocked by the film, suggesting that going to Idaho to find their spiritual destination will be a foreseeable let-down.) She dreams of a home (see figure 1.3), and since she does not love the duplicitous fellow sectarian intended for her, she breaks all conventions and chases after her hero, Jubal, to save him from his enemies and himself. The optimistic ending thus offers a clear reinforcement of the family as the foundation of the future and of America as a country. Nonetheless, the upbeat *denouement* cannot deny that the price to pay for this bright future may be the traditions that small local communities may have considered safe, but which in the long run prevented the nation from forming one large and happy family.

America is therefore a racially and ethnically homogeneous country in the world of *Jubal* – not only is there no Moor or African-American character, but even Native Americans are absent from the screen and the dialogue.

Figure 1.3 Jubal and Naomi dreaming of a home – Felicia Farr and Glenn Ford in *Jubal*. Directed by Delmer Daves, 1956. Columbia Pictures.

The conflict is artificially generated, based on personal hatred and jealousy: Jubal is shunned by Pinky, the Iago character, because he 'stinks of sheep' and therefore cannot be a proper cowherd, but mostly because Jubal soon proves to be a superior ranch hand, horseman and human being in general. The conflict is thus cooked in the home, the domestic sphere of the close-knit community of men sharing the same space – and the best excuse for trouble is the archetypal sinner-cum-victim: the one and only woman on the ranch. The film's ending shows mercilessly that 1950s American society considers such temptresses the archenemy: as Mae risked her home and hearth for the sake of inconsiderate, if innocent, flirtation, she has no place in this society. Her fate serves as a warning for such loose women who do not cherish their simple but well-meaning husbands: they will have to pay with their lives for their foolishness. The one to build a future on is the girl who knows her place: at home, by her husband's side, with a heart filled with love pure as the driven snow.

Besides the Shakespearean context, however, it is also instructive to examine the broader cinematic western context, which may explain a number of directorial choices and narrative elements through the familiarity of the genre for contemporary audiences. To see what the western without *Othello* would look like, one may compare *Jubal* with *Shane* (1953, dir. George Stevens), a film made only three years earlier, whose plotline has more than superficial similarities with that of *Jubal*. As a result, some contemporary reviewers accused the filmmakers of a lack of originality, but when looked at through a Shakespearean lens, one can easily recognise that it is precisely the *Othello* elements that are missing from the earlier film.[48] In *Shane* the conflict is between ranchers and homesteaders, and the outsider ex-gunslinger hero needs to take sides; although his lifestyle would associate him with the outlaws, his inner values make him stand by the settlers. Having to defend them, however, forces him to resort to violence, which in turn makes him unfit for acceptance in the community – thus, in the end the lonesome cowboy rides off on his own, since Shane knows that 'a man cannot change what he is'.

In *Jubal*, on the other hand, as in the domestic tragedy of *Othello*, the conflict is sown within the home, by the bored wife's behaviour, thus Pinky, her disappointed ex-lover and spiteful ranch hand, can easily incite jealousy between husband and wife, which will result in the demise of both. Jubal, the solitary outsider, is both more and less significant in the story than Shane: he upsets the delicate balance within the ranch community, and later on he is manipulated as a tool to fabricate the web of lies that will bring down Shep and his wife. At the same time, Jubal is presented as a good man wishing for an ordinary life, not a magnificent-seven-in-one like Shane, and this ordinariness also grants him a domestic future that Shane has to refuse if he wishes to retain his identity. In this way, *Jubal* joins the same argument that many 1950s westerns, including *Shane*, were engaged in, dwelling 'explicitly on whether violence is an appropriate means of resolving the various crises defined in their plots', questioning 'the ethics and relative necessity of physical conflict. While this ... does not mean that the prospect of violence ceases to be central to their plots, it signals a significant departure.'[49] But as *Shane* emphasises the price to pay for the old – however heroic – lifestyle, *Jubal* is more focused on the promise of happiness if one is willing to leave all that heroism behind, and in effect, both argue that violence might be necessary for spiritual and physical regeneration, to use Richard Slotkin's terms.[50]

Another significant non-Shakespearean element in *Jubal* (but one with a contemporary socio-cultural relevance) is the Puritan religious community that the loner cowboy joins at the end, and where he hopes to find health and happiness. What is more, the positive influence is mutual, as he also ends up activating the religious wanderers into defending truth and the values they believe in. This motif may readily bring to mind the famous Ford western, *Wagon Master* from 1950, the story of a Mormon community journeying towards the promised land they hope to find in the San Juan Valley, accompanied by two young horse traders turned wagon masters, who also end up defending the Mormons from the greater danger, the murderous Clegg clan. In *Wagon Master* we can observe the same contrast between two women as in *Jubal*: a dark-haired beauty with a sinful past in show business, but with a good heart that will save her from solitude, on the side of Travis, the more mature and experienced of the wagon masters. At the same time, there is also the innocent fair-haired Mormon girl, Prudence, who is hardly granted any utterance throughout the whole script, but whose timid smiles are receptive of the more boisterous (if slightly childish) advances of the young wagon master, antagonising an attentive Mormon young man. While the ending is left open in the way most of Ford's westerns leave questions unanswered, the young and capable protagonists are allowed at least a vague promise of domestic bliss after their years of wandering. At the same time, the narrative also staves off a tragic ending, just like in *Jubal*, which – in contrast to its Shakespearean source – shifts its focus from the victim to the saviour figure, and thus allows its eponymous hero the chance of finding the Promised Land he is seeking.

If we add to this generic backdrop the socio-cultural background of the McCarthy era, which created all-round suspicion and a general lack of trust in the American population, it is no wonder that the reinforcement of Christian belief (to counter the atheist threat of Communism) was generally accepted as vital to saving the nation. It was this atmosphere of uncertainty and the subsequent increase in Puritan religiosity that resulted in the inclusion of the phrase 'under God' in the Pledge of Allegiance during the 1950s, the reinstated presence of 'in God we trust' as a national motto, to be put not only on coins but on paper money as well from 1957, among other signs that clear and fundamental religious beliefs were seen in the age as a significant safeguard to protect America as a community. While the Mormons in *Wagon Master* or the God-fearing people in *Jubal* have to suffer mockery, even exile and other hardships for their faith, they are also represented as the meek who will inherit the earth. At the same time, all the 1950s films mentioned here exemplify, if to varying degrees, the power of mass hysteria and fear. Their scenes in which a small number of scaremongers can terrify crowds either into running away from their rightful homes or making someone a scapegoat without evidence of their guilt, echo the dark shadows the McCarthy era cast over American society as a whole. The western, Ford's work in particular, but *Jubal* likewise, puts its emphasis on the community, the way a ragtag bunch of strangers can be shaped into unity by surviving hardships and happiness together – and no other era needed this message more than the 1950s.

Comic and parodic visions – *McLintock!*

After the genre's heyday, the 1960s and 1970s certainly saw a decline in production and consumption, possibly as a result of the growing historical and political awareness of the Indian–white antagonism being plagued by outdated and politically incorrect stereotypes. Added to that, the painful lessons of the Vietnam War no longer allowed such wide-eyed visions of white supremacy, but invited more critical or ironic attitudes towards ethnic conflicts, which many reviewers refer to when explaining the change in the style of westerns made in this period. In the world of the cinema, the 1960s also brought a general crisis, a decline of the classical studio system, with audiences turning towards home-owned televisions and away from implausible historical epics, among which the western used to have its place.[51] The so-called revisionist westerns of the late 1960s and 1970s approached the genre with a more critical attitude, as we shall discuss in the following sections, but the mainstream classic western was clearly on its way out, replaced by comic or even parodic approaches to the iconic elements of the formula.

No wonder that the Shakespeare-inspired western also reflected the changing cultural and industrial contexts, partly through the choice of narratives to adapt and even more by the ways these films adopted the generic context and background. In most cases, it is not simply the general nostalgic vision of the West that may be successfully invoked by the 1960s westerns, but there are particular cinematic predecessors as well that are cited by these visual texts. *McLintock!* joins the line of earlier John Wayne westerns, and shows us the ageing hero who finds it hard to move on and away from the simple but noble world of the ranch. This is confirmed by the fact that Wayne shares the screen with Maureen O'Hara, as in some of his most famous films in the previous decade, including *Rio Grande* (1950) and *The Quiet Man* (1952). Even though the latter is no western, it also has a strong-minded female protagonist, and the boisterous Wayne–O'Hara screen relationship easily feeds into the Katherina–Petruchio match, their star appeal and previous career underscoring the theme of romance between two powerful personalities.

Comparing it only to other adaptations of Shakespeare's play, we could easily say that *McLintock!* owes just as much to the musical version of *The Taming of the Shrew*, *Kiss Me Kate* (1953, dir. George Sidney), as to the Wayne–O'Hara partnership. In particular, the slapstick wife-taming elements, mostly in the two scenes of public spanking and humiliation (one for the mother, one for the daughter, see figure 1.4), and the classic farce-like

Will in the Wild West

Figure 1.4 Wife taming in the Wild West – Stefanie Powers, Patrick Wayne, Maureen O'Hara and John Wayne in *McLintock!* Directed by Andrew V. McLaglen, 1963. Batjac Productions.

stair routines, covering the shrewish wife in molasses and goose feathers, are clearly indebted to the extremely popular Broadway musical and its Hollywood adaptation. But placing *The Quiet Man* also besides these sources of inspiration, it is hard to decide what exactly is the Shakespearean addition to the film – whether it is the western tradition that has paved the way for this film, or the legacy of early Shakespearean comedy with its marketplace slapstick traditions, or whether we should read *Rio Grande* and *The Quiet Man* also as *Shrew* variants, as Henryk Hoffmann suggests in his description of *McLintock!*:

> It does not break any aesthetic or intellectual grounds, but it is interesting as yet another version of the unusual and likeable on-screen relationship between John Wayne and Maureen O'Hara, with the intended similarity to both *Rio Grande* and *The Quiet Man* (both loosely derived from Shakespeare's *The Taming of the Shrew*), emphasised by the heroine's first name, Katherine.[52]

It is true that O'Hara's character in *Rio Grande* is called Kathleen, *The Quiet Man*'s heroine is Mary Kate – still, it may be practically impossible to go back to a single originary source for any of these films, as the possible allusions to characters and products of contemporary popular culture are simply too manifold. *Kiss Me Kate* is clearly one of the most important influences, but another type of comedy that may have left its mark on this film, just like on *Kiss Me Kate*, appears to be what Stanley Cavell calls the comedy of remarriage. In this subgenre a formerly married couple gets together again after realising that for all their differences of opinion, they belong together.[53] This is indeed what happens in *McLintock!*, since G. W. (that is, George Washington) McLintock, eponymous hero and owner of the town named after him (John Wayne), is still married to his estranged wife, Katherine (Maureen O'Hara), who has been living in the East with their daughter Rebecca (Stefanie Powers) for two years. Now Katherine is back, asking for a divorce, but after many comic twists of the plot, the film ends with the couple reunited – what is more, their daughter also realises that young homesteader Devlin Warren (Patrick Wayne) is a better partner for her than her refined banjo-playing Eastern beau (Jerry Van Dyke), and thus the conclusion brings double happiness.

More significant in the comic effect achieved by *McLintock!* is, however, the presence of genre parody, which 'subvert[s] the conventions of the Western in ways that breathe new life into the genre', and while mocking 'established formulas of the genre, it ultimately reinforces them through its acceptance of a shared set of codes'.[54] *McLintock!* clearly fits this bill, keeping the Shakespearean inspiration at bay, with the single Shakespearean line in its dialogue coming from *Macbeth*, rather than the *Shrew*: McLintock refers to the 'milk of human kindness' (1.5.17) when his charitable disposition is criticised.[55] The setting, however, is unmistakeably that of the western – ranch, cattle, rodeo and what you will – and the heroes of the narrative are those of the nineteenth-century expansion of America, the struggling small towns and booming businesses. Nonetheless, it is significant that some of the western conventions have become empty, performative devices, like the ten-gallon hat that McLintock routinely throws up at the weathervane of his house (shaped like a bull, rather than a cock), for the amusement of the local children.

This does not mean that the film is not truly invested in some of the fundamental western themes, specifically the representation of Native Americans, but also of family and marital life. In this comic vision of the West, the Other comes in two shades: on the one hand, in the usual form of Native Americans, and on the other, as new settlers who present a different lifestyle to the ranchers' community, with the true western hero mediating between the two. Although the representation of both of these groups and conflicts is still rather one-sided and schematic, and the protagonists of the film would not pass any test of political correctness according to twenty-first-century standards, it is evident that the film sides with the victims of abuse and injustice. The store clerk, Davey Elk (Perry Lopez), complains of the constant racial prejudice he has to put up with; at the same time, he is the cinematic descendant of the burlesque Native figures, akin to the Chinese cook of the McLintock family, and is allowed very little sympathy for his troubles.

More screen time is granted to the group of Native Americans who defy government regulations and choose to rebel against enforced relocation, and for whom McLintock attempts to provide justice. Their role within the narrative is no more than a backdrop against which the calamities of love can be painted, but seeing G. W. McLintock maintain a friendly relationship with them colours our understanding of his personality and enables us to recognise that the real villains are not the rebellious Indians but the duplicitous governor of the territory and his greedy agents. This is vital for letting the comedy of remarriage run its course and Katherine understand where her own loyalties lie. The group of settlers get even less of our attention, but from the sides taken by the protagonists we learn that they have mostly been misled and lured to the territory by false promises and have no chance of long-term prosperity in the land. The only members of the group that are granted individuality are the handsome young settler, Devlin, and his mother (Yvonne De Carlo), who come to be associated with the McLintock family in many ways, mostly as romantic interests. However, they also turn out to be settlers only by necessity, forced into this life by the death of the father, which also meant the end of Devlin's college years, but not that of his skills and talents. Thus he easily betters all his rivals for the hand of Becky McLintock in a way reminiscent of the Lucentio–Bianca plotline of Shakespeare's comedy. Afterwards the settlers practically disappear from the narrative; this is no longer the heyday of the western where their efforts at forging a community would be the focus, and the revisionist western has not yet quite arrived to openly question the superiority and criticise the behaviour of white ranchers. What the film promises and grants its viewers is the well-known setting and all the characters necessary for an authentic western story, but without the dramatic melancholy of the classics.

At the same time, there is no escaping the nostalgic element represented by the ageing protagonists, even within this comic vision of the West: McLintock and Katherine are no longer adventurous youngsters, and the world they wish to pass on to their daughter is one of comfort and safety, even if they lament the loss of heroism. A significant number of references are made to the good old days of the past – somewhat ironically, though, as those good old days were times of near starvation, constant struggle and sometimes suffering – when a man was still a man, and a woman was a woman who fought for her family and home (like a man) when the need arose. The older generation of characters (the phrases 'men of my age' or 'young men of your age' are repeatedly used), and possibly of filmmakers, do not rejoice in the passing of this world, but the signs of change can no longer be denied. By the end of the decade, the revisionist western will dominate the genre, and not even the Shakespeare western can remain unchanged by its effects.

Spaghetti Shakespeare – *Johnny Hamlet*

Before looking at the revisionist Anglo-American western, there is another subgenre that needs mentioning, partly because of its significance in global cinema history, but even more as it was another sign of the decline of the western genre and its representation of the Old West: the Italian or spaghetti western. The latter term, which has come into general use to describe the films shot mostly in Spain but directed by Italian filmmakers, is not a little derogative. Still, there is no denying that the great masters of the spaghetti western, legendary filmmaker Sergio Leone in particular, together with composer Ennio Morricone and many others, have shaped and revitalised the genre considerably. From such a rich tradition, it is no surprise that at least one film openly acknowledges being inspired by Shakespeare's *Hamlet*: Enzo G. Castellari's *Johnny Hamlet* (1968, shot in English, but also known in Italian as *Quella sporca storia nel West*, in a literal translation 'That dirty story of the West', and released in the USA as *The Wild and the Dirty*).

In German, the film is known as *Django: Die Totengräber warten schon*, meaning 'Django: The Gravediggers are already waiting', and the gravedigger is indeed a keyword – one that we could expect to have a purely Shakespearean relevance, but that is only half of the truth. When looking at the most significant Italian westerns from the years directly preceding *Johnny Hamlet*, it becomes clear that graveyards and gravediggers are much more central to the subgenre than either the classical western or Shakespearean drama would imply. The first film to use the name Django, Sergio Corbucci's 1966 *Django* has a considerable number of similarities with *Johnny Hamlet*, from the post-Civil War setting and the two gangs of outlaws (one Mexican, one American), through the scenes of torture, to the significance of the graveyard itself, which are all essential ingredients of spaghetti westerns. By the time *Johnny Hamlet* came out two years after Corbucci's film, the enormous commercial success of the original *Django* and its eponymous character resulted in a vast number of films being (re)titled to tie in with the box-office hit (out of the thirty-one appearances of the character, the first fifteen are in films released in 1966–1967).

Looking at *Johnny Hamlet* through a Shakespearean lens, we have to realise two somewhat paradoxical facts: first, that among the western Shakespeare adaptations this film has the most textual references to its source text, using cast members and names, locations and plot elements, even quotations, including the great soliloquy from *Hamlet*. Second, and more importantly, it is also obvious that for all its Shakespearean lineage, the film cannot be properly understood without its generic context. While the spaghetti western used a great number of elements that featured in the American western narratives as well, the local variants are still recognisable and make this subgenre a phenomenon of its own. *Johnny Hamlet* opens with a dream sequence, which combines Johnny Hamilton's (Andrea Giordana) vision of his father's ghost with a nightmare about the Civil War (in which he has just fought and from which he is on his way home). On waking from the dream, he rides home and begins to clear his name, while also clearing his town of bandits.

This being a western, the genre of quiet men, the ghost does not utter a word, and neither does Johnny say anything to the actors who have given him shelter for the night and whose recitation of Hamlet's great soliloquy can be heard during the opening sequence. It is telling that this western does not begin with a view of the wide open plains of the Wild West, as does practically every western of the classical period – it is a western of the imagination, a fiction brewed within the mind that may or may not bear any relation to reality. The film's powerful visual world is full of reflexive surfaces and reflected views, as if claiming in a self-reflexive manner that it is not the real thing, only an imitation. At the same time, the many peephole shots implying observation, as well as the abundance of mirrors and reflections, centralising the theme of appearances and fake realities, also fit the *Hamlet* theme, and are therefore natural cinematographic choices to enhance the combination of the genre with the source text.

The central conflict of *Johnny Hamlet* involves another aspect of the spaghetti western that characterised the most famous early examples of the genre, notably Leone's *Dollars Trilogy* (*A Fistful of Dollars*, 1964; *For a Few Dollars More*, 1965; *The Good, the Bad and the Ugly*, 1966), later imitated by many others. In all these films, a solitary gunslinger comes to a town which is ruled by two rival gangs, and by playing them against each other, he eventually eliminates both. In the course of the films, a hidden cache of gold or money plays a central role, and the protagonist gets involved in the fate of the suffering victims of the feud while he tries to help the locals. Before the final showdown, he even gets caught and tortured by the bandits, but successfully (or miraculously) survives, and in the end, rides off into the sunset. The compulsory element of the rival gangs explains why in *Johnny Hamlet* it is not only Claude Hamilton (Horst Frank), Johnny's uncle, who counts as the enemy of the Hamlet character, but a gang of Mexicans is equally involved in the treachery. Eventually, the Mexicans realise that they have also been betrayed by Claude, therefore it is easy to convince them to turn against him – and thus we get all necessary components for the final shootout and the cleansing of the town.

Judging the film from a purely Shakespearean perspective, we may be at a loss as to why in *Johnny Hamlet* the Rosencrantz and Guildenstern figures, Ross and Guild (Ennio Girolami and Ignazio Spalla) are shown as such cruel thugs, rather than weak and manipulable, servile courtiers misled by their willingness to serve. Here the two characters may not be very intelligent, but they are relentlessly threatening, sometimes downright brutal, although these features are not exactly inherent in their Shakespearean incarnations. However, if we see these scenes as following the generic traditions, the scene of Johnny's arrival into town resembling in many ways the well-known opening scenes and the images of the showdown from Leone's *Once Upon a Time in the West* (made in the very same year, 1968), these details fall into place more easily. A western hero does not fear gossip or the fact that his intentions are made known to his enemies, since he has nothing to hide. The only thing he fears is a gunslinger who is a better shot than himself, but there are not many of those – here it is only Horace (Gilbert Roland), the Horatio figure, and his perfect shots are always there to save Johnny's skin. Similarly, the fact that Johnny Hamilton survives the almost inhuman torture, and subsequently defeats all his enemies before riding off with Horace on his side (see figure 1.5), would sit rather uneasily in the Shakespearean tradition. It does, however, fit nicely with the best-known western cliché of the rough man, the solitary but self-sufficient hero, who is ready kill to protect others, but who will not be tied down by any community. Most spaghetti westerns are no settler narratives but they are set in the Civil War, often emphasising the cruel and senseless bloodshed of internal warfare. This also explains why Johnny is no student of moral philosophy but a soldier who has learnt the value of life and death on the battlefield.

The gravedigger scene has been mentioned as a clear link between the Shakespearean source text and the spaghetti western, but it also has an interesting social aspect. As Mariangela Tempera emphasises in her account of references to the gravedigger scene in *Hamlet* in Italian cinema, 'the Spaghetti Western … champions the underdog' and 'embraces the downtrodden peasant against the overbearing Gringo'.[56] Consequently, the social hierarchy and the relationships among various members of the

Figure 1.5 Riding off from Ranch Elsinore – Andrea Giordana and Gilbert Roland in *Johnny Hamlet* or *Quella sporca storia nel West*. Directed by Enzo G. Castellari, 1968. Daiano Film/Leone Film.

cast may undergo rather considerable modifications, as *Johnny Hamlet* illustrates perfectly. As one obvious sign of the influence of this Italian cinematic convention, the significance of the gravedigger is greatly increased in the film and he is granted a role reminiscent of the dramatic Chorus of antique tragedy.[57] The gravedigger motif is best exemplified by Leone's *Dollars Trilogy*, the first piece of which, *A Fistful of Dollars*, actually includes a number of scenes in a graveyard, with a lot of fighting (much like in *Johnny Hamlet*, where there are several gravedigger scenes, although none of them feature an actual funeral, in contrast to *Hamlet*). In this context, the graveyard is simply the macabre setting for another gunfight, with the grim reminders of death surrounding the participants. *Johnny Hamlet*'s gravedigger again shows a direct connection to the coffin-maker of *A Fistful of Dollars*, who is not simply a source for comic relief in the vein of Shakespearean tragedy, or a commenter on events, but an active participant and the sole individual who prospers in such a place of high mortality. The second instalment in Leone's trilogy, *For a Few Dollars More*, has no gravedigger among its cast, but in the final scene the pile of corpses thrown onto a little cart is strongly reminiscent of *Johnny Hamlet*'s ending, where the gravedigger arrives with a similar little cart and rejoices over the amount of work that resulted from the shootout (see the character in the background in figure 1.5). But the graveyard becomes central in the third film of Leone's trilogy, *The Good, the Bad and the Ugly*, in which the search for gold leads all three bounty hunters towards a graveyard where the treasure lies buried in a grave.

Another cinematographic connection to this particular subgenre of the western is the abundance of close-ups, even extreme close-ups, that characterise *Johnny Hamlet*, again very much like in Leone's work. The rising tension and quiet exchange of looks among these men of action (but few words) is not an exclusive feature of the Italian westerns. In the classical western, however, it is often the near empty landscape, the sleepy town and the hills in the background that have a central role, rather than the faces or eyes of the opponents that dominate the visual landscape of spaghetti westerns. These facial close-ups are often accompanied by circular panorama shots sweeping around the horizon, sometimes as point-of-view shots to imitate the protagonist taking stock of his position. Their most essential role, though, is to imply that in this world danger lies in every direction of the compass – a feeling the Prince of Denmark probably shared with these morally questionable but undoubtedly reckless heroes of the Mediterranean West.

Genre revisionism – *Harry and Tonto*

While the Italian and other European film companies were churning out one spaghetti western after another which showed no conventional regard for the sanctity of church, home or nation, but were rather characterised by an exaggerated presence of violence and nearly senseless killing, the American cinema scene turned to different paths of questioning the value system of classic westerns. Ford continued to produce a series of westerns until the mid-1960s and John Wayne starred in a number of well-known productions for another decade, but many of their later films are imbued with even more nostalgia than was characteristic of the genre. In the 1970s, the genre was brought back from its slumber, albeit in a somewhat altered manner when compared to the classical period. This was the time of 'the emergence of the so-called "revisionist" Western – the attempt by Western filmmakers, animated by a conviction of the unsustainability of traditional generic models, to reorient the Western's relationship to the history in which, at least nominally, it is grounded'.[58] The revisionist western uses the same setting and the well-known conflicts of the genre, but refuses to engage in its clichéd presentation of heroism, gender roles, attitudes to race and ethnicity, and optimistic happy endings.

Revisionist westerns brought a diminishing belief in the superiority of the white settlers and also a radically changed image of Native Americans. As John G. Cawelti summarises the underlying idea of genre revisionism: 'the conquest of the West was not a grandly simple matter of Lone Rangers bringing outlaws to justice and Indians to civilization, but a complex, dirty and ambiguous proceeding like the rest of human history'.[59] Such revisionism was born partly out of revisionist politics, forcing audiences to question their allegiances towards values and institutions previously taken for granted, and this critical attitude was also fed by events of national trauma such as the Kennedy assassination, the Vietnam War and the Watergate scandal. At the same time, aesthetic revisionism was also demanded and sought by filmmakers, most clearly by the New Hollywood generation, and similarly influential cinematographers who came directly before them, for example, Robert Altman, Sam Peckinpah, Arthur Penn, William A. Fraker and Sergio Leone. This latter group Paul Arthur characterises as 'wedged generationally between the giants of Hollywood's Golden Age and the film-school-trained, counterculture-infused New Hollywood upstarts'.[60]

It comes as no surprise therefore that in the 1970s, the Shakespeare western also reflects on these changes, and the final example in this chapter, the award-winning *Harry and Tonto* (1974), chooses to discard even the most characteristic, practically compulsory, element of the genre: its setting. The open vistas and spectacular landscapes of the Wild West are replaced by the urban jungle of the American metropolis. This lyrical film étude, which should be considered a road movie, is in many ways an odd one out in this discussion, since it does no more than touch upon the western theme, and in the same way, it only quotes Shakespeare in a self-conscious, but not necessarily systematic, manner. Directed by Paul Mazursky, and focusing on the theme of ageing, *Harry and Tonto* is nonetheless interesting in the context of the western as well, particularly as it fits into the revisionist tendencies of the 1970s. As Lanier points out, 'the road movie can be thought of as an ideological heir to the Western, since in both genres the American landscape itself promises liberation from overcivilization and bourgeois constraint, the possibility of ever-new horizons and personal renewal through self-reliance and endurance of adversity'.[61] In many ways, the film's endorsement of some of the western's characteristics and their use in a highly ingenious and creative way reminds the viewer of another unconventional western of the period, Dennis Hopper's *The Last Movie* (1971), which in Barry Langford's words 'defeats ... categorisation',[62] and despite its unique vision and uncompromising editing, 'has occasioned only intermittent critical interest'.[63] Both films showcase drifters in search of their true selves, on a journey which takes them back to the past, and rather than finding a way ahead, this backward journey prevents them from coming to terms with the reality of their present. Hopper's self-reflexive treatment of the clash between the real and the fake, the Peruvian Indians' world of belief and ritual and the cinema's world of illusion, can easily be seen as another take on Mazursky's nostalgic road movie, which follows its protagonist on a journey away from the limitations of the so-called real, even though much of the liberating power of the journey seems to be fed by a mediated fake reality of a time long past.

In a way, *Harry and Tonto* feels like a less violent, maybe kinder version of *The Last Movie* with a bit of Shakespeare added to it. The Shakespearean text that informs *Harry and Tonto* is *King Lear*, which is particularly interesting when compared to *Broken Lance*, discussed earlier in this chapter. As quoted, Lanier considers *Broken Lance* and most other American 'Lear screen spinoffs ... second-order adaptations', and argues that 'the relentlessly tragic, even nihilistic nature of the play ill sorts with the dominant ideological orientations of American culture', which is why mainstream American film genres find it hard to accommodate this dramatic source.[64] In the earlier film, it seems obvious that what makes *King Lear* particularly well suited for adaptation to the western genre is the centrality of the heath, a place whose inimical nature to life defines much of the dramatic struggle in the play. In the same way that the heath tests the endurance and humanity of Shakespeare's heroes, the open frontier of the Wild West is the place where a man can show his mettle by facing challenges presented by nature and society alike.

Interestingly enough, in *Harry and Tonto*, the symbolic heath is still in the West, but only from its protagonist's, Harry's (Art Carney), perspective. He has never before ventured so far from his home in New York, and the landscape, though wide and open, always includes a road, rather than the rugged mountains of Monument Valley or other famous western sites. The contrast between the urban desolation – the setting of Harry's futile attempts to share his life with his children – and the liberating air of the road, when civilisation seems to fall away from him, is powerful enough to remind us of Lear's journey of self-discovery through his suffering and madness. The Shakespeare elements, however, are consciously downplayed in *Harry and Tonto*, and the film's screenplay was nominated for the Writers' Guild of America Award for 'best drama written directly for the screen' (by Paul Mazursky and Josh Greenfeld), suggesting that the abundance of *Lear* motifs have become integral parts of the new textual body. However, if we consider the motifs of a tense relationship between father and children, an old man wandering in nature, accompanied only by an odd set of outcasts as companions, and going through a thorough inner transformation, from which he returns a kinder, more understanding man, we must realise how much the film owes to Shakespeare's

Lear. Harry also has a tendency to quote Lear's words, particularly in moments of high passion when he feels 'more sinned against than sinning' (3.2.60); for instance, when he is mugged on the street, he exclaims 'You heavens, give me that patience, patience [that] I need! / You see me here, you gods, a poor old man, / As full of ... [grief as age, wretched in both]' (2.2.460–2). But when he quotes 'I loved her most, and thought to set my rest / On her kind nursery' (1.1.123–4) to his daughter, she does not miss a beat before responding 'please, Harry, no Shakespeare', suggesting that Shakespeare is just as much out of place in the present society as Harry himself.

At the same time, *King Lear* is certainly not the only source from which the script springs: *Harry and Tonto* makes explicit references to *The Lone Ranger*, a popular radio and television series from 1938 (directed by John English and William Witney), whose protagonists reappeared in many later productions. These inter-cinematic references begin with Tonto, Harry's cat, named after the Lone Ranger's Native American companion, who was originally created simply to give the Lone Ranger someone to talk to – a function rather vital in a radio series.[65] Tonto the cat also performs this function, that of the reliable companion who shares every moment with his friend – but a companion who is sufficiently different in kind to emphasise the solitude of the protagonist.

The solitary western hero is one of the time-honoured character traditions of the genre, particularly the ageing gunman who represents the values of a disappearing era and whose fights for (what he believes is) truth and justice increasingly alienate him from the new world in which he finds himself. Once again, such a generalising summary underlines the reasons why *King Lear* has inspired several western productions: the same characterisation fits Shakespeare's patriarch just as well as a great number of western heroes including Tom Doniphon, the man who actually shot Liberty Valance in Ford's 1962 masterpiece, or most of the gang of outlaws in *The Wild Bunch* (1969, dir. Sam Peckinpah), one of the best-known examples of revisionist westerns. Yet there is also a touch of the Shakespearean in that the only true companion of the old man will leave him before the end of his journey, reminding the viewer of the disappearance of Lear's Fool.

When looking at the presence of compulsory genre elements in the film, the most ironic moment is clearly when Harry is incarcerated for a night after drunkenly relieving himself in public, and in the jail cell he meets Sam Two Feathers (Chief Dan George), a Native American medicine man. When Harry introduces his cat to the real Indian, it turns out that Sam has never heard of *The Lone Ranger* – he has no radio, and although he is the proud owner of a television set, he is unaware of the mediatised fame of the unlikely couple of the Lone Ranger and his friend Tonto. Still, the encounter between the real Native and the 'bestialised' fictional one is pessimistic in more ways than one: the meeting takes place in jail, as none of these figures can find a place in society. Moreover, the melancholy scene also becomes self-reflexive through the mention of the television, in line with 'the cultural shift from film to television as the primary self-articulation of American national identity' that Langford describes.[66] He points out that the theatrical western as a genre was increasingly in competition with 'the flood of TV Westerns that poured out between the late 1940s and the early 1960s and were in constant syndication throughout the 60s thereafter'.[67] This shift in the medium of self-articulation therefore neatly connects the two endangered species: the Native American and the western as a genre, and the highly self-reflexive nature of Mazursky's lyrical film, in spite of its *auteurial* qualities, still shows a sensitivity to the threats the genre was dealing with in the period.

The second half of the film, when the journey from one of his children towards another takes Harry to what he recognises as the West (he claims to be west of Chicago for the first time in his life), the western motifs suddenly become abundant and reinforce the feeling that this odd hybrid of a road movie has indeed entered its western phase. It is not only Harry's words that suggest the turn of direction, but his ten-gallon hat also visibly marks the change (see figure 1.6) (until then, he was wearing a characteristic trilby), and even more noticeably he quite literally starts singing a different tune. Throughout the film, he performs a variety of songs, mostly the Sinatra-type show repertoire, always selected for the occasion (from 'The Boulevard of Broken Dreams' through 'Chicago' to 'Tea for Two'). At the point of his turn towards the West, he is singing 'Get Along, Little Pussies' to Tonto – a 'felinised' version of the traditional cowboy ballad 'Git Along, Little Dogies' (even though a dogie refers to a motherless or neglected calf rather than a dog, but Harry carries his repertoire lightly, and adjusts it easily to the occasion). At the same time, there is no denying that the cowboy ballad entering Harry's repertoire does not revitalise the western as a lifestyle, and it will only remain a performative, rather than a lived, experience. *Harry and Tonto*, just like *The Man Who Shot Liberty Valance* in Langford's interpretation, is a chamber western, with only echoes of the sweeping vistas of Ford's classics, and Mazursky's vision implies that the landscape which used to dominate the genre is no longer there, there is only the highway that cuts through the rolling fields.[68] In this

Figure 1.6 Harry and Tonto on their way to Vegas – Tonto, Art Carney and Barbara Rhoades in *Harry and Tonto*. Directed by Paul Mazursky, 1974. Twentieth Century Fox.

way, *Harry and Tonto* offers a lyrical and melancholy lament over the disappearance of the Old West, of an old generation, of life and pleasure and community, and in some way that of Shakespeare as well. Its heroes are all loners, drifting along endless roads to unseen destinations, stopping here and there, making friends (or meeting fellow lonely drifters), but without ever actually arriving at anywhere they can call home.

All in all, this overview of the ways the western has been employed by directors and adaptors illustrates what Pat Dowell remarked in connection with the revival of the genre in the 1990s: 'Whatever a Western once was, today it seems to be all things to all people – an object of nostalgia, a chance to reclaim forgotten history, an underused vehicle for violent action, just another costume drama, or a novel setting for the conventions of other genres.'[69] Possibly so – but if this adaptability is a feature that continues to characterise the western so many decades past its prime, then we have the most convincing evidence here that Bazin was, after all, right in claiming that 'the western does not age'.[70] What it does is come back into fashion every now and again, and in the meantime it allows other genres to prosper, which are often equally receptive to Shakespearean influences, as the following chapters will illustrate.

Notes

1. A. M. Modenessi, '(Un)doing the Book "Without Verona Walls": A View from the Receiving End of Baz Luhrmann's *William Shakespeare's Romeo + Juliet*', in C. Lehmann and L. S. Starks (eds), *Spectacular Shakespeare: Critical Theory and Popular Cinema* (Madison and Teaneck, NJ: Fairleigh Dickinson University Press; London: Associated University Presses, 2002), pp. 62–85, p. 63.
2. M. Manheim, 'The English History Play on Screen', in A. Davies and S. Wells (eds), *Shakespeare and the Moving Image* (Cambridge: Cambridge University Press, 1994), pp. 121–45, p. 125.
3. B. Charry and G. Shahani, 'The Global as Local/Othello as Omkara', in C. Dionne and P. Kapadia (eds), *Bollywood Shakespeares* (New York: Palgrave Macmillan, 2014), pp. 107–23, p. 112.
4. For a detailed account of the Shakespearean elements, see Willson, *Shakespeare in Hollywood*, pp. 109–15; also S. Simmon, 'Concerning the Weary Legs of Wyatt Earp: The Classic Western According to Shakespeare', *Literature/Film Quarterly*, 24:2 (1996), 114–27.
5. Bazin, 'The Western: Or the American Film Par Excellence', p. 143.
6. E. C. Brown, 'The Bard Comes to *Yellow Sky*: Shakespeare's Tempestuous Western', in E. C. Brown and E. Rivier (eds), *Shakespeare in Performance* (Newcastle-upon-Tyne: Cambridge Scholars Publishing, 2013), pp. 138–54.
7. T. Howard, 'Shakespeare's Cinematic Offshoots', in Jackson (ed.), *The Cambridge Companion to Shakespeare on Film*, pp. 295–313, p. 306.
8. J. C. Tibbets, 'The Machine in the Garden', in Rollins (ed.), *The Columbia Companion to American History on Film*, pp. 590–5, p. 590.
9. Howard, 'Shakespeare's Cinematic Offshoots', p. 306.
10. H. Fagen, *The Encyclopedia of Westerns* (New York: Facts on File, 2003), p. xviii.
11. The name of the town may be a respectful nod to Stephen Crane's classic western short story 'The Bride Comes to Yellow Sky' (1898), which has, however, no discernible link to Wellman's film, but rather seems to anticipate the plot of one of the greatest westerns of all times, *High Noon*. *Yellow Sky*'s screenplay was written by Lamar Trotti, based on an unpublished novel by W. R. Burnett, an extremely prolific writer whose credited and uncredited work amount to nearly forty novels, and almost sixty Hollywood scripts, among them award-winning classics. The novel was later published under the title *Stretch Dawson* (New York: Fawcett Gold Medal, 1950), with some notable differences from the film's script.
12. Bazin, 'The Western: Or the American Film Par Excellence', p. 143.
13. Brown, 'The Bard Comes to *Yellow Sky*', p. 147.
14. *Ibid.*, pp. 147–8.
15. M. K. Johnson, 'Introduction: Television and the Depiction of the American West', *Western American Literature*, 47:2 (2012), 123–31, 129.

16 M. E. Wildermuth, *Feminism and the Western in Film and Television* (Cham: Palgrave Macmillan, 2018), p. 65.
17 Brown, 'The Bard Comes to *Yellow Sky*', p. 144.
18 Bazin, 'The Western: Or the American Film Par Excellence', p. 145.
19 E. Buscombe, *'Injuns!' Native Americans in the Movies* (London: Reaktion Books, 2006), p. 71.
20 Brown, 'The Bard Comes to *Yellow Sky*', p. 146.
21 All parenthetical references to *The Tempest* are to this edition: W. Shakespeare, *The Tempest*, The Arden Shakespeare, Third Series, ed. V. M. Vaughan and A. T. Vaughan (London: The Arden Shakespeare, 1999).
22 V. M. Vaughan and A. T. Vaughan, 'Introduction', in Shakespeare, *The Tempest*, pp. 1–138, p. 44.
23 S. Mintz, 'The Family', in Rollins (ed.), *The Columbia Companion to American History on Film*, pp. 352–62, pp. 358–9.
24 *Ibid.*, p. 359.
25 D. M. Lanier, '"Easy Lear": *Harry and Tonto* and the American Road Movie', in V. Bladen, S. Hatchuel and N. Vienne-Guerrin (eds), *Shakespeare on Screen: King Lear* (Cambridge: Cambridge University Press, 2019), pp. 140–54, p. 140.
26 [B. W. Kliman], '*Broken Lance* is Not *Lear*', *Shakespeare on Film Newsletter*, 2:1 (1977), 3.
27 All parenthetical references to *King Lear* are to this edition: W. Shakespeare, *King Lear*, The Arden Shakespeare, Third Series, ed. R. A. Foakes (Walton-on-Thames: Thomas Nelson & Sons, 1997).
28 Lanier, 'Easy Lear', p. 151, n. 1.
29 Y. Griggs, *Screen Adaptations: Shakespeare's* King Lear: *The Relationship between Text and Film* (London: Methuen Drama, 2009), p. 105.
30 B. F. Dick, *Radical Innocence: A Critical Study of the Hollywood Ten* (Lexington: University Press of Kentucky, 1989), p. 138.
31 Cawelti, *The Six-Gun Mystique Sequel*, p. 43.
32 Bazin, 'The Western: Or the American Film Par Excellence', p. 145.
33 S. Matheson, 'Introduction', in S. Matheson (ed.), *Love in Western Film and Television: Lonely Hearts and Happy Trails* (New York: Palgrave Macmillan, 2013), pp. 1–5, p. 1.
34 Griggs, *Screen Adaptations: Shakespeare's* King Lear, p. 101.
35 *Ibid.*, p. 108.
36 H. Hoffmann, *Western Film Highlights: The Best of the West, 1914–2001* (Jefferson, NC: McFarland, 2003), p. 60.
37 Buscombe, *'Injuns!' Native Americans in the Movies*, p. 101.
38 Tibbets, 'The Machine in the Garden', p. 590.
39 M. L. Bandy and K. Stoehr, *Ride, Boldly Ride: The Evolution of the American Western* (Berkeley, Los Angeles and London: University of California Press, 2012), p. 175.

40 Willson, *Shakespeare in Hollywood*, p. 125.
41 Ibid., p. 128.
42 Bandy and Stoehr, *Ride, Boldly Ride*, p. 179.
43 Cf. Q. Taylor, *In Search of the Racial Frontier* (New York and London: W.W. Norton, 1999); P. Durham and E. L. Jones, *The Negro Cowboys* (Lincoln: University of Nebraska Press/Bison Books, 1983); D. Flamming, 'African Americans in the Twentieth-Century West', in W. Deverell (ed.), *A Companion to the American West* (Malden, MA, and Oxford: Blackwell, 2007), pp. 221–39.
44 See Willson, *Shakespeare in Hollywood*, p. 128.
45 Bandy and Stoehr, *Ride, Boldly Ride*, p. 158.
46 Willson, *Shakespeare in Hollywood*, p. 123.
47 Bandy and Stoehr, *Ride, Boldly Ride*, p. 181.
48 E.g. B. Crowther, 'Screen: Lust Out West; *Jubal* Tells Tale of Cowboy and Female', *New York Times* (25 April 1956), www.nytimes.com/1956/04/25/archives/screen-lust-out-west-jubal-tells-tale-of-cowboy-and-female.html (accessed 26 January 2020).
49 S. Corkin, *Cowboys as Cold Warriors: The Western and U.S. History* (Philadelphia, PA: Temple University Press, 2004), p. 95.
50 Cf. R. Slotkin, *Regeneration Through Violence: The Mythology of the American Frontier, 1600–1860* (Norman: University of Oklahoma Press, 2000).
51 See e.g. J.-L. Rieupeyrout, 'The Western: A Historical Genre', *Quarterly of Film Radio and Television*, 7:2 (1952), 116–28.
52 Hoffmann, *Western Film Highlights*, p. 91.
53 S. Cavell, *Pursuits of Happiness: The Hollywood Comedy of Remarriage* (Cambridge, MA: Harvard University Press, 1981).
54 M. R. Turner, 'Cowboys and Comedy: The Simultaneous Deconstruction and Reinforcement of Generic Conventions in the Western Parody', in P. C. Rollins and J. E. O'Connor (eds), *Hollywood's West: The American Frontier in Film, Television, and History* (Lexington: University of Kentucky Press, 2005), pp. 218–35, p. 218.
55 All parenthetical references to *Macbeth* are to this edition: W. Shakespeare, *Macbeth*, The Arden Shakespeare, Second Series, ed. K. Muir (Walton-on-Thames: Thomas Nelson & Sons, 1999).
56 M. Tempera, '"Whose Grave's This?": References to *Hamlet* V.1 in Italian Cinema', in C. Dente and S. Soncini (eds), *Crossing Time and Space: Shakespeare Translations in Present-Day Europe* (Pisa: PLUS – Pisa University Press, 2008), pp. 79–87, p. 81.
57 Ibid.
58 B. Langford, 'Revisiting the "Revisionist" Western', *Film & History: An Interdisciplinary Journal of Film and Television Studies*, 33:2 (2003), 26–35, 27.

59 A. R. Lee, 'Western Sightings: John G. Cawelti in Conversation with A. Robert Lee', *Weber: The Contemporary West*, 19:1 (2001), http://weberjournal.weber.edu/archive/archive%20C%20Vol.%2016.2-18.1/Vol.%2019.1/Lee.htm (accessed 26 January 2020).
60 P. Arthur, 'How the West Was Spun: *McCabe & Mrs. Miller* and Genre Revisionism', *Cinéaste*, 28:3 (2003), 18–20, 19.
61 Lanier, 'Easy Lear', p. 148.
62 Langford, 'Revisiting the "Revisionist" Western', 32.
63 D. Nystrom, 'The New Hollywood', in C. Lucia, R. Grundmann and A. Simon (eds), *The Wiley-Blackwell History of American Cinema Vol. III: 1946–1975* (Oxford: Blackwell, 2012), pp. 409–34, p. 417.
64 Lanier, 'Easy Lear', pp. 140, 141.
65 R. Siegel, 'The Lone Ranger: Justice from Outside the Law', *NPR* (14 January 2008), www.npr.org/templates/story/story.php?storyId=18073741 (accessed 26 January 2020).
66 Langford, 'Revisiting the "Revisionist" Western', 30.
67 *Ibid.*
68 *Ibid.*
69 P. Dowell, 'The Mythology of the Western: Hollywood Perspectives on Race and Gender in the Nineties', *Cinéaste*, 21:1–2 (1995), 6–10, 6.
70 Bazin, 'The Western: Or the American Film Par Excellence', p. 141.

2

Shakespeare the tear-jerker: from woman's film to global melodrama

For an account of the Shakespeare melodrama, we must cast our eyes back as far as the 1930s, the heyday of the so-called woman's film, a genre often equated with the melodrama in the narrowest sense of the word. The most melodramatic Shakespeare film of the decade was a prestigious Hollywood super-production – MGM's *Romeo and Juliet* (1936, dir. George Cukor) – but since that film uses the Shakespearean script, and can be considered a straightforward adaptation of the drama, it falls outside the scope of this volume. There is, however, a lesser-known gem from the decade, a British reworking of the *Othello* story: *Men Are Not Gods* (1936, dir. Walter Reisch), which can prove convincingly that 'women's films aren't trivial', as many critics of the genre imply.[1] A second film discussed in this chapter is another *Othello* adaptation, one from the post-war period: Basil Dearden's *All Night Long* (1962), a British social melodrama centred on the racial tension inherent in the play. Jumping ahead in time, the next film examined is from a decade when American television was saturated with melodramatic soap operas: *A Thousand Acres* (1997, dir. Jocelyn Moorhouse), an adaptation of Jane Smiley's Pulitzer-winning novel from 1991, which sets the drama of *King Lear* in the Iowa farmlands. The last section of the chapter takes an even bolder leap ahead and looks at the way the melodramatic mode informs contemporary British-Asian Shakespeare adaptations, in particular Sangeeta Datta's 2009 *Life Goes On*, another take on the *Lear* story. Although the diversity of the examples may seem disconcerting at first sight, and the films discussed in this chapter certainly give a lesser impression of continuity than in the chapters before and after it, I believe the persistence of the melodramatic mode will provide a convincing argument that what we are witnessing is indeed one of the fundamental cinematic conventions of American, and by extension, global film production.

Woman's Shakespeare – *Men Are Not Gods*

Among the several Shakespeare films that include melodramatic elements, the one example where there appears to be no critical dissent concerning the work's genre is Walter Reisch's 1936 *Men Are Not Gods*: practically every reference to the film includes the word 'melodrama'. True, some of these references use the term in a generally pejorative sense, and therefore descriptions such as 'Starts very strongly in a lightly comedic vein but quickly descends into maudlin melodrama' are most probably intended to denote the film's perceived inadequacies rather than define its generic qualities.[2]

This reworking of *Othello* was written and directed by Austrian émigré Walter Reisch, who had previously produced a number of successful musical comedies and romances, together with melodramatic 'woman's films'. Later he was to write the scripts for such hits as Ernst Lubitsch's *Ninotchka* (1939) and Cukor's *Gaslight* (1944). Reisch left Austria earlier in the year, and this was his first film directed in England; by the following year, he was already working in Hollywood.[3] The cast of *Men Are Not Gods* includes English actress Gertrude Lawrence, who was at the peak of her career at the time, accompanied by Sebastian Shaw and a young Rex Harrison, whose career began to pick up after this role. The poster face and the real star appeal, however, were provided by American Miriam Hopkins, whose extremely versatile screen career had by this time included several roles where she was either the damsel in distress or the third corner of a romantic triangle, threatening to disrupt a marital union. Her casting may thus have increased audience expectations of the melodramatic turn of events in *Men Are Not Gods* as well.

And yet there is more to this short and largely forgotten film than a clichéd plot and typecast actresses would suggest, and certainly more than the dismissive reviews imply. If we begin the investigation by looking at the film's Shakespearean lineage, we notice an interesting combination of intentions already presented in the title, which partly acknowledges the source text's authority, while simultaneously liberates itself from under its control. The phrase 'men are not gods' is a direct quotation from *Othello* (3.4.149), and the very same words are heard twice in the film's dialogue.[4] The first time we hear it from the stage, during a performance of *Othello*, then at the very end of the film, when the line and its message have already been internalised by one of the protagonists, the actress who plays Desdemona. When she claims that Shakespeare's words are often true in real life as well, this female wisdom functions as the final message and moral conclusion of the film, which suggests a readjustment in social hierarchy, possibly bringing men down from their pedestal to a more human level. At the same time, these concluding words also highlight the melodramatic angle, confirming that the story has been told from a distinctly feminine viewpoint.

Although it may appear that the Shakespearean element is only marginal and used out of context (Michael Brooke claims that aside from the title, 'Shakespeare references are thin'),[5] this is not entirely true. The film belongs to the group sometimes referred to as a 'backstage-story' or 'mirror movie', its action revolving around the life of actors and their performances.[6] As such, it includes considerable portions of *Othello* through a variety of media, mostly seen on a theatre stage, sometimes broadcast on the radio, at times overheard, at others quoted in off-stage conversations. The film thus establishes the centrality of the Shakespearean text, and as Douglas Lanier remarks, this narrative, like other backstage dramas using the same trope of the murdering Othello, represents the nearly magical power of the Shakespearean drama. In his words, 'These films amplify the power of stage performance, presenting the *Othello* narrative as an almost irresistible text which seems to possess the actor as he performs his part.'[7] However, in *Men Are Not Gods*, it is not only the performer who is mesmerised by the Shakespeare text, but, through the mediation of the actor – who turns out to be a most unworthy channel for this sacred communication – the words enchant the young and naive female protagonist, whose viewpoint becomes the narrative frame for the film.

The plot revolves around a rather typical love triangle, comprising famous American thespian Edmund Davey (Shaw), his wife, Barbara Halford (Lawrence), who plays Desdemona to Davey's Othello, and Ann Williams (Hopkins), a young and innocent editorial secretary. After Davey's less-than-magical first night on the London stage, Barbara goes to the office of the *Daily Post* to stop an inevitably disastrous review from being published, but she only finds there Ann, secretary of fearful theatre critic Mr Skeates (A. E. Matthews), with the damning review ready to go to print. Barbara appeals to Ann 'as one woman to another', in a gesture reminiscent of countless other melodramas (see figure 2.1), to do something and save the day. When Ann looks at the silhouette of Barbara pacing up and down in front of her office door, the perfect image of the woman in distress, she no longer hesitates and knows immediately what she has to do. Out of respect for the powerful love between wife and husband, she decides

Figure 2.1 As one woman to another – Miriam Hopkins and Gertrude Lawrence in *Men Are Not Gods*. Directed by Walter Reisch, 1936. London Film Productions.

to alter the review, which gets her fired the very next day, but saves Davey's career. Interestingly enough, even the most unfeeling of men, Mr Skeates, suspects that the reason for Ann's betrayal must be none other than love, although at this point he is still unaware of the details (but his insight proves prophetic): 'you did something for this man that a woman will only do for the man she loves'.

Later Ann also goes to see the production, and becomes fascinated by the actor to the level of infatuation, but being a decent girl she refuses to act upon her feelings. Davey, however, is looking for a bit of amusement on the side, and to win her over, he presents himself as the victim of his wife's jealousy, saying that 'in private life, Desdemona is the jealous one, Othello is the victim'. After his increasingly intensive advances, Ann still finds the strength to face him, declaring what almost sounds like a manifesto of women guarding the home fires: 'I confess quite openly: yes, I do love you. But I'd never taken anything belonging to anyone else and I never will, and you belong to someone else, and to a woman I think of very highly of, just because she loves you.' Thus Ann tries to resist him in the name of all women in love, but the universe – the most powerful character of melodramas – seems to conspire against her, not allowing her to forget Davey, bombarding her with his voice and his Othello from every direction. The temptation is much more tangible here than in Shakespeare's play, but this is clearly necessary to enhance the moral stature of the woman. After all, Shakespeare's Desdemona has to defend herself from the accusation of an imaginary crime of which she is not even aware, therefore she is doomed to fail. Ann Williams, on the other hand, has to fend off the advances of the man she admires, and that takes courage and strength which all women should learn to possess, according to the rules of the melodrama.

To protect the protagonist's moral position, we witness her struggle with herself throughout a long sequence, and when she finally accepts Davey's proposition, the camera does not even show her face. It remains hidden behind her umbrella, and her voice sounds as if she were in a daze, indeed bewitched, just like Othello was accused of bewitching Desdemona. It is clearly no accident that the textual excerpt we hear most often from the play is Othello's first great speech at the Venetian Senate, where he defends himself against the accusations of witchcraft and magic – and whenever we hear these words, we see Ann's face, visually connecting the words of enchantment to their victim. But however much Ann (and the camera) tries to protect her virtue and hide her fall to immorality, Barbara soon learns about what is going on, and she goes once again to enlist Ann's help, reasoning that the girl is 'the only decent person in this business'. Decency is indeed the keyword here: when Ann learns that Barbara is expecting a child, the young girl immediately sends Davey a goodbye note. The actor does not take kindly to his plans being thwarted, and he becomes so enraged that he nearly kills his wife on-stage in the final act of *Othello* – and it is again Ann, sitting in the gallery, who saves the day by screaming out loud to break the spell and stop the performance. In the end, the couple are reunited, and Ann disappears back to the nameless crowd of the lower middle class where she came from, sacrificing her love for the sanctity of the family hearth. (As discussed in Chapter 3, a very similar situation with a less forgiving ending is exemplified in the 1947 *Othello* adaptation, *A Double Life*, where the stylistic and narrative conventions of the *film noir* require a final tragic sacrifice which cannot be resolved by such a miraculous melodramatic *denouement*.)

Elements of the Shakespearean source narrative are thus modified, but still strongly present in the film, including the outsider acquiring fame in a new place (Davey is a newcomer on the British theatre scene), turning away from his lawful and loving wife in a jealous rage, with the tension building up to a scene of near-strangulation at the end. There are also plenty of direct quotations throughout, which are typically tied in with the diegesis, and yet *Men Are Not Gods* could easily fail as an *Othello* adaptation if that was all we were looking for. Approaching it from the viewpoint of the melodrama, however, helps us to make sense of the rewritten elements of the plot and characterisation, and also explains why it is those particular parts of the text that are quoted throughout the film.

As the title of the film (and every poster, with Miriam Hopkins's face in the centre) indicates, this version of *Othello* is not interested in the self-discovery of the male protagonist, but it is the females, the commonly marginalised members of the cast, who gain wisdom and a rediscovery of their own place in (bourgeois) society. That is why we can see the two suffering females joining forces in a moral battle, finding sympathy in the most unlikely partners – each other – in their struggle to preserve the morality of their social universe. As Marcia Landy also notes, this element is central to the genre: 'The women's position is, as in many films of the 1930s, one of solidarity in keeping the wayward genius under control and thereby protecting the interests of marriage and family.'[8]

The melodrama, as opposed to the romance, does not allow love to be victorious over every obstacle, unless it is the right and proper kind of love. The real heroine of the story is therefore not the wife – we can see that she is also partly to blame for allowing her husband to go astray, and she draws this very same conclusion herself at the end. It is Ann, the young and innocent party in the triangle, who saves the day, whose love may be purer and more idealised, but who has no place in this relationship, as her presence would inevitably disrupt the sacred marital union. Still, in a sense both females share the function of the victim, a role central to the melodrama. As Thomas Elsaesser argues, 'one of the characteristic features of melodramas in general is that they concentrate on the point of view of the victim'.[9] This in turn explains why *Men Are Not Gods* chooses to present the *Othello* story not simply from the viewpoint of a suffering character, but we may even interpret Ann and Barbara as doubles for the role of Desdemona – both accused of betrayal, both sacrificing something for the man they love. It is true that in Shakespeare's *Othello* the women are also victimised (both Desdemona and Emilia are betrayed and killed in the end), but there they appear to be simply collateral damage in Iago's plot to destroy Othello. Here there is no Iago figure – the cynical old theatre critic turns out to be a wise man who gives the best advice to Ann. The most destructive force is Davey himself, the very same man who is loved by both women and who would destroy both of them if he had his way were it not for the knowledge of impending parenthood, which turns him back onto the good path in the eleventh hour. Shakespeare's words in the title sum it all up by claiming that it is all the fault of men, who pretend that they are almost divine, and enchant women, abusing their superior social position. They will nevertheless inevitably fall from their pedestal as the enchanted females wake from their passivity and realise how little of the godlike there is in their admired men.

As the focus of the melodrama is the female body in distress, displaying strong emotions, the film offers us several instances of women on the verge of or in floods of tears, with body language nearly ecstatic or hysterical, to express the depth of their emotional drama. When Barbara is pleading to Ann in the office; when Ann loses her job (even though up until that point her employer appeared to be the most horrible of bosses); when Ann watches Desdemona die on stage for the first time; or when later Ann is battling with her conscience, we always see at least one of the women crying. This tearful response is sometimes markedly in contrast with the reactions of others; in the theatre, when the whole auditorium applauds enthusiastically, a close-up of Ann's face shows her brought to tears. The real moment of distress, however, comes at the climax of the film, when Davey is about to strangle his wife on stage and Ann cries out in terror. The performance gets interrupted, Barbara is saved, but Ann is still in obvious physical anguish, her body shaking so much from her hysterical tears that a doctor is called to assist her. The words of comfort that eventually reach her come from Barbara, who tells the girl that all will be well, and to Ann's pleading she promises to stop playing Desdemona on stage.

When at this point Davey enters Barbara's dressing room, overhearing the dresser's reference to Barbara as 'a woman in her condition', it appears that the words (as much of a euphemistic cliché as any to describe pregnancy) finally break the spell that Ann and extramarital excitement had over him. To take back the melodramatic centre stage at this point, Barbara breaks down in tears to declare that it was precisely Davey's selfishness that prevented her from telling him the news earlier. As the marital disagreements appear to have dissolved into thin air, Ann silently leaves the room, while the camera closes up on the amorous faces of the newly reunited couple. The conclusion revisits the *Othello* quotation in the title; after Barbara tells Davey that 'there is nothing to forgive: when things go wrong between husband and wife, the wife is always just as much to blame as the husband', she assigns her newly acquired wisdom to Shakespeare, claiming that she has learned from the play that men are not gods indeed. We do not know how much she played the green-eyed monster at home, as Davey had accused her earlier, but we remember how at the beginning she was all too willing to downplay her own theatrical success to boost her husband's confidence (and ended up boosting only his ego). Thus the blame the film lays at the wife's feet is not exactly any morally condemnable straying from marital fidelity, but simply not being strong enough to put her husband right when she could and should have done so.

The melodramatic ending also implies Ann's miserable future; Davey asks her what shall become of her, and she answers with his earlier words: she will continue to be what she always has been, 'a representative of the gallery, the symbol of the unreserved seat, the enthusiastic audience' – a nameless nobody. Ann's class identity, her (failed) attempt to break free from her predictable and restricted life, and particularly her fixation with the married film star, a clearly unattainable object of desire, are all stereotypical components of the woman's film.[10] At the end, middle-class consciousness rules again, and although this petty bourgeois morality seemed like a prison earlier (at the last performance at the theatre, Ann's face is framed by the bars of the gallery, visualising her being trapped in a situation from which she cannot find a way out), the very same middle-class decency is what saves the day and the life of mother-to-be and her unborn child. As the theatre producer announces, 'perhaps even Shakespeare may forgive us if on this occasion only we allow Desdemona to live'. Lanier interprets the ending also in the context of the genre: 'By so explicitly refusing Desdemona's scripted demise, *Men Are Not Gods* completes its reimagining of the murderous Othello trope in terms of the protocols of a "woman's picture", exposing the mechanisms of male sexual and class privilege for what they are, selfserving hypocrisy.'[11] We may miss the providential intervention set against a blood-and-thunder backdrop, so common in early melodramas, but there is a message for both sexes here: a warning for those who do not respect the sanctity of the hearth, as well as a promise of long-term reward for those who are willing to sacrifice their passions for it. As Cawelti argues about twentieth-century melodramatic literature, 'Popular Freudianism has replaced providence as the primary means of articulating the universal moral order, but the result is essentially the demonstration of a connection between traditional middle-class domestic morality and the operative principles of the cosmos.'[12]

In line with the stylistic characteristics of the melodrama, the film employs powerful if well-known cinematic tricks and tools to enhance the message, exemplified for instance by the colour symbolism of the two women's clothes. Ann's outfits gradually darken, from predominantly light colours to a spotted dress she wears at the night of her fall for Davey's charms, even to a black costume when she has crossed over to the other side, but she is back in white again for the final performance, although a black hat hides her grief-stricken face. Barbara also appears in a shining light evening dress when she pleads for her husband, but in the scenes when we see the married couple's disagreements, she is dressed in black, and that is how she appears on stage as Desdemona, with a white-blond wig, her pretended innocence in contrast with Ann's natural blond hair and true morality. Another device familiar from the sensationalist-type melodrama is employed during the last performance, when Davey is losing control and we no longer know whether the rage shown on the stage and on our screen is that of Othello or of a murderous Davey himself. In this sequence, the camera projects the enlarged silhouette of the man over Barbara, as if a monster were coming to strike the diminutive figure of the woman. When the show is interrupted, we see Davey unable to move from the posture in which he was about to strangle his wife – the power of the performance casts a strong spell that is not easy to break. It is only the call of fatherhood that allows him to finally find 'his own voice, abandoning the theatrical language that had characterized his philandering', and re-establish belief in the decency of the universe, conforming to the requirements of the genre.[13]

British social melodrama – *All Night Long*

Possibly the least well-known film discussed in this chapter is *All Night Long*, a British adaptation of *Othello*, but whatever the reasons for its obscurity, the film is a true gem for lovers of jazz music, while not without interest as a Shakespeare adaptation either. Although reviews at the time of the film's release were mixed at best, with some critics lamenting the changes from the Shakespearean source material, others the too obvious racial element, time has earned the film laudatory comments as well, scattered among the less appreciative voices. Directed by Basil Dearden, produced and designed by Dearden's long-time partner, Michael Relph, *All Night Long* belongs to the group of films that do not wish to exploit the Bard's name for prestige or as a selling point. Whether this is a 'shameful' move, as Daniel Rosenthal argues, or indeed a courageous one, to shift the film's focus towards a contemporary social issue, is a question of perspective. Rosenthal is certainly right in claiming that 'Anyone who enjoyed Basil Dearden's showbiz melodrama *All Night Long*, but did not know *Othello*, would have thought that Peter Achilles and Nel King's script, in which drummer Johnny Cousin spins an Iago-esque web around black pianist Aurelius Rex and his white wife, was an original screenplay, not an adaptation.'[14] This is particularly easy to believe since the film has a number of selling points independent of the plot, or its Shakespearean lineage, notably the great names of jazz, from Dave Brubeck to Charles Mingus and many others, who not only contribute to the non-diegetic soundtrack, but even appear on screen as themselves. In this way one can argue that the film participates in several types of prestige narratives, downplaying the literary one and emphasising the musical element. What is more, as Paul Skrebels emphasises, out of the painful history of colonisation and racial inequality 'there arose a black cultural treasure, jazz, complete with its own aristocracy: Count Basie, Duke Ellington, and therefore, by extension, Aurelius Rex', the film's Othello figure, who can thus be accepted as a perfect representative of royalty within jazz society.[15]

By the time of the creation of this film, Dearden and Relph had collaborated on plenty of projects, and as Alan Burton and Tim O'Sullivan claim, 'a consistent theme in [their] post-war films concerns male characters forced to confront painful adjustment to new circumstances and changing social norms and expectations'.[16] Many of these films observe 'a tragic dimension, whereby the narratives result either in the death of the main male protagonist or a significant subsidiary character, or in his imprisonment, or in some such seriously diminished ambition or circumstance'.[17] The few available studies on *All Night Long* are mostly silent about the circumstances of its creation, and it is in biographies of Charles Mingus that we find further evidence concerning how it came to be and confirmation that the social, particularly the racial, aspect of the story was originally seen as the central element in the film. The idea, it would appear, came from Nel King, American writer and editor, who wanted to bring attention to what she saw were the natural acting skills of Charles Mingus. 'With echoes of Orson Welles and Paul Robeson in her head, she wanted to adapt Shakespeare's *Othello* to a jazz setting. The classic play spoke to America's contemporary racial conflicts. Jazz was an art forged mainly by black Americans. The music would be part of the drama' – just as it has always been a vital part of melodrama, we might add.[18] The creation of the film, however, was not without obstacles; the screenplay was written by King and Paul Jarrico (blacklisted in America during the McCarthy era, Jarrico was writing under the pseudonym Peter Achilles), but when they found no buyer for it in America, they turned their attention towards the British market.[19]

The obstacles to finding an American distributor resulted from the film's central theme, conflict within a racially mixed cast and between a married couple in particular. Alfred Crown, the American producer reported that:

> United Artists would distribute the movie only if Lena Horne (a light-skinned black actress) played the Desdemona-like role. Jarrico and King angrily responded that such casting defeated the whole point of the screenplay, which was the issue of miscegenation. ... Crown replied that United Artists did not want to handle a film about miscegenation.[20]

In response, Jarrico and King decided to turn to other producers, and eventually found Bob Roberts in London. The caution of potential American buyers is, of course, understandable, since, as Santoro explains, 'Interracial relationships were still a flash point for American media' and 'few mainstream filmmakers were bold enough to risk alienating audiences for a social statement'.[21] After all, several states still had legislation in force that prohibited interracial marriage and it was only in June 1967 that these were declared unconstitutional. Even after that, it took years, if not decades, for several states to officially repeal these: 'Alabama was the last state to have a miscegenation law on its books', in force until November 2000.[22] No wonder that American producers were vary of such sensitive topics, even if independent filmmakers, such as John Cassavetes in *Shadows* (1959), had already addressed interracial sexual relations, in what he described as 'a basic melodramatic situation'.[23]

The British director approached with the script was Basil Dearden, who had already 'made *Sapphire*, a thoughtful movie about a murdered black music student who'd passed for white', and who found this script also to his liking.[24] In light of Dearden's earlier work, it is hard to believe that he 'liked neither jazz nor black people',[25] but all accounts agree that the director requested significant rewriting, which the scriptwriters resented. Jarrico's biography cites one of his letters to King, claiming that he was not simply disappointed, but felt that the final product might 'turn out to say the very opposite of what we intended'.[26] The biographer still praises the final script and attributes the film's mixed initial reception to directorial failings: '*All Night Long* is actually a well-constructed version of *Othello*, with well-realized characters. Unfortunately, it is lethargically directed; there is little of the heat one would expect from an all-night jazz session involving rivalries and romantic tangles. And no one dies.'[27]

The ending is indeed a crucial aspect of the film (and the cause for much of its criticism) – and yet it must be admitted that it does not distort audience recognition or even appreciation for its Shakespearean associations.

Even though Shakespeare is often noted for his tendency to increase dramatic tension by condensing his inherited plots, King and Jarrico's script takes this condensation one step further, turning *All Night Long* into a story of a single night, albeit a long and suspenseful one. The plot takes place at a party, organised by wealthy English socialite Rodney Hamilton (Richard Attenborough), to celebrate the first wedding anniversary of black jazz pianist Aurelius Rex (Paul Harris) and his white wife, singer Delia Lane (Marti Stevens), who gave up singing for the sake of her marriage. The white drummer of Rex's band, Johnny Cousin (Patrick McGoohan) has plans to disrupt the marital harmony, partly out of general resentment of Rex's success and partly for business reasons: he wants to lure Delia back to work, to join the band he is about to start himself. He uses a saxophone player, Cass Michaels (Keith Michell), to implicate Delia in a story of infidelity, and fabricates evidence by recording snatches of conversation and editing them on a tape recorder recently bought by Rodney. The party itself is practically an all-night jam session, with some of the music involved in the diegesis, and suspense is very much in the air, even if some critics fail to recognise it, as seen from the quotes mentioned. Their complaint is that in spite of the tangible conflict and the motif of jealousy, the drama stops short of real tragedy, and indeed, Delia, the falsely accused wife survives and reconciles with her husband as they leave the nightclub together. The Iago figure, Johnny Cousin, is also spared – although not the humiliation of discovery, only death – and in his turn he also spares the life of his wife, the Emilia character, though his treachery causes her considerable suffering, and destroys their marriage.

The ending is certainly a decisive aspect in terms of the film's genre: by discarding the tragic ending of the original, the filmmakers shifted the dominant mode towards the melodrama. Skrebels, however, argues that 'Rex's throwing off of Johnny's control is given extra symbolic force, as representing something more than the triumph of a heroically individual will', and with this climax the film refuses to subscribe to racial stereotypes that would cast the black man as driven by instinct and passion rather than reason.[28] What is more, the film uses other subtle devices to reverse the inherited power structure of *Othello*. The dramatic confrontation between Rex and Johnny coincides 'with a noticeable increase in the presence of black people in the "jazz world" of the party generally and in the dramatic action itself', and in this scene 'Rex is shown framed on either side by other black musicians and guests in a "united front" against Johnny'.[29] Added to this, there is one single named character whose race has been changed from the corresponding Shakespearean one: Bianca becomes Benny (María

Velasco), and her humiliation by her boyfriend Cass, and Johnny's use of those words on his doctored tape, all add to the unvoiced, but painfully felt realities of skin colour defining a woman's desirability or lack thereof.

All these elements contribute to the final impression that instead of a tragedy what we have is a true melodrama, where individuals play out greater social conflicts hidden in the background. Interestingly enough, here the racial aspect is less explicit, although clearly significant, as in the world of jazz being black appears to be an enviable position. Johnny even mockingly refers to himself as a minority: 'oh, I belong to that new minority group: white American jazz musicians. They're going to hold a mass meeting in a phone booth' – yet in his ironic tone, one can hear his envy of black musicians, blaming his skin colour for his secondary rank, even though the narrative makes it clear that Delia, the whitest of whites, is considered as outstanding a singer as her husband, Rex, is a pianist (see figure 2.2).

Figure 2.2 Victims of society – Paul Harris and Marti Stevens in *All Night Long*. Directed by Basil Dearden, 1962. The Rank Organisation.

There is, however, even more emphasis given to the position of women, who are subtly shown to be victims of various types of direct or indirect stereotyping. Delia has given up work for her love, but misses the music and her talent remains concealed as a result; Emily, Johnny's long-suffering wife, has a husband in name only, as Johnny makes it clear that he has never really cared about her, not even at the time of their marriage. Benny, the Bianca character, girlfriend of Cass, is also fully and painfully aware of her own marginal position in Cass's heart and this (almost) all-male club. All these women are shown in sometimes understated but obvious distress, fighting back tears, at other times giving vent to their emotions, only to be scolded by their partners for showing how they feel. Emily's constant and visible humiliation by Johnny becomes an important undercurrent in the melodrama, matching Delia's and Benny's suffering – the three women together present a powerful image of female position, comparable to the unvoiced but no less tangible racial inequalities persisting in society. In a way, *All Night Long* merits consideration already for the way it can direct our attention to the female characters among so many male faces, many of them celebrities in and out of the diegesis as well.

The role of music in melodrama has been often described, yet, as several scholars argue, this connection to music may be tangible even in works which have no musical sequences and whose dialogue is predominantly spoken. Yet the rapid alternations between turns of fate and extremes of passion, signalled with the excessive gestures that characterised theatrical melodrama in the eighteenth and nineteenth centuries, are also essential in the cinematic iterations of melodrama. Moreover, non-diegetic or diegetic music is often used to full effect in these works, to underscore the heightened emotions and suspense. *All Night Long* is exemplary in this regard: it uses music not simply as a background soundtrack but as a diegetic element; it is only the final chords that are non-diegetic, when Johnny's drum solo is rounded off by the sounds of a big band playing in the background.

In effect, music functions as a language of its own, as significant as the cinematography and the dialogue. Two of the songs included in the film are performed with their lyrics as well, both sung by Delia ('All Night Long' and 'I Never Knew I Could Love Anybody Like I'm Loving You'), which naturally emphasises their centrality in the narrative – but the rest are no less meaningful. Rex is invited to join in the jam session, but also initiates several songs on his own. The first one he begins to play, before the seeds of jealousy are planted in his brain by Johnny, is Duke Ellington's 'In a Sentimental Mood', a plaintive melody, full of longing and desire. Yet not much later, when Johnny's words begin to worm their way into his mind, and the Brazilian drummer's exotic and passionate solo raises tension to an explosive level, Rex takes over the piano and starts playing another classical Ellington hit, 'Mood Indigo', which signals even in its title the change in atmosphere. We can thus see the way Rex and Johnny clearly communicate, illustrating that music is indeed a language that is comprehensible as part of the visual spectacle, as the best of melodrama has always been able to show.

Women's drama in the Midwest – *A Thousand Acres*

Jane Smiley's Pulitzer Prize-winning novel, *A Thousand Acres* (1991), a feminist retelling of the *King Lear* story, was received enthusiastically by readers and critics alike, bringing her immediate fame (and scoring what Susan Elizabeth Farrell calls 'a major literary coup in the United States by winning both the National Book Critics' Circle Award for fiction and the Pulitzer Prize').[30] The book was praised not only for its centralising of the previously marginalised feminine aspect, giving the two elder daughters a chance to tell the story from their point of view, but also for its setting in the Iowa farmlands, where the adaptation seems to have found a natural place for this story of divided properties and clashing generations. In this '*King Lear* in the cornfields',[31] the family patriarch, Larry Cook (the Lear character), decides to sign over his thousand-acre farm to his three daughters, Ginny, Rose and Caroline (stand-ins for Goneril, Regan and Cordelia), the youngest of whom expresses her concerns about the idea and is consequently cut off. Throughout the ensuing period, while Larry descends into more and more arrogant irrationality, it turns out that he used to beat and sexually abuse his elder daughters when they were young, something their younger sister is unaware of, and therefore Caroline continues to take her father's side when he is trying to revoke the contract dividing the farm. A neighbour, Harold Clark (the Gloucester figure) gets blinded in a farming accident; his recently returned prodigal son, Jess (Edmund) has affairs with both Ginny and Rose before he leaves, taking his modern ideas of organic farming with him. The plot follows *King Lear* quite closely, but the narrative viewpoint of the eldest daughter, Ginny, radically changes our awareness of the characters' self-discoveries, and as we follow the family's and the farm's gradual disintegration, Smiley offers the previously marginalised evil daughters a chance to win the reader over to their side.[32]

Discussing the many influences that led her to the composition of the novel, the author mentioned – apart from her readings of Shakespeare and other classics, including Icelandic sagas – that 'three other threads that tied up for me in *A Thousand Acres* were feminism, environmentalism, and a vaguely Marxist materialism'.[33] The reason I quoted Smiley's characterisation of the novel's central themes is that I believe these aspects help us to identify how Jocelyn Moorhouse's 1997 adaptation liberated itself from its textual source and imbued the story with a different focus, toning down most of the ideological concerns and replacing them with a melodramatic interest in 'woman's drama'.

The film adaptation, written by Laura Jones, earned a few awards and nominations for the performances of the main cast (mostly Jessica Lange, playing Ginny, and Michelle Pfeiffer, playing Rose), but the film as a whole left most critics disappointed, some very explicitly so. Roger Ebert included his review in his volume on the films he openly hated, and described the film as 'an ungainly, undigested assembly of "women's issues" milling about within a half-baked retread of *King Lear*'.[34] Already in this short dismissal we can feel the critic laying the blame for the film's shortcomings on its displacement of the *King Lear* narrative with a commercial melodrama. Another review makes the film's generic lineage equally clear by evoking the stars and the peak decade of the genre's popularity:

> It's a tragedy of domestic proportions about family and illness and trauma and betrayal and abuse. The genre reaches back to the '40s when actresses like Joan Crawford and Bette Davis played the martyred divas of the matinee. *A Thousand Acres* is a little more modern (though I swear the women in it engage in the making of pies), but it shares one important trait with its predecessors—it's all about self-sacrificing, angelic women who don't get what they want.[35]

In this review, Stacey Richter summarises most of the key concerns of the melodrama: the domestic environment and the centrality of female sacrifice, both in the form of self-sacrifice for the greater good of the community, but also victimisation by (predominantly) patriarchal society. In another contemporary review, Russell Smith refers to the psychological interest at the heart of the classical woman's film and its later descendants as well, but he also connects it with another close relative of 1990s melodrama, the television soap opera:

> This is a hard, angry, morally unforgiving movie with dominant sensibilities more similar to the current wave of 'therapy fiction' than to the classical tragedy genre. Superimposing these raw, primal emotions onto amber-hued scenes of bucolic splendor creates a satisfying tension that sustains interest even when the story veers uncomfortably close to primetime soap territory.[36]

Ramona Wray, however, points out how the film adds to the *Lear* story a previously marginalised, but very much topical, issue, through its preoccupation with the long-denied bodily realities of female existence in traditional society. In essence, this again connects the film to the melodrama and its focus on the distressed female body: 'the film elaborates a storyline centring upon the coercion of women and the ways in which female bodies, and their reproductive potential, are dictated to by the combined forces of patriarchy and industry'.[37] Indeed, the central world order of the melodrama, the sanctity of the domestic sphere, is shown here to have been endangered by the poisonous practices of men. Yet, whereas Smiley's novel makes it clear that the farming methods of Larry Cook (Jason Robards) are not only responsible for Ginny's repeated miscarriages and resulting childlessness, but also for Rose's (and possibly their mother's) breast cancer as well, the film only makes the connection explicit in the case of Ginny, the narrator, making her the only true melodramatic protagonist. Rita Kempley mentions that *A Thousand Acres* features 'the first-ever close-up of a mastectomy scar',[38] but in other ways it follows the more timid visual conventions of the melodrama, reluctant to show the ugly physical realities of the body, choosing to imply them through long-term and long-suppressed psychological consequences.

The cinematography also fits this interior viewpoint, and all the revelations concerning the girls' molestation are verbal (sometimes even slightly verbose), rather than visual, with only a few images of Ginny's recollection of her father standing in her doorway at night. The horrific story of abuse and violation is told in a very much understated manner, the camera shying away from all scenes of violence, showing only the consequences.[39] Most of the time we see even less, and only hear Ginny's voiceover narration, suggesting an internalised resolution of long-suppressed conflicts (she never tells her younger sister Caroline what Rose revealed about their father), while looking out on endless vistas of cornfields. The corn, as James Keller argues, is more than characteristic Midwest setting or beautiful landscape: it is both evidence for the poison in the fields and witness to the suffering of land and people. It even becomes 'voyeur in the Cook family tragedy, peeping through windows and appearing at the screen door of Ginny's kitchen'; it even 'suggests a vegetable prison, a discipline and a lifestyle'.[40] Images of confinement haunt the film's visuality, in its narrow, mostly interior, spaces, as the bedrooms, fitting rooms or kitchens, but even within natural settings – a striking effect to achieve amid so many green open fields.

The natural environment is particularly significant in marking out the place of the film among variations within the melodrama. Superficially, *A*

Thousand Acres seems to be set in a period whose struggles were surpassed by the late 1990s, since it shows women in need of second-wave feminism, confined in the domestic environment and to a life of servitude, without property or control over their own fates. There are no women of colour in this Midwestern community, and women's bodies, particularly their reproductive organs, play a central role in their struggles. At the same time, the narrative conclusion suggests that these fights might legally be over – but signing over the property to the girls does not solve their problems; on the contrary, it accelerates the family's disintegration. Similarly, Caroline's independence in terms of education and employment (she is a lawyer, of all symbolic vocations) only contributes to her blindness to the suffering of her sisters. In this situation of silent drama, therefore, the symbolism of nature's exploitation gains epic and topical proportions and adds an ecofeminist voice to the disenfranchised, to show how exploitation of both land and women by patriarchal society are inherently linked. It is true that there is no mention in the film of the higher rate of toxicity in environments with an African-American or Native American population, but the Midwestern setting universalises both the threat and the continued resistance to its elimination by focusing on this most stereotypically American environment. Moreover, the film emphasises the shared plight of women and raises viewers' awareness to 'the existence of gender-related differences in reactions to environmental toxic substances', without blurring diverse women's stories into one stereotypical narrative.[41]

The reactions of the male members of the cast to female suffering range from ignorance through insensitivity to active violence, underlining the oppressive nature of the patriarchal society where females can only find comfort and understanding in each other's company. This solidarity of the victims with the downtrodden, the marginalised and the abandoned is one of the main themes of the film, reinforced at the conclusion once again when Ginny laments having to leave Rose behind, missing her already: 'all our lives we'd looked out for each other in the way that motherless children tend to do'. The significance of this sentence is noticed by critics as well, which indicates that the words are not only aimed at empty tear-jerking, but point out melodrama's focus on female companionship in a world hostile to the powerless.[42] In such a world, Larry's verbal poison – his curse on both of his elder daughters – functions as a repetition and confirmation of the years of physical abuse that the girls had to go through. Again, the sacrificial position of the victimised female becomes particularly clear when Rose explains how she put up with her father's molestation in order to save the truly innocent: her younger sister, Caroline.

In an interview, Smiley lists a number of differences between her novel and the screenplay, which had significant consequences as regards the meaning and context of several aspects of the narrative. Yvonne Griggs, however, notices the consistency of the changes with the genre of melodrama, and claims: 'As such, what Smiley sees as fundamental flaws in the film may be construed as conscious inclusions and omissions related to the governing codes and conventions of on-screen melodrama, written for a cinema-going audience in a post-feminist era.'[43] Griggs also sees the melodramatic qualities of the film primarily in the foregrounding of the female characters already mentioned, and she emphasises how this focus on the female experience even results in downplaying the male–female relationships within the context of the (patriarchal) family unit compared to Smiley's novel. Furthermore, Ramona Wray remarks that

> Crucial here is the fact that Ginny/Goneril dominates the proceedings via her retrospective interpretation of events: it is her perspective that is privileged, and the whole amounts to an elaboration of her autobiography. Informed engagement with what was prior ('I remember' and 'I was remembering' are loaded refrains) permits the emergence of a new-found female self-confidence, while the narrative more generally unfolds in such a way as to grant the woman, for the first time, a shaping voice. Of course, in elaborating these points of view, and as it befits the genre to which it subscribes, *A Thousand Acres* is sentimental …[44]

Thus, the changes in focus and plot fit perfectly with the world of the melodrama, endowing the film with the atmosphere of feminine emotionality.

The increased significance given to the female characters comes at the price of suppressing the subplot, not only when compared to the Shakespearean source text, but even to Smiley's novel, where the secondary characters are granted a considerably more rounded treatment. The accident that blinds Harold Clark, the Gloucester character, is missing entirely, and Jess (Colin Firth), the Edmund figure, is significant here only as a philanderer, rather than as a representative of a new generation of organic farmers, engaged in a wider reaching battle over the mismanaged American land that is poisoning the people it is meant to support.

The figure of the patriarch, Larry Cook, remains in this way practically the sole representative of the tyrannical old world that is responsible for the suffering of the females, which means that his demise and eventual punishment must also come as if by a universal force. One way to strengthen our impression of the melodrama's belief in a predominantly benevolent universe is visible in the way Larry's mental disintegration is represented.

While Smiley's novel explicitly talks about the dementia of the Lear figure, in the film this change from ruler to outcast comes more abruptly, without the rational explanation of the medical diagnosis. Since this sudden change happens at the trial scene, where the judge subsequently rules for Ginny and Rose, it fits more into the melodramatic world of fateful reversals of fortune, illustrating the universe's power to set right what has been destroyed. Nonetheless, no sense of triumph is allowed, since the wounds inflicted on the girls are beyond healing, and the film makes it abundantly clear that the conservative Midwestern society is also slow to respond to change.

Even more significant is the absence of narrator Ginny's guilt in the film: in the novel she is clearly culpable for attempting to poison her sister Rose out of jealousy for her more successful affair with Jess Clarke. There is no can of poisoned sausages made by Ginny for Rose, and in this way Ginny's central position as melodramatic victim is not compromised. It is true that Ginny is tempted by immorality – she also has a short affair with Jess – but when she realises that he does not respond to her feelings, she stops pursuing him and does nothing to actively get him back from her sister. At the same time, it is also true that Ginny's conclusion is not a resounding victory, but rather a renewed acceptance of her (silent) position in the world. As Griggs summarises: 'In line with the conventions of melodrama as a film genre, the status quo is maintained at a societal level, and the female voice, though found, is then silenced.'[45] The maintenance of the status quo and the keeping up of appearances are equally explicit issues within the film. Before the trial, their lawyer advises Ginny and Rose to make sure they look the part they have to play in society, by putting on a dress and sweeping the porch every day if necessary, as this may decide their case rather than what actually happened between them and their father.

Yet, by the end, it would appear that Ginny and her nieces are freed from all the poisonous psychological and material realities of the farm. On closer look, it is evident that their liberation comes at a high price: the loss of the farm and the death of Rose, whose final words also imply that she considers her life to have been a waste and her 'sole, solitary accomplishment' a passive one. Looking back on her life, she claims: 'All I have is that I saw without being afraid, without turning away, and that I didn't forgive the unforgivable.' With her death, her voice is doubly silenced, as Ginny cannot bring herself to say the words she promised Rose, unable to tell Caroline about their father's abusive habits. Ginny's inability is rooted in her acceptance of her own unchanging position as victim, but it is also the result of a lack of strategies to cope with her awareness of victimhood.

She says in the final moments of the film: 'Rose left me a riddle I haven't solved, of how we judge those who have hurt us when they have shown no remorse, not even understanding.'

This is not, however, a weakness on the part of the filmmakers, but rather their understanding that the melodrama does not offer an escape for women: if they achieve self-disclosure and self-recognition, it rarely comes with a changing of their actual circumstances, as they typically return to the sphere they were trying to escape from in the first place. In Ginny's case, this is not the farm itself – that has been lost – but the position of caregiver, the one who provides for others, rather than the one provided for. And yet the film ends on a moderately optimistic note, with the hope that the tragedies, the vicious circles of abuse, incest, poison and betrayal, cease with their generation, and the next one – Rose's daughters – will have a better chance of a happy life. The last line of the film thus ends the narrative in true melodramatic fashion: 'in them I see something new, something my sister and I never had – I see hope'. Again, in the novel we are granted a few more details that strongly qualify this optimism, as there we learn that one of the girls, Linda, 'is especially interested in vertical food conglomerates', preparing to join the powers that brought about the end of the family farm.[46] In the film, however, Ginny's voiceover narrative has the final word, appreciating her true inheritance in her nieces (see figure 2.3),

Figure 2.3 Ginny and her legacy – Michelle Williams, Jessica Lange and Elisabeth Moss in *A Thousand Acres*. Directed by Jocelyn Moorhouse, 1997. Touchstone Pictures/Propaganda Films/Prairie Films/Beacon Pictures/Via Rosa Productions.

whom she can finally watch over and help to grow in an environment away from the toxic thousand acres of her and Rose's childhood. One could not describe this ending as comic – all the survivors have lost someone and everyone carries scars of various kinds – but Ginny as melodramatic protagonist can offer her true nurturing spirit to the next generation of women, in the hope of giving them a better future.

Shakespeare in East Ham – *Life Goes On*

The final part of this chapter will not only jump ahead another decade in time, but, more importantly, will discuss a film whose genealogy includes a tradition radically different from Western European and Hollywood filmmaking: Bollywood cinema. The argument justifying the inclusion of a London-based but Bollywood-inflected British-Asian film is the critical commonplace that popular Indian cinema is predominantly melodramatic in mode, a feature that Western criticism never fails to observe and tends to criticise, equating this central narrative and stylistic element with cheap kitsch and untamed, simplistic excess of emotionalism. This chapter focuses on a single example, *Life Goes On* (2009, dir. Sangeeta Datta), a film shot in London, with a predominantly English dialogue, but depicting both Eastern and Western social traditions and clearly targeting a diasporic audience.

At the same time, it is important to acknowledge that Datta's work is not the only one of its kind, and together with Jeremy Wooding's *Bollywood Queen* (2002), a *Romeo and Juliet* story, or Jon Sen's *Second Generation* (2003), a made-for-television adaptation of *King Lear*, it could be seen as a sufficiently important subgroup to merit discussion in this context. All these films, although set and produced in London, make use of easily recognisable characteristics of Bollywood filmmaking, including song-and-dance sequences, and a tendency towards melodrama, to encourage audience identification with their ethno-cultural community. At the same time, both Bollywood and British-Asian films have begun to adapt the compulsory musical elements 'to Western tastes, as hip-hop and drum'n'bass compete with bhangra', in Kaleem Aftab's words.[47] This controversial hybridity is reflected in the way certain technical features, from slow-motion cinematography to song-and-dance sequences, are represented in the films. However, in contrast to the traditional predominance of non-diegetic musical elements, contemporary Bollywood and British-Asian films tend to incorporate the traditional song-and-dance element in their plot, and they also show their diasporic origins through the recurring themes of intergenerational and intercultural conflict. Several of these films have also gained recognition beyond the boundaries of British-Asian communities and have reached a global film market. Pascale Aebischer even refers to 'the "Asian chic" of Bollywood' tangible in the contemporary mediascape, and describes how the success of several British-Asian films, including *East is East* (1999, dir. Damien O'Donnell) and *Bend It Like Beckham* (2002, dir. Gurinder Chadha), has paved the way for a number of British-Asian, or Bollywood-style, Shakespeare adaptations as well.[48]

Sangeeta Datta's 2009 adaptation, loosely based on *King Lear*, is an interesting example of melodramatic Shakespeare films not produced within, but influenced by, the Indian mediascape. The tangible evidence of this influence includes plenty of local and culture-specific particularities, the musical language and cinematic style, dress code and choice of names, but even more significantly the symbolic presence of the mother figure and her consistent identification with nature, which confirms the film's generic identity as a melodrama. Not only does the mother appear at the heart of the narrative, emphasising the universality of female experience (see figure 2.4), but the three daughters of the Lear character are all presented in a more sympathetic light. Each in their own way, they represent independent British-Asian young women who are struggling to find their way among clashing socio-cultural expectations, inherited traditions and a liberal multicultural environment.

Life Goes On concerns itself with the life of the South Asian diaspora in Britain, as is quite conspicuous through the film's London setting,

Figure 2.4 Remembering the mother – Sharmila Tagore in *Life Goes On*. Directed by Sangeeta Datta, 2009. SD Films/Stormglass Productions.

the metropolis having an integral part in director-screenwriter-producer Sangeeta Datta's concept, as she emphasises the significance of the cultural scene of the British capital as the film's backdrop. In the midst of the globalised diversity of London, *Life Goes On* highlights one specific group, an immigrant family of three generations from the Indian subcontinent, and this diaspora identity informs the film's narrative and cinematography as well, relying as much on Bollywood's visual vocabulary as on Western traditions of filmmaking. The Bollywood association is actually denied by the creators' manifesto, but I believe that the dissociation is more concerned with issues (and prejudices) of quality, rather than (trans)national identity. Stormglass Productions, the production company behind the film, claims to have been 'set up to promote meaningful cinema and theatre in the British-Asian culture-scape … [i]n the face of Bollywood cinema and its onslaught of mindless comedy and candyfloss romance'.[49] While for non-Asian audiences the differences may be less noticeable, *Life Goes On* is clearly more accessible to the global viewer than the stereotypical candyfloss romance musicals of earlier decades, partly owing to the way it fits into the well-known conventions of the melodrama.

The film focuses on a respectable middle-class Hindu family, parents and three young adult daughters, living in London, and follows their lives for six days, from the unexpected death of the mother, Manju (Sharmila Tagore), until her funeral. The middle-class background is a common feature of classical Hollywood melodrama, since this social order is what needs to be upheld at all costs, its value system proving more enduring than the temptations of rebellion against its confines. The plot can easily be read as an updated variant of *King Lear*, as we witness the father, a Hindu physician, Sanjay Banerjee (Girish Karnad) divide his wealth among his three daughters, then fall out with the youngest and most caring one, Dia (Soha Ali Khan). Sanjay then ends up wandering around London in a stormy night and eventually finds himself alone on the heath – in Hampstead – but, in the end, he succeeds in reconciling with everyone around him. The Shakespearean legacy is also manifest throughout the film in direct meta-theatrical references, when Dia, a student at the Royal Academy of Dramatic Arts, plays Cordelia in the end-of-term student performance of *King Lear*. The script also includes textual quotations, mainly in voiceover, but at times visually reinforced by the cinematography, as in framing Sanjay and Dia in an archway while the words 'come, let's away to prison' (5.3.8) are heard.

However, the differences between the Shakespearean characters and their counterparts are significant in emphasising the film's contemporary diasporic setting and in paving the way for its melodramatic conclusion. While the first daughter is married to a white Englishman, repeatedly expressing her dissatisfaction with her life, and the second daughter is a lesbian, Dia is not facing the stereotypical conflict between an arranged marriage or true love, but a choice between holding on to her Muslim boyfriend, Imtiaz, father of her yet unborn child, or letting him go, in obedience to her father's wishes.[50] An old family friend, Alok (Om Puri) is assigned the role of the Fool, but his role and relation to other members of the cast is considerably more complex than in Shakespeare's play, particularly through his past romantic involvement with Manju. Most importantly, it is the figure of the mother whose character and role is burdened with a variety of meanings. Not only does her presence signal an increased role for the feminine principle in the film, mostly aligning it with the cinematic traditions of the melodrama, but the centrality of the maternal within the narrative is also a constant reminder that it is the Bollywood variant of the melodramatic that informs the film. She is also associated with one of the key markers of Indian cinema, that is, music, but in *Life Goes On*, song-and-dance sequences are no longer the extra-diegetic Kashmiri spectacles that provide so much fascination in traditional Bollywood musicals. As typical in British-Asian cinema, such inserts are given a diegetic justification; thus we see the daughters dancing in family celebrations, while singing is typically connected to Manju, when she teaches traditional songs to children, accompanying herself on her sitar.[51]

The inclusion of the mother in a *Lear* narrative can also be seen as a natural decision to reinforce the dominant melodramatic mode of the film's atmosphere. As a series of flashbacks make it clear, Manju's whole life was dedicated to her family, and her constant positioning of herself in the background, always prioritising the needs of her loved ones, makes us reinterpret her death as a necessary sacrifice. Only after her loss is her family able to regain a social equilibrium both within the domestic environment and in the broader context of the British-Asian diaspora. In this way, we are constantly reminded of classical melodrama's focus on female suffering, the sacrifices made within and for the domestic environment, to pave the way for a more conciliatory conclusion that characterises most films within the genre. Significantly, Diana E. Henderson emphasises a generic context other than the melodrama: that of the Shakespearean romance, with its foregrounding of forgiveness and reconciliation, especially between fathers and their daughters.[52] At the same time, in spite of the obvious correspondences between the narrative structures of the late Shakespeare plays and *Life Goes On*, I believe the dominant generic conventions visible throughout the film are consistently associated with the melodrama.

It is a commonly known peculiarity of Shakespeare's *King Lear* that all mother figures are absent from the drama; in *Life Goes On*, however, the figure of the mother lingers on, and it is an image presented with unquestioning nostalgia. The postcolonial family is fraught with conflict and tension, very much in line with the social concerns of 'the British Asian Shakespeare-inflected films, on the big screen and on television, that flourished amid the growing awareness, following the 9/11 attack on the World Trade Center, that the multicultural make-up of British society was not entirely harmonious', as summarised by Aebischer.[53] Moreover, in contemporary British-Asian cinema the depiction of traditional social structures, as well as clashes between expected and desired gender roles and socially required sacrifices, belong to the staple elements of narratives. Sanjay Sharma even argues that British-Asian films 'in their representational form appear to be more "conventional" and do not intend to disrupt narrative genres or deconstruct hegemonic cinematic aesthetics'.[54] More specifically, the social issues in these films are more recognisable for their increasingly multicultural and transnational global viewership than by potential audiences in the 'mother country'. Their plots present a less idealised image of the West, and focus particularly on the clash of value systems, racism and the negotiation of new identities as experienced by diasporic communities.[55] While 'these films do question mainstream, stereotyped representations of South Asians',[56] they also fit into the equally stereotypical portrayal of 'young British Asians as experiencing stress, identity crises and conflict as a result of tensions between their hybrid/Western outlook and their parents' South Asian cultural values'.[57] One particular embodiment of these crises appears to be 'the scenario of the arranged, forced or forbidden marriage as cultural and generational conflict', a situation which fits perfectly into the melodramatic plight of female victims of an oppressive social structure.[58] In *Life Goes On*, as mentioned, the family as a whole is torn between tradition and social progress, but all tensions come to a head in connection with the younger generation's marital choices.

While Manju is not a metaphorical mother (but already spiritual and therefore intangible), our only access to her is through discrete images, flashback recollections of earlier conversations and encounters. These images are inspected severally, through the eyes of individual members of the family, and it is only the film's narrative that can link the images together into a continuous story, to be told and thus understood.

Alternatively, we may claim that it is only the mother's constant presence that binds the separate threads together into one colourful tapestry. When comparing her position to the self-sacrificing mother figures of classic melodrama, it is true that Manju appears less a suppressed and downtrodden housewife than a happy and satisfied mother. She is not forced into her role, and her choice of remaining within the household and the domestic sphere is clearly her own (the only suggestion that once she had aspirations to subvert this order is the vague reference to her past romantic association with Alok). Nonetheless, the final sequence of the film, immediately preceding the end credits, shows Manju disappearing in a forest, stepping out of the frame, which cannot hold her captive any longer. Yet the real rebels against the oppressive patriarchal world order are her daughters, the second-generation immigrants, who resist the traditional middle-class roles in diverse ways.

However, this resistance and fight for liberation, displayed by all female characters, are restricted by the conventions of the melodrama, and the film ends on a note of acceptance of traditional family values, as the generally 'benevolent, humanly oriented world order' of the melodrama is restored through the sacrifices of the women.[59] Again it is symbolic that the film ends with Manju's funeral – on the one hand, an institutionalised ritual which marks the end of her role in the family narrative; on the other, an occasion for the whole family to get together and display by their participation and their traditional clothes that the human sacrifice, Manju's death, was worthwhile. These communal and family rituals always play a significant role, both in Shakespearean drama and narrative cinema, to consolidate the work's general atmosphere and in this way confirm its genre as well. Interestingly, Jeremy Wooding's *Bollywood Queen* chooses a wedding, rather than a funeral, for its final scene of reconciliation, even though the plot's association with *Romeo and Juliet* would imply otherwise. Naturally, as the film refuses the drama's tragic ending and turns towards a comic – and partly melodramatic – resolution, no one is killed during the plot and there are only minor injuries in the fights. The decision of both young lovers, however, to reconcile with their own families, shows how the British-Asian diaspora narrative diverts the emphasis from the conflict between rival families towards the intergenerational conflict, potentially no less lethal, and no less vital to restore, in order to create a future for the second-generation immigrant community.

As I have already referred to the social background of the melodrama, it is also important to remark that while in Western societies women's participation on the job market has increasingly become the norm even in the middle classes, this does not seem to be the case in the nostalgic visions of Bollywood cinema. Even in British-Asian films, when we see women holding jobs they are typically participating in the family business as the only socially acceptable form of employment, especially for unmarried girls. In *Bollywood Queen*, Geena works in a sari shop, which requires her to be dressed in a sari, while also hindering her escape from the confines of the Indian community, both physically and emotionally, as she feels out of place as soon as she leaves her 'native' environment. Catherine L. Innes claims that 'in India and other postcolonial nations, the dichotomy between public activity defined as male, and feminine roles defined as private and domestic, have prevailed', which is a more than accurate description of the family structure in *Life Goes On* as well.[60] The home as inclusive territory works perfectly for Manju, she is hardly ever seen either leaving, let alone outside, the home (which includes the garden), and the film's narrative never even attempts to deny her acceptance of the role of women in patriarchal society. When a colleague returns her personal belongings to the family, we learn that Manju did have a job outside the home, in a library, but we never actually see her performing it, and thus for the viewer this part of her life does not acquire any significance. We also learn of her marital unhappiness, but only indirectly and as a thing of the past, for which we tend to blame her husband, the self-centred Sanjay, since he did not offer her companionship while the children were young. As a result, even after the acknowledgement of her infidelity, Manju's status as the nurturing centre of the family and her acceptance of the roles of wife and mother remain unquestioned.

Another visual sign of women's role in society is their dress, which is markedly and consistently traditional Indian in Manju's case: whenever she is not wearing a sari, she is dressed in salwar kameez, the most hybrid of apparels of Indian origin. Her daughters, on the other hand, are mostly seen in Western clothes, jeans and jackets, Dia even in a short skirt, signalling their move away from the traditional role of woman as the silent accessory in the household. However, towards the conclusion of the film, the three girls are seen nostalgising over their mother's wardrobe, and all of them don one of Manju's saris for the funeral, as a sign of their reconciliation with their Indian parentage. (Similarly, in *Bollywood Queen*, Geena returns to the family wedding in a sari, rather than the rebellious Western clothes she and her friends appear in whenever they rehearse.)

In close association to motherhood is nature, known as 'Mother Nature' in many cultures and present typically as a female figure in most mythologies, and closely connected to femininity in the language of the cinema as well. *A Thousand Acres* relies on the images of cornfields to emphasise the extensive damage female bodies had to suffer, but in *Life Goes On* nature is almost exclusively tamed and domesticated, and appears predominantly in the form of the family's garden. However, the constant presence of this version of nature is so emphatic that it draws attention to itself in a variety of ways: we learn that the garden has been created by Manju (the mother is the source of all life) and the girls are reminded of their duty to tend the herbs she planted. Visually, there are practically no shots of Manju where nature is not included in some form: most often as setting, since she is almost exclusively shown in her garden, and on rare occasions in a public park, while it is also her healing power and wise advice that her daughters seek. Already in the very first sequence of the film, moments before her fatal heart attack, she is inside her kitchen, but surrounded by plants, preparing dinner for her family and friends, in a way offering her vital energies by providing the means of life to everyone around her.

Nature is also present in the cinematography in the form of cutaways between scenes, highlighting the presence of nature's healing power, the presence that will restore the balance and recharge energies. Nature also provides the place where everyone can be at home, the starting point of all human endeavours and the final destination where all human flesh will eventually return. *Life Goes On* thus argues that it is no longer a matter of importance whether the divine forces whose healing power can cure breaches within communities are the gods of Hinduism or Christianity. What remains a universal truth is that in the same way as Cordelia's nature – 'both her human nature and the nature in which she believes, which is a potentially benevolent *super*nature – opposes the *un*natural in this world, those who vie for political, material, and sexual advantage', the melodrama believes in the possibility of returning to a harmonious and benevolent universe.[61] Manju in *Life Goes On* embodies maternal love that creates unions above all divisions, love that heals all wounds, and that is the most powerful source of life, capable of opposing the destructive forces of the world as well. At the same time, it is equally significant that – contrary to the tragic fate of half the cast in Shakespeare's drama – in this British-Asian melodramatic retelling of *King Lear* the only character who dies is the one who was not even supposed to be there. This alteration in turn makes the mother figure a symbolic saviour of the traditions of the family, the whole of the diasporic community and even the cinematic conventions of the melodrama.

Notes

1. See F. Leibowitz, 'Apt Feelings, or Why "Women's Films" Aren't Trivial', in D. Bordwell and N. Carroll (eds), *Post-Theory: Reconstructing Film Studies* (Madison: University of Wisconsin Press, 1996), pp. 219–29.
2. Stephen, '*Men Are Not Gods* Review', *Letterboxd* (8 October 2016), www.letterboxd.com/film/men-are-not-gods/ (accessed 26 January 2020).
3. A. Loacker and M. Prucha, 'Österreichisch-deutsche Filmbeziehungen und die unabhängige Spielfilmproduktion 1933–1937', *Modern Austrian Literature*, 32:4, Special Issue: *Austria in Film* (1999), 87–117, 102.
4. All parenthetical references to *Othello* are to this edition: W. Shakespeare, *Othello*, The Arden Shakespeare, Third Series, ed. E. A. J. Honigmann (Walton-on-Thames: Thomas Nelson & Sons, 1997).
5. M. Brooke, '*Men Are Not Gods* (1936)', *Screenonline*, www.screenonline.org.uk/film/id/439260/index.html (accessed 26 January 2020).
6. K. Rothwell, *A History of Shakespeare on Screen: A Century of Film and Television* (Cambridge: Cambridge University Press, 2004), p. 209.
7. D. Lanier, 'Murdering *Othello*', in D. Cartmell (ed.), *A Companion to Literature, Film, and Adaptation* (Chichester: Wiley-Blackwell, 2012), pp. 198–215, p. 199.
8. M. Landy, *British Genres: Cinema and Society, 1930–1960* (Princeton, NJ: Princeton University Press, 1991), p. 249.
9. T. Elsaesser, 'Tales of Sound and Fury: Observations on the Family Melodrama', in Grant (ed.), *Film Genre Reader IV*, pp. 433–62, p. 457.
10. Cf. *Ibid.*, p. 455.
11. Lanier, 'Murdering *Othello*', p. 207.
12. Cawelti, *Adventure, Mystery, and Romance*, p. 47.
13. Landy, *British Genres*, p. 249.
14. D. Rosenthal, 'The Bard on Screen', *Guardian* (7 April 2007), www.theguardian.com/film/2007/apr/07/stage.shakespeare (accessed 18 January 2020).
15. P. Skrebels, '*All Night Long*: Jazzing Around with *Othello*', *Literature/Film Quarterly*, 36:2 (2008), 147–56, 150.
16. A. Burton and T. O'Sullivan, *The Cinema of Basil Dearden and Michael Relph* (Edinburgh: Edinburgh University Press, 2009), p. 89.
17. *Ibid.*
18. G. Santoro, *Myself When I Am Real: The Life and Music of Charles Mingus* (New York: Oxford University Press, 2000), p. 183.
19. Santoro's book has Peter Jericho, which is clearly an error. Moreover, the book may have some further bias, for example in its argument that Mingus's marginalisation in the project was racially motivated, since this claim is hard to support in light of the film's theme and the presence of so many other actors and musicians of colour.
20. L. Ceplair, *The Marxist and the Movies: A Biography of Paul Jarrico* (Lexington: The University Press of Kentucky, 2007), pp. 180–1.

21 Santoro, *Myself When I Am Real*, p. 183.
22 K. W. Weierman, *One Nation, One Blood: Interracial Marriage in American Fiction, Scandal, and Law, 1820–1870* (Amherst and Boston: University of Massachusetts Press, 2005), p. 171.
23 R. Carney (ed.), *Cassavetes on Cassavetes* (London: Faber and Faber, 2001), p. 55.
24 Santoro, *Myself When I Am Real*, p. 183.
25 Ceplair, *The Marxist and the Movies*, p. 181.
26 Ibid.
27 Ibid.
28 Skrebels, 'All Night Long', 152.
29 Ibid.
30 S. E. Farrell, *Jane Smiley's* A Thousand Acres: *A Reader's Guide* (New York and London: Continuum, 2001), p. 74.
31 R. Kempley, 'In *A Thousand Acres*, A Tired Feminist Plot', *Washington Post* (19 September 1997), www.washingtonpost.com/wp-srv/style/longterm/movies/review97/thousandacreskemp.htm (accessed 26 January 2020).
32 Diana E. Henderson reminds us of a critically undervalued *Lear* variant, *Hobson's Choice* (1953, dir. David Lean), which also directs the viewer's sympathy to the eldest daughter, as opposed to the traditional folkloric focus on the youngest child. D. E. Henderson, 'Romancing *King Lear*: *Hobson's Choice*, *Life Goes On* and Beyond', in Bladen, Hatchuel and Vienne-Guerrin (eds), *Shakespeare on Screen*, pp. 125–39, p. 126.
33 J. Smiley, 'Shakespeare in Iceland', in J. Bate, J. L. Levenson and D. Mehl (eds), *Shakespeare and the Twentieth Century: The Selected Proceedings of the International Shakespeare Association World Congress Los Angeles, 1996* (Newark: University of Delaware Press; London: Associated University Presses, 1998), pp. 41–59, p. 52.
34 R. Ebert, *I Hated, Hated, Hated This Movie* (Kansas City: Andrews McMeel Publishing, 2000), p. 344.
35 S. Richter, 'A Thousand Acres', *Tucson Weekly* (29 September 1997), www.filmvault.com/filmvault/tw/t/thousandacresa1.html (accessed 26 January 2020).
36 R. Smith, 'A Thousand Acres', *Austin Chronicle* (19 September 1997), www.austinchronicle.com/calendar/film/1997-09-19/a-thousand-acres/ (accessed 26 January 2020).
37 R. Wray, '*King Lear*: Performative Traditions/Interpretative Positions', in A. Hiscock and L. Hopkins (eds), *King Lear: A Critical Guide* (London and New York: Continuum, 2011), pp. 56–77, p. 65.
38 Kempley, 'In *A Thousand Acres*, A Tired Feminist Plot'.
39 Interestingly, as Anne-Kathrin Marquardt draws attention to it, the film was still rated 'R' in the USA, as a result of 'strong sexual language', but most other countries were much more lenient in their ratings, France even recommending

it for general audiences. Cf. A.-K. Marquardt, 'Unlearning Tradition: William Shakespeare's *King Lear*, Jane Smiley's and Jocelyn Moorhouse's *A Thousand Acres*', in M. Dobson and E. Rivier-Arnaud (eds), *Rewriting Shakespeare's Plays for and by the Contemporary Stage* (Newcastle-upon-Tyne: Cambridge Scholars Publishing, 2017), pp. 11–30, p. 15, n. 13.
40 J. R. Keller, *Food, Film and Culture: A Genre Study* (Jefferson, NC: McFarland, 2006), p. 99.
41 K. J. Warren, 'Taking Empirical Data Seriously: An Ecofeminist Philosophical Perspective', in K. J. Warren (ed.), *Ecofeminism: Women, Culture, Nature* (Bloomington and Indianapolis: Indiana University Press, 1997), pp. 3–20, p. 10.
42 Y. Griggs, '"All Our Lives We'd Looked Out for Each Other in the Way That Motherless Children Tend to Do": *King Lear* as Melodrama', *Literature/Film Quarterly*, 35:2 (2007), 101–7.
43 Griggs, *Screen Adaptations: Shakespeare's* King Lear, p. 146.
44 Wray, '*King Lear*: Performative Traditions', pp. 70–1.
45 Griggs, *Screen Adaptations: Shakespeare's* King Lear, p. 149.
46 J. Smiley, *A Thousand Acres* (New York: Alfred A. Knopf, 1992), p. 369.
47 K. Aftab, 'Brown: The New Black! Bollywood in Britain', *Critical Quarterly*, 44:3 (2002), 88–98, 91.
48 P. Aebischer, *Screening Early Modern Drama: Beyond Shakespeare* (Cambridge: Cambridge University Press, 2013), p. 189.
49 'Stormglass Productions', *Mandy.com*, https://crew.mandy.com/uk/company/3975/stormglass-productions (accessed 26 January 2020).
50 Diana E. Henderson refers to a significant insight made by Preti Taneja that neither of the elder daughters' unconventional partnerships are seen as scandalous, as opposed to Dia's choice of a Muslim boyfriend. Henderson, 'Romancing *King Lear*', p. 138, n. 25.
51 On the significance of Rabindranath Tagore's poetry in the film, see Henderson, 'Romancing *King Lear*', p. 132.
52 Ibid.
53 Aebischer, *Screening Early Modern Drama*, p. 196.
54 S. Sharma, 'Teaching British South Asian Cinema: Towards a "Materialist" Reading Practice', *South Asian Popular Culture*, 7:1 (2009), 21–35, 22.
55 See Dwyer, 'Planet Bollywood', p. 369.
56 Sharma, 'Teaching British South Asian Cinema', 22.
57 Aebischer, *Screening Early Modern Drama*, p. 197.
58 Ibid.
59 Cawelti, *Adventure, Mystery, and Romance*, p. 45.
60 C. L. Innes, *The Cambridge Introduction to Postcolonial Literatures in English* (Cambridge: Cambridge University Press, 2007), p. 140.
61 H. R. Coursen, *Shakespeare Translated: Derivatives on Film and TV* (New York: Peter Lang, 2005), p. 116.

3

Dark-minded Othellos, mobster Macbeths: *film noir*, gangster, gangster *noir*

In the introduction to Part I of the book, I have attempted to provide a brief summary of the concept of *film noir*, the characteristics of the gangster film and the strong connections between the two conventions. It is of course unsurprising that within Shakespeare's dramatic *oeuvre* it is typically the tragedies that find the most welcoming adapting environment in *film noir* and gangster narratives, as several versions of *Hamlet*, *Othello* and *Macbeth* can testify in the analyses later in this chapter, even though other source texts have also been transformed into *film noir*, following its well-known visual and technical conventions. These stylistic and technical features are succinctly summarised in Harry Keyishian's genre-based analysis of four *Hamlet* films, which points out the typical meanings assigned to these devices: '*Film noir* is most easily identified in terms of its visual style and camera strategies: low key lighting, shadows and fog; a *mise-en-scène* that makes settings as important as people; canted camera angles (expressing subjectivity), tight framing (showing entrapment) and slow tracking shots (suggesting the unravelling of mystery).'[1] When *film noir* is mentioned in connection with films based on Shakespearean drama, it is mostly in reference to Laurence Olivier's 1948 *Hamlet*, or Orson Welles's 1952 *Othello* adaptation, emphasising their black-and-white cinematography and distinctive camerawork that fit perfectly Keyishian's quoted description. Here, however, I focus on a range of lesser-known films that also follow the conventions of *film noir* or gangster films, and are primarily seen as such, rather than as vehicles for Olivier, Welles or other great actor-director-*auteurs*.

The chapter begins with a discussion of two classic examples of *film noir* from the immediate post-war period, roughly spanning the decade between

1945 and 1955. After the analysis of *Strange Illusion* (1945, dir. Edgar G. Ulmer) and *A Double Life* (1947, dir. George Cukor), the next group comprises works that display conventions of not (only) the *film noir* but even more so the gangster film, although the overlaps between the two formulas are undeniable. Some authors tend to use the terms interchangeably, and Spencer Selby also implies that *film noir*, which he calls 'a historical, stylistic and thematic trend ... took place primarily, but not exclusively, within the generic complex of the American crime film of the 1940s and 1950s'.[2] Other descriptions suggest that *film noir* from its inception embraced a number of other genres, from police procedurals to gangster films and many more, therefore precise lines of distinction between these topically clearly related groups are almost impossible. A perfect example of the stylistic connections between the two genres is *Joe Macbeth* (1955, dir. Ken Hughes), particularly when contrasted with a later take on *Macbeth* within the genre, *Men of Respect* (1990, dir. William Reilly). While these films' cinematography shows their indebtedness to *noir*, their protagonists are no longer the victims of crimes, but rather the perpetrators. At the same time, they also provide convincing evidence of the complexity of the moral universe of both *film noir* and the gangster genre, a conflict best exemplified by the final work included in the chapter, James Gray's indie drama from 2007, *We Own the Night*. This neo-*noir* police and gangster narrative confirms that this genre framework continues to function as a perfect adaptation framework for Shakespearean drama, where appearance and reality are never in harmony.

Classic psychological *noir* – *Strange Illusion*

A little-known, low-budget film that is a particularly interesting example in this context is Edgar G. Ulmer's *Strange Illusion*, released at the very beginning of the *noir* era, in 1945 by Producers Releasing Corporation (one of the so-called 'Poverty Row' studios of the era). The studio typically granted extremely short time and very little in terms of material background, but offered great artistic freedom to its directors, which in this case clearly paid off. Douglas Lanier points out the work's indebtedness to a popular theme of the age: psychology, arguing that 'the film is a fascinating, well-made film noir adaptation of *Hamlet* that concentrates on the play's Oedipal psychology, and it deserves to be much better known'.[3]

To spot the structural similarities between the film and its Shakespearean source is not difficult, as Lanier also mentions abundant 'plot and character parallels to *Hamlet*', even though there are no direct textual quotations from Shakespeare's drama.[4] Spencer Selby's one-sentence summary may ring a bell to anyone familiar with *Hamlet*: 'Adolescent believes that his widowed mother's suitor may have murdered his father',[5] and a slightly more detailed description of the plot highlights further aspects that remind the viewer of the tragedy. A young man, Paul Cartwright (James Lydon), who has a recurring nightmare about the death of his father, a former lieutenant governor of California, goes home for a holiday to realise that his mother (Sally Eilers) is about to marry a man called Brett Curtis (Warren William). Paul suspects that the suitor is more interested in the family property than in the widow, but his nightmares also suggest Curtis's potential involvement in the death of Paul's father, a judge of high esteem.

Instead of one Horatio figure, Paul has two friends by his side, a somewhat clownish but trustworthy young man called George (Jimmy Clark) and an elderly father figure, Doctor Vincent (Regis Toomey), a psychiatrist by profession. The latter is particularly helpful in digging up suspicious details from Curtis's past (Curtis's real name later turns out to be Claude Barrington, whom Paul's father already suspected of criminal activities). Paul's girlfriend, Lydia (Mary McLeod), represents an Ophelia-like romantic interest, and like the Danish Prince's inability to trust Ophelia, initially Paul also has problems communicating his true feelings towards her. Lydia narrowly escapes falling victim to Curtis's advances; in the course of the plot, we learn that young girls are this villain's weakness, and his criminal history even includes the murder of several females.

Paul's recurring nightmares seem to be coming true step by step, and he has a series of fainting spells, after which he is sent to recover in a sanatorium – a mental asylum – run by a Professor Muhlbach (Charles Arnt), Curtis's former therapist and current partner in crime. Paul plays along, sometimes pretending to be more troubled than he is, to be able to keep an eye on Curtis and the whole operation, again recalling Hamlet's madness and his treading of the borderline between pretence and reality. Gradually more and more suspicious facts come to light that implicate Curtis in a series of crimes, including the death of Cartwright Sr, but the investigation also raises the vigilance of the criminals. In the final scenes, after a sequence of car chases and narrow escapes, Curtis is shot dead by a policeman, but not before throwing Paul violently across the room. The young man lies unmoving on the ground, and the final scene of the film takes us to another of his dream visions, similar to the nightmare scene at the beginning. Here he no longer sees the fatal accident, but meets his father, who then takes his wife's arm in a loving embrace, and Paul moves away from them, happily joining his girlfriend instead, envisioning the long-awaited closure of his cycle of investigation and revenge. Although with much fewer casualties than *Hamlet*, the plot thus includes most of the significant characters and even the diegetic conflicts of the Shakespearean source play. Yet the way these inherited elements are reborn in the context of a *noir* production exemplifies how the director found a perfect match in the updated version of the *Hamlet* plot for the genre's characteristic interests in psychology and investigations. As the blurb on the DVD cover explains, 'at the time, the director was fascinated with psychoanalysis, and he put together an eery mystery concerning a father–son relationship', and after some creative twists and turns, the final 'picture contains as much *Hamlet* as it does Freud, along with some stunning camerawork'.[6]

The truly ingenious qualities of the film include, on the one hand, the expansion, indeed the transformation, of the play's inherent psychological element into a central theme. In *Strange Illusion*, the motivation for the crime, the nature of the evidence and the investigation all involve aspects of psychology. On the level of characterisation, the psychological interest is also enhanced: the confidant figure, Dr Vincent, is a psychiatrist, and young Paul, a law student, is equally interested in continuing his father's research in criminology. The motif of dreams could be seen as a compulsory element for a *Hamlet* adaptation, but I believe it could be even better explained by the post-war period's general belief in the reality of subconscious messages sent by one's mind in the form of dreams and nightmares. Filmmakers also made use of this notion, as 'The emphasis on psychological motivation, including psychoanalytic theories of psychology (the 1940s saw the adoption of so-called vulgar Freudianism by Hollywood), was often associated with or presented as an increased realism', and therefore helped to strengthen audience engagement with films.[7]

To fit this realism, instead of the fear of military invasion, the real threat here comes from the psychologically disturbed criminal, and potentially an abuse of psychological knowledge and control, as represented by the shadowy spaces of the sanatorium. While psychologists are typically depicted as wise and benevolent characters, especially in *film noirs* made during or immediately after the war, the threat of abusing this sort of knowledge is often there in the background. This darker aspect of psychology may also reflect the influence of German expressionist cinema, particularly *The Cabinet of Dr. Caligari* (1919), 'which depicts a disturbing portrait of an asylum and a series of murders told from an insane narrator's subjective point of view', a pattern later developed by other films as well.[8] As Sheri Biesen refers to the mental institution depicted in another post-war *noir* film, *Behind Locked Doors* (1948, dir. Budd Boetticher), such a setting is no longer a place for healing in the period, but 'a criminal hideout depicted as an abusive, dangerous prison where people are beaten near death'.[9]

In *Strange Illusion*, we are not yet forced to question psychology as a real science, since it is represented as an authentic and reliable discipline by Dr Vincent; at the same time, it also appears as a power that can be abused by the evil-minded. As a result, viewers can easily understand why young Paul's life may be in actual danger in the hands of Professor Muhlbach (the German name potentially embodying 'the postwar American cultural tensions and xenophobic fear of foreigners in a growing paranoid Red Scare climate')[10] and his accomplices. Lanier also emphasises the film's careful navigation between various types of psychoanalysis, as in his view, 'it stages a crossing of energies between an Oedipalized Hamlet narrative (which dominates the film's first half) and the debunking of European psychiatry and its displacement by American ego psychology (which dominates the second half)'.[11]

This familiarity with psychology, combined with a fear of the foreigner and the criminally insane, is one of the sources that fed into the postwar popularity of *noir* films (another prime example is *Whirlpool* from 1949, dir. Otto Preminger, which shows a murderous hypnotist exerting psychological control over the heroine). The anxiety over psychological troubles was enhanced by the then familiar genre of hard-boiled detective fiction, similarly easy to identify with in the increasingly alienating urban lifestyle characterising American society from the beginning of the twentieth century. At the same time, the psychological focus is undoubtedly a regular feature in classical Hollywood genres, which connects *film noir* to its female counterpart, the melodrama. As Cowie argues, '*Film noir* can therefore be viewed as a kind of development of melodrama so that whereas earlier the obstacles to the heterosexual couple had been external forces of family and circumstance, wars or illness, in the *film noir* the obstacles derive from the characters' psychology or even pathology as they encounter external events.'[12]

Apart from the film's interest in psychology, the visual world of *Strange Illusion* also fits the *film noir*'s characteristics, although on a smaller scale and with less spectacular results than George Cukor's award-winning *A Double Life*, discussed later in this chapter. The mirror, a multifaceted visual metaphor in Cukor's film, also plays a key role here, embodying the self-reflexive (and self-questioning) tendency of the male protagonist, and employed as a device to express the complex surveillance structures in an oppressive system. For instance, when Paul arrives at the sanatorium (called Restview Manor, in a not-too-subtle combination of references to spying and eternal rest), the first time he is left alone, we are immediately struck by the presence of a large mirror in the room. The mirror reflects only a part of his body at the time, but – in true *noir* fashion – it fills us with the premonition of even stranger illusions. The reflective surface soon turns out to be a two-way mirror behind which Curtis and Muhlbach can hide and spy on their patient, a plot Paul tries to thwart, but to no avail. Eventually, however, the mirror will also serve as his means of escape: when locked into the room, his only way out is by breaking through the mirror, shattering any leftover illusion of pretended innocence. *Strange Illusion* thus shows its sensitivity to the mirror as not simply a visual tool that can extend the camera's vision, but also as an object of metaphorical significance, manifesting the themes of (self-)reflection, appearance and reality, and even the fragmentation of personality.

Another setting where the black-and-white cinematography is employed in cleverly orchestrated ways is the prison-like environment of the mental institution. Even though it is supposed to be morning when Paul arrives at Restview Manor, the *chiaroscuro* lighting makes the place appear almost nocturnal and positively threatening. Both the shadows cast by the window bars, and Paul's own shadow following him on the corridor walls, hint at imprisonment and surveillance, a feeling turning into conviction when he comes to a heavily barred dead end (see figure 3.1). The Venetian blinds on the window, another staple element of *film noir* settings, allow him to take a peek at what may be awaiting him on the outside, but their striped shadows also bring to mind the police investigation rooms, a staple location in *noir* films.

In the prison-like setting, the *film noir* motifs of isolation and alienation are enhanced by the realisation that Paul's telephone line is monitored by the doctor and his assistant, and therefore his communication with the outside world is practically impossible (later the line is physically cut off). The updated setting thus offers a natural framework, readily incorporating the Hamletian themes of Denmark's prison-like atmosphere, making Paul the 'observ'd of all observers' (3.1.156), justifiably unable to trust anyone around him.[13] But however much we are aware of Paul's conscious ploy to throw his opponents off the scent, the environment creates real anxieties in the viewer, while it also confirms the protagonist's complete social isolation.

Psychological illness is, of course, a favourite motif of *noir* films, and the threat of the disintegration of the male psyche is a common theme in many contemporary works. In *Strange Illusion*, madness and the investigation

Figure 3.1 Bars everywhere – James Lydon in *Strange Illusion*. Directed by Edgar G. Ulmer, 1945. Producers Releasing Corporation.

into the criminal mind is elevated into a central theme, as we have already implied, but again its use is often subtler than the all-too-obvious presence of the mental asylum suggests. Paul is described by Curtis as 'a neurotic type', and at one point, his mother also remarks that Paul 'hasn't been himself lately'. The phrase subtly combines the psychological with an allusion to Hamlet's musings on how he has 'of late ... lost all [his] mirth' (cf. 2.2.295–6), or even his later insistence to Laertes before the duel that there is an inner rift inside his personality that allows him to act against his true self. At the same time, Dr Vincent's mounting suspicions seem all the more justified in this dark post-war world where there is no one to trust, and it is almost more natural to doubt one's own mental capacities than to believe one's own eyes.

The film also makes clever use of another visual element that fits the American social drama just as much as a performance of *Hamlet*: the huge portrait of the deceased father, which is first seen hanging above the fireplace in the living room of the Cartwright family, but is soon removed to the father's (now abandoned) study.[14] In stage or film productions of Shakespeare's play, Hamlet's admonitions of his mother in the closet scene are often accompanied by his pointing at some image of the father and his treacherous brother ('Look here upon this picture, and on this, / The counterfeit presentment of two brothers', 3.4.53–4). Likewise, in *Strange Illusion*, young Paul Cartwright and his mother's new suitor, Brett Curtis, are both shown standing in front of the huge painting, being compared and contrasted to its model. At the same time, the portrait and its later displacement from its pride of place to a less intrusive part of the home serve also as a somewhat clichéd but effective tool in *film noir*, which tends to give visual form to the increasing suspicions of foul play in precisely such alterations in the setting. Since the removal of the portrait was initiated by Paul's mother, even the Hamletian motif of the mother's potential implication in the crime is established.

For all the Shakespearean elements, the film remains and primarily functions as a *film noir*, which becomes evident mostly in the second half, and particularly in the final sequence, where the previously purely psychological investigation turns into a police drama. Viewers can enjoy the car chase and the race against time, during which the authorities struggle to collect and identify fingerprints and car registration plates, and get hold of search and arrest warrants from attorneys and court officials, while criminals do their best to destroy all incriminating evidence and people who are potential threats for them. The car itself is a motif inherited from early gangster films, in which it 'is at once a refuge and an escape', both for the victim and the villain.[15] Here a car provides the most damning form of evidence, hidden in an abandoned farm building, and its recovery confirms the previously suspected but unproved aspects of the original crime.

Since *Strange Illusion* is not fully set in a police environment, the Hamlet character is not a member of the forces, therefore in the final shootout it is not he but an armed police officer who gets the chance to deliver the fatal shot that silences the perpetrator once and for all. True, in an even more stereotypical *film noir*, the central character leading the investigation would be a private eye, but a young law student with an interest in criminal psychology, who is just as much an outsider even within his own world as Raymond Chandler's hardboiled detective figures are, sufficiently fits the bill. Whether the reason for the considerably lower body count (than in *Hamlet*) is attributable to the Hays Code, which cautioned filmmakers against the depiction of crime and violence of all kinds, or the desire for a simpler, and more melodramatic than tragic, *denouement*, is hard to say. Still, the uncertainty of the final scene, in which Paul is lying unconscious on the ground envisioning the meeting with his parents in something resembling the afterlife, can be read either as a successful, although slightly late, accomplishment of filial revenge, or a final selfless sacrifice. Either of the two may be acceptable as a Hamletian, but even more as a *noir*, conclusion, which tends to choose psychologically motivated conclusions, avoiding unnecessary bloodbaths and the killing of (at least partially) innocent women and men all around. Here it is not Fortinbras but American law enforcement that has the final word, and that word is a reassuring one: even though post-war society has not yet been cleared of all corruption, there is one less pair of criminals around to endanger the sanctity of the family and the legacy of truly great ancestors.

Post-war male anxieties – *A Double Life*

It was not only low-budget B-movie directors who searched for inspiration in Shakespeare's *oeuvre* for their *film noir* scripts, as we can see in the film discussed in this section, Cukor's multiple award-winning *A Double Life*.[16] The film relies on the generic conventions of *film noir* in many ways, although some interpreters find elements of other genres, particularly the melodrama, in the way the film 'represents the impact of external forces on the internal psyche'.[17] The melodramatic features are undeniable, but also unsurprising, as contemporary criticism often uses the term *noir* melodrama to describe such dramatic explorations of social pressures on the solitary individual. At the same time, the predominant interest of the *film noir* in issues of (male) psychology makes this genre the most appropriate context in which the film can be fruitfully discussed.

A Double Life is set in New York, where a Broadway star, Anthony John, known as Tony (Ronald Colman), is offered the leading role in *Othello*. He is tempted, but both he and his ex-wife, Brita (Signe Hasso), the company's leading lady, are aware that his tendency to identify wholly with each role is a constant threat to his mental balance whenever he leaves the safe territory of the comedy behind; thus the *noir*'s interest in mental instability is established right from the start. Despite his misgivings, Tony accepts the role, and his performance is a resounding success, as a result of his extremely plausible impersonation of *Othello*. Part of this brilliant performance is Tony's ingenious idea to murder Desdemona by 'kissing her to death' rather than strangling her, and this becomes a signature element of the show. In the long run, however, the actor starts to become increasingly prone to jealousy and madness, confirming his worst fears about tragic roles, and at one point he nearly strangles Brita on stage in the murder scene. The abyss of madness is irretrievably pulling him in, and not long after this, in a near trance, he goes to the apartment of Pat Kroll (Shelley Winters), a waitress he occasionally visits for comfort, and kills her with his famous kiss of death. As Lanier points out in his analysis of *A Double Life* and similar *Othello* adaptations, Tony's actions are not only prompted by his envisioning the waitress as a fickle Desdemona, but also by seeing in her his jealously desired ex-wife, Brita.[18] On the subsequent theatre performance, realising both his guilt and the inevitability of punishment, Tony kills himself in the final scene as the regretful Othello. The film's general atmosphere and the *denouement* therefore successfully invoke the tragic spirit of the Shakespearean source text, while the updated language and plot connect the film to its mid-twentieth-century American social context and the generic framework of the *film noir*, reflecting postwar social anxieties.

Although the theatre is neither a mental institution nor a police station, this space can be dominated by dark shadows and labyrinthine spaces as much as the traditional *noir* settings. The pool of light in which *noir* characters so often appear or disappear finds its perfect place on stage, emphasising the actor's isolation and the pressure of the limelight.[19] The overwhelming darkness casts a menacing spectre of crime and passion over the story, which emphasises the alienation of the main hero from human society, represented by the brightly lit private spaces surrounding Brita. But, as *film noir* demands, the darkness of the soul is not simply an illusion: *A Double Life* culminates in real, though off-stage, murder, followed by the on-stage suicide of the protagonist.

This decision to adapt the drama as a *film noir* murder story explains the way the Shakespearean source material is used and incorporated into the script, and why the film never shows more than the murder scene in full. Since *A Double Life* is another mirror movie, a story of actors whose off-stage lives reflect their stage personas, such references to *Othello* in the scenes showing theatre rehearsal or performance come as no surprise. However, the textual identification between the frame narrative and the meta-theatrical plot goes much deeper in the film, presenting the murder scene as the culmination of a maddening creative process and the result of an equally maddening jealousy. The film focuses on the journey towards that stage (in both senses of the word, since the performative aspect is always involved in this investigation of post-war male anxieties), placing madness at the centre of the frame narrative, underscoring it with appropriate textual references. Several earlier passages of the play, including the well-known references to the 'green-eyed monster' (3.3.168), are used to imply the psychological process through which the protagonist loses his grip on reality. The quotations are often internalised by the frame narrative, either as voiceover, or as accidental asides, suggesting the protagonist's inner voice, at other times they appear woven into off-stage dialogues. In particular, it is the ignorant little waitress who provides the actor Tony with unintentional cues, for example, when asking 'What's the matter?' (5.2.47) and 'Do you want to put out the light?' (playing on Othello's 'Put out the light, and then put out the light!' in 5.2.7).

One of the distinctive tools of *film noir* cinema is clearly at work here: the acting style that allows the audience to glimpse at the mounting tension under the surface and the hidden anxieties troubling the protagonist, while leaving other members of the cast unaware of the same. As already implied, the film reflects on the dissonance between the inner and outer perceptions of reality that the disintegrating psyche of the protagonist can no longer hold together. In Ronald Colman's nuanced performance, this imbalance is represented by the subtle vocabulary of facial and bodily gestures characteristic of *film noir* (see figure 3.2). As Cynthia Baron describes the language of *noir* performance: 'it is the crafted selection and combination of differing poses, gaits, movements, gestures, facial expressions, vocal intonations and vocal inflections that let audiences, but not the other characters, see how smart, socially compromised tough guy characters think and feel as they encounter the physical and emotional dangers presented by noir scenarios'.[20] Anthony John is not the stereotypical tough guy character, but the discrepancy between his initial swagger and easy-going flirtatious charm, and the visions and sound effects that begin to trouble him during his engagement with the Othello role, allows the audience an awareness of the effort required of him not to give in to the turmoil in his psyche.

Although the cast of *A Double Life* does not include corresponding characters for the entire dramatis personae of *Othello*, there are a number of easily recognisable pairs apart from matching Othello and Desdemona to Tony and Brita, respectively. The figure of the *femme fatale*, a stock character in *film noir*, is represented by the young waitress who tries to comfort Tony by offering him food and more intimate bodily attentions. And yet she is not completely a Bianca character, for all her loose morals, not simply because she is unattached and has no connection to the only Cassio-like figure, but also since she will eventually turn into the real Desdemona, the victim killed by Tony in his murderous rage. The characterisation of the females thus follows the *film noir* conventions rather than the Shakespearean source.

Similarly coded in the characterisation of both females, in *A Double Life* no meaningful friendship is available for the protagonist, since both potential confidants are female and are therefore compromised by the past or present sexual attraction between them and Tony. Pat, the blonde waitress, lacks the intelligence and insight to be able to offer advice, and her function as *femme fatale*, drawing the protagonist into dark alleys and into her unlit bedroom, makes her representative of danger rather than comfort. The other stereotypical female role in *film noir*, the reliable and more domestic woman, is embodied by the ex-wife, Brita. This relationship also recalls Steve Neale's reference to the crisis in the domestic sphere, the 'failed or doomed romances', manifestations of a 'crisis in male identity'.[21] The protagonist of *A Double Life* clearly displays signs of such a personal crisis, particularly through his dysfunctional family life: however attractive he may appear to women, including Brita, he is unable to perform successfully the role of responsible family man that is required of a positive hero in the idealised world of classical Hollywood cinema.[22]

Unlike in *Men Are Not Gods*, *A Double Life* features a Iago character as well, who betrays Tony by notifying the police of his suspicion of the great actor and in this way brings about his downfall. This is Bill (Edmond O'Brien), a journalist and the theatre's press secretary; alternatively, he is the only one who could be classified as a Cassio, who incites Tony's revenge by being the new admirer of his ex-wife. Again, this suitor is not completely evil – the *noir* no longer believes in perfectly black-and-white characters – but since he joins forces with the institutional, social threat that the *noir* protagonist typically fights against, he cannot be seen as wholly good either. Robert F. Willson offers another theory, suggesting that 'the role of Othello ... is Anthony John's Iago', pointing out that in the film, at least in part, the menace is internal and thus impossible to avert, again perfectly fitting the favourite concerns of *film noir*.[23] I believe nonetheless that the very palpable external threat of the criminal investigation started off by the jealous romantic rival is equally powerful in turning the film into a *noir* thriller, beside the numerous other generic features described here.

This impression of imminent danger is enhanced by the darkly passionate, award-winning music composed by Miklós Rózsa, together with numerous cinematographic devices that we can read as tell-tale signs pointing to the adapting genre. This is partly tangible in the pace of the narrative, particularly in the last sequences, where the parallel montage scenes, alternating between pursuer and pursued, investigation and cover-up, criminal and detective, are deployed in an effort to increase the tension to breaking point. Throughout the film, all the necessary stock characters of thrillers make an appearance, including snoops and decoys, manipulated forensic pathologists and vulture-like journalists, ready to sell their mother's soul to boost circulation numbers.

Apart from the characteristic themes of crime and personal crisis and the predominantly dark atmosphere of *noir* films, *film noir* is also known for its tendency to comment on the action visually as well.[24] It is certainly true that in *A Double Life* a surprising amount of shots add to the tension by presenting human existence as essentially isolated, threatened, even imprisoned. The film also creates a strong nocturnal impression, and the recurring images of overpowering architectural structures, particularly the elevated train tracks and steep flights of stairs, also help us to associate the film with *noir* productions. It is under these dark, high-rise or shadowy structures that Tony prowls the streets, typically late at night, after the performances, among frightening sound and light effects, and he makes clear references to ghosts haunting him day and night. Lanier argues that 'Tony's wandering through the bleak cityscape becomes a visual correlative for what he has repressed, the seedy streets from which he had escaped and to which he is drawn' and points out the connections between the character of Othello, American Shakespeare and the crisis within the male identity as displayed by Tony.[25] Marguerite Rippy also finds this representation of the male psyche not only typical of the period, but part of the American tradition of interpreting *Othello*: 'In a series of films ranging from 1931 to 1985, the American screen has repeatedly depicted *Othello* exclusively in terms of the degeneration of the white male psyche.'[26]

Apart from its embodiment of an American performative tradition of *Othello*, it is also interesting to note that *A Double Life* seems to have exerted its influence on other *noir* filmmakers as well. Half a year after Cukor's film, another *film noir* was released with the title *Kiss of Death* (1947, dir. Henry Hathaway), most probably feeding on the marketing opportunities offered by the success of *A Double Life*.[27] Apart from the title, *Kiss of Death* has no resemblance to *A Double Life*, neither does it include a kiss of death, only in the metaphorical sense of betrayal – it is a typical gangster *noir* film that illustrates the blurred moral lines between right and wrong. But the deadly kiss as a selling point was not abandoned by Hollywood producers; even several years later two films recall the same image of the fatal embrace. *Kiss Me Deadly* (1955, dir. Robert Aldrich) is a *noir* thriller of the hard-boiled type, where the deadly kiss is simply a metaphorical reference to the threat of death constantly following the protagonist.

Released a few months after Aldrich's film, however, Stanley Kubrick's second feature direction, the 1955 film *Killer's Kiss*, contains elements that may look familiar, either from *Othello* or from *A Double Life*. Here we have a love triangle, a jealous man nearly killing the woman he claims to love and a chase after a stolen scarf that ends in murder – yet none of these is in actual fact a Shakespearean parallel. The brilliance of Cukor's film is tangible precisely in the way it could add the *Othello* motif to these stereotypical *noir* conventions. Peter Hutchings notes a much later echo of Cukor's work in a 1970s horror film, *The Flesh and Blood Show* (1972, dir. Pete Walker), in which a former Shakespearean actor turns into a serial killer after murdering his own 'unfaithful wife and her lover in the theatre'.[28] According to Hutchings, with the murderous Othello motif 'the film seems to be referring back to George Cukor's ... *A Double Life*, which also presented the part of Othello as one capable of driving insane the actor who plays it'.[29] While these films are not adaptations of either *Othello* or *A Double Life*, in the Hollywood studio system references to earlier successes were vital in maintaining the popularity of genres, and the kiss of death motif could easily have been used for the purpose.

Beside textual and cinematographic devices, objects and imagery may acquire significant roles, enhancing our perception of the genre. As suggested in the analysis of *Strange Illusion*, the fragmented psyche of the protagonist that the *noir* revels in can find visual expression in the mirror, often exploited for its metaphorical and meta-theatrical potentials as well, and *A Double Life* also abounds in mirrors of all kinds. The main protagonist, the leading actor of the theatre, is first seen looking at his own portraits, as if he were looking into mirrors, in the theatre lobby – and we soon realise he is searching for his own identity, which keeps eluding him, especially when he is between roles. He encounters reflective surfaces, often real mirrors, wherever he goes, and they not only present him with the image of his own anxieties but also project his fears and his imagination, his all-too-powerful identification with the role. It is in the window of a travel agent's (advertising trips to Venice, of all places) that he first sees himself in the costume of Othello. There is a mirror next to his table in the Italian restaurant, coincidentally called Café Venezia, where he meets Pat, the Italian waitress; another one at the first-night reception, when he is beginning to hear voices. He also looks into a mirror in the small apartment of Pat, in a way that suggests that the boundary between external reality and his internal world has become dangerously blurred (see figure 3.2). Mirrors acquire a menacing quality in the office of the wigmaker who helps to lay a trap for Tony, and the artificial identity constructed with the help

Figure 3.2 Mirroring Othello and the *femme fatale* – Ronald Colman and Shelley Winters in *A Double Life*. Directed by George Cukor, 1947. Kanin Productions/Universal.

of mirrors precipitates his downfall. When the actor looks into a mirror, he sees his other, fictional, unreal self, which preys on his mind – and whenever mirrors are used to create extra reflective surfaces they shatter the illusion of a safe and protective environment and add to the oppressive atmosphere of destruction. In *A Double Life*, therefore, mirrors have the power to fragment and destroy the central male identity, and what they reflect will never bring about self-knowledge but only result in disturbing a pathologically troubled mind. Yet this doomed existence has found such powerful visual expression through the generic framework of the *film noir* that it is no longer possible to separate the influence of the Shakespearean source and the *noir* cinematography from one another.

Shakespeare the gangster – *Joe Macbeth*

As the introduction to this chapter discussed, the stylistic and thematic conventions of *film noir* are often tightly interwoven with gangster narratives, and an interesting example to show this transition would have been *House of Strangers* (1949, dir. Joseph L. Mankiewicz), a *film noir* with a strong leaning towards the gangster genre, as also noted by Yvonne Griggs.[30] The film's connections to Shakespeare are strongly debated, and despite its obvious relevance, spatial limitations of this book did not allow me to include it in the chapter. Moving on to the post-war decades, I will focus my attention on films where the emphasis on psychology is overshadowed by the elements of crime and punishment, and as a result, these works are better classified as gangster films. Apart from two variants on the *Macbeth* theme – *Joe Macbeth* (1955, dir. Ken Hughes) and *Men of Respect* (1990, dir. William Reilly), the chapter also discusses *We Own the Night* (2007, dir. James Gray), a reworking of the *Henry IV* plays. Were it not for the oft-lamented spatial constraints, several other films could also be included here, among them *My Kingdom* (2001, dir. Don Boyd), a *King Lear* story set in Liverpool's ganglands, or a *Richard III* adaptation entitled *Street King* (2002, dir. James Gavin Bedford), or even *The Godfather* trilogy (1972, 1974, 1990, dir. Francis Ford Coppola), particularly the third instalment, a work inspired by *King Lear* and other Shakespearean dramas,[31] as acknowledged by Coppola himself.[32] There are indeed a number of correspondences between the *Lear* plot and Coppola's mafia family, but since I believe that these are general thematic resonances rather than traces of significant creative inspiration, *The Godfather* has not been granted a place in this chapter.

Possibly the film with the most textually straightforward relationship to its Shakespearean source discussed here is Ken Hughes' 1955 adaptation of *Macbeth*. Although it proudly acknowledges its Shakespearean origins, critical appreciation of the film has been scarce and rather mixed; Thomas Cartelli and Katherine Rowe only mention it as a 'notable example' of 'completely updated filmic transformations of Shakespeare's plays',[33] while Tony Howard calls it a 'cheap transatlantic gangster film' with 'fading American actors'. In comparing it to the other works of its scriptwriter (*Broken Lance* and *The Last Patriarch*), Howard goes as far as claiming: 'This is the most "loyal" of Philip Yordan's Shakespeare adaptations, and for that very reason the worst; though it has deliberately ironic overtones for "sophisticated" viewers, this is simplified Shakespeare'.[34] At the same time, I believe that the film successfully adopts the conventions of the gangster genre, therefore the alterations of plot and characterisation are easier to justify from the vantage point of post-war gangster *noir* than from the aspect of textual fidelity.

The film's Shakespearean lineage is declared in its visual frame, by placing textual quotations on title cards at the beginning and at the end.

Interestingly, the two quotations imply no development or change in the personality of the eponymous hero (Paul Douglas), which might explain why the order of the quotes is reversed when compared to the play – but, as we shall see, another reason for that may be the gangster film's alliance with the belief systems of a secular Puritanism and Social Darwinism.[35] The opening title card, which appears directly after the camera has switched from the silhouette of the dark city – stereotypical *noir* and gangster setting[36] – to the location of the first scene, reads as follows: 'Not in the Legions of Horrid Hell, Can come a Devil more damn'd In evils to top Macbeth. Act 4 Scene 3 Macbeth, William Shakespeare'. The quotation thus establishes the protagonist's clear identification with Shakespeare's hero, almost in the style of Laurence Olivier's *noir*-style *Hamlet*, which begins with the well-known (non-Shakespearean voiceover) statement: 'This is the tragedy of a man who could not make up his mind.' What is more, the title card in *Joe Macbeth* suggests that the film offers no redemptive reading of the tragedy; the story that is about to unfold is not that of a fallible victim, but one of a monster on his way to eternal damnation.

And yet the film itself presents a much less clear-cut reading of the personality and guilt of the central character, and stays closer to the Shakespearean interpretation, laying part of the blame for the Macbeths' fall on the wife, Lily (Ruth Roman), but also on fate, with a fortune-teller named Rosie (Minerva Pious) standing in for the witches. Nonetheless, this ambivalence and the final outcome can also be seen as compulsory requirements for gangster films, which 'are the home of the conflict between good and evil',[37] but without a morally clear stance, since, as Mitchell argues,

> the elements of Puritanism, Social Darwinism, and the Horatio Alger myth are hopelessly contradictory. And it is precisely these contradictions which the American gangster film embodies and which, because they remain unresolved in America's collective consciousness, provide the imbalances, ambiguities, and ambivalences with which the gangster film abounds.[38]

True, some of these elements in themselves seem more than familiar from the tragedy of *Macbeth*: that 'there has always been something "fated" about the main character in American gangster films' and that 'death comes to the gangster not as a result of a social or legal process, but because he has sinned'.[39] This affinity between the gangster film as a genre and the predicament of Macbeth may be the reason why several gangster adaptations of Shakespeare's plays have chosen the Scottish play as their source. Griggs argues convincingly for overlaps between Jacobean tragedy and the gangster genre, both 'in terms of their ideological and thematic preoccupations, especially when coupled with notions of "revenge"', and even the fundamental structure of early modern tragedy, which is easily reflected in 'the rise and fall trajectory of the classic gangster film'.[40] She is absolutely right in her assumptions that apart from the thematic proximity between gangster films and *Macbeth* or *Richard III* (although the latter is not a Jacobean play, its medieval structure of rise and fall is obviously related), *King Lear*'s regular adaptation to the same cinematic genre must also reflect this relationship.

In *Joe Macbeth*, another possible function of the title cards and the first scene is, however, to align the film with the classical gangster narrative, a connection emphasised by the Columbia pressbook in its recommendations for marketing the film alongside earlier gangster classics.[41] One of the best-known – pre-Code-era – gangster films which defined the genre for decades was *Little Caesar* (1931, dir. Mervyn LeRoy), with Edward G. Robinson in the lead role. LeRoy's film, together with a number of its contemporaries, established the core of the genre's conventions: the Italian-American hero, whose rise and fall constitutes the main action. *Little Caesar* also opens with a title card, displaying a quotation not from Shakespearean drama but the *Bible*: 'for all they that take the sword shall perish with the sword. Matthew 26.52', stating the moral of the story before we even get to know our protagonist. The action begins right after this with a small-scale robbery which we witness only from outside, the safe distance of the street, in a similar way to *Joe Macbeth*'s first job, which we hear mediated through others' words – the camera only enters the scene to show the aftermath, rather than the actual act of violence. The dissatisfaction that both films' protagonists and their partners express in the ensuing dialogues will then lead both of them to take more ambitious and daring steps, setting them on a path that can take them to the top, but will also lead to their inevitable downfall.

Joe Macbeth uses another title card with a Shakespearean quotation at the end of the film, when the last line of dialogue has been spoken by Lennie (Bonar Colleano), the Macduff/Fleance figure. The camera still lingers on the final scene, over the dead bodies of Joe and Lily Macbeth lying side by side on the ground, when the following words are superimposed over the gory image: 'It will have blood, they say, Blood will have blood. Act 3 Scene 4 Macbeth William Shakespeare.' Lennie closes the dialogue, saying to Angus, the butler: 'this is the end of the line, better lock up and get yourself a new job', implying that he is in control, but also that he is stepping out of the vicious circle of violence, by effectively committing suicide; as he steps out of the house, the offscreen sounds of sirens and gunshots make it clear that 'he allows the police to kill him'.[42] Lennie's conclusion about the end of the line works equally as a Shakespearean reminder of the childless Macbeths, who had no one to carry on their legacy, and as a reminder of the cold and heartless rule of the world of gangsters that we have seen represented in a number of ways. In this universe, it takes longer for neon lights to be replaced over the bar doors than it takes to get rid of the bar's owners. As the scene of the first murder, the restaurant will change names and owners, from Tommy's to Duca's, then to Mac's, in quick succession. In the same way, the villa on Lakeview Drive (the film's version of Forres, Inverness and Dunsinane combined) changes owners quickly, although Angus, the butler remains, and serves one master after another, as they fall in and out of power. Therefore it seems fitting that Angus is still visible in the background at the end, contemplating the two corpses, when a return to the Shakespearean source sums up the moral of the story: whenever and wherever, the rules of the game do not change: the gangster has to fall if he is too steeped in blood.

The statement thus reinforces the conclusion clearly visible before us, that it was their own bloody life and decisions that brought about the Macbeths' bloody end. Yet what is even more interesting, and what links the final quote back to the starting one, is that while this last quotation is a line of Macbeth's in Shakespeare's play (spoken after the fateful dinner when he encounters Banquo's ghost, realising that he has no way out), the first one is from Macduff, thus Lennie's character (and as mentioned, the quote is taken from later in the play). Thus the film implies a similar reverse order of a flashback structure to that which characterises so many *film noirs*, which often begin with the narrator's voiceover reflection on the significance of what they are about to relate. At the same time, leaving the viewer with the final image of the gangster's dead body, and possibly a moral message, is also a convention found in the genre's classics, including *Little Caesar* and *Public Enemy* (1931, dir. William A. Wellman). *Joe Macbeth*'s Shakespearean moral is therefore fulfilling audience expectations based on the genre's conventions while also confirming its literary lineage. The film's dialogue is an equally clever combination of recognisable Shakespearean quotations and allusions (listed in detail by Lanier), all embedded into the vernacular of the post-war American metropolitan underworld, with even a few tongue-in-cheek meta-references to the world of Shakespearean performance.[43]

Just like the Wild West seemed to be an appropriate setting for *King Lear*, particularly by representing the inhospitable heath in western films, the dark and rainy nights of the metropolis, with shady locales and rubbish-strewn streets, easily accommodate the Scottish play. Lanier stresses that 'the film repays repeated viewings, and within the limitations of B-film production in Britain in the 1950s, it makes a good case for analogues between barbaric Scotland and the mean streets of film noir'.[44] A central element of this visual parallel is clearly the villa, symbol of the rise and fall of one gangster after another, which at one point becomes the Macbeths' castle. Nature and its responses to human action are just as symbolic as they were in Scotland; the birds surrounding Lakeview Drive gather above the lake at the moment of Duca's death, and they cry out, just like 'the obscure bird / Clamour'd the livelong night' (2.3.58–9).

In an ingenious reversal of spatial characteristics, the most claustrophobic of spaces, the royal chamber in which King Duncan is murdered in Shakespeare's tragedy, unseen, in the dark, the murder only related to us by the Macbeths, here becomes the most open of spaces: Duca is murdered outside, in nature, in the lake during a swim. Interestingly, Courtney Lehmann refers to the lake as a swimming pool, which 'is repeated in a different context in *Scotland, PA*',[45] although here the lake is clearly not a status symbol in itself, as in director Billy Morrissette's black comedy, but rather the eeriest element within the Gothic landscape that penetrates the safe cocoon of the metropolitan gangland. The familiar, dark and confined space of gangster *noir* therefore reveals the unfamiliar place of the unacceptable crime to be outside of its traditional urban sphere where a 'kingpin' can always be protected by his boys. Here the kingpin meets his downfall in his most exposed state of undress, unprotected, without any witnesses, where there is nothing to save him from his inevitable downfall. (Near) nakedness is all the more relevant here since the gangster is traditionally defined by his clothes, the black suits of the Italian-American mafia that combine the allure of elegance and attraction with the archetypal darkness of crime characterising this lifestyle.

Elegance and brute force are both needed to maintain the gangster's position, but neither of these are sufficient to protect him from the anxieties and visions that later begin to trouble Joe Macbeth. In another ingenious combination of the Shakespearean source text with the gangster film's concerns, and the psychological issues so much at the heart of *film noir*, the film implies that at the heart of the trouble is the gangster's greatest fear: effeminacy. The narrative takes us close enough to witness the dynamics of the relationship between Lily and Joe, how their love turns into dependence on each other, particularly how Joe begins to include Lily in the decision-making and let her ambition cause the destruction of both of them. Looking back at the history of the gangster film, it becomes clear how the earliest examples of the genre 'portrayed gangsters as degenerate and overly feminized men losing their independence in the new capitalist society, but later films recast them as men who wielded power through sexuality and guns'.[46] A displacement of gender qualities between the Macbeths is expressed in some of the best-known passages in Shakespeare's play, in Lady Macbeth's reference to her husband as one 'too full o'th'milk of human kindness' (1.5.17), and her own desire to lose her femininity: 'Come, you Spirits / ... unsex me here' (1.5.40–1). Yet in *Joe Macbeth* this threat of emasculation is reinforced by the conviction that a gangster is one who can least afford to be emotional and caring. In line with the changing notions of manhood in the pre-war decades, 'the gangster figure helped shift ideal masculinity away from traditional qualities, such as honor, to traits such as violence, independence, and the ability to exploit the social system'.[47] Lanier also mentions how 'the film focuses primarily on the tense relationship between Joe and Lily ..., Joe's crisis of conscience and manhood, and the escalating violence of his rule as "king of the city"'.[48]

Yet it is not only masculinity that is in crisis; following the genre's traditions, female characters have also little to expect from their lives. The *femme fatale* figure of *film noir* is also doomed to die, and here this is aptly manifested when Lily is destroyed by her own husband's accidental bullet – and her own greed, in effect. Her fall, I believe, is not necessitated by some misogynistic intention, 'getting "what she deserves"',[49] as Lehmann implies, but it appears to be her unavoidable destiny. *Joe Macbeth* is not alone within the genre in considering the controversial female roles in this context, as a much later gangster film, *Prizzi's Honor* (1985, dir. John Houston) 'annexes two competing generic traditions to consider what acceptable role a woman might play in the world of crime', and ends up with the conclusion that gender equality is not possible within this genre's framework.[50]

Another well-known character in gangster *noir* is the criminally inclined psychopath that Joe turns into, although once again, following the conventions of the *noir*, we can here witness a gradual blurring of lines between good and evil. Like *A Double Life* and Tony's inner struggles, which push him into criminality, in *Joe Macbeth* we are allowed to see the psychological disintegration of the great man, undermined by feminine greed. Howard points out how the low budget of the production may have contributed to the film's 'weird somnambulist tone', its economy appearing metaphorical: 'as Mac becomes more isolated, darkness embraces him and he shoots desperately into total blackness'.[51]

Another connection between *Joe Macbeth* and its *film noir* aspects can be witnessed in the film's use of the mirror, a symbolic object in the *noir* productions discussed. While the mirror does not have such a central role here as in the previous two films, its appearances are still meaningful. The character who is visually associated with the mirror is not the gangster, but his wife, Lily Macbeth, whose preoccupation with her own position and her reflection on her husband's role makes her a key figure in the narrative. In an early scene, set in the privacy of their bedroom, we see her looking into her mirror. The camera shows the back of her head and also her face in medium close-up, as if visualising her two-faced personality, emphasising her ability to perform and pretend to further her own aims (see figure 3.3). Behind her, in the mirror at the back of the screen, the small figure of Joe appears, and as Lily finishes her line, the camera zooms in on him. Joe is therefore the focus of Lily's (and the viewer's) attention, but Lily is turning her back towards Joe, and looking at herself, rather than directly facing her partner. From this scene we cut right to the exterior of the house, shrouded

Figure 3.3 Joe and Lily Macbeth in the mirror – Ruth Roman and Paul Douglas in *Joe Macbeth*. Directed by Ken Hughes, 1955. Columbia Pictures/ Film Locations.

in dark night, with the first guests already arriving at the party, then back to the bedroom, with Lily now clad in a white evening gown standing in front of another, full-length, mirror. In a remarkable move, the camera leaves the mirror and turns to the side, to include half of Lily's body on the right, and half of her reflection in the mirror on the left. At this point Joe comes in, crossing right in front of the mirror, blocking Lily's view. The implication is clear: Joe with his bodily integrity would stand in the way of Lily's self-serving ambition if he were strong enough to stand up against her, but after a split second of looking at each other, Joe steps out of the frame, allowing Lily to continue carrying out her fantasy.

Another staple element, characteristic within the gangster genre, but given new meaning and significance here, is alcohol, which serves to test the mettle of the tough guy; in *Joe Macbeth* it certainly helps to evaluate a number of characters, particularly Lennie, Banky's son (also standing in for Macduff by virtue of his murdered family). But the most ingenious combination of the gangster's staple dietary item, that is, spirits, and *Macbeth*'s central theme, happens at the party scene when Banky's ghost appears. Here the strong drink makes the host's hallucination perfectly plausible and therefore the supernatural finds its place in the diegesis of this most down-to-earth of genres. The scene shows that Joe has already begun to slide down on the slippery slope towards his unavoidable destiny, partly as he shows no restraint and asks Lennie to double up his drink even before drinking the first one; but most of all as he apparently loses all control of himself and the situation. If he is drunk, which Lily offers as an excuse for his odd behaviour, that is bad enough, but if he is delusional from the gradual psychological disintegration, losing his grip over reality, then he has even less place at the top of the game.

Ken Hughes' *Joe Macbeth*, although it remained mostly unnoticed by critics and scholars (or when it is mentioned, it is sometimes dismissed as a 'cherishable oddity',[52] with the cast blamed for the film's failure), is therefore a prime example of how a Shakespearean classic can be incorporated into a hard-core American cinematic context. Some of its elements are even evoked by later works within the genre, for instance, Carolyn Jess-Cooke observes how *Joe Macbeth* is referenced in *Scotland, PA* (2001, dir. Billy Morrissette) through the first name of the main character, Joe Mac.[53] Yet an even more specific reference – an acknowledged remake – manifests itself in the next mafia *Macbeth* film discussed: William Reilly's *Men of Respect*, released in 1990, the year of the gangster film's great revival.

Gangster revival – *Men of Respect*

Reilly's *Men of Respect*, although in many ways not as characteristically *noir* as the films discussed thus far in this chapter, is an obvious continuation of the themes raised by *Joe Macbeth* (Howard explicitly refers to it as 'the more upmarket remake' of the former, both being produced by Columbia Pictures).[54] It is also an openly declared retelling of the Scottish play: 'Adapted from the tragedy of Macbeth by William Shakespeare', as announced by its title card. Following this card, the next screen makes a statement, once again reminiscent of the way *Joe Macbeth*'s quotations set the tone of the film: 'There is nothing but what has a violent end or violent beginnings.' This sentence, however, is not a direct quote from *Macbeth*, but recalls Friar Laurence's 'these violent delights have violent ends' (2.6.9), a line taken from *Romeo and Juliet* where violence is equally lethal and senseless, and where death is often the result of a blood feud and honorary obligations, rather than necessity.[55] As will be seen, the film is indeed steeped in the late gangster and neo-*noir* tradition, both stylistically and thematically, but it makes clever use of its acknowledged Shakespearean source, even including a few fragments of the dialogue, including Lady Macbeth's 'Who would have thought the old man had so much blood in him?' in the sleepwalking scene.[56] Although Buchanan views the script's Shakespearean correspondences in a different light, claiming that 'the lines, often sounding like an unpolished experiment in prosaic parallelism, are only allowed to flirt in the vicinity of their far weightier Shakespearean original', she also notes how the film's cinematography is able to successfully evoke the '*noir*-esque universe' fitting the underworld of New York.[57]

Looking at *Men of Respect* and its forerunner, and placing the two mafia *Macbeths* next to each other, as if in a retrospective investigation, the continued themes and motifs allow us to highlight even further aspects of the gangster genre that characterise both productions. At the same time, *Men of Respect* also reflects on the development of the genre itself, and the new wave of gangster films released in 1990, shortly before Reilly's film, which premiered in October that year at the Chicago International Film Festival, before opening in cinemas the following January. The year indeed saw a cornucopia of cinematic gangsters; the last part of Francis Ford Coppola's *Godfather* trilogy, Martin Scorsese's *GoodFellas*, Abel Ferrara's *King of New York*, the Coen brothers' *Miller's Crossing*, and *State of Grace*, directed by Phil Joanou and Michael Lee Baron were all released in 1990.

Such timing cannot be an accident: the gangster movie was clearly living its renaissance – sometimes this period is also referred to as the neo-gangster era – resonating well with the contemporary socio-political issues, including 'the recession of the early 1990s'.[58] As Mark Nicholls argues, this was a time when films like these mafia narratives 'have a great deal to tell us, not only about the accumulation and loss of wealth and power in the early 1990s but also about the way filmmakers and their audiences respond to periods of financial depression and economic hardship'.[59] He even finds thematic connections to *King Lear* in several of these films, particularly the ones directed by the group of so-called 'New York Fabulists', Martin Scorsese, Francis Ford Coppola and Woody Allen. Even though most of these links seem to be rather tenuous, the thematic connections within the group seem well established.

Set against this backdrop, the character of the Shakespeare gangster seemed also ready for revival, responding not only to its earlier manifestations, but at least as much to the contemporary cultural context. Writing about *Men of Respect*, Lanier observes how 'Reilly melds Shakespeare's *Macbeth* with the atmosphere and motifs of contemporary New York gangster films', adding that 'The cast is stuffed with well-known "tough-guy" character actors, and the milieu and graphic violence strongly recall Scorsese.'[60] This resurgence of the gangster film as a genre also affirms what new genre theory claims, that films in each cycle of production should be considered 'as intertexts rather than independent texts', reflecting on each other and on the socio-cultural context that brought them into existence.[61] This cyclical and intertextual consideration of films is particularly relevant when we examine the various adaptations of the same text within the same genre, since references to previous products are inevitable, as the following discussion will illustrate.

At the heart of the gangster film is a particular set of racial stereotypes, characteristically laying the blame for the rampant violence in American streets at the feet of non-assimilated minority groups. While the classic gangster films, 'such as Mervyn Leroy's *Little Caesar* (1930) and Howard Hawks' *Scarface* (1932) established a lasting association in popular culture between the gangster and particular ethnic groups',[62] this connection was not always in the foreground: in *Joe Macbeth*, despite the obvious Italian-American background of Duca, the New York kingpin, racial/ethnic stereotypes are not emphasised. The cast is comprised of predominantly white Anglo-Saxon actors, the film relies on no recognisable Italian accents and Joe Macbeth's story, as expected from the gangster *noir* narrative of the 1950s, focuses 'on the death of the gangster personality. There are effectively no more big shots and it is in gangster *noir* that the final death of the big shot can be seen.'[63]

In *Men of Respect*, however, we can witness the wars of an explicitly Italian-American gang; the Macbeth figure is called Mike Battaglia (John Turturro), the Banquo family are Bankie (Dennis Farina) and Philly Como (David Thornton), and the head of the mafia is Charlie D'Amico (Italian for 'friend', played by Rod Steiger). Several of the actors also bring their own Italian-American heritage to enhance plausibility for this ethnic background, particularly Turturro and Farina, beside Stanley Tucci playing Mal (the Malcolm figure), to name but a few of the most prominent cast members.

The Italian-American cultural context has resulted in such generic typecasting that it has severely restricted the cinematic representation (and in turn, downplayed the actual intention and ability of assimilation) of the community. The stereotype seems to have gained such wide and general acceptance 'that Italian Americans on screen are most often connected to working class culture regardless of the temporal period of the film's narrative. Furthermore, when they are not associated with the working class, they are gangsters.'[64] At the same time, Italian-American women are always depicted in the domestic sphere, mostly in one of two roles: either as the rotund Mamma, endlessly cooking huge pots of spaghetti, or the Sophia Loren-type dark and alluring beauty, not too different from the two stereotypical female roles of *film noir*.[65] The dark and dangerous beauty is a central character in *Joe Macbeth* and *Men of Respect* alike, both of which display Lady Macbeth figures who are capable of evoking desire in many men, but whose beauty hides darkness and danger.

Men of Respect's association of gangsters with immigrants of Italian origins also becomes clear from the title, as the concept of 'respect' was fundamental in the hierarchical domestic environment of the immigrant community. Robert Casillo refers to this notion in his description of the social background of Martin Scorsese, which influenced his upbringing and eventually his cinematic output, saying: 'What maintained the hierarchy was respect or *rispetto*, a mixture of love, fear, duty, and loyalty towards the family order.'[66] In *Men of Respect*, 'respect' is repeatedly emphasised by both the head of the operation and practically everyone who is arguing for or against certain characters. In this world, someone who has respect deserves promotion and position, while those without respect have to be eliminated, as they have brought shame on the whole community. There are two ritual occasions when loyalty is sworn and the brotherhood is bound by blood, first at the very beginning of the plot, marking the rise of

Mike's career, and at the end, when Mal is reinstituted into his own. The *Macbeth* narrative accommodates such a ritual easily, as the ceremonial expression of gratitude echoes Duncan bestowing his thanks on the hero of the day, to which Macbeth replies:

> The service and the loyalty I owe,
> In doing it, pays itself. Your Highness' part
> Is to receive our duties: and our duties
> Are to your throne and state, children and servants;
> Which do but what they should, by doing everything
> Safe toward your love and honour. (1.4.22–7)

The similarity of the wording of the oath Mike swears to what Macbeth promises to his king is obviously partly rooted in the affinity between the muscle-based societies depicted in Shakespeare's drama and in Italian gangster cinema. A parallel scene is almost entirely absent from the 1955 *Joe Macbeth*, where the official recognition for Joe's achievement takes the form of a gift to Lily, whom Joe is about to wed, and the nomination of Joe to the position of first boy. Yet by then the position of first boy has proved to be a vicarious, indeed temporary, one, and so the honour is equally dubious. In *Men of Respect*, however, this swearing of blood brotherhood finds its natural place, and there are several occasions when similar rituals are observed, particularly in the second half of the film, when Charlie D'Amico's sons, Mal and Don, gain back the support and allegiance of their father's former men one by one.

What is more, the parallel scene at the end, when Philly Como swears allegiance to the sons of the former kingpin, is much more articulate in its ritual renewal of the bond than in the final scene of *Macbeth*. Lanier even argues that 'Mal's ceremonial induction of Philly into the "men of respect" at film's end implies that the cycle of ambition and murder is about to begin again',[67] an ending strongly reminiscent of the bleak outlook of Roman Polański's 1971 *Macbeth*, as Howard points out.[68] In Shakespeare's play the emphasis is on the purification of the kingdom and the nation from sin, and while Macduff also declares his acknowledgement of Malcolm's title, the new king makes it clear that the Scottish nobility will also turn over a new leaf, signified by their adoption of the title of 'earl' instead of 'thane'. Yet the drama ends with only an invitation to the coronation, but not the actual ritual, while *Men of Respect* insists upon the visualisation of the renewed bond, and in this way manifests a return to the old ways that were abandoned by Mike, bringing destruction to the whole community. In this sense, the film's conclusion is more pessimistic than the play, implying that the mafia has evidently been restored to its days of power and glory.

Tradition in itself is always shown to be a keyword in the Italian-American community, which is built on the tight-knit relationship of the family, fighting with all their might to rebuild or replicate the Old World relations, which are central to the dynamics of the group. The Old and New Worlds are not simply contrasted as pre- and post-lapsarian states in any gangster narrative, but their opposition is particularly relevant in the context of the immigrant community. As Ilaria Serra argues, 'Emigration was a disgrace for the Italian family, a curse that weakened its unity and crumbled its foundation.'[69] As the gangster film shows, this breach of tradition, the disruption of the family bond and the dislocation of people from their nurturing home regions, has to be reversed, and the loyalty and respect on which the hierarchy is founded must be ceremonially re-acknowledged. Interestingly enough, this reconnection with tradition is characteristic of the 1990s cycle of gangster films, as they depict the lives of (and were made by filmmakers who are themselves) third-generation immigrants, the children of those who did everything to assimilate, even by denying their ethnic roots.

One symbolic location that is often displayed to emphasise the clash between tradition and assimilation is the heart of the home: the kitchen. The theme of cooking and the kitchen appears at the centre of the gangster operation as the most domestic of environments, functioning both as the source of life and as the end of life. While roadside diners have featured in the earliest gangster films as well (in the opening scenes of *Little Caesar* or *The Killers*, among others), these 1990s kitchens and restaurants are the beating heart of the Italian-American family, both in the sense of blood relatives and the larger mafia operation.[70] As Casillo argues, the domestic sphere, or *domus*, which is as sacred as the church for the Italian-American community, is therefore also a space where religiosity is taken for granted.

> For southern Italians, as for Italian Americans, the sacred overflows the church and extends beyond to the family itself, where sanctity crystallizes in the most essential and intimate form of Italian American spirituality. This is the religion of the house or domus conceived as both an enclosed spatial entity and a hierarchical system of relationships, each invested with sacred significance.[71]

The kitchen, while clearly an enclosed spatial entity, can equally appear as a semi-public space, in the form of the restaurant, the business operation of the gang (or its cover for other, shadier lines of business), as featured in *Joe Macbeth*. In *Men of Respect*, the motif of the kitchen and the small Italian restaurant takes on even greater significance; whereas in *Joe Macbeth* the bars simply signified the territorialised form of power and investment, in *Men of Respect* the restaurant represents the liminal sphere where life and death, tradition and ruthless ambition, entertainment and entrapment all meet. More than just a symbol of domesticity, the theme of cooking is in itself a trademark of the Italian-American gangster figure; in *Men of Respect* the Italian gangster and his wife are expected to entertain their guests in a restaurant that is their home, their business and their show of allegiance to their Italianate culture at the same time. The commonplace expectation of women's place being in the kitchen – 'women's work is never done' – is the perfect excuse for Ruthie (Katherine Borowitz), the Lady Macbeth figure, to be up in the middle of the night, when she is actually paving Mike's way for the murder. When Charlie, the *padrino* (literally 'godfather', the head of the mafia family), arrives at the feast held in his honour at the Battaglias' restaurant, and praises Ruth's beauty – 'she still looks like a fox' – she responds by putting herself down: 'slaving away here, making everything you like'. Her witty repartee with Charlie is simply another way for her to confirm that not only is she capable of fulfilling the traditional role of the Italian-American housewife, but she has wit and intelligence as well, and can stand up for herself, thus she is a better candidate for the darker female role in gangster *noir*, the *femme fatale*.

The role of women within the gangster genre, though essentially similar to the two female stereotypes observed in *film noir*, has also undergone some change since the post-war years. In *Joe Macbeth*, Lily Macbeth's acknowledged strength and regular intervention in the gang's business is seen as a dangerous subversion of the mafia code; yet by 1990, the genre's classics, particularly *The Godfather Part III*, with Michael Corleone's sister taking an executive decision at a crucial moment, grant women potentially greater powers, both within the immediate family and in the broader Family business. Nonetheless, children, particularly babies, are still anathema in the genre, and in *Men of Respect*, the absent child of the Battaglias is turned into a story of horror. Apparently, Ruth aborted an earlier pregnancy for the sake of Mike's career, and she is ready to remind Mike of her suffering to teach him this kind of merciless determination.

Even though *Men of Respect* is half a century removed from the classic *noir* period, it still relies on plenty of elements that can be associated with the *noir* tradition, among them the motif of the mirror. The split reflections of Ruthie in the bedroom show her power to embrace and overpower Mike with her stronger ambition; she subsequently uses the bathroom mirror to force Mike to confront his own image. Another mirror follows the steps of Charlie and his men into the restaurant – the fateful journey that will not be reversed. This very same circular mirror affords Ruthie (and the viewer) control over the movements of every guest in the house, and in its diminutive reflection of the film's universe every action appears to be determined by fate. Similarly interesting is the use of the mirror in the short discussion between Mike and Banky Como when they reflect on the prophecy they have heard from an old woman. When Mike makes a vague suggestion to Banky, implying that his future support to further Mike's career would be appreciated, Banky gives an equally unspecific promise, with the caveat that 'just so I don't have to do anything where I can't look at myself in the mirror'. The mirror is thus not only a physical object and a cinematographic tool to create reflective surfaces, but also a metaphorical manifestation of the identity of the man of respect.

Another tradition of *film noir*, indeed, a central thematic element, as discussed, concerns the psychological anxieties of the male protagonist, and the Italian-American gangster tradition emphasises the social marginalisation of its characters through their immigrant background as well. The blurred line between good and evil, psychologically troubled victim or psychopathic criminal, is very much present in *Men of Respect*, and stylistically this is also supported by *film noir*'s characteristic cinematography. Even if the film is shot in colour, most of the scenes are set at night, when the cover of darkness and the uncanny city lights make colours nearly irrelevant, and what remains is the nocturnal play with light and darkness. Added to this are the contrasts between white and black clothes, the ubiquitous presence of slanted light beams, flashes of lightning and dark pools of shadow, which end up bleaching most of the colour from the film, reinforcing a *chiaroscuro* impression.

There is one additional colour, however, which forces itself at our attention repeatedly throughout the film: red, the colour of blood. The otherwise predominantly dark film, in which shades of grey and black dominate the colour palette, gives a shockingly powerful role to red, establishing it as the key to the story of the rise and fall of Mike Battaglia. It also confirms the central role of Ruth in the events, since her hair is a dark red – Charlie compares her to a fox – which makes her stand out even more spectacularly among the dark-haired Italian-American gang. Red is the single noticeable colour in many other scenes, and it is the colour of the walls on the street front of the Fedora Restaurant, Mike and Ruth's joint. It is often used as a background shade, as in the first shootout scene in a restaurant with red upholstery. In a later scene, during the night when Ruth and

Mike are waiting for the opportunity to get rid of Charlie, we can see Ruthie's attentive face in close-up, silhouetted against a red background, as opposed to Mike in medium close-up, his black suit contrasted to the white background, showing that he has not yet left his position in the gang, not even in thought. Then, when he envisions red blood dripping from the ceiling onto his palm, his mental immersion in the crime acquires powerful visualisation.

After the murder, when Ruth convinces Mike how easily blood is washed out of their clothes, she appears in a bright red dressing gown, as if dressed in the colour of the murder itself. Yet afterwards her gradual disintegration is also shown in her choice of clothes, no longer the dominant gold or black; by the end she is seen wearing a white silk nightdress, all colour bleached out of her, while she continues to scour the all-too-white bath where she washed the bloodstained clothes on the fateful night of the murder. It is in this very same, freshly cleaned bath where Mike finds her at the end, this time covered in her own blood. At the party where Mike sees Banky's ghost, the greens of the garden are all faded into an almost greyish hue, and the bright red tablecloths, the reddish glow of the lanterns, the red paint of the iron railing behind the table all stand out. The witch character – the old woman with the 'second sight' – is also dressed in a red gown; and after Mike's second visit to her, we see him in a rust-coloured jacket, instead of his customary black one.

In this almost monochrome film, the most colourful scene at the end acquires the significance of a ritual, where the final showdown between Mike Battaglia and his opponents takes place under a firework display, which not only fulfils the prophecy of falling stars (replacing Birnam wood), but simultaneously elevates the gang retaliation to the level of divine retribution. In this sense, it ties in with the melodramatic streak often observable in *noir* and crime stories as well – the fantasy of the universe returning to a morally restored state as a result of human sacrifice. Even if the rise-and-fall narrative of gangster stories is fundamental to the re-establishment of this moral world, these two versions of *Macbeth* exemplify how adaptations have always been able to tell their own stories and reflect their own ages, with their particular concerns and anxieties, with the help of inherited plots and genre conventions.

Neo-*noir* indie criminals – *We Own the Night*

The last film that has strong enough ties to the gangster film to be included in this chapter may at first glance seem somewhat out of place in the volume, as it is considered an *auteur* film, rather than a product of genre cinema. *We Own the Night*, indie director James Gray's 2007 neo-*noir* crime drama, has also been analysed by Lanier as a film that resists generic categorisation. As Lanier argues, 'Gray's utterly unironic tale of redemption runs against the grain of most neo-*noir* crime dramas with which it shares so many superficial traits'.[72] While it is hard to disagree with this claim, I still believe that the film is worth examining in the context of the *noir* as well, particularly as those superficial generic traits are still relevant to audiences' viewing experience.

The film tells the story of a group of NYPD police officers cracking down on a large-scale drug operation run by the Russian mob, but what makes *We Own the Night* a more complex drama than an average police procedural is the moral journey of one of its protagonists, nightclub manager Bobby Green (Joaquin Phoenix). Bobby's father, Burt Grusinsky (Robert Duvall) and brother (Mark Wahlberg) are both members of the NYPD, his father Chief of Police, and his brother Joe a decorated captain in the force. Bobby is clearly the black sheep in the family, who even adopts his mother's name to distance himself from the officers, but he becomes an undercover informant for the police after his brother is nearly killed by the Russian mob. The plot thus follows the ambivalent movements of Bobby between his law-abiding family and his darker sphere of action, the nightclub, which is a favourite haunt of the Russians and their drug dealers.

This shifting of allegiances, and the back-and-forth movements between two worlds, however, is not simply in line with the undercover crime story, in which a member of the law enforcement agency has to blend into the world of crime in order to bring it down. The two contrasting worlds are also a recreation of the two settings in the *Henry IV* plays, of which the film can be seen as an adaptation. One of these worlds appears to offer more in terms of warmth, friendship and camaraderie: the nightclub is characteristically shot in mellow, reddish-brown tones, while the other sphere demands hard and harsh duty, and so the NYPD precincts are dreary, bleak and grey; even the party in honour of Joe seems at first a formal, lifeless affair.

The issue of divided loyalties between Bobby's two families – his blood relatives and the seemingly more welcoming and warm-hearted Russian mobsters – is a staple element of gangster films, as repeatedly mentioned earlier in this chapter. Even Lanier agrees that in comparison with the Shakespeare films of another post-millennial indie *auteur*, Michael Almereyda, 'Gray aims for a more classic Hollywood style marked by clarity of narrative line and character arc, continuity editing, and meticulous attention to framing and *mise-en-scène*'.[73] With these aspects in mind, the film may seem less of an exception than a creative example, not least as it makes no direct textual references to its early modern inspiration – *Henry IV, Parts 1* and *2* – which may even go unnoticed by audiences unless they look out for similarities. But once the viewer has been made aware of the connection, which was explicitly acknowledged by the director in an interview,[74] the film actually gains added depths and layers of meaning, rather than being dismissed as a derivative product.

In his article, quoted in the previous paragraphs, Lanier goes on to describe a number of ways in which Gray creates complex, even composite characters in which traits of several Shakespearean figures are combined. Bobby Green is the obvious Prince Hal figure; yet, in my reading, it is also Bobby who has a Hotspur-like tendency to disregard both the laws of civility and common sense. While his brother Joe's domestic relations can remind us of Hotspur's seemingly cold-hearted treatment of his wife, the passionate extremes of love and rage that we can witness between Hotspur and his Kate characterise Bobby's relationship with his girlfriend Amanda rather than that of Joe and his wife. It is indeed Amanda who tries to dissuade Bobby from getting involved in what is a potentially lethal assignment, while Joe eventually makes the decision to move to an administrative position for the sake of his family. In this sense, and in the dynamics of Bobby and Joe's relationship and their shifting positions in their father's affections and expectations, I see much more of the Prince Hal and Lord John of Lancaster parallel, also mentioned by Lanier, but little that would make Joe a Hotspur figure.

The two brothers' conflicting and colliding paths also help the film's alignments with another genre within mainstream Hollywood cinema, as David Greven argues in his essay about a previously unnamed generic group that has produced a considerable number of significant films since the 1980s. Greven calls this group of films the 'double-protagonist film', in which 'the central conflict is a complex negotiation for power between two protagonists, each played by a star, both of whom lay legitimate claim to narrative dominance'.[75] While the thematic group comprises examples from a range of traditional genres, and while there are also examples of two female protagonists, Greven's analysis indicates that the generic antecedents of this group are not only the so-called 'buddy film', but even more the traditional masculine genres. These include 'the western, the noir, the Hitchcockian psychosexual thriller, and its imitators of the 1970s and the 1980s', which often relied on two male stars for the manifestation of their fundamental thematic concerns, such as the split masculine identity, which is particularly central to *film noir*.[76] Greven's identification of *We Own the Night* as a member of this group also confirms that the film can and indeed should be seen within the framework of mainstream Hollywood cinema, rather than a predominantly independent production, even though it bears undeniable traces of its *auteur*'s artistic concerns.

Apart from the various interpretations of the two central characters in terms of the film's Shakespearean source, I believe there are a number of other possibilities, not mentioned by other critics, to align the cast of *We Own the Night* with that of *Henry IV*, particularly when it comes to the Falstaff figure. While it is true that Bobby's friend Jumbo Falsetti exudes the most comic charm of all, and he is directly responsible for the death of Bobby's father by his betrayal, at the end of the day he is no more than a pawn in the game. It is the Russian drug kingpin Marat Buzhayev (Moni Moshonov) who is explicitly identified as a father figure to Bobby, and thus the manifestation of the other world that tries to lure Bobby away from the law and order his real father stands for. Amanda, Bobby's girlfriend, although undoubtedly the one 'who represents to him the possibility of love, a life of pleasure, and independence from his powerful, aloof father',[77] shows no real comic traits, and certainly no surrogate or alternative father tendencies, which would make her a Falstaff variant. In my view, she could be seen more as a companion figure in the mould of Ned Poins, Hal's closest confidant, who allies himself with the Prince even in opposition to Falstaff.

Amanda's own character development is also worth tracing in the film, which shows her change from a call girl at Bobby's club to a caring partner who is morally and emotionally more involved in Bobby's distress over the attempts on his brother's and father's lives than any other character. The cinematography and costume design also emphasises this change, from the first shots focusing on her body, very much on display and there for the taking, through her gradual adoption of darker, simpler and more conservative outfits, with the camera allowing us to witness her own pent-up emotions and suffering. She may also be seen as a combination of the two female character types of *noir* cinema: from the *femme fatale*, whose attraction blinds the protagonist to the standard values of family and society, she becomes the abandoned victim-like lover, who is swept away by the larger forces of evil that the protagonist has to stand up against.

We Own the Night is particularly useful in this chapter for another reason: it highlights the thematic and stylistic connections between *film noir* and crime films, particularly in its invocation of nostalgia 'that noir so often takes as a theme and engenders in its spectators', as argued by Jennifer Fay and Justus Nieland.[78] *We Own the Night* establishes itself as a backward-looking product right from the start, partly through the inclusion of a selection of black-and-white photographs from *Police Work*, a 'volume of New York Police Department photographs' by photojournalist Leonard Freed, which Gray refers to as having provided the initial spark for the film.[79] The still images acquire further significance as they help the viewer identify the film's title as the unofficial motto of the NYPD's Street Crime Unit, a plain-clothes elite anti-crime unit operating between 1971 and 2002.[80] After the introductory sequence, the narrative steps into the end-of-century underworld, explicitly defining its setting as 1988, Brooklyn, New York, moving nearly twenty years into the past from the film's release. The film's theme also recalls the (mostly failed) war on drugs initiated by the Reagan administration in 1982; however, this time the war is fought in a radically changed ethnic environment, no longer targeting predominantly African-American gangsters and communities.[81]

As already mentioned, the two senses of the family – a classic element of the gangster genre – here also collide, although in a different way to the Italian-American mafia stories. Here the blood family and the business Family, that is, the gang, are on opposite sides of the law, and Bobby's commitments to both worlds make him at first a reluctant mediator between the two. Yet when his own brother is injured by a gunman in front of his family home, and later when their father gets killed, Bobby's loyalties become clear, and he chooses the right side of law and order. He does so not only by putting himself in danger, acting as an undercover informant, to help the police crack down on the international drug operation of the Russians, but in the end he officially dons the uniform and thus joins the NYPD at the side of his brother, following in his father's footsteps (see figure 3.4).

We Own the Night, while in many ways displaying standard characteristics of the genres it relies on – a hybrid of *noir* crime and the gangster film – is also obviously a product of the post-millennial decade, rather than the classic gangster era or the 1990s revival of the genre. One clear sign of the different times is visible in the racial composition of the characters; it is no longer the semi-assimilated immigrant who is the protagonist, and the gangsters, for whom no sympathy is spared, are no longer Italian or Hispanic, but Russian. This is perfectly in line with what Ingrid Walker writes about the turn-of-the-century reality of American mobsters, as she claims: 'While a few mob microcosms persist, ... gangster life prevails not so much in the Italian American Mafia but in less pervasive manifestations of Russian and Asian organized crime.'[82] What this change in ethnic composition also means is a shift in sympathies – of cinema audiences and society in general – away from the mobster; it is hard to think of any representations of the Russian mob which would incite sympathy from

Dark-minded Othellos, mobster Macbeths 139

Figure 3.4 Brothers in arms – Mark Wahlberg and Joaquin Phoenix in *We Own the Night*. Directed by James Gray, 2007. Columbia Pictures/2929 Productions/Industry Entertainment.

viewers. It is true that Bobby also comes from a family of immigrants, as his Russian-sounding name (Grusinsky) testifies, which is a source of embarrassment for him, causing him to become Bobby Green by adopting his mother's name. By the end of the film, however, he is once again proud to bear his father's name, in acknowledgement of the whole family's legacy in upholding the American value system. Since the Russian mob is seen as less established in American society, without previous generations of immigrant ancestors, their trade also focuses on less family-friendly areas. Russian gangsters are typically shown to be familiar with the rough trade, dealing not in casinos or politics, but violence and drugs, which was never seen as a viable road to legitimacy, either in *The Godfather*, or in *GoodFellas*, where the central character attempts to meddle in the drug business.

Here the Russians may pretend to be familiar and friendly, but by the end they turn out to be less than human, downright monstrous, betraying Bobby and murdering his father. *We Own the Night* is in many ways reminiscent of another gangster film released in the same year in the UK. In *Eastern Promises* (2007, dir. David Cronenberg), a midwife's search for the family of an orphaned newborn takes her into the depths of the London Russian mob, and eventually gives her an unlikely ally in the form of the gang's driver, who turns out to be an undercover agent, working on bringing down the gang. Using children to emphasise the ruthlessness of the

Russian mobsters is another common theme between the two films, implying that the world has changed significantly since the age of the godfathers. While the Italian-American mafia films typically show parents' tendency to make decisions with the long-term benefit of their children in mind, in *We Own the Night* the last bit of sympathy is lost for the seemingly benevolent Russian gang leader when it turns out that he uses his own grandchildren as a cover for drug trafficking. Just as Falstaff's disregard for law and lack of respect for the royal family gradually take on an embarrassing quality, Marat Buzhayev's figure also gains monstrous proportions and has to be brought to spectacular justice in order to re-establish audiences' belief in society, a critical concern in the first decade of the new millennium. At the same time, *We Own the Night*'s genre heritage ties it to the classical studio era, rather than the postmodern blockbusters that came into prominence in the 1990s, discussed in Part II of this book.

Notes

1. Keyishian, 'Shakespeare and Movie Genre', p. 75.
2. S. Selby, *Dark City: The Film Noir* (Jefferson, NC, and London: McFarland Publishing, 1984), p. 1.
3. D. Lanier, 'Film Spin-Offs and Citations', in R. Burt (ed.), *Shakespeares after Shakespeare: An Encyclopedia of the Bard in Mass Media and Popular Culture*, vol. 1 (Westport, CT, and London: Greenwood Press, 2007), pp. 132–365, p. 153.
4. *Ibid.*, p. 152.
5. Selby, *Dark City*, p. 182.
6. Roan Group, Edgar Ulmar's *Strange Illusion*, DVD cover, 2000.
7. E. Cowie, '*Film Noir* and Women', in J. Copjec (ed.), *Shades of Noir* (London and New York: Verso, 1993), pp. 121–65, p. 130.
8. S. C. Biesen, 'Psychology in American Film Noir and Hitchcock's Gothic Thrillers', *Americana: The Journal of American Popular Culture (1900–Present)*, 13:1 (2014), www.americanpopularculture.com/journal/articles/spring_2014/biesen.htm (accessed 26 January 2020). (The film's release date is given as 1920 in most other sources.)
9. *Ibid.*
10. *Ibid.*
11. Lanier, 'Shakespearean Rhizomatics', p. 32.
12. Cowie, '*Film Noir* and Women', p. 130.
13. All parenthetical references to *Hamlet* are to this edition: W. Shakespeare, *Hamlet*, The Arden Shakespeare, Second Series, ed. H. Jenkins (London and New York: Methuen, 1982).

14 Although within the conventions of the western, *Broken Lance* also makes use of two portraits of the family patriarch, one in the bank and another in the abandoned family home, initiating the film's flashback sequences.
15 Silver, 'The Gangster and Film Noir', p. 314.
16 Academy Awards for Best Actor in a Leading Role (Ronald Colman), and Best Music, Scoring of a Dramatic or Comedy Picture (Miklós Rózsa); Golden Globe Award for Best Actor; also nominated for Academy Awards for Best Director (George Cukor) and Best Original Screenplay (Ruth Gordon, Garson Kanin) and the Grand International Award at the Venice Film Festival in 1948.
17 M. H. Rippy, 'All Our *Othellos*: Black Monsters and White Masks on the American Screen', in Lehmann and Starks (eds), *Spectacular Shakespeare*, pp. 25–46, p. 32.
18 Lanier, 'Murdering *Othello*', p. 209.
19 Cf. Silver, 'The Gangster and Film Noir', p. 315.
20 C. Baron, 'Film Noir: Gesture under Pressure', in Cornea (ed.), *Genre and Performance*, pp. 18–37, p. 27.
21 Neale, *Genre and Hollywood*, p. 151.
22 Cf. R. Wood, 'Ideology, Genre, Auteur', in Grant (ed.), *Film Genre Reader IV*, pp. 78–92.
23 Willson, *Shakespeare in Hollywood*, p. 93.
24 R. Ottoson, *A Reference Guide to the American Film Noir: 1940–1958* (Metuchen, NJ, and London: Scarecrow Press, 1981), p. 1.
25 Lanier, 'Murdering *Othello*', p. 209.
26 Rippy, 'All Our *Othellos*', p. 31.
27 In 'Murdering *Othello*', Lanier even hints at the possibility that the 1947 success of *A Double Life* might have paved the way for the Academy Award of Laurence Olivier's *noir Hamlet* the following year, see p. 213.
28 P. Hutchings, 'Theatres of Blood: Shakespeare and the Horror Film', in J. Drakakis and D. Townshend (eds), *Gothic Shakespeares* (Abingdon: Routledge, 2008), pp. 153–66, p. 165.
29 *Ibid.*
30 Griggs, *Screen Adaptations: Shakespeare's* King Lear, p. 121.
31 *Ibid.*, esp. pp. 126–33.
32 M. Nicholls, 'From Divestment to Due Resolution: *King Lear* and the New York Fabulists, 1989–92', *Journal of Film and Video*, 65:3 (2013), 3–13, 3.
33 T. Cartelli and K. Rowe, *New Wave Shakespeare on Screen* (Cambridge and Malden, MA: Polity, 2007), p. 17.
34 Howard, 'Shakespeare's Cinematic Offshoots', p. 311.
35 Cf. E. Mitchell, 'Apes and Essences: Some Sources of Significance in the American Gangster Film', in Grant (ed.), *Film Genre Reader IV*, pp. 255–64.
36 Silver, 'The Gangster and Film Noir', p. 304.

37 Mitchell, 'Apes and Essences', p. 258.
38 *Ibid.*, p. 263.
39 *Ibid.*, p. 258.
40 Y. Griggs, '"Humanity Must Perforce Prey Upon Itself Like Monsters of the Deep": *King Lear* and the Urban Gangster Movie', *Adaptation*, 1:2 (2008), 121–39, 121.
41 R. F. Willson Jr, 'The Selling of *Joe Macbeth*', *Shakespeare on Film Newsletter*, 7:1 (1982), 1, 4.
42 *Ibid.*, 1.
43 Lanier, 'Film Spin-Offs and Citations', pp. 202–3.
44 *Ibid.*, p. 203.
45 C. Lehmann, 'Film Adaptations', in Burt (ed.), *Shakespeares after Shakespeare*, pp. 74–131, p. 101.
46 F. L. Gardaphé, 'The Gangster Figure in American Film and Literature', in G. Muscio, J. Sciorra, G. Spagnoletti and A. J. Tamburri (eds), *Mediated Ethnicity: New Italian-American Cinema* (New York: John D. Calandra Italian American Institute, 2010), pp. 55–63, p. 56.
47 *Ibid.*, p. 57.
48 Lanier, 'Film Spin-Offs and Citations', p. 203.
49 Lehmann, 'Film Adaptations', p. 101.
50 T. Welsch, 'Yoked Together by Violence: *Prizzi's Honor* as a Generic Hybrid', *Film Criticism*, 22:1, Special Issue: *Genre* (1997), 62–73, 62.
51 Howard, 'Shakespeare's Cinematic Offshoots', p. 311.
52 D. Rosenthal, *Shakespeare on Screen* (London: Hamlyn, 2000), p. 75.
53 C. Jess-Cooke, 'Screening the McShakespeare in Post-Millennial Shakespeare Cinema', in M. T. Burnett and R. Wray (eds), *Screening Shakespeare in the Twenty-First Century* (Edinburgh: Edinburgh University Press, 2006), pp. 163–84, p. 176.
54 Howard, 'Shakespeare's Cinematic Offshoots', p. 311.
55 All parenthetical references to *Romeo and Juliet* are to this edition: W. Shakespeare, *Romeo and Juliet*, The Arden Shakespeare, Second Series, ed. B. Gibbons (Walton-on-Thames: Thomas Nelson & Sons, 1997).
56 An almost literal quotation of 'Yet who would have thought the old man to have had so much blood in him?' (5.1.37–8).
57 J. Buchanan, *Shakespeare on Film* (Harlow: Pearson Education Limited, 2005), pp. 105, 106.
58 Nicholls, 'From Divestment to Due Resolution', 4.
59 *Ibid.*
60 Lanier, 'Film Spin-Offs and Citations', p. 209.
61 Lam, 'Gangsters and Genre'.
62 Gardaphé, 'The Gangster Figure in American Film and Literature', p. 56. (*Little Caesar* was released in the USA in January 1931.)
63 Mason, *American Gangster Cinema*, p. 81.

64 L. E. Ruberto, 'Where Did the Goodfellas Learn How to Cook? Gender, Labor, and the Italian American Experience', *Italian Americana*, 21:2 (2003), 164–76, 166.
65 D. Golden, 'Pasta or Paradigm: The Place of Italian-American Women in Popular Film', *Explorations in Ethnic Studies*, 2:1 (1979), 3–10.
66 R. Casillo, *Gangster Priest: The Italian American Cinema of Martin Scorsese* (Toronto, Buffalo, NY, and London: University of Toronto Press, 2006), p. 89.
67 Lanier, 'Film Spin-Offs and Citations', p. 209.
68 Howard, 'Shakespeare's Cinematic Offshoots', p. 311.
69 I. Serra, 'Italian American Cinema: Between Blood Family and Bloody Family', in Muscio, Sciorra, Spagnoletti and Tamburri (eds), *Mediated Ethnicity*, pp. 189–99, p. 189.
70 Cf. Silver, 'The Gangster and Film Noir', p. 299.
71 Casillo, *Gangster Priest*, p. 88.
72 D. M. Lanier, 'Shakespeare and the Indie Auteur: Michael Almereyda and James Gray', *Shakespeare Bulletin* 34:3 (2016), 451–68, 464.
73 *Ibid.*, 465.
74 Quoted by Lanier, *ibid.*, 463.
75 D. Greven, 'Contemporary Hollywood Masculinity and the Double-Protagonist Film', *Cinema Journal*, 48:4 (2009), 22–43, 22.
76 *Ibid.*, 23.
77 Lanier, 'Shakespeare and the Indie Auteur', 463.
78 J. Fay and J. Nieland, *Film Noir: Hard-Boiled Modernity and the Cultures of Globalization* (London and New York: Routledge, 2010), p. 125.
79 D. Lim, 'An Auteur for a Neglected New York City', *New York Times* (9 September 2007), www.nytimes.com/2007/09/09/movies/moviesspecial/09lim.html (accessed 30 January 2020).
80 T. Lynch, '"We Own the Night": Amadou Diallo's Deadly Encounter with New York City's Street Crime Unit', *Cato Institute Briefing Papers* 56 (31 March 2000), 4, www.cato.org/sites/cato.org/files/pubs/pdf/bp56.pdf (accessed 30 January 2020).
81 See e.g. W. Knapp, 'The War on Drugs', *Federal Sentencing Reporter*, 5:5 (1993), 294–7.
82 I. Walker, 'Family Values and Feudal Codes: The Social Politics of America's Fin-de-Siècle Gangster', in Silver and Ursini (eds), *Gangster Film Reader*, pp. 381–405, p. 382.

Part II
Contemporary blockbusters

Introduction

After the discussion of classical Hollywood genres and their appropriation of Shakespearean narratives, Part II of the volume investigates three genres that represent more recent colours on the cinematic palette. While the three genres included in these chapters – teen films, undead horror and biopics – are not regarded as classics of commercial cinema, it is undeniable that they also had antecedents either in the pre- or post-war decades of filmmaking. They have typically (re)gained popularity and thus significance in and around the 1990s, the great decade of filmmaking, whose impact on Shakespeare films is well known and documented. Kenneth Branagh's *oeuvre*, Franco Zeffirelli's *Hamlet*, Baz Luhrmann's *William Shakespeare's Romeo + Juliet*, Michael Hoffman's *A Midsummer Night's Dream* and several other outstanding works have not only changed the Shakespeare film scene for good, but also reached mass audiences and thus popularised screen Shakespeare to a previously unprecedented extent. Samuel Crowl, in his survey of what he calls 'the long decade' between 1989–2001, defines the period as 'the Kenneth Branagh Era'; at the same time, he also makes it clear that besides the phenomenal success associated with Branagh's and other *auteurs*' work, this 'decade consists of the most concentrated release of sound films based on Shakespeare's work in the century, similar to, but surpassing, the decade that followed the end of World War II'.[1]

What is even more important, however, is that this was not only an increase in quantity, but that the nature of Shakespeare adaptations also changed during the decade. As Douglas Lanier sums up the most significant difference between this decade and previous eras of filmmaking: 'Whereas before the 1990s screen Shakespeare was predominantly an art film phenomenon, recent adaptations have by and large aimed to reach a mass market audience and recast Shakespeare as popular entertainment. … Crucial to that enterprise has been assimilating Shakespeare to popular film genres.'[2] As discussed in the following section, by this decade, the demographic composition of audiences had also shifted towards the dominance of teenagers and young adults. It appears, therefore, that a fortunate constellation of various socio-economic and industrial factors created an unsurpassed supply and demand for films based on literary sources, Shakespeare among them, while this new industrial and commercial context also impacted the emerging cinematic style, catering for a more popularly inclined and predominantly young audience which preferred to be entertained rather than educated.

That is why out of the diverse selection of existing genres, this part of the volume discusses three distinct groups: teen films, specifically the high school subgenre; followed by the subgenre of horror employing undead creatures (zombies or vampires), also most appreciated by young audiences, irrespective of whether the films' protagonists are teenagers or not; and finally, a seemingly very different, but no less significant group: biopics, that is, biographical films depicting some aspect or period of William Shakespeare's life and work. This group is particularly interesting as it offers perfect examples of how recent filmmaking thrives on generic hybridity while maintaining well-known genre frameworks. It has, of course, long been a commonplace of film studies that the genre structures of classical Hollywood cinema have gradually given way to a hybridity characteristic of modern (and especially postmodern) film. This is partly a consequence of genres evolving in a way that follows and reflects on the socio-cultural reality of their periods of creation; partly a general tendency of the entertainment industry to keep offering novelties to its consumers. Genres' reflection on their socio-historical context can be diverse: teen films need to be able to speak the language of the contemporary young generation to attract their attention; zombies and vampires, on the other hand, are allegorical means of expressing current anxieties and social concerns; and biopics often fuse the atmosphere of the era depicted with the period of their creation, to emphasise the topicality of their subjects.

Another aspect that connects all these genres is their postmodern attitude towards authority; as discussed in the individual analyses in the following three chapters, contemporary films tend to question Shakespeare's high cultural status and authority in general, while also participating in it by adopting and adapting his works for new audiences. Their indulgence in the commercialised aspects of popular culture, tangible sometimes in mockery, and more often in self-referential meta-cinematic elements, also results in shared stylistic, aesthetic, narrative or structural solutions. When looking at the attitude of the films to the source material they rework, we can see how they conform to what Fredric Jameson described as the aesthetic of postmodernity.[3] They all display a predilection for pastiche, quotation either without context, or at least without the intention to engage in in-depth dialogue, an imitation without an attempt at actual rediscovery, but also parody 'amputated of the satiric impulse'.[4] This approach is manifest in most teen flicks discussed in Chapter 4; it is more than characteristic of the films employing the undead, which always represent some aspect of society that cannot be expressed through realistic images. Even in the seemingly most reverential group of films, the biopics, we can find a predominantly entertaining, rather than educational, attitude, with plenty of in-jokes, without the expectation that they will all be recognised by audiences.

There is also a reason why these genres have often been accused of 'dumbing down' their source materials, offering viewers the fridge-magnet length of apparently random quotations, or simplified, psychologically over-explained and often historically distorted backstories. They are criticised for diluting the stakes that create suspense in tragedies, or for lacking the dimensions of social criticism that remain tangible even behind the romantic resolutions of conflicts in Shakespearean comedy. While contemporary genre films mostly operate within narrower social layers (set practically in a bourgeois universe), it is untrue that these adaptations are without social context or that they lack engagement with their source material and target audience. As the following discussion intends to show, their engagements with the contemporary world often take formulaic and predictable, but clearly defined, forms.

The teenpic

Probably one of the most characteristically contemporary genres is the teen film, even though it is not an entirely new invention. Since the beginning of film history, there have been films with teenage characters, or films employing young actors, and particularly films targeting young audiences, and yet the revival of the form in the 1990s seems to have been unprecedented in many ways. As Wheeler Winston Dixon claims at the beginning of his account: 'In the late 1990s, films aimed at a younger teenage audience, ages thirteen to nineteen, exploded on theatrical motion picture screens with a wave of productions'.[5] Melissa Croteau describes a similar sudden burst in the production of teen films adapted from literary classics: 'This genre exploded after the 1995 and 1996 box office hits *Clueless*, *Scream*, and

Romeo + Juliet proved to filmmakers and studios that teen films could be extremely lucrative because of their low production costs and large audience with plenty of free time and discretionary cash.'[6] This recognition – that even though teenagers do not constitute the majority of the population, they definitely make up the largest segment of cinemagoers – is again not new: cinema production and marketing have been relying on young audiences at least since the 1950s. This 'progressive "juvenilization" of film content and the film audience that is today the operative reality of the American motion picture business' is in turn 'best revealed in the genesis and development of what has become the industry's flagship enterprise, the teenpic', as Thomas Doherty argues in *Teenagers and Teenpics*.[7] Since the 1950s, however, considerable changes in American society have also left their mark on the genre of the teen film, and the upsurge of teen Shakespeare adaptations since the mid-1990s constitute a distinct group, not unrelated to its historical predecessors, but justifiably treated as a new phenomenon.

The teen film as a genre – in contrast with the classical Hollywood genres discussed in Part I of the volume – is not characterised by its thematic focus, although the most popular topics addressed by youth films are inevitably connected to the interests of the target audience. Timothy Shary summarises this peculiarity of teen films: 'the youth genre is based on the ages of the films' characters, and thus the thematic concerns of its subgenres can be seen as more directly connected to specific notions of different youth behaviors and styles'.[8] As a result, the influence of teenagers, if not as characters, then as prime consumers, is palpable in practically every genre and mode of contemporary cinema.

Still, even though teenagers comprise the core of teen films' audiences, it is not utterly impossible that films depicting young characters draw audiences from other age groups as well, particularly from the young adult population, extending possibly as far as forty-year-olds. Just as young adult literature is often described to have a crossover readership, with children, teenagers or young adults equally able to identify with certain elements in the stories of Harry Potter or Katniss Everdeen, teen films, particularly when they are adaptations of literary classics, may have a similar power to attract several age groups.[9] This crossover attraction partly relies on the different expectations of various demographic sections, but also on the specific age groups' abilities to recognise or relate to their source material. As teenagers may be drawn to these films for their depiction of high school life and characters, other age groups with an awareness of the literary sources turn to them with possibly double nostalgia. On the one hand, such films may invoke their memories of high school life (or simply being of high school age), but also remind them of their high school readings, the literary classics. It is no accident therefore that the texts typically used as source materials in these films belong to the core reading materials in English literature, and rarely include less commonly known works.[10] As we shall see, it is not uncommon for filmmakers to emphasise this aspect by visualising the English literature classroom, or school performances of Shakespeare plays, or even the classroom experience of viewing a film adaptation of some literary classic, in an (often mocked) attempt to provide better motivation for students.

At the same time, we may note that specifying the age group of characters similarly determines typical situations and conflicts, relationships and character types, and even a number of predictable settings, while excluding a certain set of conventions or interpersonal relationships that are less likely to concern this generation. In this way, the American high school or its sports grounds become elements almost as compulsory in the genre as the Wild West in western films, or dark and overpowering high-rise architectural structures in *film noir*. The school environment determines a number of situations as well: anxieties over school performance, peer friendship and rivalry, even bullying, homecoming or prom dances, sports contests, clashes with parents and/or school authorities.

As is expected from commercial cinema, we can witness how the genre reflects changing social reality in several of these listed aspects, but most noticeably in the representation of authority figures and institutions. While youth films in the 1950s often depicted strong and powerful authority figures, and the young protagonists engaged in rebellion against these controlling forces, from the 1960s onwards, 'the most fascinating trend in teenpics has been their palpable desire for parental control and authority, not their adolescent rebellion and autonomy'.[11] This in turn gave way to a more independent generation of screen teens in the 1990s. In recent teen films the majority of authority figures – teachers, parents, institutional representatives – are depicted as weak or incompetent, often ignorant and typically ridiculous characters who are completely out of touch with teenagers' concerns and whose absence serves as a catalyst for youth to take responsibility for their lives. As Kevin J. Wetmore Jr claims, following Thomas Leitch's argument, teen films since the 1980s, influenced especially by the work of John Hughes, no longer express any real anxiety concerning the pressures of the adult world. Yet even less do they reflect any desire on the parts of youngsters to take their places in this world of adult responsibility and conformity: 'the teenpic keeps the adolescent central, marginalizes the adult world and insists not only on the values of the teenage generation but in the value of not leaving that generation'.[12] But the absent (or absent-minded) parental figures can also be blamed for the unresolved issues within the troubled adolescent psyche that lead to tragedies, as two of the films discussed in Chapter 4, O (2001, dir. Tim Blake Nelson) and *Lost and Delirious* (2001, dir. Léa Pool), will illustrate.

First and foremost, teen films are structured around the obvious – and predominantly heteronormative – school romances and sexual encounters, with the conflict mostly focusing on adolescents discovering their sexual identities. Nonetheless, the small but significant group of queer teen films should also be mentioned, whose main concerns are similar to those of regular teenpics, with the exception of (one or more of) the protagonists' sexual identities, and the conflicts arising from an often homophobic environment. Romantic relationships are shown to develop from distant desire through courtship to actual physical connection, whether that means holding hands, kissing or even having sex (although the latter is rarely depicted explicitly in mainstream teen films) – but long-term relationships formally sanctified by marriage are practically absent. Nonetheless, all films end in some highly regulated festive event that replaces the wedding celebrations of Shakespearean comedy – in a high school environment this is most often the prom, or sometimes a debutante ball, or, in a specific subgroup of films, a sports final. These may seem run-of-the-mill events of adolescent life, but they share many of the features of Shakespearean *denouements*: they represent each individual in their respective roles within their micro-society. At the same time, these events also function as conclusions, providing opportunities for taking sides, revealing friends or exposing foes, and acknowledging romantic interests or betrayals in the most significant public setting of the peer group, where adults are either completely absent or simply play the role of witnesses.

These concerns may be predictable, yet it is essential to acknowledge them, since reviews and critical interpretations, particularly when it comes to literary adaptations, often lament the lightening of pressures and conflicts. Thus R. S. White remarks of Tim Blake Nelson's O how, compared to *Othello*, 'A high school student is not a plausible vehicle for the insecurities that the play represents, which are those encountered within marriage, not juvenile courtship.'[13] Such judgements, however, seem to reflect somewhat irrational expectations; as this book argues, what we can and should observe is whether the target audience will experience the film's conflict as a characteristically (or at least plausibly) teenage issue, and whether that conflict is capable of manifesting tensions which are considered serious and potentially lethal within the age group. Judging from the tragic regularity with which high school conflicts, ranging from bullying to academic underachievement, lead to actual fatalities, particularly in the United States (where the majority of these films are produced), it could be argued that the stakes can be high enough even in classrooms, on prom dance floors or football fields, without setting the action on actual battlefields or in marital relationships.

Moreover, the films are often invoked in debates concerning the 'series of "moral panics" around young people and social behaviour' whose source has typically been the cinema, 'not only due to its function as a social gathering place, but more so in generating concerns about the ways that popular media influence youth'.[14] Hugh H. Davis also claims a direct and potentially positive influence when he argues that teen film adaptations of literary classics 'have helped shape teen culture in the twenty-first century and help inform and educate their audience on the basics of canonical stories'.[15] Yet Emma French is right in pointing out the contradictory intentions behind teen adaptations' reliance on classical source texts. In her view, teen Shakespeare films' marketing strategies appeal 'to the teen audience's assumed knowledge of Shakespeare, through in-jokes and quotation, although the same films' marketing evinces a contrary current, anti-intellectual and revelling in its own self-conscious irreverence, and appealing to the "teenager as rebel" stereotype'.[16] This paradox will be referred to in the analyses that follow, with more details of the typical decontextualised quotations and often covert (or absent) identification with the source works testifying to the complexity of the issue.

Another question that often comes up in discussions of teen adaptations is whether the process necessarily involves 'dumbing down', as is often expressed by both conservative educational critics and pessimistic academics.[17] The question is whether it is rather a procedure similar to all other types of adaptation, involving inevitable alterations of source text, style and even cultural status, or something more damaging, from which young and impressionable audiences should be protected. Adapting Shakespeare and other canonical works into popular media has often invoked such anxieties, but perhaps no other genre has been so much in the crossfire of value-centred debates as the teen film. As Ailsa Grant Ferguson notes, 'Accusations of "dumbing down" Shakespeare dogged the heyday of the teen Shakespeare "update" (*She's the Man, Ten Things I Hate about You, O*, among others). These films used accessible elements of Shakespeare's plays, the plot, the characters, the basic themes, to create teen narratives'[18] – the operative word being 'accessible'. But, as French remarks, such accessibility is often seen as simplification, and therefore one of the common views is 'that reducing the intellectual challenges posed by engagement with the play is an inevitable corollary of updating the play for the MTV generation'.[19] The most concerned critical voices may be rooted in an overprotective attitude towards young generations (and the inevitable, if ancient, lament over deteriorating cultural values in society) – but the denigration directed at the teen genre as a whole often seems exaggerated. I hope to show in what follows that what many perceive as a lamentable dumbing down of something precious and intelligent is part and parcel of the adaptation process necessary to transform literary texts into the specific generic framework of the teen film.

In yet another view, the predilection of popular culture for the performative may also be seen as a process away from the verbally expressive, as Richard Burt argues:

> A 1990s American popular Shakespeare is precisely a dumbed down Shakespeare. The stress in recent Shakespeare film adaptations is on the performative rather than the rhetorical. *William Shakespeare's Romeo and Juliet*'s [sic] editing is MTV-inflected. Two journalists ... compared the film to an MTV rock video.[20]

I believe, however, that the expression 'dumbing down' should be used with caution, as it invokes the type of elitist conservative critical attitude that is hardly conducive to mutual discourse between popular culture and the academia, without which no real understanding of contemporary culture is possible. Equally important is that not all popular Shakespeare films employ similar strategies of updating or making the text accessible to a specific target audience through simplification of plot, characterisation or language. Besides, it also needs to be acknowledged that these films often display considerable verbal wit – albeit admittedly a very different kind of wit from that of Shakespeare. Yet, since the comic wordplay and verbal puns are among the most easily outdated elements of Shakespeare's work, and therefore regularly updated even in theatre performances, it might not amount to actual sacrilege to replace the obsolete repartees by elements of the contemporary teen vernacular.

Another significant issue of teen adaptations comes to light precisely when examining the classroom scenes in which the Shakespeare quotations and interpretations are included. It is true that these scenes where cultural authority figures – teachers – initiate discussions of Shakespeare rarely offer any innovative or even complex interpretation of the text. What they do offer instead, however, are examples of identification, of possible points of entry and applicability in texts to which most teenagers find it hard to connect. In this way, the films are also idealistic and implicitly educational as well, suggesting that it is worth engaging with the canonical high cultural works that comprise the curriculum. Since teen films' central concern is adolescent identity and the way teenagers find role models, groups they can belong to, paths they can follow, in order to discover and confirm their own identities, the seemingly dumbed down use of Shakespeare quotations encourages identification with social roles and in this way serves a vital purpose.

What is important here is clearly the tendency of contemporary filmmaking to turn well-known, even authoritative, texts into teen films centred on the problems and everyday conflicts of adolescence and growing up, without relying on any potential marketing value offered by the cultural prestige of the original texts. Reina Green also refers to this tendency when she notes that 'while a few fans may recognize Shakespeare beneath the surface of a teen romantic comedy, the film industry is nervous about marketing teen adaptations of Shakespeare through their association with the Bard, preferring to position them through the audience's recognition of movie stars, hit songs, and a school setting'.[21] Moreover, eliminating Shakespearean language from a teen film's script is not simply a necessary adjustment for the sake of a less than erudite audience, but, as Doherty argues, the allegedly 'dumbed down' language is precisely one of the signature elements of the teenpic that allows a certain generation of viewers to identify the genre as theirs. 'In pinpointing the year of release for any given teenpic, the slang, fashion, and music soundtrack of the moment are more accurate than carbon dating.'[22] Music is just another form of teen vernacular, also mentioned by French as one of the key elements of the genre in connection with Luhrmann's *William Shakespeare's Romeo + Juliet*:

> Popular music forms one of the most potent means of marketing filmed Shakespeare adaptations to a teen audience: in addition to its stand-alone appeal, it performs the distinctive function within Shakespeare film marketing of reassuring the teen audience that difficult themes and language can be made comprehensible by judicious use of explicatory, familiar music.[23]

This emphasis on the soundtrack will be noticeable in all Shakespeare productions discussed in Chapter 4, and in some cases even the cross-generational appeal of the films is established predominantly through the musical elements.

What all the films discussed in Chapter 4 have in common are, therefore, the setting of the (American) high school, a cast of predominantly young actors, many of them teen idols of their generation, and a story that is modelled on some Shakespearean dramatic plot, although the films' title and even their promotional materials rarely mention this literary inspiration. The narrative similarities are often superficial, and the dialogue mostly updated, to adopt a convincingly teen vernacular both in vocabulary and style, in which Shakespeare quotations and explicit references appear either in completely decontextualised form or within the confines of the classroom. The society depicted is predominantly middle class, although intricately layered into various cliques and groupings, with protagonists typically starting out either as marginalised outcasts or rebels, but by the end of the narrative achieving recognition and acceptance. The only exceptions are *Lost and Delirious* and *O*, in which the protagonists' fate shows a downward spiral, from the centre towards the margins, from inclusion to exclusion and tragedy.

Revival of zombies and vampires

Like the other generic categories discussed in Part II, zombies and vampires are not new phenomena on cinema screens in the twenty-first century. Among the earliest masterpieces of cinema history we can find Friedrich Wilhelm Murnau's *Nosferatu* (1922) with an undead creature as its protagonist, an iconic film which established (or rather popularised) the conventions of a specific type of horror film, the vampire narrative.[24] Meghan Sutherland goes even further in asserting undead films' unoriginality when she makes the strong statement that 'every zombie film is a kind of remake. The undead have been lumbering around recycled B-film sets and Hollywood lots since the days of silent cinema'; she further argues that 'it is not just the dead bodies that are reanimated and proliferating in zombie cinema; it's the films themselves, too'.[25] Still, Outi Hakola maintains that 'undead characters did visit the silent screens of the United States and elsewhere, but horror films were more or less isolated productions before the sound era', the best-known ones, like *Nosferatu*, mostly coming from Germany.[26] As she explains, it was only 'with the advent of sound' that 'the living dead features became part of the horror genre'[27] and then remained staple characters in all periods of film history, before the recent 'zombie renaissance' in the twenty-first century brought them into the mainstream of popular culture.[28]

Yet, since the earliest days of horror cinema, there have been instances of cross-fertilisation between Shakespeare, the most canonical of authors, and horror, allegedly the most debased of all genres. Peter Hutchings, in his analysis of some of these meeting points, with reference to the 1931 *Dracula* (dir. Tod Browning) draws attention to the fact that 'there might be a more complicated and context-specific set of intermedial and commercially driven relationships at work here between apparently disparate areas of culture, cutting across cultural hierarchies in unpredictable ways'.[29] In this volume, however, I do not intend to collect and describe scenes in straightforward film adaptations of Shakespearean drama that rely on the conventions of horror cinema, such as certain parts of Roman Polański's *Macbeth*, Julie Taymor's *Titus*, or even Branagh's *Hamlet*,[30] all of which 'align themselves (or can be aligned with) the horror genre'.[31] Instead of such moments of generic influence in *auteur* films, Chapter 5 looks at genre cinema productions that use recognisable elements of Shakespearean drama as their inspiration, incorporating Shakespearean plot devices or characters in works that are identified as horror films.

As Hutchings notes, since the earliest days of silent cinema, 'Shakespeare and horror have tended to go their separate ways, with examples of interaction still few in number', and yet the seemingly 'uncrossable cultural divide' between the two has been bridged more than once, and with confidence and creativity.[32] 'There is no awkwardness or embarrassment here, no snobbishness or cap-doffing to high culture, and no sense either of Shakespeare slumming it with the horror proles.'[33] What we can find instead is mutual inspiration and potential for cross-fertilisation, as exemplified by a number of post-millennial films using the generic framework of vampire or zombie cinema.

Although the endemic presence of monsters in our contemporary culture may invite us to treat them as a unified group, looking at the origins of such characters that inhabit a grey zone between life and death, we may note an interesting difference between the various types of undead creatures. Many of them have their roots in superstition, folklore or mythology, but only the vampire is a characteristically literary figure, and the early vampire films were practically all adaptations, based on Bram Stoker's 1897 novel *Dracula*. As regards the figure of the zombie, however, it is important to note that although its pre-history includes Haitian and African folklore and popular beliefs, 'unlike other monsters, the zombie has no literary antecedents' but owes its currently familiar image to the cinema.[34] James McFarland claims that for all the obvious generative sources, 'the zombie-image has a single, unique origin: George A. Romero's 1968 film *Night of the Living Dead*. It is in this film, a film in which the word "zombie" does not occur, that the elements of the image assemble in their significant potency and begin their remarkable historical career.'[35] Nonetheless, as

McFarland adds in a note: while zombies have appeared in slapstick parody versions and even romantic comedies, 'the zombie-image belongs to none of these genres essentially – and indeed is never entirely at home in any narrative structure – but is an apocalyptic image, situated in the dislocation generated by the apocalyptic rupture in history characteristic of the present'.[36] As a result, the zombie image can make itself at home in any narrative structure, and 'The zombie tradition presents almost a tabula rasa space, a text remarkably free of generic convention or complex heritage, and this blankness makes it an open, accessible, or even democratic popular cultural phenomenon.'[37] This phenomenon is then readily exploited by filmmakers to express various forms of social criticism, from anti-war propaganda to a general critique of consumer society.

Whatever their origins, the recent return of undead characters to haunt television and cinema screens is undeniable. Moreover, it is not simply an increase in quantity that makes vampire films or the genre of the zombie apocalypse a topic of interest, but rather the fact that these previously marginalised subgenres have apparently become mainstream, A-list staples of youth and adult cinema consumption. At the same time, the post-millennial zombie is no longer one of many characterless and (literally) faceless rotting corpses, but is often endowed with something of a personality. Similarly, the vampire as protagonist has undergone remarkable change since the early 1990s, and the recent trend in handsome, humane and empathetic, even 'vegetarian', vampires has turned the nightmarish Dracula-type figures into likeable and loveable idols of adolescents and young adults.

Although it is hard to pinpoint the exact starting point of this trend, a number of young adult novels and subsequent media franchises, such as Anne Rice's *Vampire Chronicles* (1976–2016), were among the first to humanise the monster protagonist. The 1994 film adaptation of Rice's *Interview with the Vampire* (dir. Neil Jordan), with its stellar cast and high production values, clearly contributed to the higher position of the vampire story in subsequent years. This was followed by Joss Whedon's *Buffy the Vampire Slayer* (1997–2003), Charlaine Harris's *Southern Vampire Mysteries* (2001–2013), Stephenie Meyer's *Twilight* saga (2005–2008, on film 2008–2012), instrumental in expanding the genre's reach to younger audiences, and HBO's *True Blood* (2008–2014), adapted from Harris's novels, to name but a few of many works that prove that the vampire as a positive hero has become endemic in popular culture.

It is also true that the vampire is and has always been closer to the human – their attraction for us, according to Christian Moraru, is precisely 'a psycho-cultural matrix of self-identification, the vampiric *in* the human. ... Admittedly, they are monsters. But in their monstrosity – in their botched metamorphosis – we view ourselves.'[38] Whether it is our post-millennial anxieties that have allowed us to find such alliances in the monstrous, making us see and represent the monsters of previous ages as our own kind, or our jadedness and disbelief in anything beyond humanity, the Gothic has certainly taken over our imagination. Following up on what appears to be a lucrative trend, these days practically all television programme providers, streaming services and cinemas offer a variety of feature films or series whose protagonists or conflicts are associated with undead characters, and apparently there is still life left in the undead.[39]

One popular explanation for the so-called zombie renaissance can be found in 9/11 and the terrorist threat that has become more tangible for the American population since the 2001 attacks. Kyle Bishop, in his article 'Dead Man *Still* Walking', explicitly argues that the twenty-first-century 'renaissance of the subgenre reveals a connection between zombie cinema and post-9/11 cultural consciousness'.[40] This connection may appear in the form of clear visual recollections of natural or man-made disasters, or in the genre's central themes, but 'the movies' relevance has become all the more clear – a post-9/11 audience cannot help but perceive the characteristics of zombie cinema through the filter of terrorist threats and apocalyptic reality'.[41]

Doherty reaches further back in his reference to the 1990s craze for the undead when he argues for a connection with the AIDS crisis of the mid-1980s and the subsequent suppression of on-screen representations of sexuality. Teen films were purged of sex by the end of the millennium, as Doherty notes: 'To eliminate sexually transmitted audience discomfort, Hollywood's teen-targeted films covered up the nudity and closed down the sex play.'[42] To combine the threat of contagion with a compensation for the general absence of nudity from popular films, the horror genre provided the perfect opportunity:

> Drenched in a venereal horror, a flood of vampire films and blood-infected chillers – *The Lost Boys* (1987), *Bram Stoker's Dracula* (1992), *Innocent Blood* (1992), and *Interview with the Vampire* (1994) served as transparent allegories for the omnipresent fear of fluids. Driving a stake through the heart of a vampire was a less threatening form of physical contact than other types of penetration.[43]

As opposed to the surprisingly chaste teen movies, films featuring the undead indeed revel in the goriest forms of bodily (un)reality, as if to compensate for what is absent from the other favourite genre of teen audiences.

It has to be noted, however, that other scholars dispute such simple equations between 9/11 and the zombies' return, supporting their claim partly with non-American zombie narratives, partly with the fact that 'the main generic conventions are actually characterised by a greater longevity and durability than this argument suggests'.[44] Instead of the socio-cultural explanation, they emphasise the significance of digital technologies and fan practices that have undergone a more recognisable change in the new millennium and that offer participation in ways never seen before. According to Paul Manning, 'The blank democracy of the zombie text offers an open field for fan practices and fan inscription, processes which are accelerated in the age of digital technologies.'[45] Although this could in theory apply to any or every other cinema or TV genre, it appears that certain genres tend to inspire more fan productions than others, and the darker forms of science fiction and horror often lead the unofficial charts. Unsurprisingly, it is particularly the younger demographic, well versed in digital technologies that enable low-budget production, distribution and marketing, who seem to relish these opportunities to visualise their own apocalyptic nightmares.

Although it has been stated that the humanoid undead that appear to be all the rage in the 2010s do not necessarily have literary origins, this does not mean that such monsters would have any aversion to canonical works of literature. As a result, zombies, vampires, werewolves, ghouls, mummies or other terrifying figments of the imagination have appeared in adaptations of the widest range of literary classics. Nothing and no one seems immune to the viral infection of zombification, as titles such as *Grave Expectations, Android Karenina*, or the trend-setting novel recently turned into a blockbuster movie, *Pride and Prejudice and Zombies* (2016, dir. Burr Steers) show all too well.[46] No wonder that the already much-abused body of Shakespeare's work has also become food – if not always for thought, then for parasitical creatures intent on sucking out the last drops of blood of the author's lifeless corpse, either for inspiration or simply to enhance marketing. The aesthetic consequence is again unsurprising: most of these works are ironic, parodic or subversive to some extent, either mocking the high cultural position of their revived source material, or even more often making fun of themselves and their genre, the whole undead craze and the mindless fans who flock to see and feed on such entertainment. While several of the works discussed in Chapter 5 are low-budget, even amateur, productions, some of them painfully so, they all share this tongue-in-cheek attitude, which makes it easier to forgive them their intellectual shortcomings.

The postmodern biopic

The inclusion here of the literary biopic – films dramatising the biography of historical personalities, in this case, the historical William Shakespeare, supposed (or disputed) author of thirty-odd plays, several narrative poems and a substantial sonnet cycle – may at first sound somewhat at odds with the intentions of the rest of the volume. And yet, when we look at the Shakespeare-related films released since the late 1990s, it is hard to deny that the ones that left the deepest impression on the general viewing public have probably been *Shakespeare in Love* (1998, dir. John Madden) and *Anonymous* (2011, dir. Roland Emmerich): works that provide a cinematic retelling of the author's life. True, the reception of the two films by audiences was worlds apart, *Shakespeare in Love* being a commercial and popular success, while *Anonymous* hardly made up half of its production budget. Nonetheless, the public response to the stories has been much more significant than in the case of either adaptations of Shakespeare's history plays (similarly based on fictional versions of history) or many written accounts of Shakespeare's life. Moreover, most biographical films rely to some extent on the author's works, and Shakespeare biopics are no exception: they typically include references to one or more of the canonical works, effectively functioning as adaptations.

Such strong popular and critical reactions are in many ways connected to the controversial nature of the genre itself. The biopic has actually been a staple in traditional Hollywood filmmaking since the beginning of the twentieth century; Jeffrey Richards even calls it 'one of the earliest genres of feature films'.[47] But together with teen flicks and undead movies, it also returned to popular screens in the last decade of the twentieth century, even if these new iterations of the genre were extremely varied in terms of production budgets, artistic qualities and critical or popular successes. What they share is diversity: they often display other genres' influences, confirming that generic hybridity is a characteristic feature of contemporary filmmaking. Yet, despite its long history, the biopic's attention to artists in general and Shakespeare in particular has been uneven, to say the least. As Hila Shachar begins her account of the genre: 'Literary biographical films ... have become increasingly popular since the early 1990s. While literary biopics have always featured in cinematic history, it is only in recent times that they have boomed into a considerable cinematic trend.'[48] In a discussion of films about British artists in particular, Jim Leach argues how the Thatcherite era's low output of biopics may be connected to Prime Minister Thatcher's commonly known Victorian middle-class view of national identity, and the fact that her understanding of the great achievers of the nation – as represented by portraits on the walls of 10 Downing Street – did not include artists, 'not even Shakespeare'.[49]

The reasons for the newfound popularity of biopics since the 1990s may be manifold; apart from political changes, the cultural climate of postmodernism may also be partly responsible for this trend, which has clearly affected the way we approach the representation of the factual and the fictional, including an understanding of the embodiment of historical characters by actors. According to Dennis Bingham, 'It seems no accident that the biopic performance would reach a point of perfection in the postmodern period when the simulacrum, the synthesis, becomes the standard.'[50] This does not mean, of course, that all films discussed in the volume could be categorised as postmodern – some of them clearly resist that label, and all of them display a conservative tendency as regards linear biography and cause-and-effect relations in explaining how inspiration comes from the lived experience of the author. But some, notably *Shakespeare in Love*, can be described as postmodern on account of their stylistic irreverence, and can be classified with other postmodern biopics that 'utilize ideologies of western selfhood only to subvert them through a postmodern self-consciousness of the cultural specificity of identity construction'.[51] At the same time, the textual strategies and the cinematographic devices employed by the films discussed in Chapter 6 vary to a great degree, some clearly revelling in the subversive or playful qualities of postmodernism, but others remaining conservative in their attitude to biography and its cinematic retelling.

Apart from the increased interest of postmodernism in all things simulacrum, we can also observe a parallel phenomenon that may even be a consequence of the argument just proposed: a change in the critical esteem of the biopic as a genre. Throughout most of its considerable history, the biopic has been a target of criticism, rather than critical study, yet this scholarly neglect has been counteracted by a gossip-hungry popular interest in the private lives of the historical personalities depicted.[52] Whatever sparked audiences' curiosity, the fact remains that *Shakespeare in Love* surpassed the commercial success of any other Shakespeare-related film in the history of filmmaking, including Luhrmann's *William Shakespeare's Romeo + Juliet*, or even the animated *Gnomeo and Juliet*, directed by Kelly Asbury in 2011, which are the financially most successful Shakespeare adaptations to date.[53] (At the same time, none of the other biopics discussed in the volume have made it even close to their production budgets, some spectacularly failing to do so, which would at least qualify Deborah Cartmell's claim that 'the "presence" of Shakespeare, or rather Shakespeare as movie star, rather than Shakespearean content, seems to be what sells Shakespeare on screen'.[54] As it appears, Shakespeare's selling power also needs to be placed within the framework of an otherwise market-worthy film.)

There is, however, a curious contradiction between critical esteem and public recognition, since it is undeniable that 'the biopic is a proving ground'[55] for actors and 'a prestige genre, with films made in hopes of winning awards and earning respect'.[56] Joshua Clover adds to the biopic's shortcomings the notion that most films produced within the genre's frameworks are 'not biographies per se, but treatments that agree in advance on a conventional and banal understanding of psychological mechanism'.[57] This, of course, is often true, but that does not necessarily make the biopic an outstanding (or outstandingly poor) group within Hollywood filmmaking, since in American culture, everyday psychologising is the norm rather than the exception. This in turn perfectly fits into the structure of classical Hollywood cinema narrative, which equally appears to be structured on a strictly logical, mostly chronological and always psychologically motivated plotline. On the other hand, the sometimes over-psychologised nature of biographical fiction lends itself to self-parody, as in the famous scene in *Shakespeare in Love* when the author visits the quack shrink Dr Moth (Antony Sher), who quickly recognises – for a small fee – that young Will's writing block is related to his romantic disappointments and sexual failures, as good old Freudian analysis implies.

Clover is right, however, in observing that many of the biographical films are not biographies in a traditional sense of the word and offer no more than a superficial glimpse of the private, often intimate, aspects of famous lives. One of the new developments of the genre is that beside the historical figureheads of monarchy and empire, more recent, and possibly less widely known celebrities, have also been granted their own biopics. Jerome de Groot, in his discussion of written autobiographies and biographical writings, notes that in our culture, 'obsessed with contextualising and historicising the immediate rather than a broader contemplation of events', 'momentary significance is more important than any notion of wider importance'.[58] Even though this may not apply to the literary biopic, particularly that of canonical authors such as Shakespeare, it is still noteworthy how the success stories of long-dead authors and other historical personalities are often made to resemble celebrity (auto)biographies. They focus on the intimate and gossip-worthy elements, love lives and family dramas, the struggles of the small man – the underdog – against obstacles and inimical circumstances. At the same time, biopics rarely emphasise education and lifelong endurance, or other less spectacular forces that undoubtedly contribute to their protagonists' rise to fame. It is also no wonder that the majority of biopics prefer to focus on the young, pre-star personas, or on the ageing and failing body and mind, as *The Iron Lady* (2011, dir. Phyllida Lloyd), *Iris* (2001, dir. Richard Eyre), and Ben Elton's *All Is True* about the last years of Shakespeare (2018) – but rarely do they offer 'from-the-cradle-to-the-grave' accounts.

The celebrity aspect of biopics is tangible also in the way the genre attracts popular star actors to roles where the double fame of the personality depicted and their own star persona may easily result in blockbuster productions. However, the reason why the biopic is such a proving ground and therefore 'a magnet for well-known actors' is precisely why it also lends itself to criticism from disappointed viewers.[59] The central performance of the protagonist is based on the image of a historical personality, an image often commonly available and therefore comparable to the fictional representation. Particularly when a film handles the life of recent historical figures whose lives have been either well documented, or even publicly available in visual media, it invites similar criticism as adaptations of well-known textual sources do. Based on the same fidelity argument, there is a superficial level of comparison that most often finds expression in the phrase 'it wasn't like that in the book', or the complaint that the actor does not sufficiently resemble the real-life person.[60] While in literary adaptations, the introduction of new faces, creating previously unseen bodily representations to the canon of fictional character embodiments, may be seen as an actual advantage for new products, the case is quite the opposite in the biopic, where a certain amount of physical similarity between actor and character is often expected. (True, the inter-cinematic history of previous representations of fictional characters is also used as a touchstone against which new performances are measured, and earlier performances are often clearly alluded to, as in Branagh's open references to Laurence Olivier's iconic Shakespeare roles, but in such cases, physical similarity is not an expectation, rather a special treat for the initiate.)

In the biopic, the specific bodily reality – and audiences' familiarity with the public image – of the character to be represented creates serious restrictions on casting and performance as well, necessitating the suppression even of star personas for the sake of the adoption of the historical subject. At the same time, contemporary biopics often opt to discard the anxiety concerning what Jean-Louis Comolli in his seminal essay calls 'a body too much', that is, the remembered historical image and that of the actor, also commonly recognised.[61] In an almost subversive postmodern move, contemporary biopics often include either documentary footage or still images of the depicted historical person to contrast with the enacted version, or remind the viewer in other ways of the created, and therefore fictional, nature of the cinematic work. A slideshow of photographs during the end credits is, of course, not a way forward for the Shakespeare biopic, but the unashamed contrasting of commonly held views against new depictions characterises these films as much as any other work in the genre. At the same time, a desperate desire for bodily similarity may turn out to be even counterproductive in some cases. One of the reasons, I believe, why the two least successful films discussed in Chapter 6, *A Waste of Shame* (2005, dir. John McKay) and *All Is True*, left audiences dissatisfied was the fact that their respective Shakespeares (Rupert Graves and Kenneth Branagh) were made up to look more like the seventeenth-century portraits than the twenty-first-century actors. As a result, contemporary audiences may have found it hard to identify with, or care about, let alone fall in love with, these images of the Bard.

Because of the nature of the source material – if the film wants to sell itself as an account of a historical life, its creators are also expected to be aware of what is known of that life – the preparations for biopics may differ considerably from original screenplays. Bingham claims that 'the biopic involves research more obviously than does any other genre'[62] – but then what happens in the case of a life like William Shakespeare's, popularly known for its gaps and ellipses (but not for his particularly handsome visage)? The majority of Shakespeare biopics opt for the typical narrative solution of focusing on the 'rise to fame' part of the story, with a 'not-yet-famous' image of the artist, authenticated through an often hyper-realistic setting and references to well-known contemporary characters, most typically Queen Elizabeth,[63] often parodied in Shakespeare biopics, and fellow playwrights.[64] This strategy is characteristic of many recent literary biopics, which 'seek to recover and invent lost histories via a particular focus on gender and sexuality' – typically centralising the figure of the female muse of the author.[65] As Shachar explains, 'Most literary biopics are aware of their own fictionality and flaunt the fact that they have invented the "truth" through their process of recovering untold histories.'[66]

This somewhat off-focus presentation of the most famous name is also connected to another feature of the biopic, mentioned earlier: its generic hybridity. As is common practice, particularly since the post-war period, the biopic is often mixed with other genres, depending on the aspect of the historical life on which the filmmakers wish to focus. Bingham argues that as biopics denote 'drama rather than documentary, [they] almost inevitably overlap with other genres, which is one reason for the form's longtime lack of recognition as a genre in its own right'.[67] Thus the most important generic framework that informs *Shakespeare in Love* is the romantic comedy, but *Anonymous* works within the conventions of the thriller, while also intending to impress as a historical film. *Bill* (2015, dir. Richard Bracewell) aims at pure entertainment with the musical comedy genre, and openly takes itself less seriously, although it does not fully cut its ties with historical authenticity. It also displays an inclination for educational entertainment, directed at a younger audience, and however light-heartedly, it still endeavours to authenticate itself through association with historical facts.

Another interesting aspect to investigate in the biopic is the films' textual policies: while they may be based on printed or unpublished, factual or quasi-literary sources, from biographies through letters, memoirs and other archival material, they invariably rely on more or less recognisable quotations from the author whose life they depict. Such quotations (often in the form of pastiche or parody, as mentioned) also serve the purposes of authentication: by aligning the fictional figure on screen with the texts associated with a historical personality, the films achieve a level of realism. The quotations, however, need not be connected to each other in a way that narrative cohesion in a dramatic adaptation would necessitate. As we shall see in Chapter 6, Shakespeare biopics' use of such randomly arranged textual fragments aligns them with contemporary genre cinema, including teen and horror films' fragmented quotations, confirming that biopics are not an entirely different phenomenon from the films based on dramatic sources, and that they have a rightful place in this discussion of Shakespeare adaptations.

Notes

1 S. Crowl, *Shakespeare at the Cineplex: The Kenneth Branagh Era* (Athens: Ohio University Press, 2003), p. 1.
2 D. Lanier, 'Will of the People: Recent Shakespeare Film Parody and the Politics of Popularization', in Henderson (ed.), *A Concise Companion to Shakespeare on Screen*, pp. 176–96, p. 180.
3 Cf. F. Jameson, *Postmodernism, or, The Cultural Logic of Late Capitalism* (London and New York: Verso, 1991), esp. pp. 16–25.
4 *Ibid.*, p. 17.
5 W. W. Dixon, '"Fighting and Violence and Everything, That's Always Cool": Teen Films in the 1990s', in W. W. Dixon (ed.), *Film Genre 2000* (New York: State University of New York Press, 2000), pp. 125–41, p. 125.

6 M. Croteau, 'Kat and Bianca Avenged: Or, Things to Love about *10 Things I Hate About You*', in L. Wilson (ed.), *Americana: Readings in Popular Culture* (Los Angeles: Press Americana, 2006), pp. 65–9, pp. 65–6.
7 T. Doherty, *Teenagers and Teenpics: The Juvenilization of American Movies in the 1950s* (Philadelphia, PA: Temple University Press, rev. edn, 2002), p. 2.
8 T. Shary, 'Teen Films: The Cinematic Image of Youth', in Grant (ed.), *Film Genre Reader IV*, pp. 576–601, p. 578.
9 See e.g. two recent studies on the phenomenon: S. L. Beckett, *Crossover Fiction: Global and Historical Perspectives* (New York and London: Routledge, 2009); R. Falconer, *The Crossover Novel: Contemporary Children's Fiction and Its Adult Readership* (New York and London: Routledge, 2009).
10 Apart from Shakespeare's work, successful teen films have been inspired by G. B. Shaw's *Pygmalion*, Jane Austen's novels, Charles Dickens's *Great Expectations*, to name but a few.
11 Doherty, *Teenagers and Teenpics*, p. 196.
12 K. J. Wetmore Jr, 'Shakespeare and Teenagers', in M. T. Burnett, A. Streete and R. Wray (eds), *The Edinburgh Companion to Shakespeare and the Arts* (Edinburgh: Edinburgh University Press, 2011), pp. 377–87, p. 379.
13 R. S. White, 'Sex, Lies, Videotape – and Othello', in J. R. Keller and L. Stratyner (eds), *Almost Shakespeare: Reinventing His Works for Cinema and Television* (Jefferson, NC: McFarland & Company, 2004), pp. 86–98, p. 91.
14 Shary, 'Teen Films', pp. 581–2.
15 H. H. Davis, 'I Was a Teenage Classic: Literary Adaptation in Turn-of-the-Millennium Teen Films', *Journal of American Culture*, 29:1 (2006), 52–60, 59.
16 E. French, *Selling Shakespeare to Hollywood: The Marketing of Filmed Shakespeare Adaptations from 1989 into the New Millennium* (Hatfield: University of Hertfordshire Press, 2006), p. 101.
17 See e.g. R. Burt, *Unspeakable ShaXXXspeares* (New York: St. Martin's Press, 1998), esp. pp. 1–28; R. Green, 'Educating for Pleasure: The Textual Relations of *She's the Man*', in Brown, Lublin and McCulloch (eds), *Reinventing the Renaissance*, pp. 32–46, esp. p. 32; G. M. C. Semenza, 'Teens, Shakespeare, and the Dumbing Down Cliché: The Case of the Animated Tales', *Shakespeare Bulletin*, 26:2 (2008), 37–68.
18 A. Grant Ferguson, *Shakespeare, Cinema, Counter-Culture: Appropriation and Inversion* (New York and London: Routledge, 2016), p. xxv.
19 French, *Selling Shakespeare to Hollywood*, p. 115.
20 Burt, *Unspeakable ShaXXXspeares*, pp. 4–5.
21 Green, 'Educating for Pleasure', pp. 42–3.
22 Doherty, *Teenagers and Teenpics*, p. 190.
23 French, *Selling Shakespeare to Hollywood*, p. 110.
24 The film's original title was *Nosferatu, eine Symphonie des Grauens*, translated into English as *Nosferatu: A Symphony of Horror*, or simply *Nosferatu*.

25 M. Sutherland, 'Rigor/Mortis: The Industrial Life of Style in American Zombie Cinema', *Framework: The Journal of Cinema and Media*, 48:1 (2007), 64–78, 64.
26 O. Hakola, *Rhetoric of Modern Death in American Living Dead Films* (Bristol and Chicago, IL: Intellect, 2015), p. 9.
27 *Ibid.*
28 On the possible causes for the unprecedented popularity of zombies on both cinema and television screens, see e.g. L. Hubner, M. Leaning and P. Manning (eds), *The Zombie Renaissance in Popular Culture* (Basingstoke: Palgrave Macmillan, 2015).
29 Hutchings, 'Theatres of Blood', p. 155.
30 See e.g. S. Crowl, 'Flamboyant Realist: Kenneth Branagh', in Jackson (ed.), *The Cambridge Companion to Shakespeare on Film*, pp. 226–42.
31 Hutchings, 'Theatres of Blood', p. 156.
32 *Ibid.*, p. 165.
33 *Ibid.*, p. 166.
34 P. Manning, 'Zombies, Zomedies, Digital Fan Cultures and the Politics of Taste', in Hubner, Leaning and Manning (eds), *The Zombie Renaissance in Popular Culture*, pp. 160–73, p. 164.
35 J. McFarland, 'Philosophy of the Living Dead: At the Origin of the Zombie-Image', *Cultural Critique*, 90 (2015), 22–63, 22.
36 *Ibid.*, 59.
37 Manning, 'Zombies, Zomedies', p. 164.
38 C. Moraru, 'Zombie Pedagogy: Rigor Mortis and the U.S. Body Politic', *Studies in Popular Culture*, 34:2 (2012), 105–27, 114 (italics in original).
39 L. Bradley, '*Zombieland: Double Tap* Proves the Zombie Craze Will Never Die', *Vanity Fair* (16 October 2019), www.vanityfair.com/hollywood/2019/10/zombieland-double-tap-zombie-movies-trend-history (accessed 5 January 2020).
40 K. Bishop, 'Dead Man *Still* Walking: Explaining the Zombie Renaissance', *Journal of Popular Film and Television*, 37:1 (2009), 16–25, 17.
41 *Ibid.*, 24.
42 Doherty, *Teenagers and Teenpics*, p. 200.
43 *Ibid.*, p. 202.
44 Manning, 'Zombies, Zomedies', p. 163.
45 *Ibid.*, pp. 166–7.
46 S. Browning Erwin and C. Dickens, *Grave Expectations* (New York: Simon & Schuster, 2011); B. H. Winters, *Android Karenina* (Philadelphia, PA: Quirk Classics, 2010); S. Grahame-Smith and J. Austen, *Pride and Prejudice and Zombies* (Philadelphia, PA: Quirk Books, 2009).
47 J. Richards, 'Gender and Authority in the Queen Victoria Films', in H. B. Pettey and R. B. Palmer (eds), *Rule, Britannia! The Biopic and British National Identity* (Albany: State University of New York Press, 2018), pp. 67–84, p. 71.

48 H. Shachar, 'Authorial Histories: The Historical Film and the Literary Biopic', in R. A. Rosenstone and C. Parvulescu (eds), *A Companion to the Historical Film* (Chichester: John Wiley & Sons, 2003), pp. 199–218, p. 199.
49 J. Leach, 'A Matter of Life and Art: Artist Biopics in Post-Thatcher Britain', in Pettey and Palmer (eds), *Rule, Britannia!*, pp. 163–82, p. 164.
50 D. Bingham, 'Living Stories: Performance in the Contemporary Biopic', in Cornea (ed.), *Genre and Performance*, pp. 76–95, p. 78.
51 Shachar, 'Authorial Histories', p. 200.
52 See e.g. Neale, *Genre and Hollywood*, p. 54.
53 Based on available box-office data; see also R. Paterson, 'Box Office Poison?', *Shakespeare in Southern Africa*, 25:1 (2013), 13–29. It is true that a film's success can be measured in terms other than box-office takings, yet *Shakespeare in Love* proved remarkably successful in collecting Academy Awards and other acknowledgements as well.
54 D. Cartmell, 'Marketing Shakespeare Films: From Tragedy to Biopic', in D. Shellard and S. Keenan (eds), *Shakespeare's Cultural Capital: His Economic Impact from the Sixteenth to the Twenty-First Century* (Basingstoke: Palgrave Macmillan, 2016), pp. 57–76, p. 59.
55 Bingham, 'Living Stories', p. 78.
56 *Ibid.*, p. 77.
57 J. Clover, 'Based on Actual Events', *Film Quarterly*, 62:3 (2009), 8–9, 9.
58 J. de Groot, *Consuming History: Historians and Heritage in Contemporary Popular Culture* (London and New York: Routledge, 2009), p. 35.
59 Bingham, 'Living Stories', p. 78.
60 Cf. B. McFarlane, 'It Wasn't Like That in the Book', in J. M. Welsh and P. Lev (eds), *The Literature/Film Reader: Issues of Adaptation* (Lanham, MD: Scarecrow Press, 2007), pp. 3–14.
61 J.-L. Comolli, 'Historical Fiction: A Body Too Much', trans. B. Brewster, *Screen*, 19:2 (1978), 41–54.
62 Bingham, 'Living Stories', p. 77.
63 On the use of historical materials in biopics about Queen Elizabeth, cf. E. Stróbl, 'The Tilbury Speech and Queen Elizabeth: Iconic Moments of English History on Film', in É. Antal, Cs. Czeglédi and E. Krakkó (eds), *Contemporary Perspectives on Language, Culture and Identity in Anglo-American Contexts* (Newcastle upon Tyne: Cambridge Scholars Publishing, 2019), pp. 251–67.
64 See H. B. Pettey, 'Elizabeth I and the Life of Visual Culture', in Pettey and Palmer (eds), *Rule, Britannia!*, pp. 41–66, p. 62.
65 Shachar, 'Authorial Histories', p. 202.
66 *Ibid.*
67 D. Bingham, 'The Lives and Times of the Biopic', in Rosenstone and Parvulescu (eds), *A Companion to the Historical Film*, pp. 233–54, p. 247.

4

Back to school, Will: Shakespeare the teen idol

In the introduction to Part II of the book, we have seen the significant impact of youth culture on filmmaking through the increased economic independence and purchasing power of teenagers, particularly since the 1990s. As a result, the teen film can be seen as the flagship genre of the new cinematic boom, and of particular interest for this volume, as a number of popular Shakespeare-based films discussed here have outperformed major Shakespeare adaptations at the box office, which in itself is a noteworthy achievement.[1] On the other hand, the critical reception of these films has been uneven, mostly because the Shakespearean source material can easily disappear among the conventions of the high school subgenre of teen films. Yet, if we give the genre the benefit of the doubt, it is easy to notice how these conventions, which reinforce the films' generic identity, can be combined with Shakespeare's *oeuvre* in a variety of ways and use the popular genre's framework to turn teen viewers into Shakespeare fans.

The first films discussed are the obvious ones: *10 Things I Hate About You* (1999, dir. Gil Junger), *Never Been Kissed* (1999, dir. Raja Gosnell) and *She's the Man* (2006, dir. Andy Fickman). It is of course true that these films have received more than sufficient critical attention since they were released, but precisely for that reason they provide the best opportunity to establish the general features that characterise the whole group. These films are followed by a discussion of *O* (2001, dir. Tim Blake Nelson) and *Lost and Delirious* (2001, dir. Léa Pool), two films that represent the tragic side of teen social reality, in which romantic happiness is not allowed to overcome the obstacles posed by an oppressive, white supremacist or conservative patriarchal society.

As discussed in the introduction, the teen film is dominated (and often marketed) by its soundtrack at least as much as its narrative, but the final film discussed here places an even greater emphasis on the role of music. *Were the World Mine* (2008, dir. Tom Gustafson) borrows from the conventions of the high school musical subgenre, in which the Shakespearean material is not only used for a narrative template or as a topic for classroom discussion, but as a performance within the high school setting. The film's plot revolves around a performance of *A Midsummer Night's Dream*, but *Were the World Mine* is also a queer production, in which the homophobic world of a small town and its even smaller high school needs to be challenged to allow the happy ending of the comedy. Together with *Lost and Delirious*, these queer teen films exemplify the ways in which Shakespeare can be used to represent social conflicts and express personal desires that do not fit into the dominant heteronormative discourse of global film production.

With the inclusion of rather diverse variations on the teen film, from more straightforward adaptations like *10 Things* and *O* to less obvious reworkings, such as *Lost and Delirious*, we can also see how the decontextualised use of the literary source material can transform the genre qualities of the text, turning a comic source into a tragedy and vice versa.[2] Likewise, the same text can inspire tragic and comic teen adaptations as well, as Elizabeth Klett shows in her analysis of *She's the Man* and *Lost and Delirious*, both based on *Twelfth Night*.[3] It is no accident, however, that the more daring genre-bending films belong to the queer subgroup, which are typically more inclined to queer their source material in innovative ways.

The common core

As we can expect, the most important element of the genre's conventions is the age group of characters, but age in itself does not determine the genre, as clearly not all *Romeo and Juliet* adaptations are teen films, despite the protagonists' youth. Within the teen genre, this chapter will focus on the high school subgenre, and thus it will not include the arguably most famous example of Shakespeare teen pictures, Baz Luhrmann's iconic *William Shakespeare's Romeo + Juliet* (1996), even if the film's influence on the development of the genre is undeniable. As Emma French notes, although Luhrmann's film is often credited with launching the 1990s wave of teen Shakespeares, the rest of the group chose to follow different textual and marketing strategies. 'Subsequent teen film adaptations, appearing on the back of Luhrmann's success, display a much more cautious referencing of Shakespeare and a desire to market the films primarily as teen movies rather than Shakespeare adaptations.'[4] The best-known queer teen Shakespeare film, Alan Brown's *Private Romeo* (2011), is also absent from the discussion, mostly as an in-depth evaluation of its unique textual strategies would be beyond the scope of this chapter.[5]

The introduction has claimed that the central concern of the teen film, with its self-contained world of adolescence, poised between childhood and adulthood, is the expression of teen or young adult anxieties about identity and coming of age, including the discovery of sexual identities. The queer teen film as a subset of this genre is no different, with the exception that obstacles in the course of true love are often presented as more real and insurmountable than in the case of heterosexual teen romances, where social (or even micro-social) conflicts may raise obstacles, but the seriousness of these difficulties is rarely sustained. As Catherine Silverstone also notes, several critics have reproached mainstream teen Shakespeare films for their 'conservative feminist and heteronormative limits'.[6] Nonetheless, there are examples of teen films that employ Shakespeare in a queer context, often in classroom scenes where Shakespeare is used to empower queer characters in their quest for a non-heteronormative gender or sexual identity. Such empowerment, however, is rarely complete, and the two queer films included in the chapter, even if they follow radically different strategies in terms of their adaptation of the Shakespearean source material, appear to conform to many of the conventions of the mainstream (heteronormative) teen genre, and their optimism is confined to a fantastical, non-realistic layer of the narratives. Queer cinema typically involves more realistic and in-depth explorations of social issues, and often refuses to shy away from representing them as simply fictions that can be revised, rewritten, edited out as in a queer fantasy narrative. In *Were the World Mine*, the Shakespearean performance provides a solution and a cure to social ills and prejudices, as opposed to *Lost and Delirious*, where the Shakespearean element does not prove to have universal and miraculous healing power. In the latter, the pressures of patriarchal, heteronormative society destroy not only a queer relationship but also a queer character, although the film's final scene combines a realistic representation of a tragic outcome with a non-realistic metaphorical visualisation of the protagonist's legacy.

Trendsetters – *10 Things I Hate About You*

In the wake of earlier successful literary teen adaptations, primarily *Clueless* (1995, dir. Amy Heckerling), based on Jane Austen's *Emma*, and Luhrmann's in many ways subversive *Romeo + Juliet*, the more conventional high school version of the teen genre also opened its arms to Shakespearean adaptations. One of the first, and certainly one of the most influential, works in this combination was *10 Things I Hate About You*, Gil Junger's retelling of *The Taming of the Shrew*. Since the film is probably the best-known teen Shakespeare adaptation, critically evaluated to within an inch of its life, I will here focus on the genre itself, referring to the most important staple elements that are exemplified by this film, and some (or most) of the others mentioned in this chapter, but I will not provide a close reading of the film as a whole.

The central character in the film – Kat Stratford (Julia Stiles), the shrew figure – is a non-conformist, therefore socially (that is, romantically) isolated rebel, exemplifying a generic staple character. In Timothy Shary's analysis, 'Rebels are best defined by what they do not want to do – conform – but if they are to make it in school (or society) they must find some means of surviving with their adamant individuality intact, which necessitates the sophistication of their techniques.'[7] Kat's rebellion is similar in many details to that of Viola Hastings (Amanda Bynes) in *She's the Man*, as both are directed against what these girls perceive as 'archaic' and 'antiquated mating rituals': the debutante ball and the prom, respectively, and both characters resist the oppression of a society where a girl needs a heterosexual romantic partner to make her complete. But even the clumsy overage heroine of *Never Been Kissed*, Josie Geller (Drew Barrymore), enacts her own little post-teenage rebellion by going back to high school in order to hack the system, become popular and get a boyfriend – something that she would never be allowed to achieve in the normal course of events.

It is no accident that it is precisely the prom at which the rebel characters' anger is targeted – as Frances Smith argues, the prom is not simply a staple event in the genre; it is much more than a straightforward translation of the wedding scenes with which Shakespearean comedies often conclude. As she points out, 'the prom not only provides the central focus of these films, but also permeates the narratives throughout', mostly because the prom 'constitutes a privileged space of gender and class interpellation, respected even by those whose subcultural positioning would usually lead them to shun such an event'.[8] In *10 Things*, the centrality of the prom is noticeable from the first scene, in which Kat's arrival at Padua High shows her outrage against the whole tradition, and a very similar debate is included at the beginning of *She's the Man* concerning the debutante ball. The latter film, however, uses the ball as a more conservative finale, in which Viola's presence among the debutantes and on the arms of her newly acquired boyfriend (see figure 4.3) argues that it is possible for a contemporary teenager to achieve her goals and conform to social expectations of femininity, with the possible sacrifice of a few yards of gown material. (This is not without significance, of course, as the traditional full-bottomed dresses still used in such coming-of-age rituals have their origins in an emphasis on female fertility, and as such, show the young females' readiness for marriage and subsequent motherhood.)

In *10 Things*, however, the prom is only a partial success – the more stereotypical couple, Bianca (Larisa Oleynik) and Cameron (Joseph Gordon-Levitt) cement their relationship here, but Kat and Patrick (Heath Ledger) do not. In a possible wink at the 1980s great trendsetters in the teen genre, particularly *Pretty in Pink* (1986, dir. Howard Deutsch), the rebel couple's romantic conclusion happens in the school car park, outside the institutional walls and boundaries, on their own terms (see figure 4.1). Like the protagonists in *Pretty in Pink*, Kat and Patrick's 'relationship is seen to flourish only in … non-places',[9] although the fact that it is broad daylight and a bustling crowd of teenagers surrounds the kissing couple at the end of *10 Things* suggests an open and public acknowledgement of their submission to heterosexual dating rituals.

The textual policy of *10 Things* is again typical of the genre as a whole, which tends to confine direct quotes to classroom scenes, or otherwise

Figure 4.1 Rebel love in the parking lot – Heath Ledger and Julia Stiles in *10 Things I Hate About You*. Directed by Gil Junger, 1999. Touchstone Pictures/Mad Chance/Jaret Entertainment.

distinguishes them from the everyday teen vernacular of the script. Written by Karen McCullah Lutz and Kirsten Smith, *10 Things* includes one single line of the original Shakespearean dialogue ('I burn, I pine, I perish', 1.1.155[10]) to signal Cameron's love at first sight, although there is another brief exchange from *Macbeth* between the nerd character Michael (David Krumholtz) and Mandella (Susan May Pratt), completely twisted out of context, as L. Monique Pittman points out.[11] Shakespeare as a source for these quotes is not even identified in the film, and when a school assignment asks for an adaptation of Shakespeare's Sonnet 141, Kat's poem is both a nod to the authorial status of Shakespeare and a freely adapted version of Katherine's much debated submission speech from *The Taming of the Shrew*. Another standard textual joke that we can find in the film is the 'faux-Shakespearean'[12] phrase uttered by Michael, who is at that point dressed as Shakespeare: 'The shit hath hitteth the fan-eth', illustrating the fake 'antiquated language' which is a significant element in the adaptation (and marketing) politics of the film and the genre as a whole.[13] French convincingly shows how 'The film's marketing exploits the film's "girl power" message and its relationship to other teen films far more than its status as a Shakespeare adaptation.'[14]

Crucial to all teen films are figures of authority, mostly parents and teachers, but as already mentioned in the introduction, the post-1990s teen film assigns no real authority to any adult character, but reveals their lack of control, often turning them into targets of ridicule. This is the treatment that befalls the father of the Stratford girls (Larry Miller), an overworked gynaecologist who is clearly light years behind the times when it comes to the rules of dating, sexual education and parent–child relationships in general. Parental authority in teen films is typically restrictive, but it is also a means of manifesting 'the natural liminality of adolescent home life, one in which the individual is both materially and emotionally dependent upon parents, but also resentful of the restrictions that accompany such dependence'.[15]

Ms Perky (Allison Janney), the school's guidance counsellor, with her forced wit and her writer's career apparently built on sexual wishful thinking, can only represent a caricature of power. Again, Steve Bailey and James Hay observe that in many teen films 'the teachers are often comically irrelevant figures, blustering pointlessly in the face of indifferent students or … being secretly manipulated by them'.[16] The other representative of (intellectual) authority is Mr Morgan (Daryl Mitchell), the English teacher, who is also a failure at sorting out teenage emotional and intellectual dilemmas and distinguishing between real and fake attitudes of rebellion and obedience. In one respect, he is the only authentic figure, though: his being African-American puts all student rebellions into perspective, as he reminds Kat as well that it is not only females that are absent from the curriculum, but all non-white male authors in general. His rapping Shakespeare's Sonnet 141, and his comments on the text (about Shakespeare knowing 'his shit'), also make it clear that being streetwise does not hinder him from appreciating greatness when he sees it.

As a result, Kat's submission speech, even though it is performed at school, in the form of a school assignment for the English class, is not directed at these fake sources of authority, but is an open acknowledgement of what is really at stake: being in love. But in a somewhat unexpected gesture, Gil Junger's film returns the authority to Shakespeare, whose canonical status is instrumental in achieving the romantic conclusion of the plot. This type of meta-reference is quite common in teen adaptations, where the school environment allows filmmakers to directly reflect on the status of literature and Shakespeare in particular, sometimes contrasting performative and textual media and their abilities to involve or even inspire teenagers. Thus, while *10 Things* includes a rewriting assignment, the plot of *Were the World Mine* revolves around a school performance of *A Midsummer Night's Dream* and in *Never Been Kissed* 'the class reads *As You Like It*, and Josie and Michael Vartan (Sam Coulson), her English teacher, connect through the text'.[17] Interestingly, the Shakespearean texts invoked in these classroom scenes are often not identical with the source text of the film (*10 Things* uses the *Sonnets*, in *O*, the teacher quotes from *Macbeth*, and asks her students about Shakespeare's poems; in *Lost and Delirious*, the classroom analysis focuses on *Antony and Cleopatra* and *Macbeth*, rather than *Twelfth Night*, the primary narrative source for the film). The teen film thus evokes or questions Shakespeare as a general authority, rather than a specific point of origin or textual reference.

Another characteristic feature that is typically determined by the target audience is the films' soundtrack. In *10 Things* the particular choice of musical performers, both intra- and extra-diegetic, provide an essential part of the setting, not simply as atmospheric background, but also offering thematic relevance through song lyrics and socio-cultural information through the easily recognisable performers' ideological positions. On a broader level, the amount of music, particularly the number of intra-diegetic musical performances in themselves, signifies an essential key to identifying the film as a representative of the teen genre – yet musical hits are often the first elements to seem out of date within a few years of the film's release. More particularly, however, critics have often pointed out how the soundtrack is also a powerful tool in positioning Kat within society, signifying her movement from Riot Grrrl towards a representative of Girl Power by the end of the film.[18] This status in turn is tied in with discussions on the type of feminism and neoliberalism, and the conservative or empowering attitudes, that the protagonists, mostly Kat, embody.

Pittman's discussion of student responses to *The Taming of the Shrew* and *10 Things I Hate About You* is particularly telling in this regard. She notes that 'rather than renovate Shakespeare's play with updated and enlightened notions of self and gender, *10 Things* silences questions on both topics and assigns agency in the most traditional of ways – to the young men determining their destiny and coming of age'.[19] While these conservative aspects are undoubtedly there, I would disagree with Pittman's suggestion that as a result 'the film fails to achieve the status of its Renaissance source'[20] – what I see in the responses of Pittman's students and other uncritical comments is a confirmation of the power of the adapting genre. The high school romance in particular is characteristically a vehicle that celebrates heterosexual relationships, presenting them as the ultimate (or the only) way to achieve personal happiness and social success as well; therefore, a mainstream film adopting the genre's conventions is unlikely to question such norms. As we will see later in the chapter, even queer teen films maintain and reflect on heterosexual romance as the ultimate (if not the only) realistic path to happiness.

Sexuality, however, particularly casual sex, has no place in the genre, and that is why the two teenage female protagonists of *10 Things* appear sexually just as inactive as Josie Geller in *Never Been Kissed* or Viola Hastings in *She's the Man*. The film's mild displays of nudity are also denied to the viewer (in a similar vein to Viola's and Sebastian's flashes to prove their genders in *She's the Man*), and no character who prefers casual sex to true love is held in high regard by the end of the narrative. The issue of young adult sexuality, its role in defining position within the high school society and the educational message of the genre encouraging chastity is fully explored in *Never Been Kissed*, to be discussed next.

Back to high school, back to Shakespeare – *Never Been Kissed*

Never Been Kissed, a teen film (very) loosely based on *As You Like It*, made it to the cinemas in the same year, hardly more than a week later, as *10 Things I Hate About You*, and achieved even greater box-office success. Indeed, in 14th position, *Never Been Kissed* is ranked as the financially most successful Shakespeare adaptation in the 'high school comedy' genre to date, ahead of *10 Things* (ranked 23rd) – but preceded by *She's All That* (1999, dir. Robert Iscove), based on G. B. Shaw's *Pygmalion*, and *Clueless* (1995, dir. Amy Heckerling), the trendsetter teen version of Jane Austen's *Emma*.[21] It is hard to say whether the success of any of these films depended on their 'tried and trusted'[22] source material, that is, literary originals whose cultural status can be expected to draw a considerable audience and therefore guarantee financial success, or, on the contrary, their conscious lack of references to such textual authority. At the same time, these examples provide ample proof that the strategy of reworking a few, often superficial, elements of literary classics in the teen genre, without explicit textual references to the source texts, seems to be financially lucrative. The success of *Never Been Kissed*, at least according to Brandon Gray, is mainly attributed to Drew Barrymore, whose 'rising star power' allowed the film 'to overcome very poor timing, coming out after a glut of teen pictures, and a mediocre advertising campaign'.[23]

The star power at work here does not emanate from Shakespeare, but from the female lead, an actress already better known than Julia Stiles of *10 Things* or Amanda Bynes of *She's All That*, and not even the plot summary implies that Shakespeare plays any significant role in the whole enterprise. The protagonist of *Never Been Kissed*, Josie Geller, copyeditor for the *Chicago Sun Times*, is put on an assignment to go back to high school as an undercover journalist and write about teenagers' life, but she is mostly expected to present an angle that would make her experiences newsworthy, preferably full of juicy scandals. In the course of her assignment, she has to relive her rather traumatic memories of her own high school years, when she was continually mocked and tormented for her nerdiness. Eventually, with the help of her brother, she is accepted by the in-crowd, and even gets elected as prom queen (see figure 4.2). She also falls in love with her English teacher, and eventually, after her disguise has been lifted and her article published, the two are able to find happiness together.

The single plot device that may link *Never Been Kissed* to Shakespeare's *As You Like It* is the element of disguise, but quotations from the play appear only within the confines of the English classroom, where Josie is happy to show off her general knowledge and extensive vocabulary. As usual, it is no particular familiarity with Shakespeare that the classroom scenes illustrate; they emphasise instead Josie's literacy and maturity, especially when contrasted with others in her class. The English classes are more significant for showing the development of the romantic story – a growing attraction between Josie and her English teacher, Sam Coulson – than as

Figure 4.2 High school happiness – Jordan Ladd, Drew Barrymore, Michael Vartan and Martha Hackett in *Never Been Kissed*. Directed by Raja Gosnell, 1999. Fox 2000 Pictures/Flower Films/Bushwood Pictures/Twentieth Century Fox.

a key to the dramatic source text. Coulson's trust in Josie's writing skills, and his subsequent disappointment at finding out her real identity, are vital in catalysing her skills into writing a moving personal story about her own journey of self-discovery, turning her into a real journalist at last.

Here, as in all other teen films, as indicated in the introduction to Part II, Shakespeare is used to encourage identification and a search for one's true identity, rather than the film providing a complex interpretation of the drama. The main topic of discussion in Coulson's classes is the liberating power of disguise, but this does not lead to an in-depth analysis of the Shakespearean text, which does not even feature in the actual dialogue of the film outside the classroom. The single Shakespeare line (used outside the school) is from *The Merchant of Venice*, which Josie quotes on the night of the prom: 'look how the floor of heaven / Is thick inlaid with patens of bright gold' (5.1.58–9).[24] The excised plot retains only what is vital for the teen film: high school life, with student cliques, friendship and enmity, romance and the prom, but finding deeper parallels is mostly based on speculation. Still, the two opposing worlds of *As You Like It* are retained, together with the journey as a rite of passage, but rather than a contrast between the inhuman world of the court and the liberating green world, Josie's real acceptance in the adult (urban) world comes only after her understanding and surviving the adolescent (suburban) world. As Bailey and Hay argue, her success 'is the result of a careful mastery of the critical knowledge associated with youth culture: navigating the social structure of the high school, appropriate taste in music, clothing and cars, and dealing with adult authorities'.[25] Josie's desperate attempts at finding the appropriate car and clothing style, and most of all, friends, play a vital role in signalling her transformation, and are typical elements in the teen genre, without Shakespearean overtones. Even the hangout of 'cool' students, the so-called Court, which may resemble the scene of exile of Duke Senior in the Forest of Arden, is less significant as a Shakespearean reference, and more as a staple item of teen films, representing 'the social stratification into distinct and heavily marked cliques'.[26] Josie's real experience of growing up is signalled by her final refusal to be intimidated by adolescent society, wisdom achieved through her painful experiences in disguise.

But possibly just as significant are the film's other intertextual references, not to Shakespeare, but iconic works in the teen genre itself. Josie's brother, Rob appears at the prom dressed in a white shirt and his underwear, identifying his costume as Tom Cruise's iconic image from *Risky Business* (1983, dir. Paul Brickman). *Risky Business*, a near-cult viewing experience of a slightly older generation (to which Rob himself belongs), shares some of the concerns of *Never Been Kissed*: the 'distinctly affluent suburban settings', the contrasting world of the city (in both cases Chicago, a 'space of both liberation and menace'), and the effect of this on the protagonist's self-development.[27]

Cross-dressing is entirely absent from the text (even at the prom, although Hugh H. Davis refers to a scene of cross-dressing, claiming that 'Josie, in a metacinematic moment, attends dressed as Ganymede from the source material for this film',[28] Josie explicitly states she is Rosalind and is dressed accordingly). Yet one aspect of high school reality may be connected to the restrictive, rather than liberating, power of the disguise; as Douglas Lanier also remarks: 'like Rosalind, Josie finds that her disguise is also an impediment to romance'.[29] Just as in *As You Like It* Rosalind's male disguise prevents her from being united with her lover, here Josie's position as a student places just as much of an insurmountable obstacle between her and her teacher, who is fully aware of the immoral, even illegal, nature of a student–teacher relationship. Yet the barrier must be maintained as long as the job lasts, and Josie is hardly in the position to come clean about her real identity, since this relationship is the most marketable part of her experience, a scandalous idea that her journalist colleagues would be happy to exploit for a juicy story.

When searching for the deeper or more complex thematic elements of teen films, one must remember that the single most important narrative drive in the genre is the desire of the (mostly female) protagonist to enter into a romantic relationship. As Ariane M. Balizet quotes Thomas Leitch, teen films' structure reflects 'the pattern of teenaged subjects overcoming financial, parental, or institutional obstacles to reach their ultimate goal: each other'.[30] This film's title – *Never Been Kissed* – emphasises this desire by defining its protagonist as one who has not had any meaningful heterosexual relationship so far, a situation that needs to be remedied as soon as possible. Therefore, it is just as much a belated coming-of-age story as so many other films in the genre, where the central plot revolves around losing one's virginity or at least acquiring a partner for the prom, both of which are meaningful in the context as forms of finding one's status and identity. As usual, the film does not address any real class issues – none of the characters appear to suffer from a lack of financial resources, as the whole school is populated by affluent upper-middle-class students, and the marginalisation of certain characters, especially Aldys (Leelee Sobieski), is the result of their nerdy behaviour and style, rather than poverty.

The three central settings of high school films all make an appearance in the film: the school as the central location, including scenes in the cafeteria and at the lockers, but also the suburban home and the shopping mall. The latter becomes a place of transformation, where Josie's official acceptance takes place, when, in a reverse makeover, the most popular girls at school begin to imitate her style. Bailey and Hay argue that the school in *Never Been Kissed*, as in a number of other teen films, functions 'as a kind of sociological microcosm of a wider society' and 'acts as a space in which power dynamics evident in larger social formations – which usually involve bullying, snobbery, humiliation and other forms of social domination – are played out on a more modest scale'.[31] The parallel between wider society and the school is made explicit in the prom scene, when Josie throws away her crown and reveals her real identity. Yet although she argues that school dramas are insignificant when compared to real life, the film itself implies the opposite. It is the psychological injuries acquired during her school years that have prevented her from reaching full adult status, and it is only her finding – and losing – a romantic partner that helps her to overcome the traumas that apparently hurt no less now than the first time. Yet Bailey and Hay are right in their implication that the 'unofficial' knowledge acquired in the school environment proves to be more beneficial and essential in solving real-life problems than any academic achievement. As the most telling example, Josie's brother has no outstanding intellectual skills (at the age of twenty-three, he has the reading skills of a fifteen-year-old), and his character puts into question Josie's whole quest for acceptance. Not even the film's exaggerated representation of Josie's weirdness and Rob's ability to speak the language of the crowd hides the fact that Rob is stuck on a level of development that makes him the real loser anywhere outside the artificial society of the school.

The most important symbol of freedom, the car, also gets a central role – it is partly a status symbol, partly a means of mobility (sometimes escape). The teen film often assigns meaning to vehicles, not simply through characters' ownership (or lack thereof), but also the particular make, even year, which all contribute to the definition of one's social position, referencing wealth, style, individuality. As Jack DeWitt claims in his reading of *American Graffiti*: 'Each car is an extension of its driver that reveals key aspects of character – because in teen culture you are what you drive.'[32] While the boarding school settings in *She's the Man*, *Lost and Delirious* and even *O*, to a certain extent, emphasise the closed, even isolated, settings, and teenagers' dependence on adults or peers with a special status for their mobility, the vehicles in *10 Things*, as in *Never Been Kissed*, certainly emphasise the role of cars in defining personality. That is why the latter film spends so much screen time with car issues, and why Josie needs to swap cars with her brother Rob, as her conservative grey Buick would give away her identity before she could set foot in the school building. Her car gets the same treatment as her – mockery and ridicule – before she is accepted by the in-crowd, and even though the car is relatively marginal in this film, it is also suggestive of the ways one can be defined as cool.

The choice of classroom scenes is also telling: although gymnastics or sports play practically no role in the film, sports classes are a common sight, as ever. It would seem that even in films in which the protagonist is not engaged in any serious sports activity, unlike the footballer heroine of *She's the Man* or the basketball players in *Were the World Mine*, sports can offer an easily recognisable field of humiliation and physical suffering. But even when the protagonist is not such an incapable, clumsy non-athlete as Josie Geller, gym scenes abound with typical slapstick-style freak accidents and minor disasters, either suffered or initiated by the central characters. Eventually, the battlefield of the stadium is, almost without exception, used as a contrast, either with the deeper emotional levels of art and Shakespeare in particular (the latter being always superior), or with the true aim of the teen film – finding one's own true self. As we shall see next, even Viola in *She's the Man*, whose true identity requires her prowess on the football field, needs to learn to get back to her 'woman's weeds' (5.1.271) to achieve true happiness, in the form of heterosexual romance.[33]

Not afraid of Shakespeare – *She's the Man*

Andy Fickman's 2006 teen adaptation of *Twelfth Night* employs strategies that are closer to Junger's *10 Things* than to *Never Been Kissed*, both in its acknowledgement of the source text and its treatment of plot and character relationships. (This may come as no surprise, seeing that McCullah Lutz and Smith wrote the screenplay of both *10 Things* and *She's the Man*, in the latter case together with Ewan Leslie, who gets credited for the creation of the story.) Although there is no clear reference to the dramatic source in the title, the movie poster and the DVD cover include the following line at the bottom: 'inspired by the play *Twelfth Night* by William Shakespeare'. The rest of the marketing campaign, however, including 'the preview and the website before the film's release, the opening credits in the film itself, and the film's DVD materials all tout the Shakespearean inspiration', in Laurie E. Osborne's view possibly building on the earlier success of *10 Things I Hate About You*.[34] The DVD also includes a bonus track with the title 'Inspired by Shakespeare ...', and therefore it appears that filmmakers were less cautious than with their earlier enterprise and had already added the references to Shakespeare's authority at the time of the film's first release. As Osborne shows, 'the insistent promotion of *She's the Man* as a Shakespeare-inspired version of *Twelfth Night* clearly registered with viewers' (even if the association did not necessarily win their appreciation), and after the established popularity of the film, the filmmakers were ready to confirm this success by emphasising the classical reference even more on the DVD marketing materials.'[35]

While this is undoubtedly true, it is also significant that Shakespeare is not the most important association used as a selling point, but the teen film again. The DVD cover places the film in its generic context with '*Mean Girls* gets a classic twist!' *Mean Girls* (2004, dir. Mark Waters) did spectacularly well at the box office and even collected a number of awards along the way. Yet the semantic ambiguity of the word 'classic' is not dispelled in a way that would tell us whether the classic twist is Shakespearean, and therefore 'of the highest quality and outstanding', or simply something 'very typical of its kind'.[36] In her analysis, Osborne shows how the echoes of *As You Like It* in *Just One of the Guys*, *Motocrossed* and *She's the Man* similarly complicate the films' relationships to their Shakespearean source texts, while underscoring the significance of previous teen films, in actual fact ones the filmmakers' generation may have grown up on. Several reviewers note the similarity between *She's the Man* and *Just One of the Guys*, which Osborne argues even gained in popularity retrospectively after the release of *She's the Man*, while its 'unacknowledged debt' to Shakespeare, previously unremarked by reviewers, became visible after '*She's the Man* insisted on its own Shakespearean origins'.[37]

Another film in the teen genre that clearly informs *She's the Man* is *Bend It Like Beckham* (2002, dir. Gurinder Chadha), similarly a high school romantic comedy with a sports angle, where girls have to defy social traditions, particularly traditional gender roles, to have their talent on the football pitch acknowledged. As Reina Green emphasises, 'Both these films also targeted the same young audience, and while this audience may have been unaware of these intertextual connections, they demonstrate how teen Shakespeare films do not simply draw on Shakespeare's plays and prior adaptations, but on other contemporary teen films in many different genres.'[38] Both films, however, like the majority of films in the genre, focus more on the adolescent female heroine's search for her own identity, in which a balance between traditional female roles, as demanded both by the family and broader society, and non-typical talents and aspirations is eventually found. The journey to self-acceptance characteristically takes the heroine through a denial of her own interest in femininity (mostly expressed in dress choices) and romantic relationships (dumping the unsympathetic male or avoiding dating occasions). But the final success is always a double one: an official recognition of (sporting or other professional) talents and the acquisition of the most desirable romantic partner from the cast (see figure 4.3). The bottom line is therefore very much the same as even that in *Never Been Kissed*: finding professional success must always be accompanied by learning to dress and behave appropriately, and the reward will be happiness in (strictly heterosexual) love.

In *She's the Man*, the patriarchal (or at least male-oriented) rules are introduced right at the beginning: the main conflict is not a loss of home or security, as for Viola in *Twelfth Night*, but the cutting of the girls' football team by the school. Yet in one sense Viola's decision to don male disguise and try to make it in the world of boys puts her in a similar position to Shakespeare's heroine, since both of them have an opportunity (and the necessity) to carve out a new identity for themselves. Their male disguise soon becomes a source of confusion and a hindrance to both girls' happiness, yet the gender-based obstacles make the society depicted in the film more explicitly backward than Shakespeare's, where girls are not denied their social position or even choice of bride. In *She's the Man*, however, the narrative conflict is expressed partly through a number of stereotypical prejudices about girls being weaker, slower, effectively poorer players on the football field. Viola, although not forced to leave her school, wants to

Figure 4.3 Success in both roles – Channing Tatum and Amanda Bynes in *She's the Man*. Directed by Andy Fickman, 2006. DreamWorks/Lakeshore Entertainment/Donners' Company.

prove herself on the pitch and therefore takes her brother's place in the rival boarding school, Illyria High, and its football team. The final showdown between the two teams also sets the two coaches in opposition to each other, and here the more aggressive, definitely more masculine Illyrian coach (Vinnie Jones) turns out to have the more enlightened attitude – or the more pragmatic one, realising that Viola's talent can help them win the game – when he asserts that they do not 'discriminate based on gender' and allows Viola to remain a member of his team.

The film shows a society with extremely conservative gender roles, but since we mostly observe this from the viewpoint of adolescent females it is obvious that there is no attempt to provide a complete exploration of gender positions. The set of twins at the centre of the narrative, even though including one male and one female teenager, are not given equal screen time, with the narrative foregrounding female identity, as is usual in Shakespeare teen films – and, in this case, following the dramatic source. Richard Burt finds the genre's focus in what he calls '"lesbosocial" relations: a girl and often a group of girls occupy the film's romantic center, with the heroine poised between bad girls who are sexually active (sluts) and good girls who are (naive) virgins'.[39] This is undoubtable, although I believe the expression 'lesbosocial' implies a self-contained female group, where defining relationships are among females, whereas here the primary aspiration of practically all females (and certainly all teen Shakespeare protagonists) is to be partnered in a successful heterosexual romantic relationship.

In *She's the Man*, Viola's twin brother Sebastian (James Kirk) is established as one who is uncritical of social traditions, even when they are unpleasant or do not make sense to him (including dating a girl just because she is hot, although she is also awful – simply because 'It's a guy thing'). At the same time, he is also effeminised by his lack of athletic ability and particularly by his choice of music over football, although his identity as a musician is established through gendered visual signs as well. When we first see him, he is wearing a T-shirt with the image of the single 'Gone Daddy Gone' from the 1983 debut album of folk punk band Violent Femmes, a group composed of three men, although their name would also fit a Riot Grrrl-type of feminist self-representation. The song may carry a number of associations, primarily as a reference to Sebastian's farewell, since this is the T-shirt he is wearing as he is climbing out of his window to escape to London. Yet the song's lyrics also include lines such as 'Beautiful girl, lovely dress / High school smiles, oh yes / Beautiful girl, lovely dress / Where she is now I can only guess', which firmly situate the conflict within the high school subgenre of teen films.[40] The lyrics also point out the problematic aspect of clothing and appearances with which particularly Viola, but to some extent even Sebastian, struggle, and the text effectively foreshadows the disappearance of both twins from the closely controlled society of boarding schools and country clubs into which they find it equally hard to fit.

But as Paul (Jonathan Sadowski), Viola's gay hairdresser friend reminds her: 'Inside every girl, there's a boy', which is not a reference to Viola's potential intersex or transgender features, but, in the context of *She's the Man*, it implies that what is at stake here is a revolutionary sense of gender equality. What the narrative sets out to prove is the notion that girls are better than boys at everything, even being a boy. Viola's influence at Illyria High includes convincing her teammates to use tampons to stop nosebleeds and to imitate her (spectacularly feminine) victory dance on the pitch; she also gets Duke (Channing Tatum) to admit that he is sensitive and feels protective towards girls, respecting them more than is fashionable. It appears also that this type of feminine behaviour is necessary for boys to achieve masculine maturity (making them desirable romantic partners). Not only does Viola fall for Duke when she discovers that he has feelings, but Olivia's crush on (Viola dressed up as) Sebastian is also explained by 'him' being 'not the goonish handsome' but 'he is delicate, ... even refined handsome'. At the same time, the conservative gender aspect is not entirely absent from the narrative, as Viola is dependent on Duke's help to improve her performance and make it to the first string of the football team. Yet there are more uncertain masculinities on display: Justin (Robert Hoffman), the bad guy (Viola's ex-boyfriend) cannot tolerate defeat and throws a hysterical temper tantrum, an obvious sign of his lack of manliness, and so justifies Viola's choice of Duke over him.

It appears therefore that the film does not wish to offer a more contemporary, or post-feminist, approach, even if that would be possible in twenty-first-century high school society, but is satisfied with radical feminist fights, declaring legal and physical equality – allowing girls to play football without debating the predominantly binary gender positions. But, as Klett also argues, 'She's the Man deliberately eschews homoerotic readings of the Olivia/Viola and the Viola/Duke relationships',[41] and whenever there is 'the least suggestion of homoeroticism' between two male characters, 'their mutual response is revulsion and fear'.[42] True, there are several gay characters in the film, but Paul, the hair stylist, is the gay best friend, an honorary girl, his sensitivity making him the perfect coach for Viola's transformation – although Paul's less than convincing male sensibilities may also be the reason for the limitations of Viola's performance as a male. The headmaster of the school, however, is simply a ridiculous effeminate man who refuses to come out of his own closet, whose inability to accept his own identity also signals his cluelessness as an authority figure.

Furthermore, the film does not get involved in intricacies of Shakespearean interpretation, either the questions of identity represented by Viola's fictive male persona Cesario (in *She's the Man* she pretends to stand in for an actual male, her own brother, although it is true that she does not learn to be a man from Sebastian, but from other, randomly picked, males) or the potential homosexuality between Antonio and Sebastian. The shadow of mourning is also absent, clearly in line with the teen comedy's more light-hearted conventions, and therefore Viola's general good cheer is only threatened by her anger over male injustice on the football pitch. Olivia's recent bad breakup leaves no visible signs to anyone apart from Viola (certainly not to the camera), therefore the plausibility, let alone relevance, of this grief is rather limited.

The film's Shakespearean references, however, are explicit – as the way they are used in *10 Things* – in the names of most characters. The cast names include Viola, Sebastian, Olivia, Duke Orsino, and a tarantula called Malvolio, owned by the actual Malvolio figure, named Malcolm Festes ('the only reference to Feste the clown in the film').[43] Duke's friends are called Toby and Andrew, Olivia's friend is Maria, and Malcolm is even seen wearing yellow socks, recalling Malvolio's infamous yellow stockings and cross-garters from *Twelfth Night*. Like the added identifiers of Shakespeare-related material, the debutante/country club is called Stratford Junior League and the rival schools are called Cornwall and Illyria, the latter recalling the exotic location of Shakespeare's play, although both in *Twelfth Night* and in the film the name is 'more mythical than geopolitical, and its best-known associations ... intertextual rather than international'.[44]

Just like *10 Things* or *Never Been Kissed*, the dialogue of *She's the Man* includes a single recognisable quotation. Here it is the best-known sentence from the drama, heard at the final game, when all disguises have been shed and Duke is willing to give Viola a chance to prove herself (since she admits that 'I just wanted to prove that I am good enough'). As captain of the team (and betrayed friend), Duke is expected to give his assent to Viola's participation in the second half of the game, which he does by saying: 'Some are born great, some achieve greatness, and some have greatness thrust upon them' (2.5.145–6). The moment is extremely cheesy and the quotation just as decontextualised as the lines used in the other teen films, without any of the mockery infusing Maria's letter to Malvolio. The film's Duke even feels it necessary to add an explanation by saying that what he means is their best chance of winning is with Viola on the team. The function of the quotation is therefore simply to signify the 'classic twist', the Shakespearean lineage, and it exemplifies contemporary tendencies of textual poaching, the random lifting of quotes from their contexts for the sake of a superficial association, here given by the keyword 'greatness' rather than anything else.

The final scene, standing in for the double marriage rites of Shakespearean comedy, is a bona fide ball in *She's the Man*, the debutantes' event in the country club, again reinforcing the genre's focus on affluent upper-middle-class society. Yet this scene does not stand by itself, as Pittman observes: 'Rather than a dual wedding, the film builds toward dual communal events – the match between Cornwall and Illyria and the Stratford Junior League Debutante Ball.'[45] Since success as a debutante is not what Viola was primarily striving for, her appearance at the ball on the arm of Duke (see figure 4.3) only signals that her successful assertion of her own identity makes her capable of performing both a male-assigned role on the football team and a traditionally female role as the virginal beauty. As the film's main narrative drive is her proving herself as a football player, the more important event is the final game. At the same time, as Pittman argues, the film consistently presents Viola in a way that 'confirms for viewers that Viola is not opposed to girliness in general, just to her mother's bizarrely 1950s notion of the feminine and the home' or her ex-boyfriend's repressive ideas of how girls are supposed to behave.[46] Pittman also refers to the way Bynes (or Viola/Sebastian) slips in and out of character and gender performance, arguing that 'because these slips of the tongue and flicks of the wrist so consistently happen in moments where Viola expresses emotion that the film registers as genuine through an often sentimentalized score, the preoccupation remains to present a core self for Viola rather than pursue gender identity as an improvised performance'.[47]

Tragedy on the court – O

Tim Blake Nelson's 2001 film is a clear example that youth films not only address the most light-hearted aspects of life, superficial parties and dating challenges all turning into romantic successes or coming-of-age stories with positive moral conclusions. O has the dubious honour among teen films of being able to recall real-life tragedies and Shakespeare's great fictional tragedy, *Othello*, at the same time. Transforming Othello into O (Mekhi Phifer), short for Odin James, the African-American basketball player star of an all-white high school team, who secretly dates Desi (Julia Stiles), the dean's daughter, Nelson's film has found a setting in which the racial conflict of Shakespeare's play can be realistically represented among teenagers. Avoiding the well-trodden paths of teen comedy, the film is still clearly recognisable as a high school drama, and as such, allows us to highlight strategies shared by teen films, even if the general atmosphere of the film avoids any comic associations.

The setting of a high school, and more specifically, a suburban upper-middle-class boarding school, immediately defines the film's association with its genre, as all accounts emphasise. It is true that this high school is also set in the broader context of the Deep American South, which has not only a geographical, but much more a cultural, significance, and which informs the film's adaptive strategy in a significant way. Vanessa Corredera constructs her analysis on the argument that through the director's choice of turning *Othello* into 'a distinctly American tale' and diverse 'adaptive choices the film trades in and ultimately reifies malignant American fantasies – both historical and modern – about black men that overwhelm the film's attempts at positive representation'.[48] Her careful reading of the film underlines its stereotypical representation of blackness, yet I believe this only confirms the film's strong adherence to its generic conventions as well, since the teen genre rarely represents fully rounded and socially equal non-white characters.

O has everything in its setting and narrative that characterises the American high school film, including its rituals, house parties with drinking and rowdiness, and in general, a type of education that encourages self-expression and argument over lexical knowledge. Within the high school genre, O is also a sports film, and here, as in many other teen films, the sports stadium is superior to the classroom, as we saw in *She's the Man*. The formally perfect, but in reality dysfunctional, family background is equally present – Coach Duke Goulding (Martin Sheen) and his family share the dining room as a space, but hardly any word, during dinner, and this background is given as the most important explanation for Hugo (Josh Hartnett), the Iago character, turning out the way he did. This 'presence as absence' in parenting is perfectly in line with the way other teen films represent their authority figures, although, as will be discussed in more detail, O does not see adults as ridiculous, but expresses an almost nostalgic longing for the more tangible and nurturing presence of parents, both biological and symbolic, in the lives of adolescents.

This setting in turn produces its typical characters and groups, mostly in cliques, which are representative of social stratification and society's tendency to create smaller, self-contained units based on similarities of family background, particularly race, income, profession, recreational interest, taste and style. The presence of cliques is a common staple, and the token black guy in most films is often no more than that (as it is explicitly parodied in *Not Another Teen Movie*, dir. Joel Gallen, 2001). Odin, however, is not an empty token or a nod to multiracial representation, as his presence is undoubtedly explained by his prowess on the basketball court. Even if it was his talent that granted him the opportunity to get out of his birth environment, it soon becomes obvious that no one pretends to have forgotten his origins and previous history of drug abuse. He is welcomed (or tolerated) as long as the school needs him – the role of high school sports is significant here as it rarely is outside America. But it is more than clear that at the time of the institution's foundation, and for many subsequent decades, Odin's talents would not have been enough to make him a member of the basketball team in such an all-white environment. It is again no accident that his extraordinary skills are those of an athlete, rather than a scholar, not simply because the basketball court serves as a better adaptation of Shakespeare's battlefield, but principally because sports are among the few areas in which students of colour are expected to excel in mainstream Hollywood cinema. Yet O's Otherness is never completely eliminated, and his inability to fully belong to this world, though stereotypical, is clearly rooted in American historical and cultural reality.

As usual within the teen film, the Shakespearean language is completely absent from the dialogue, but just as typically Shakespeare is mentioned in a classroom scene. The embedded Shakespearean text, however, is not *Othello*, but *Macbeth* (again, not unusually in the genre), and a question the two protagonists are asked concerns the poems rather than the plays. Yet Hugo's witty reply: 'I thought he wrote movies' is often mentioned in criticism as a self-referential nod to the shifting position of Shakespeare from a canonical high cultural text to a popular visual medium. For all the lack of literal quotations, the plot closely follows that of the Shakespearean tragedy, down to the details of Desdemona's handkerchief, Iago's manipulation of Roderigo and even Cassio's drunken behaviour. As usual, the motif of marriage is absent, but it is replaced by what is equally typical, the narrative of a first sexual encounter, imbued with the genre's characteristically 'deep anxieties regarding teenage sexual activity'.[49] The handkerchief, which is presented as 'more than a hundred years old', which has been in Odin's family all this time and which is 'supposed to stay that way', allows O to declare that he feels he and Desi are already family. The seriousness of both the gift and the comment suggests a relationship that is rather out of place in the teen environment, but Desi's first reaction to the present: 'over your price range, that's what it is', makes it clear that she is well aware of their relative social (and financial) statuses – and is also spoken in a lighter tone, directing the conversation away from long-term commitments.

The inclusion of a scene of explicit sexuality, however, marks this film out as different from the others included in the chapter – the only other exception is *Lost and Delirious*, discussed next. While this could simply show that these films are more daring in discussing the issue, the tragic consequences of these sexual encounters in both films can also reinforce the conservative message characteristic of the genre, warning adolescents that the price for premature sexual activity is high. While sexual (self-)discovery is often a part of teen narratives, whenever the actual physical encounter is shown on screen it usually implies higher stakes, either concerning the finality of the choice that protagonists have made or their loss of reputation. This condemning attitude towards sexually active teenagers confirms what Burt describes in great detail in his quoted discussion of teenage female protagonists. As he claims, girls are practically subdivided into two groups: good girls (losers) and sluts, also known as hotties, and even if he focuses on romantic comedies and horror films, the same conservative feminism he describes seems to apply to practically all teen Shakespeare films.[50]

The plot's parallels with its Shakespearean source are again similar to the way *10 Things* follows *Shrew*'s plot, even including the recognisable counterparts of some of the better-known speeches. Nonetheless, neither Odin's acceptance speech at the award ceremony, nor the discussion in the dean's office concerning how Odin started dating Desi, can establish him as such a monumental figure as Shakespeare's Othello. Tim Blake Nelson's film does not complicate his protagonist in the way *Othello* does, with the Moor's contradictory self-description about being rude in his speech coming right before he wins over the whole senate with a rhetorical tour de force. O's speech is clearly black English, displaying many substandard features of the American vernacular, which indeed marks him out as different, even among his school companions, but without giving him a superior standing in his surroundings. In the mentioned classroom scene, when neither boy knows the right answer to the English teacher's question (which appears to have no connection to the classroom material), Odin's silence only 'reinforces the illiteracy of [the] main character', forcing him into a position of powerless silence.[51] Hugo, however, is quick to retort, appearing in control of the situation. Odin's speech is also stylistically inappropriate when he has to give an account of his behaviour in front of the dean and the coach, and the dean makes no qualms about turning his words back against him. Yet however wrongfully accused Odin is in this situation, he comes across as an outsider who does not know the rules of the game. In Desi's bedroom, when she tells him 'you've got the best stories', the story he tells about his lowly origins – a C-section baby who got a scar from the doctor's knife as his mother could not afford the best doctors – is refuted in the next second. For a moment, though, we see that Desi is ready to believe everything O tells her, and he is ready to make himself interesting to her, not by a narration of his own true self, but a made-up version.

The dilemma facing Michael (Andrew Keegan), the Cassio figure, regarding how to restore his reputation, also cleverly combines the Shakespearean source text with the teen film's concern of finding one's own identity: it boils down to a choice between being part of the in-crowd and/or an independent, self-reliant personality. 'The only person you have to answer to is yourself', Hugo tells Michael when chiding him for being 'a mommy's boy', and – following the genre's logic – parents are indeed noticeably absent from the narrative, so a mommy's boy has no chance in this world. The ones who appear in person (Hugo's parents and Desi's father) are clueless as to what goes on in their children's lives, although neither are even marginally comical figures. Desi's father as the dean of the school and

Hugo's father, the basketball team's coach, embody the authority figures who represent formal control over the teenage society – but both of them are responsible for the creation, rather than the resolution, of the narrative's main conflicts.

In one example of the subtle cinematography characteristic of the whole film, Hugo is invited over to his father's office at dinnertime, and although he clearly arrives with the hope of reconnecting with his father, the coach's first question reveals that he is only worried about Odin. What is particularly telling, however, is that during the whole scene, while we hear the voice of the coach, we never actually see him – the camera stays outside the office, on the corridor, and shows Hugo, framed by the door, sitting practically in the doorway, while his father is only present as a visible absence (see figure 4.4). The first and only time the coach comes into the picture is when he gets up and leaves the office, absent-mindedly patting his son's head, telling him to stay and finish his supper in the now empty office. Yet the camera does not move, it remains focused on Hugo, and does not for a moment follow the father, who barely shares the screen with his son. Only when we hear the door close behind the father does the viewpoint change, and suddenly we are inside the room, looking at Hugo as he is left alone in an almost dark, closed space – after a moment's silence, we see him put

Figure 4.4 Framed son – Josh Hartnett in O. Directed by Tim Blake Nelson, 2001. Chickie the Cop/Daniel Fried Productions/Dimension Films/FilmEngine/Rhulen Entertainment.

down the tray on the floor and then pull up the zipper of his raincoat to his chin, literally closing in on himself.

Nevertheless, it is not only the everyday psychology of parental neglect that the film employs in making its story topical to its target audiences. The story of a black star athlete, dating the blond star then eventually killing her, is another way of placing the story in painfully familiar contemporary reality, as the trial of O. J. Simpson for the alleged murder of his former wife and her friend garnered the broadest possible media publicity in 1994 and in subsequent years. Odin James's initials cannot be accidental therefore, particularly in the shortened form, as he is addressed as O throughout the film, making sure to reawaken audience memories of recent events.[52] Even more topical and therefore painfully actual was the 1999 Columbine School massacre, which – as is commonly known – forced the film's release to be delayed by two years, since the finale appeared to resemble the real-life tragedy too closely. Equally powerful is the final images' ability to recall Luhrmann's *Romeo + Juliet*, with the all-too-familiar images of ambulances and police cars surrounding a scene of contemporary tragedy, similar to the shocking scenes which the news media bombard us with every day. Yet the relevance that real life provided for the film implies to me not only the filmmakers' attempt to emphasise the modernity of their version of the tale, but a confirmation of their sensitivity to everyday American reality – with all the prejudices that are still rife in society, the media, upper-middle-class schools and particularly in the Deep South.

Another nod to Luhrmann's film can be detected in the film's musical score, which contains predominantly contemporary pop music, as would be expected in the genre, yet the film does open with the 'Ave Maria' from Verdi's *Othello*, creating a symbolic setting. The aria effectively isolates the scene from the contemporary world and recalls the ending of Luhrmann's *Romeo + Juliet* on the notes of the 'Liebestod' from Richard Wagner's *Tristan und Isolde*. In both films, the incorporation of a piece from a high cultural register implies the filmmakers' wish to associate their works with more layers than simply teen popular culture. Although both musical pieces belong to the better-known examples of operatic repertoire, neither of them offer a direct textual connection, but reward the connoisseur who is willing to do a bit of research to discover the association between the soundtrack and the film. Yet, as has become common since MTV's rise 'to prominence in the 1980s and 90s',[53] the soundtrack of a popular film is part of the merchandising campaign that automatically accompanies the film's marketing, therefore it is not unlikely that audiences will be made aware of the less commonplace musical numbers as well, particularly on fan websites.

When looking at the marketing strategies employed for the film's promotion, once again we find no surprises. Instead of relying on the authority and high cultural status of Shakespeare, the marketing campaign emphasised the film's generic qualities – its participation in the teen genre, with all its stereotypical locations and themes – and the young actors' star status. French also notes how 'the casting of Mekhi Phifer may also be situated in the broader context of young actors familiar in popular culture being cast in Shakespearian roles'.[54] Julia Stiles, a central character in three of the best-known Shakespeare youth adaptations (*10 Things, Hamlet, O*) combines her teen idol appeal with her position as a Shakespearean, thus appears to be a superior star in contrast to countless other young upstarts. French also notes how 'the cast of O is a commercially minded combination of budding teen stars such as Josh Hartnett, Rain Phoenix and Julia Stiles and an older and recognisable actor, Martin Sheen, to add gravitas, appeal to an older market and enhance audience recognition'.[55]

Audience recognition in teen films, as we can see in all the examples given, is keyed to the actors and the components of the genre: the high school as a main setting and all locations playing a central role there, all of which function as signifiers through which viewers can identify a film as belonging to the group. Shakespeare, however, does not need to be recognised – whether out of a 'desire to hide Shakespeare' or indicating 'a flattery of the teen audience, suggesting that they are capable of recognising on their own that this film is a Shakespeare adaptation' is hard to tell, but apart from a few notable exceptions, this strategy has proved to be successful since the teen film's return to popularity in the 1990s.[56] Shakespeare is, nonetheless, always assigned a function, either signalling social or intellectual superiority, or providing an outlet for channelling otherwise repressed desires, as exemplified by the tragic *denouement* of Lost and Delirious.

No escape from queer tragedy – *Lost and Delirious*

Lost and Delirious, a queer teen film inspired by *Twelfth Night* and other Shakespeare plays, offers a convincing example of why a simple equation between source and adaptation, based on textual or narrative elements, may fail to show the whole picture and often miss the real depths of the film itself. This is especially the case here since the direct textual source for the film is a contemporary novel, Susan Swan's *The Wives of Bath* (1993), whose inspiration came from the novelist's own experiences in a Canadian boarding school in the 1960s.[57] Yet when placed among other Shakespeare-inspired high school films, *Lost and Delirious* also stands its ground, showing how the added Shakespearean intertextuality fits perfectly with the contemporary plot. The queer relationship at the heart of the film marks it out as different from the best-known representatives of the genre, yet its focus on adolescent coming of age, and even the nostalgic tone created by the narrator's retrospective account of the events that have defined her identity, emphasise its embeddedness in the teen genre.

Peter Dickinson points out the film's connections to several literary and cinematic antecedents exploring lesbian relationships, but the title may also be a reflection on the 1993 teen comedy *Dazed and Confused*, another film focusing on the desperate search for adolescent identity. The themes of friendship and the exploration of sexuality, not to mention the nostalgic backward look, feature significantly in both films, implying that such an echo may have been intended in the title of Léa Pool's tragic coming-of-age narrative. This nostalgic narrative viewpoint, in Lesley Speed's opinion, results in a characteristic 'assertion of a retrospective, and potentially conservative, adult perspective [... that] can be foregrounded by considering a theoretical association between adolescence and freedom'.[58] This association between adolescence and freedom is indeed central to *Lost and Delirious*, which explores three girls' struggles within the confines of a girls-only boarding school, although its conclusion qualifies the meaning of freedom in the lives of all three characters.

The film presents the struggles of Paulie (Piper Perabo), a rebel figure brought up by foster parents, as resulting from 'teenage lesbian desire and internalized homophobia'.[59] While the passion she feels for Tory, short for Victoria (Jessica Paré), knows no bounds, Tory is responsive only in the privacy of their dormitory room, but unwilling to sacrifice her superior social position for the sake of the relationship. The film's central concern is Paulie's quest for freedom from confinements of all sorts, and after Tory pushes her away, Paulie's self-destructive spiral leads to the tragic *denouement*. However, by employing a retrospective narrator, speaking with the adult voice of Mary (Mouse) Bedford (Mischa Barton), their innocent but loyal roommate, a new arrival in the dorm, conformity and adulthood have the final word. Another significant generic element is the foregrounding of the bedroom as the primary space of existence of teenage girls. As opposed to many other movies' insistence of youth's preference for spaces of transition, constituting 'locations for teenagers to assert a collective identity, establishing a physical and cultural distance from adult institutions',[60] in *Lost and Delirious* the only space with relative freedom is the park. Yet this is no public space either, but a controlled imitation of a natural environment, in which most young characters remain isolated. Even Tory's sexual encounters in the park cannot liberate her from her entrapment between contradictory social and inner pressures, and Mary, although she tries to accompany her friends on their forays into nature, is unable to offer either of them real companionship.

One seemingly minor but fundamental difference from the genre's conventions informs the more subversive direction *Lost and Delirious* takes: whereas it is set in a high school, just like all other films discussed in the chapter, it is the only film set in a single-sex institution, an all-girls boarding school. This is, first of all, an autobiographical fact in the source narrative, and it may also seem a practical decision on the part of the director for the depiction of budding queer female sexuality, but this element is in reality also part of a broader tradition. As shown by Maria San Filippo, 'the female institution in its various permutations (boarding school, mental hospital, prison, gang) and depictions (as oppressive reformatory or utopian refuge from a hostile external world) provides an enduring setting for negotiating and occasionally subverting those social forces generative of heteronormativity'.[61] The setting itself therefore foreshadows the potential for subversive sexual experimentation, even though, by subscribing to the teen genre's conventions, it promises a return to heteronormativity, which in this case will inevitably require the sacrifice of the most vulnerable and least conformist character, Paulie.

Into this complex web of intertextuality, including 'conscious references to previous lesbian representations in literary and cinematic history',[62] the Shakespearean elements are introduced in much the same way as in most other teen films: in classroom settings and in narrative parallels, even if the latter are noticeable only in the second half of the film. Some commenters note the appearance of *Macbeth*, particularly Lady Macbeth's 'unsex me' (1.5.41) speech in the English class, and Paulie's sensitivity to the endless passion that transgresses gender boundaries.[63] Another text that the girls study is *Antony and Cleopatra*; Cleopatra's declaration of her love to her dying lover in Act 4 acquires particular significance with regard to Paulie's own refusal to let go of her own attachment to Tory.

But the dramatic character that Paulie consciously imitates in several crucial scenes is Viola from *Twelfth Night*, who woos another female, Olivia, in the disguise of Cesario. However, the disguise that offers protection to Viola is regarded as offensive by the homophobic society, which eventually destroys Paulie through its refusal to accommodate her as an equal member. When she challenges Tory in her fencing gear, imitating early modern male garb, and later fights Tory's boyfriend with a sword, her dress does not liberate her. On the contrary, it seals her fate as an outsider who has no place to belong, unless she leaves this whole world behind, which she does by leaping from the roof after reciting Viola's words: 'make me a willow cabin at your gate, / And call upon my soul within the house' (1.5.272–3) (see figure 5.5). Yet her use of the Shakespearean quotation is far from straightforward or simplistic, although on the surface it sounds like a request for a place on the doorstep of her beloved. But, when complemented by the previous part of the statement ('If I did love you in my master's flame, / With such a suff'ring, such a deadly life, / In your denial I would find no sense, / I would not understand it' 1.5.268–71), it becomes a statement and even a promise of remaining true to her sworn passion, and leaving an indelible mark on the life of her lover. In a later classroom scene, when Paulie is no longer present, we can also see how Mary learns to follow her lead and use Shakespeare to speak up for herself, just like other teen heroines, whose appreciation of Shakespeare always signals emotional maturity and a coherent identity.

As mentioned, out of all the films discussed here, *Lost and Delirious* and *O* are the only ones that depict sexual encounters explicitly, as visualisation of naked youths and the bodily reality of sexuality is typically absent from this fundamentally chaste and conservative genre. Yet it is no accident that it is these two films and none other which decide to go all the way, and refuse to represent only a childish or utopian romantic idealisation of love, since they are the only narratives ending in tragedy. The tragic ending is less surprising for *O*, which is based on *Othello*, but *Lost and Delirious* proves how an originally comic dramatic source, in this case *Twelfth Night*, may also reach a tragic *denouement*. It is true that the potential for the inclusion of real tragedy in popular teen adaptations is often debated, as we have already implied in connection with *O*. *Lost and Delirious* also distances the tragic *denouement* from the rest of the plot, but without recourse to irony or parody, as often seems to be the most viable alternative for Shakespop, for instance in the case of *Scotland, PA* (1994, dir. Billy Morrissette).[64]

In Léa Pool's queer teen tragedy, the final scene lifts off from the plane of realism and looks at the tragic heroine's suicide in an allegorical light. The tamed raptor who has become Paulie's only true companion after Tory's dismissal of her love, alerts the whole school community to the realisation that Paulie has climbed onto the rooftop (see figure 4.5). When she jumps to her death, the camera does not follow her descent, but with a point-of-view shot, reflecting the skyward-turned eyes of Mary and the whole school, follows the bird, reinterpreting Paulie's tragedy as flight, both in the sense of flying and escape, that is, liberation from the confines of a society where there is no place for the likes of her. While the camera is 'tracking the

Figure 4.5 Flying away – Piper Perabo in *Lost and Delirious*. Directed by Léa Pool, 2001. Cité-Amérique/Dummett Films.

bird as it circles the school before freezing the frame just as it appears to be flying directly into the camera ..., we see the agent of repressive authority being vanquished by a resistant minority gaze'; at the same time, 'we arguably witness the self-martyrdom of a free spirit who refuses to be looked at, affixed, and judged in any terms other than those she sets for herself'.[65]

Lost and Delirious, although seemingly going against mainstream teen films, uses precisely its tragic ending to confirm the supremacy of the heteronormative middle-class world that appears as the single possible way to happiness in the genre. The inclusion of explicit queer sexuality serves a complex set of intentions: to shock – partly the narrator character, Mary 'Mouse' Bedford, but, by adopting her viewpoint, the shock is also meant for audiences – but mostly to warn its target audiences of the potentially tragic consequences of such an illicit infatuation, and thus encourage conformity to heteronormative sexual norms.

Queer utopia – *Were the World Mine*

Were the World Mine, a high school musical version of *A Midsummer Night's Dream*, also belongs to the category of queer film, but as opposed to the tragic *denouement* of *Lost and Delirious*, it 'is representative of how this group of Shakespeare-inflected films tend to drive toward "happy" endings for their subjects, even if these endings are often tinged with sadness'.[66] The choice of *A Midsummer Night's Dream* is no accident, since the forest scenes of mistaken and confused identities offer the potential for the performance of queer and reimagined sexual identities, although surprisingly few mainstream films have opted for this interpretation so far. One recent example is a television production, directed by David Kerr for the BBC in 2016, in which the momentary confusion in the forest, together with the love potion in the hands of a naughty Puck, causes Lysander for a moment to fall for Demetrius; although this joke is cleared up in a second there are two actual homosexual couples among the characters.[67] Typical (or stereotypical) teen films, however, rarely address teen coming-of-age and sexual awakening in other than heterosexual terms, unless they clearly identify with queer cinema – it comes as no surprise that most such films, including *Private Romeo*, *Were the World Mine* and *Lost and Delirious*, have been independently produced and marketed, without any mainstream Hollywood studio backing.

Looking for opportunities for queering *A Midsummer Night's Dream*, it is easy to see how the core of queer readings would focus on the forest scenes, 'a dreamscape lush with sexual possibilities: not only the homoeroticism that sometimes encumbers, sometimes oils the marriage machine of Shakespearean comedy, but also child-love, anality, and bestiality'.[68] Richard Rambuss even claims that 'Human interest in seeing someone perform or be treated – abjected, disciplined, coddled, desired, feared – as an animal is widely reflected throughout *A Midsummer Night's Dream*.'[69] Another example of a queer interpretation of the play is that of Kirk Quinsland, whose argument focuses on the mechanicals and the reception of Pyramus by the on-stage audience. He claims that 'What Shakespeare reveals through Pyramus is theatre's capacity to disrupt and defer heterosexuality, quite literally, but more importantly in the sense that Pyramus's badness exposes heterosexuality's dependence on homophobia in order to reassert and reassure itself of its own dominance.'[70]

Many of these analyses dig deep into the textual layer of the play and point out potentially subversive readings of what is either suppressed or often edited out of the text, or simply concealed in favour of more heteronormative interpretations. Several adaptations, however, take the dramatic situation as their starting point and transform it to allow queer potentials to emerge from the social situation depicted. Such a revision of the plot presents the viewer with a dream scenario: what if the application of the love potion affected Lysander's eyes in such a way that his affection turned towards a male object of desire? This is the idea that *Were the World Mine*, a queer teen musical adaptation of *Dream*, takes and runs away with. Here a high school student, Timothy (Tanner Cohen), the butt of cruel homophobic jokes in his all-male class, when cast in the role of Puck in the school production of *A Midsummer Night's Dream* miraculously discovers the recipe for a love potion. He manages to concoct the potion, then spreads it to all and sundry, turning the formerly most homophobic members of the Bible-bashing local community into besotted homosexuals. After a short carnivalesque interval, Timothy eventually reverses the world to normality, although fearing that the reversal would also mean the end of his newly found romantic happiness. But to his great joy, his boyfriend Jonathon (Nathaniel David Becker) remains by his side, happy in his queer identity. As seen from this brief summary, *Were the World Mine*'s vision of the confusion of identities focuses on the young lovers' mix-and-match troubles and downplays the Bottom-as-an-ass aspect of physical love with which the previously quoted queer readings of *A Midsummer Night's Dream* are typically concerned.[71] In a way this focus on the social rather than the sexual aspect also confirms that the primary interpretive context for the film is the teen flick, rather than the queer film.

Were the World Mine thus follows the narrative clichés of the high school musical subgenre, and its plot resembles *Get Over It* (2001, dir. Tommy O'Haver), a commercially less successful adaptation of *A Midsummer Night's Dream* in many ways, only this time the plot and the subsequent performance are given a queer twist. Apart from the usual trappings of the teen flick, in this metadramatic setting conflict often arises from a perceived social hierarchy, including possibilities for romantic pairings. This hierarchy gets miraculously subverted and rearranged through the power of the Shakespeare performance, and particularly through the previously concealed artistic talents (mostly of those who were cast as losers in the school's social drama) that it allows to blossom. The only significant difference between the two films is that in *Were the World Mine* the protagonist is an outsider and therefore loser because of his homosexuality and consequent effeminacy, which makes him appear as incompetent on the rugby field and when playing other competitive sports. From his fantasies that the camera shares with us, we are aware that his lack of skill is rather a desire for an aesthetically superior order, to create a sense of beauty and harmony out of the world of the gym, which he experiences as chaotic and violent.

It appears, therefore, that the power of the Shakespearean performance is magical and universal, it brings peace and love, order and harmony not only to the troubled young teenager or the whole group of students involved in the performance, but even to the entire community of the small town. It miraculously heals all rifts and injuries, allowing the previously neglected and harassed protagonist to be fully accepted, even appreciated, by gaining a central and superior position in the local hierarchy. Yet it is also essential to acknowledge, as Matt Kozusko points out, that it is not the Shakespearean poetry that is presented as universal, not even 'the rich, famously flexible content that allows Shakespeare to be mobilized on behalf of potentially contradictory positions, but the archaic syntax and diction that give the lines a "Shakespeareness"'.[72] Timothy, the protagonist, clearly struggles to make sense of the words, yet Miss Tebbit (Wendy Robie), the drama teacher in charge of the production, calms him with suggestions which imply that an understanding comes from an immersion in the world of the play, just like her supportive sentences encourage him to discover himself and his real sexual identity.

Were the World Mine is in other ways a rather traditional teen narrative, set in a white middle-class American society, without any apparent racial conflicts. The only non-white character is Max (Ricky Goldman), a friend of Timothy's, one of the few who support his search and acceptance of his identity from the start, and Max encounters no difficulties on account of his racial or ethnic background. The broader social concerns that often appear in queer cinema are also associated with the issue of queer identity: Timothy's single mother tries to find employment to support her son and herself, but is met with refusal wherever she goes. Yet this social criticism is also a reference to the far-reaching consequences of homophobia, since this is all tied back to her abandonment by her husband, who apparently left because he could not accept his son's homosexuality. Thus the class and economic problems are presented as resulting from the gender issue; as no other student's social background is revealed, and we have absolutely no idea of Jonathon's class standing, the obstacle between the romantic couple thus has no social component but is clearly an issue connected to Timothy's identity. As it turns out, the mother struggles because society also shuns her, together with her son, until he finds acceptance as a result of his performance. But her involvement in the school play, significantly by her decision to sacrifice her wedding dress to turn it into a fairy costume for Timothy, begins her own transformation and self-acceptance: both as a single parent, and more importantly, as a mother of a queer, but very talented, young boy.

In *Were the World Mine*, the authority figures are no different from those of the typical teen film: powerless parents (apart from the single mother, an absent, but admittedly abusive, father), and either brutally homophobic, or conservative and clueless, principals. The single exception is the drama tutor, a female teacher, surprising in an all-male classroom, and a character who seems to be rather out of this world, yet able to exercise power over both students and colleagues. She represents the artistic and academic traditions of the Shakespearean performance that not even the patronising representatives of the patriarchal micro-society (the sports coach and the principal) have the power to question. The fact that her character is not turned into a parody, even if it does sometimes verge on the comic, clearly represents the film's sympathies with non-heteronormative identities. Yet as a facilitator and a liberator, her eccentricities are seen as signs of her singular vision, which allows her to see beyond the surface and find what is concealed – not only the hurt and the pain, but also the hidden talent – she is thus associated with the rulers of the fairy kingdom of *A Midsummer Night's Dream*. In line with the majority of the musical numbers, these somewhat metadramatic scenes are presented almost as dream visions from which the protagonist must be dragged back to reality (see figure 4.6). The only exception is the last, and most crucial, time, when the reordering of the broader social universe is initiated by the teacher herself, but Timothy learns that it is possible to be awake and be accepted at last.

As regards the cinematography of the queer teen film, one thing is distinctly noticeable: while queer characters in ordinary teen films are often presented using mockery or irony, the camera rarely adopting their

Figure 4.6 Queer fantasy – Tanner Cohen in *Were the World Mine*. Directed by Tom Gustafson, 2008. SPEAKproductions/The Group Entertainment.

viewpoint, in *Were the World Mine* it is the queer protagonist's viewpoint that we interiorise most of the time. As a result, we see and recognise Jonathon as the object of Timothy's desire precisely because he is photographed in a similar manner as the love interests in heterosexual romances. At this point in the film, it is yet undecided whether Timothy's longing for the unreachable popular and handsome star of the rugby field will turn into tragedy, or at least distinct failure, but the film's visual language supports the young protagonist, who is silenced by the mockery and abuse he receives from his social surroundings. The explicit acknowledgement of Timothy's queerness comes much later than the public shaming, but by then the 'queer I/eye' of the camera has done the work of representation. As Susan Driver claims in her analysis of queer teen romance films, 'If words are weapons of public shame, the gaze becomes a realm of subversive possibility for queer youth.'[73] When the gaze is denied – Timothy's audition is conducted behind curtains and even closed doors separating him from the rest of his peers – it is the queer voice that penetrates the silence and signals his first tentative steps in claiming an identity for himself. Moreover, the scene also establishes that Jonathon can appreciate Timothy's undoubtedly superior voice, forging a connection of understanding that begins to bridge the gap between Timothy and his peer group.

Jonathon's role in the film is also significant in the sense that while he is presented as a facilitator and a supporting character, Timothy's self-liberation also motivates his coming out and finding himself. At the beginning, Jonathon is represented as the most desirable heterosexual male, being admired by two girls at the same time – and his experience in physical contact (we see him kissing his girlfriend) is also observed with pain and envy by Timothy. This experience in sexuality is what he can offer to Timothy while under the spell of the love potion. Nonetheless, the acknowledgement that the experience of a queer relationship helped him to find himself also points retrospectively to his macho performance as no more than that: a show put on for the sake of strengthening his position within the peer group, but possibly also a way of experimenting with his own uncertain sexual identity. This fits perfectly with the idea of gender theorists that 'gender is not a state of "being" but an action, a doing, and a doing that is not for oneself but for an assumed audience and therefore is a social, political and dramatic act'.[74] Jonathon's more secure position in the community forces him to maintain a performance of the expected gender role, and this conscious and successful performance prevents him from discovering his own sexual identity until Timothy's love potion forces him to shed the mask.

In terms of locations shown within the film, *Were the World Mine* follows the trend of teen films, particularly female-centred ones, by emphasising the significance of the private space of the bedroom for displaying Timothy's isolation but also his non-normative masculine – that is, queer – features. He prefers the closed domestic space to the public arena of the rugby field or the gym, partly because his bedroom is a safe cocoon, and also because he feels unable to perform the masculine activities the public and very much physical spaces of the sports fields require. These are also the fields of his regular public humiliation (the film begins with the sports coach shouting abuse at the boys' weak efforts, and when the camera points to Timothy's feet and his pair of patterned Converse sneakers, a girlish choice in comparison to the others' regular trainers, we have no trouble associating his choice of footwear to the coach's deprecation of 'fancy feet').

However, the turning point in Timothy's journey to find and claim his identity is also associated with a specific space: that of the stage and the Shakespearean performance. It is telling, therefore, that while the auditions are conducted on the stage behind the half-open curtains, casting him into complete 'hegemonic public invisibility'[75] as a result of his budding queer identity, the final performance will not only open up the stage itself, but miraculously incorporate the audience and, with them, the whole of society. Timothy's story thus mirrors the journey taken by the queer girl protagonist of *Show Me Love*, described by Driver as a 'process of coming out as a movement from interior secret spaces' (the bedroom) 'to shared intimacy', first behind the scenes on stage, and then later in the open air, in nature, 'from the homophobic bigotry of small-town teen cultures, as well as from the socially isolated realm of [the] bedroom toward a rebellious public declaration of girl-on-girl romance'.[76] Instead of the usual celebratory ritual of the prom, *Were the World Mine* concludes in a public acknowledgement of the protagonist's whole self on the stage, enabled by the Shakespearean narrative, and the film ends with an invitation to an after-show party that signals the community's acceptance and acknowledgement of Timothy's stardom, in a fairy-tale-like, unrealistic but ultimately optimistic conclusion.

Notes

1 Cf. Paterson, 'Box Office Poison?'
2 An example for the tragic source used in a non-tragic plot is *Private Romeo* (2011, dir. Alan Brown), not discussed in the chapter.
3 Klett, 'Reviving Viola'.

4 French, *Selling Shakespeare to Hollywood*, p. 116.
5 For an extended discussion of the film in the context of queer Shakespeare cinema, see A. G. Patricia, *Queering the Shakespeare Film: Gender Trouble, Gay Spectatorship and Male Homoeroticism* (London and New York: Bloomsbury Arden Shakespeare, 2017), esp. pp. 73–84.
6 C. Silverstone, 'Shakespeare, Cinema and Queer Adolescents: Unhappy Endings and Heartfelt Conclusions', *Shakespeare*, 10:3 (2014), 309–27, 325, n. 8. The critics she refers to are Richard Burt, Elizabeth A. Deitchman and Elizabeth Klett.
7 T. Shary, *Generation Multiplex: The Image of Youth in Contemporary American Cinema* (Austin: University of Texas Press, 2002), p. 50.
8 F. Smith, *Rethinking the Hollywood Teen Movie: Gender, Genre and Identity* (Edinburgh: Edinburgh University Press, 2017), pp. 69, 79.
9 *Ibid.*, p. 79.
10 All parenthetical references to *The Taming of the Shrew* are to this edition: W. Shakespeare, *The Taming of the Shrew*, The Arden Shakespeare, Second Series, ed. B. Morris (London and New York: Routledge, 1994).
11 L. M. Pittman, *Authorizing Shakespeare on Film and Television* (New York: Peter Lang Publishing, 2011), p. 105.
12 French, *Selling Shakespeare to Hollywood*, p. 118.
13 *Ibid.*
14 *Ibid.*, p. 122.
15 S. Bailey and J. Hay, 'Cinema and the Premises of Youth: "Teen Films" and Their Sites in the 1980s and 1990s', in S. Neale (ed.), *Genre and Contemporary Hollywood* (London: BFI Publishing, 2002), pp. 218–35, p. 219.
16 *Ibid.*, p. 223.
17 Davis, 'I Was a Teenage Classic', 55.
18 E. A. Deitchman, 'Shakespeare Stiles Style: Shakespeare, Julia Stiles, and American Girl Culture', in B. Hodgdon and W. B. Worthen (eds), *A Companion to Shakespeare and Performance* (Oxford: Blackwell, 2005), pp. 478–93.
19 L. M. Pittman, 'Taming *10 Things I Hate About You*: Shakespeare and the Teenage Film Audience', *Literature/Film Quarterly*, 32:2 (2004), 144–52, 148.
20 *Ibid.*, 150.
21 Based on Box Office Mojo data (accessed 18 August 2019).
22 J. Ellis, 'The Literary Adaptation', *Screen*, 23:1 (1982), 3–5, 3, quoted in Hutcheon, *A Theory of Adaptation*, p. 5.
23 B. Gray, 'Matrix Weekend Two', *Box Office Mojo* (12 April 1999), www.boxofficemojo.com/news/?id=1030&p=.htm (accessed 26 January 2020).
24 W. Shakespeare, *The Merchant of Venice*, The Arden Shakespeare, Second Series, ed. J. R. Brown (London and New York: Routledge, 1993). The quote is identified in R. Burt, 'Afterword: T(e)en Things I Hate about Girlene Shakesploitation Flicks in the Late 1990s, or, Not-So-Fast Times at Shakespeare High', in Lehmann and Starks (eds), *Spectacular Shakespeare*,

pp. 205–32, p. 229, n. 30, although he writes 'patinas' instead of 'patens' or 'patines', Malone's commonly accepted emendation.
25 Bailey and Hay, 'Cinema and the Premises of Youth', p. 231.
26 *Ibid.*
27 *Ibid.*, pp. 219, 228.
28 Davis, 'I Was a Teenage Classic', 55.
29 Lanier, 'Film Spin-Offs and Citations', p. 144.
30 A. M. Balizet, 'Teen Scenes: Recognizing Shakespeare in Teen Film', in Keller and Stratyner (eds), *Almost Shakespeare*, pp. 122–36, p. 127.
31 Bailey and Hay, 'Cinema and the Premises of Youth', p. 224.
32 J. DeWitt, 'Cars and Culture: The Cars of *American Graffiti*', *American Poetry Review*, 39:5 (2010), 47–50, 47.
33 All parenthetical references to *Twelfth Night* are to this edition: W. Shakespeare, *Twelfth Night*, The Arden Shakespeare, Second Series, ed. J. M. Lothian and T. W. Craik (London and New York: Routledge, 1975).
34 L. E. Osborne, '*Twelfth Night*'s Cinematic Adolescents: One Play, One Plot, One Setting, and Three Teen Films', *Shakespeare Bulletin*, 26:2 (2008), 9–36, 13.
35 *Ibid.*
36 'classic', adj. in *English Oxford Living Dictionaries* (Oxford University Press, 2017), https://en.oxforddictionaries.com/definition/classic (accessed 1 December 2017).
37 Osborne, '*Twelfth Night*'s Cinematic Adolescents', 15.
38 Green, 'Educating for Pleasure', p. 34.
39 Burt, 'Afterword: T(e)en Things I Hate', p. 206.
40 G. Gano and W. Dixon, 'Gone Daddy Gone', *Metrolyrics*, www.metrolyrics.com/gone-daddy-gone-lyrics-violent-femmes.html (accessed 26 January 2020).
41 Klett, 'Reviving Viola', 75.
42 *Ibid.*, 76.
43 *Ibid.*, 73.
44 K. Elam, 'Introduction', in William Shakespeare, *Twelfth Night*, The Arden Shakespeare, Third Series, ed. K. Elam (London: The Arden Shakespeare, 2008), pp. 1–154, p. 72.
45 L. M. Pittman, 'Dressing the Girl/Playing the Boy: *Twelfth Night* Learns Soccer on the Set of *She's the Man*', *Literature/Film Quarterly*, 36:1 (2008), 122–36, 125.
46 *Ibid.*, 130.
47 *Ibid.*
48 V. Corredera, 'Far More Black than Black: Stereotypes, Black Masculinity, and Americanization in Tim Blake Nelson's *O*', *Literature/Film Quarterly*, 45:3 (2017), https://lfq.salisbury.edu/_issues/45_3/far_more_black_than_black.html (accessed 26 January 2020).
49 A. M. Balizet, 'Just Say Yes: Shakespeare, Sex, and Girl Culture', *Women's Studies*, 44:6 (2015), 815–41, 816.

50 Burt, 'Afterword: T(e)en Things I Hate'.
51 E. C. Brown, 'Cinema in the Round: Self-Reflexivity in Tim Blake Nelson's O', in Keller and Stratyner (eds), *Almost Shakespeare*, pp. 73–85, p. 80.
52 Interestingly enough, Mekhi Phifer also appears as Omar Jones in several episodes in the 2005 season of *Curb Your Enthusiasm*, where again the name seems hardly accidental.
53 L. Westrup, 'Merchandising Gen X: The *Singles* Soundtrack Album (1992/2017)', *Film Criticism*, 42:2, Special issue: *Film and Merchandise* (2018), https://doi.org/10.3998/fc.13761232.0042.204.
54 French, *Selling Shakespeare to Hollywood*, p. 126.
55 Ibid.
56 Ibid., p. 128.
57 S. Swan, *The Wives of Bath* (New York: Knopf, 1993). For an in-depth comparison between the novel and the film, and the film's broader intertextual background, see P. Dickinson, *Screening Gender, Framing Genre: Canadian Literature into Film* (Toronto, Buffalo, NY, and London: University of Toronto Press, 2007), esp. pp. 172–85.
58 L. Speed, 'Tuesday's Gone: The Nostalgic Teen Film', *Journal of Popular Film and Television*, 26:1 (1998), 24–32, 27.
59 Dickinson, *Screening Gender*, p. 173.
60 Speed, 'Tuesday's Gone', 28.
61 M. San Filippo, *The B Word: Bisexuality in Contemporary Film and Television* (Bloomington and Indianapolis: Indiana University Press, 2013), p. 133.
62 Dickinson, *Screening Gender*, p. 180.
63 S. Martin, 'From Book to Screen: A Story in Three Acts', *Globe and Mail* (7 July 2001), www.theglobeandmail.com/arts/from-book-to-screen-a-story-in-three-acts/article1032156/ (accessed 6 January 2020).
64 For a detailed discussion of the strategies for combining *Macbeth* with a contemporary pop sensibility and parody in Morrissette's film, see Lanier, 'Will of the People', esp. pp. 192–4.
65 Dickinson, *Screening Gender*, p. 184.
66 Silverstone, 'Shakespeare, Cinema and Queer Adolescents', 311.
67 Cf. K. Földváry, 'Trendy or Topical? Sexual Politics and Panopticism in the 2016 BBC *Midsummer Night's Dream*', *Cahiers Élisabéthains: A Journal of English Renaissance Studies*, 99:1 (2019), 137–46.
68 R. Rambuss, '*A Midsummer Night's Dream*: Shakespeare's Ass Play', in M. Menon (ed.), *ShakesQueer: A Queer Companion to the Complete Works of Shakespeare* (Durham, NC, and London: Duke University Press, 2011), pp. 234–44, p. 234.
69 Ibid., p. 241.
70 K. Quinsland, 'The Sport of Asses: *A Midsummer Night's Dream*', in G. Stanivukovic (ed.), *Queer Shakespeare: Desire and Sexuality* (London and New York: Bloomsbury Arden Shakespeare, 2017), pp. 69–85, p. 85.

71 Cf. Rambuss, 'A *Midsummer Night's Dream*'; Quinsland, 'The Sport of Asses'.
72 M. Kozusko, 'Shakesqueer, the Movie: *Were the World Mine* and *A Midsummer Night's Dream*', in P. Holland (ed.), *Shakespeare Survey*, vol. 65: *A Midsummer Night's Dream* (Cambridge: Cambridge University Press, 2012), pp. 168–80, p. 170.
73 S. Driver, 'Girls Looking at Girls Looking for Girls: The Visual Pleasures and Social Empowerment of Queer Teen Romance Flicks', in T. Shary and A. Seibel (eds), *Youth Culture in Global Cinema* (Austin: University of Texas Press, 2007), pp. 241–55, p. 248.
74 T. Power, *Shakespeare and Gender in Practice* (London: Palgrave, 2016), p. 9.
75 Driver, 'Girls Looking at Girls Looking for Girls', p. 249.
76 *Ibid.*, p. 248.

5

Shakespeare the undead: a renaissance of vampires and zombies

As the introduction to Part II has already pointed out, there are many reasons why a new wave of undead films has come to populate cinemas since the 1990s. By the end of the second decade of the new millennium, the latest boom of zombie and vampire films has even reached the stage when self-ironic and parodic treatments are almost more common than serious and straightforward ones which use the undead as metaphors for direct social criticism, and this parodic intention is also characteristic of the Shakespeare-inspired works. The cross-pollination between Shakespeare and the undead has produced a whole range of literary fiction as well, among them a few bestsellers; even the zombie film *Warm Bodies*, discussed in this chapter, first appeared as a young adult novel by Isaac Marion in 2010, before conquering Hollywood. Other bestsellers include Lori Handeland's 2010 novel *Shakespeare Undead* and its sequel *Zombie Island* (2012), an adaptation of *The Tempest*; or *The Taming of the Werewolf* by Sylvia Shults from 2011. Not even the theatre has escaped the zombie virus, as testified by Zombie Joe's Underground Theatre's production *Hamlet, Prince of Darkness*, which offered 'a sixty minute reduction of Shakespeare's *Hamlet* in which the ghost was replaced with a vampire, Denmark was overrun by zombies and Hamlet summoned Satan to find out what is really happening in Elsinore'.[1]

As we can see, post-apocalyptic undead Shakespeare is everywhere, and while it may be a fad that does not last, it is also symptomatic of the adaptation process as a whole. Therefore, in what follows, I intend to illustrate, with the help of four films (and passing references to a few more), how Shakespearean drama has been adapted into two types of undead cinema: vampire and zombie films. As we shall see, it is almost exclusively the best-known tragedies, *Hamlet* and *Romeo and Juliet*, that appear to have found their way into these genres. Whether the reason for that is the relatively young age of target audiences (or the production teams), who may not be familiar with other Shakespeare dramas, or the relatively young age of the Shakespearean protagonists with whose typically adolescent or young adult problems the key demographic finds it easier to identify, is hard to tell. *Hamlet*, as many critics have pointed out, has a number of thematic links to the vampire as a motif, and the play influenced the nineteenth-century creation of the classic vampire itself, but even contemporary vampire figures can be seen as the 'melancholy romantic anti-heroes in the mode of twentieth-century Hamlets'.[2] Yet the continued popularity of these two primary texts also implies that the intention of the filmmakers was not an engagement with the Shakespearean representations of the Other, since in that case, *Othello* or *The Merchant of Venice*, possibly *The Tempest*, would provide much more suitable examples. What we have in the works discussed here instead is a concern with the undead themselves, rather than their Shakespearean correspondences. As a result, the films focus on the elements of the dramas that can be associated with their chosen version of horror – primarily the ghost, or Hamlet's reference to how he could 'drink hot blood' (3.2.381), or Juliet's 'ill-divining soul' that provides her with a vision of her husband 'as one dead in the bottom of a tomb' (3.4.54, 56).

At first sight, transforming *Romeo and Juliet* into a zombie-infested setting requires quite a stretch of our imagination, as the two households in the drama are in no way meant to be representations of any Norm against some form of the Other. On the contrary, the dramatic text takes pains to show the feud as being without rational or even explicable origins, and it rages between equals: 'households both alike in dignity' (Prologue, 1), where we are not allowed to see either side as being more justified in its violence than the other. As a result, turning one side of the conflict into the monstrous Other necessarily depends on the contemporary monster's humanised features, pointing out that we have more in common with them than we like to admit. Even if the various forms of undead are metaphors for racially or otherwise marginalised social groups or individuals, by introducing a romance plotline, a sense of equality is created between humans and the non-human. The bond between the lovers, forged in opposition to the rest of society, effectively emphasises the hostile, even monstrous, elements within the so-called human environment.

What is generally true, however, is that none of these adaptations intends to give a respectful reading of the plays; they are characterised instead either by a superficial or a light-hearted and parodic approach to their sources of inspiration. Even the most straightforward examples take their cinematic genre, rather than the Shakespearean text, seriously, and use the latter to comment on, or at best parallel, their own narratives. To illustrate vampire Shakespeare crossovers, the chapter will discuss one comic and one dramatic example: *Rosencrantz and Guildenstern are Undead* (2009, dir. Jordan Galland), a comic reworking of *Hamlet* in the form of a vampire film, and *Let Me In* (2010, dir. Matt Reeves), a remake of a Swedish film with meaningful parallels to *Romeo and Juliet*. Nonetheless, it is worth noting a few other examples that can be associated with Shakespeare and vampires in one way or another, therefore the chapter will begin with a brief examination of the first film in the *Underworld* franchise (2003, dir. Len Wiseman), often referred to as a love story in the style of *Romeo and Juliet*, however marginal the Shakespearean element is in the film. After the vampires, the chapter discusses two zombie narratives, *Zombie Hamlet* (2012, dir. John Murlowski) and *Warm Bodies* (2013, dir. James Levine), the latter another *Romeo and Juliet* adaptation.

There are obviously other Shakespeare-inspired vampire and zombie films, such as the *Treehouse of Horror* series, the Halloween specials of *The Simpsons*, which in the 29 October 1992 episode included a zombie William Shakespeare and made references to both *Hamlet* and *Macbeth*.[3] Similar references to *Romeo and Juliet* have been found in the popular *Twilight* series and explored, among others, by Glennis Byron, although some of her arguments may be less tenable in the light of the complete saga.[4] All in all, I believe that these connections show rather the way the concept of the 'star-crossed lovers' has acquired independent life of its own, with very few ties to the Shakespearean inspiration required to identify such doomed love stories as imitations of *Romeo and Juliet*.

Here, however, as in the rest of the volume, my concern is only with the full feature films that include recognisable elements of Shakespearean narratives, and at the same time, can be considered vampire or zombie films as well. Some further adaptations never saw the light of day, or are unavailable today, like an amateur project, *Hamlet the Vampire Slayer* (2008, dir. Jason Witter), a low-budget production inspired by the extreme popularity of the TV series *Buffy the Vampire Slayer*. Based on its trailer, the film seems to include a number of creative combinations of thematic elements from the play, particularly the nocturnal scenes and Hamlet's self-deprecating tendencies, occasionally displaying elements of linguistic humour reminiscent of other postmodern parodies, although usually executed on a much lower level.

This preponderance of parodic or at least comic versions, however, may be less of an accident than it first appears. Since introducing zombies, vampires or other undead characters into Shakespearean narratives in itself may be described as disrespectful or parodic as an adaptation strategy, it is hard to imagine serious presentations of Shakespeare plays using the generic conventions of some of these subgenres of horror. More importantly, as several scholars have argued, post-millennial horror has already expanded to embrace the conventions of the comedy as well, as the significant number of vampire and zombie comedies exemplifies. Even the non-comic treatments of the undead have undergone considerable changes, with the result that the modern undead tend to be more humanoid, even humane, if not yet entirely admirable. The real threat is no longer manifested in the Gothic monster from the dark past or the dark spaces of the imagination, but the monstrous element living inside every human, or represented by contemporary social institutions. Even *Let Me In*, the darkest of all the films discussed here, which cannot be described as a comedy in any sense of the word, conforms to this pattern by presenting its vampire protagonist as a victim of society rather than a downright villain. All films discussed in this chapter observe the narrative conventions of their chosen cinematic genre (or at least the clichés of plot and characterisation), and these narrative and cinematographic frameworks are usually preserved to allow audience identification with them as genre films, even despite the recognisably literary storylines. They also display the genre's common intention to offer social criticism, which is often at the heart of undead narratives even when they present these serious messages in a comic narrative framework. This in itself provides confirmation for the theory that it is the adapting cinematic genre which defines the new work, not the literary work used as its source of inspiration.

Bloodsucking Shakespeare

Given the more aristocratic origins of the vampire and the longer history of its cinematic representation, it is fitting to begin the discussion of undead Shakespeare figures with this group, particularly since the cinematic Shakespearean vampires appeared slightly earlier than their fellow zombies. Even though the short introduction to this chapter treated zombies and vampires as if they belonged to the same category (as so-called undead creatures populating subgenres of horror cinema), there are obvious differences between their symbolism and meaning, and equally in the target audiences drawn to their screen representations. The new millennium has seen a resurgence in the popularity of both types of screen monsters, even if in different ways and for various reasons, but they still retained some of their distinct features.

After the nineteenth-century vampire craze, at the end of the twentieth century a few individual authors and works began to reintroduce vampires to new generations of readers and viewers. Susan Chaplin argues in her account of the post-millennial vampire that 'Far from "wearing down", the vampire has come to dominate postmillennial popular culture to an extraordinary extent, generating fluid narratives across diverse media and guaranteeing huge profits for publishers, TV companies, film studios and the manufacturers of computer games.'[5] Importantly, however, these new vampires were no longer the creepy old men of Gothic literature or German expressionist cinema. As Brian H. Onishi argues, 'the current form of the vampire as white suburban teenager' reveals partly 'an attitude toward racism as something that is believed to have been overcome'; at the same time, 'contemporary vampiric images reflect a desire for enhanced bodies associated with technological innovation', a desire he sees as 'reshaping racism'.[6] No longer repulsive or even marked as the racial Other, the postmillennial vampire is endowed with a sexually attractive body, and this aestheticisation also downplays the threat it represents, while forging a connection to the films' human focalisers. In this vein, Owen in *Let Me In*, just like Bella Swan in *Twilight*, is not only attracted to his vampire friend, but they share a number of external traits as well, among them their pale skin and somewhat androgynous facial features.

It is worth noting that the general characteristics of post-millennial vampires – their sympathetic, sometimes even tragic qualities that make them suitable for heroic roles – associates them with another popular genre (or generic hybrid) of the 2000s: post-apocalyptic dystopia. It is no wonder therefore that 'postmillennial vampire films such as *Blade, Underworld, Daybreakers* and *30 Days of Night* have taken vampire narrative into darker, more apocalyptic territory',[7] a territory also familiar from zombie narratives, as this dominant genre of popular cinema has affected both types of undead representations. Apart from their brooding, somewhat Byronic nature, which characterises Edward Cullen in the *Twilight* series just as much as Selene in *Underworld*, these contemporary vampires suffer from their affliction and see themselves as victims, rather than predators. This in turn shows them in a more favourable light than the aristocratic bloodsuckers of Dracula's ilk, and invites more subtle comparisons between humans and so-called monsters. As Thomas Leitch states of 'the twelve-year-old vampire of *Let the Right One In*', she 'is considerably more appealing than most of the film's human characters',[8] and the same is true of the protagonist of the English-language remake, *Let Me In*, discussed in this chapter. Besides, the social criticism implied by the vampire figure has also undergone considerable change: the post-millennial vampire is no longer a metaphor for white upper classes preying on the lower groups of society, nor the racialised Other that threatens the nation state with invasion, and neither does it embody moral threats against Christian virtue. At the same time, it shares the somewhat melodramatic tendency of post-millennial young adult heroes: a refusal to accept their victimisation by social institutions and a desire to change their plight, or at least save the world, even if it involves sacrificing themselves in the process.

This feature calls to the heart of the post-millennial generation, which economist Noreena Hertz dubbed in her study Generation K, after Katniss Everdeen of *The Hunger Games*,[9] and whom Hertz describes as not only full of anxiety about the present and the future, but also creative and generous.[10] The anxiety of teenagers over their future, both personal and global, and young adult popular culture catering for such anxiety, is seen as one of the prime reasons for the popularity of both dystopian and horror narratives. Yet it is instructive to note how post-millennial narratives are no longer willing to acquit human society and its dominant institutions of their inadequacy when dealing with global threats to humanity. Nonetheless, in the third decade of the twenty-first century, the vampire craze seems to be on the wane – James Hibberd argued already in 2014 that spoofs and parodies are certain signs of the genre's demise. As he claims, these comic versions of the genre imply that the vampire has become a household figure, which obviously works against its primary intention: creating horror in the viewer, since 'Nothing kills scary monsters like laughter and familiarity', although even Hibberd suggests that the vampire as a figure is unlikely to disappear for good.[11]

Shakespeare deep down – *Underworld*

The first part of the *Underworld* series was released in 2003, directed by Len Wiseman, and in a manner reminiscent of the Lear story's survival in the *film noir* and western films discussed in Part I of the book, has provoked some debate as to its Shakespearean lineage, reviewers referring to it as 'Romeo & Juliet – Vampire & Werewolf Style'.[12] The film turned out to be successful enough to generate four more instalments, all of which became box-office successes, and characteristic products of the post-millennial vampire fashion, presenting a world of vampires and their enemies, the werewolves called Lycans, in a generic hybrid of horror and action-adventure. Stacey Abbott places the franchise in the company of other contemporary films that combine horror with elements of science-fiction cinema: 'In particular, the *Blade* films, *Underworld* (2003), *Van Helsing* (2004), and *Underworld: Evolution* (2006) have contributed to a reconception of generic conventions and iconography that undermines the laws of religion and folklore in favor of the laws of science and technology.'[13]

The *Underworld* films feature several dark and doomed love plots, which is the single thematic element actually reminiscent of Shakespeare's *Romeo and Juliet*, but this connection is regularly mentioned by reviewers and fans. On the Wikia site of the franchise, reference is even made to the fact that the story was consciously based on the Shakespearean drama. 'According to series creators Kevin Grevioux, Len Wiseman, and Danny McBride, the love story between Selene and Michael is based off of [*sic*] the romance seen in William Shakespeare's *Romeo and Juliet*: "Romeo and Juliet for Vampires and Werewolves".'[14] If hard-pressed, the viewer can discover further elements, including an unwanted suitor, a female helper in the family home and a father figure who stands in the way of the romance between enemies. There are a number of comparable plot turns, such as smaller and greater clashes to mark the warfare between the two clans, occasionally resulting in civilian casualties, recalling the drama's prologue and its reference to 'civil blood' making 'civil hands unclean' (line 4), and such generic similarities are apparently sufficient to warrant the Shakespearean label. The film includes a single explicit visual reference to Shakespeare in a scene when, during target practice, Selene takes visible pleasure in destroying busts of Shakespeare (see figure 5.1).

Interestingly, as if to emphasise the impossibility of tracing the origins of such archetypal plots as that of the doomed lovers, a legal suit was issued in 2003 against *Underworld* and its producer, Sony Entertainment. Author Nancy Collins and White Wolf Inc., publisher of several vampire- and werewolf-themed role-playing games, claimed in a lawsuit 'that the movie infringed upon their copyrights and plagiarized from a short story written by Collins that focused upon a *Romeo and Juliet*-type relationship between a vampire and werewolf'.[15] However, Sony countered that not only were the approximately seventy characteristics listed in the lawsuit not unique to the World of Darkness universe of White Wolf, but 'almost all of the characteristics had appeared in the previous fifty years of vampire movies and literature, most on multiple occasions'.[16] The case ended in a settlement out of court, but it is telling how labels of originality and authenticity function

Figure 5.1 Target practice with Shakespeare – Kate Beckinsale in *Underworld*. Directed by Len Wiseman, 2003. Lakeshore Entertainment/Subterranean Productions/Underworld Produktions GmbH/Laurinfilm.

to mark potentially lucrative enterprises in the contemporary world of popular publishing.

Comparing *Underworld* to *Romeo and Juliet* would indeed be rather futile or frustrating, since – as mentioned – the two share no more than the most basic elements in plot and characterisation. It is, however, interesting to note that in order for fans (or producers) to see *Underworld* as a *Romeo and Juliet* story, it is not necessary for the film (or even the later franchise) to preserve the original tragic ending. Like many other genre films incorporating a doomed love affair denied by parents or authorities, if the single element of forbidden love between members of two warring groups, clans, factions, tribes or species is present, the ending can adopt whatever conventions required by the genre, rather than the *denouement* of the source text.

Underworld and the peculiar qualities of its world-saving protagonists also fit the post-millennial version of undead narratives in the sense that instead of complete eradication of one race of monsters in order to achieve racial purity for the other – something that is often at the heart of vampire stories – it is the mixed-race, hybrid characters, born out of true love, that turn out to be the key to the future of humanity and the undead alike. As we will see later in this chapter, a similar trend can be observed in zombie cinema: 'only a savior that partakes of the nature of both the living and the undead can possibly save post-human humanity'.[17] In the *Underworld* universe, this blurring of boundaries is not only a thematic element but it is also visible in the cinematography and what Abbott calls a 'cyborg-warrior aesthetic', which 'embodies Selene's rejection of the frivolousness of the traditional vampire lifestyle, in which most of the other female vampires dress in sparkly – thus highly visible – loose-fitting evening gowns'.[18] Abbott goes on to argue that this hybridity is part of the central meaning and message of these films, as in effect such films 'undermine ... the opposition between flesh and technology, passive and active, good and evil, living and dead, human and non-human by having their lead vampire/zombie hunters take on a posthuman form, highlighting the empowerment that lies within this hybrid identity'.[19] This hybridisation between previously antagonistic forces – Shakespeare and the undead – takes consciously metadramatic form in the more explicit adaptations discussed next.

Vampire parody – *Rosencrantz and Guildenstern are Undead*

A very different take on the vampire as a character and the vampire film as a genre can be seen in Galland's 2009 comedy *Rosencrantz and Guildenstern are Undead*. In this case there can be no doubt as to the film's relation to Shakespeare: the title already acknowledges the plot's indebtedness to *Hamlet* and to Tom Stoppard's *Rosencrantz and Guildenstern are Dead*. Stoppard's play is invoked only by the title, although it implies a similarly irreverent attitude to the canonical text as its great postmodern forerunner. Yet this film is explicitly about a vampire adaptation of *Hamlet* (with the same title as the film) that the protagonist, useless loser Julian Marsh (Jake Hoffman), is hired to direct in a rundown off-Broadway theatre. Galland's work can therefore be regarded as another example of what Kenneth Rothwell called the mirror movie, but it treats the play-within-the-play structure with little respect, not so much as a complex and meaningful meta-theatrical device, but rather in a parodic nod to the time-honoured tradition.

At the same time, even in this mocked form, the play-within-the-play is capable of reflecting on the work and its whole context of creation as well, and asking pertinent questions on the apparent undead state of Shakespeare and the theatre in the contemporary cultural context. On the one hand, the way the team of vampires run the theatre and only need a 'young, controllable human director' is easy to interpret as a sarcastic reference to the cinema industry as a whole, where directors are disposable members of the machinery, whose main task is to carry out the wishes of the producer rather than to realise their own creative dreams. Julian Marsh is a failed would-be-director, who has neither been able to grow up (he still lives and entertains an endless line of casual girlfriends in a room in his father's surgery), nor possesses any particular talent or dedication whatsoever. He cannot distinguish between life and art, fact and fiction, appearance and reality – he constantly reprimands his vampires for their implausible acting, saying 'I don't think that's how a vampire would really do it', but allows the most talentless of his human actors walk over him. When Julian praises Theo Horace (John Ventimiglia), the original Horatio (turned vampire) with the words 'there's no separation between him and his character', it sounds like the highest praise for method actors trained in the Stanislavski school, whereas what we see is not art but reality, no fiction but simple fact. The film also mocks the way independent theatre (just as indie cinema, including this film) can put the most outrageous nonsense on show, without any regard for convention or marketability, and how snobbish audiences will take it all at face value. The vampire is the perfect symbol for this type of 'art', which is not motivated by financial greed or survival, but 'immortality' – yet the state of nearly complete dilapidation of the theatre questions the validity of such pretence.

Another cliché that is turned into a joke in the film is the commonly used excuse that filmmakers like to employ to attract audiences: the magic phrase referring to the (auto)biographical origins of a narrative, summed up as 'based-on-a-true-story'. Yet the script exposes this device of justifying bad fiction as an overused joke in several ways; first when the introduction shows a ballet dancer (soon to be killed by a vampire) rehearsing for the performance called *Toothfairy vs Candyland*, which she calls an autobiographical play. Her dance with a huge tooth (the symbolism of fangs not to be overlooked in a vampire comedy), visualises the comic contrast between the simplicity of the narrative and the serious form it is granted. But later on, the vampire version of Hamlet and Horatio's story is also revealed to be an autobiographical work by Theo Horace, that is, Horatio himself, indicating that Shakespeare's *Hamlet* is no work of fiction, but historical truth. Moreover, its characters have been alive (or rather, undead) since the 1600s – and Shakespeare was no more than a pawn in the hands of the vampire who wanted his story to be told (see figure 5.2).

If not a serious and meta-cinematic 'mirror-movie', *Rosencrantz and Guildenstern are Undead* is, however, a perfect example of the postmillennial horror (romantic) comedy, and when seen from this angle it is also a remarkably creative reworking of its Shakespearean source of inspiration. The filmmakers display a clear knowledge and awareness of even minor textual details of *Hamlet*, and find verbal constructs that can be turned into puns related to the new generic context. For all the outrageous vampire references in the plot, Julian's friend, Vince (Kris Lemche), who is cast to play Hamlet, takes the vampire threat as a joke, until he finds

Figure 5.2 Shakespeare under vampire command – Mike Landry and John Ventimiglia in *Rosencrantz and Guildenstern are Undead*. Directed by Jordan Galland, 2009. C Plus Pictures/Off Hollywood Pictures/Offhollywood Digital.

the confirmation in the text – not in the scenes inserted into the play by Theo, but the original Shakespearean line 'Now could I drink hot blood' (3.2.381). The way the Shakespearean text is appropriated to gain new meaning here is often creative and entertaining – a tendency characteristic of postmodern film, including horror comedies. Another example is when the vampire Horatio asks on stage 'How did you know that I was a vampire, fair Ophelia?' to which she replies: 'Look at you, pale as your shirt, your knees knocking each other', giving her words from *Hamlet* (2.1.81) a new vampire-themed meaning.

Another typical stylistic device shows that the post-millennial adaptation – particularly if it is a parodic one – readily relies on textual poaching, as has been shown repeatedly. The thematic relevance or original context of the (mis)quoted texts is less interesting for such a parody than the comic effect based on simple recognition and the extreme flexibility with which the script mixes literary quotations and fragments into its text, but clearly there is no expectation of comparative analysis of the works evoked by the twisted puns. This is the way the title cards in *Rosencrantz and Guildenstern are Undead* make references to literary and cinematic classics, for the simplest of vampire puns, creating chapter titles such as 'Job interview with a vampire', 'Grave new world', 'As I lay undying', 'Long day's journey into fright', 'Death of a pale man' or the concluding 'Breakfast is Tiffany'. The straightforward and unashamed parasitical exploitation of classical literature, particularly the great undead, Shakespeare and his work, illustrates how contemporary culture tends to decontextualise and remediate fragmented remains of classics in nearly random ways.[20]

While the film is on the one hand a light-hearted comic one-off, it can also be seen as an ironic reference to the current state of cultural affairs, with the lifeless dusty corpse of theatrical Shakespeare in need of reanimation by input from popular cinema. The fact that the theatre is taken over by vampires – creatures of the dark, who live in a world long gone by – is, of course, telling in this regard. But so is the film's ending, when the real-life, centuries-old Hamlet (Joey Kern), who has come to fight his nemesis, the vampire Theo, is completely ignored by audience members, who all flock to admire the clueless director Julian. After the show, Julian willingly turns himself over to his love Anna (Devon Aoki), already a vampire, so that they can be together and feast on their admirers forever. Anna's cheesy line, claiming that 'a vampire doesn't need to save her soul when she has a soulmate' also confirms the film's hybrid origins, the romantic comedy spicing up the parody of vampire films (or the other way around).

At the same time, the vampire as a symbol can be rather more meaningful than simply a joke: feasting on the greatest literary corpses of the past and reanimating them into another, seemingly living, version recalls the process of adaptation itself. Leitch, in his famous 2011 essay, has explicitly compared adaptations to vampires, as parasitical creatures kept alive by the blood they suck out of younger and fresher hosts.[21] In *Rosencrantz and Guildenstern are Undead*, the theatre is arguably a medium in a state of suspended animation, nearly as lifeless as the dead flowers picked out of the dustbin in the dark alley behind the building. But when injected with a bit of popular culture, it will be ready for presentation, as audiences are apparently willing to consume anything that is flavoured to their taste. As the film's Horatio reminds Hamlet, he is 'directly responsible for not only Hamlet's immortality as a vampire but also his immortality as a figure of world literature' – without this vampire's contribution, neither Shakespeare nor Hamlet would be remembered today.[22]

The film thus exemplifies how the former aristocratic figure of the vampire has become no more than a parasite by the twenty-first century, and more importantly, it also represents the claim that the literary corpus it keeps – if not alive, at least undead – is no longer a viable presence in itself, unless popular culture injects it with some fresh blood. Yet, as we also realise in the short film-within-the-film, the 'Rosecrucian and Goldenstonian' secret society's revelations concerning vampires, the undead may be able to hold onto some past beauty in this utterly ordinary world. As the simplistic animated cartoon shows how the former vampire Prince Hamlet (cured by drinking from the Holy Grail) travelled the globe, 'curing other vampires of their curse', we witness how attractive and spectacular-looking vampires are transformed into (less than) ordinary humans, with nothing desirable about them or their lives. This is how the film mocks Shakespearean theatre by equating it with the (un)dead body, but it also represents popular cinema as a pile of clichés and laughs at viewers and reviewers by showing how controllable they are. Yet the verbal and visual jokes and the sheer pleasure the film takes from poking fun at itself and its medium suggest that pastiche and parody are also natural forms of survival for Shakespeare today.

Blood-crossed young lovers – *Let Me In*

The most recent film combining Shakespearean themes with vampires is another example of the lengthy chains of adaptations whose original source is nearly impossible to unearth. Matt Reeves's *Let Me In* (2010) is a remake of a Swedish film, *Let the Right One In* (2008, dir. Tomas Alfredson), itself an adaptation of a Swedish novel, John Ajvide Lindqvist's *Låt den Rätte Komma In* (2004). *Let Me In*, a British-American co-production and one of the first films by the revived Hammer Films, was both a financial and a critical success, making a modest profit at the box office, and even when compared to its Swedish predecessor it is acknowledged as a worthy companion piece. The Shakespearean traces appear in all three works in the form of quotations from or references to *Romeo and Juliet*, the titles recalling Juliet's exclamation that her window 'let day in and let life out' (3.5.41). The last link in the chain of adaptations, *Let Me In*, discussed here, complements the textual quotations with further visual elements, underlining the significance of the Shakespearean source.

Greg M. Colón Semenza points out in his sensitive comparative reading of the novel and the two films how they all 'amplify the play's haunting echoes across the centuries, recycling its major themes for a contemporary audience suspicious of, but also desperate to believe in, the possibility of everlasting love'.[23] These echoes include iconic moments from the play's film history, mostly in the diverse ways the post-war adaptations comment on the 'enculturation argument', that is, the claim 'that if youth act violently, the adult culture in which they are reared must bear some part of the blame'.[24] This idea of violent youth as victims of adult society is particularly potent in *Let Me In*, which centres on a young boy, Owen (Kodi Smit-McPhee), bullied at school and neglected by his divorcing parents.

When he befriends a young vampire called Abby (Chloë Grace Moretz), he learns from her how to fend off his attackers and he ends up seriously injuring one. Eventually, Abby saves him from the older boys by killing the bullies in the school swimming pool. In the meantime, Abby's familiar, an elderly man (Richard Jenkins), who used to assist the girl in quenching her bloodthirst, suffers an inexplicable and gory death, and the police are soon on the trail of the vampire. Following a series of increasingly gory encounters, the film ends with the two youngsters leaving the isolated community, Owen travelling on a train with a large wooden chest, which we understand to be Abby's daytime hiding place.

Already this brief summary suggests that the primary interpretive context for the film must be found in horror cinema, and Peter Hutchings, in his analysis of various encounters between Shakespeare and cinematic horror, lists a number of new trends characteristic of horror since the 1960s and 1970s, distinguishing this wave from the earlier, 'more stylized Gothic approach'.[25] Most of the points he lists are clearly present in *Let Me In*, and even explain some of the changes to the Shakespearean material that Shakespeare film critics tend to mention as significant and potentially alienating from the source.

One such issue is the very young – clearly pre-sexual – age of the protagonists, which works against the film's identification as a *Romeo and Juliet* narrative, as the child characters mean that several crucial elements, including physical attraction, marriage and its consummation in the wedding night, are absent. At the same time, when seen in the context of horror cinema, which since the 1960s and 1970s has begun to display 'a focus on young people, who are often destroyed in the course of the film', the function of the extreme youth of these protagonists becomes clear.[26] Another item on Hutchings' list, 'a cynicism about the efficacy of social institutions and the powers of good, often resulting in open endings where evil remains undefeated', confirms the significance of this interpretive context.[27]

Yet, interestingly, the issue of sexual innocence – virginity or abstinence – can also serve as a potential link between *Romeo and Juliet* and vampire films, not only *Let Me In* but also *Underworld*, where the two enemy species' sexual union provides a turning point for the narrative comparable to the wedding night of Shakespeare's play. In the play, the overhasty marriage of the young couple is often commented on by contemporary rewritings as representative of a conservative attitude to virginity in love, thus the narrative of sexual abstinence until a legally sanctioned consummation can easily be translated into the vampire lover's self-sacrificial refusal to drink the human lover's blood. Moreover, this theme is also a central feature in the most fashionable contemporary young adult vampire narratives: *Twilight*'s handsome vegetarian vampire hero Edward Cullen also shows in- or non-human strength in withstanding Bella Swan's attraction, partly out of his desire for her protection but also out of a gentlemanly concern for her purity. It is true, as Patrick Gray points out, that in contemporary vampire narratives 'the sanctity of marriage, in the Christian sense, is simply not a concern'.[28] At the same time, the self-denying abstinence, refusing to partake of the other's blood, is introduced as a clearly moral decision, and *Let Me In* adds the Christian element as well, even if in the form of criticism. As Owen's mother is emphatically represented as a bigoted Christian, the film implies that her beliefs are incapable of saving the child, while it also shows the church as another institution that fails the younger generation.

Let Me In, however, does not engage in the beautified fantasy world of *Twilight* and other twenty-first-century vampire series, but it follows what Hutchings calls a realist approach in terms of visual style and cinematography. Its setting is the eerily familiar small town in the middle of nowhere – Los Alamos, New Mexico, in this particular case – but the temporal setting is made specific by Reagan's so-called 'Evil Empire' speech from 1983 addressed to the National Association of Evangelicals, broadcast on television screens within the diegesis. While the speech is famous for its rejection of equal responsibility in the nuclear arms race, designating the Soviet Union as the evil empire and the military efforts of the United States as the moral battle of good against evil, in *Let Me In* the phrase acquires additional overtones.[29] The short excerpt foreshadows the presence of unexpected forces of evil in the world, but more importantly, it associates this hypocritical urge to fight against evil with the hypocritical leaders of society, whose moral slogans are no more than a masquerade for their business interests.

The hypocrisy of the protective adult world also gets embodied in the character of Abby's familiar, who turns out to be no father, which is his cover story, but rather a paedophile. As a result, we see not only Owen but also Abby as a victim, rather than simply a violent perpetrator of unnameable crimes – even though we witness her performing those, too. Yet neither of the children can escape their own personal circumstances, and they easily fall through the cracks of the uncaring social system, with no adult or institution offering them real help (see figure 5.3). Hutchings' last item on the list, 'more explicit gore and violence',[30] is no longer visible as an exclusive characteristic of the post-1960s horror genre, but has become nearly endemic in several genres today, including historical films and thrillers, let

Figure 5.3 Romeo and Juliet abandoned – Chloë Grace Moretz and Kodi Smit-McPhee in *Let Me In*. Directed by Matt Reeves, 2010. Overture Films/Exclusive Media Group/Hammer Films/EFTI.

alone fantasies. In this way, the film sits easily within its generic context, while maintaining its investment in the *Romeo and Juliet* narrative at the same time.

The film's relation to its Shakespearean source is intricate and complex, as Semenza shows both the ways textual echoes appear in Lindqvist's novel already, but Reeves's script adds a further level of cinematic echoes, including a classroom scene (reminiscent of the teen genre's staple moment of studying Shakespeare at school). However, in *Let Me In*, the short scene from Franco Zeffirelli's *Romeo and Juliet* makes it clear that it is not a simple cinematic echo that is evoked here. While the class is watching the film, Owen does not pay any attention to the screen, therefore his recognition of his and Abby's story as co-dependence and partnership in the middle of a hostile world is associated entirely with his reading and Abby's quoting of the dramatic text in a note. As the image on screen is the wedding night, with Olivia Hussey's body on display, Owen's lack of attention confirms the absence of any sexual desire for Abby. The cinematic echoes within the film, however, are still instructive in underlining certain aspects of the plot and its interpretation.

One potentially problematic moment may be the film's ending, which does not see the young protagonists die, but shows them on a train, getting away from it all. And yet there is no sense in which this chance to escape would turn *Let Me In* into a comedy, romantic or otherwise. This resolution rather allows the film to explore and expand the 'escape fantasy' that Semenza connects to *West Side Story*'s famous song 'Somewhere', mediated through the funeral scene of Baz Luhrmann's *Romeo + Juliet*, and finally manifested here as a possibility that they 'discover their "somewhere" in life together after death'.[31] Even if their escape to the unknown can only be seen as a temporary victory – Owen may soon turn into another familiar of the vampire, if not himself a vampire – Leitch refers to an aspect of vampires' parasitical existence that may be relevant here.[32] As he suggests, by becoming vampires, the lovers are no longer capable of a biologically fruitful consummation of their love, therefore they are denied a future in the form of having children. This vampire existence is thus in effect comparable to the absence of a future granted to Romeo and Juliet, or the Capulet and Montague families in general: the only survival in this inhuman world for the young generation, whose lifeblood has been prematurely drained by their elders, is becoming undead. In this sense, the vampire love affair becomes the ultimately romantic representation of undying love, which embodies the hopeless and futureless prospects of contemporary young generations, while maintaining their belief in the endlessness of love.

The walking corpus – zombie Shakespeare

Following in the footsteps of the aristocracy of the undead, the new millennium has seen the resurgence of another, more democratic, kind of horror monster, the zombie, both in Shakespeare-related films and mainstream genre cinema. Phil Hoad refers to this class distinction in his comments on the revival of the zombie genre: 'Where vampires preened with lingering 19th-century aristocratic individualism, zombies are the 20th-century proletarian masses given a Halloween makeover.'[33] Moreover, although the nearly hysterical craze over vampires seems to be on the wane, zombies are arguably still here to stay, on screens and on the pages of pulp fiction. The thematic underpinning of the new craze is the idea that zombies are meant to tell us something about ourselves, showing 'how messed up we are', and beside the 'gore and violence and all that cool stuff ... there's always an undercurrent of social commentary and thoughtfulness' in these narratives, as Robert Kirkman emphasises the common features between his work, the *Walking Dead* graphic novel series and good zombie cinema.[34]

Bearing such thematic concerns in mind, the rest of the chapter will examine the ways Shakespeare has been accommodated in zombie cinema, and see how the individual films combine their Shakespearean heritage with the framework of this particular subgenre. As Meghan Sutherland argues, 'the mainstream zombie remake signifies as it does in part because the themes and subjects it narrates intersect with the political and industrial institutions that produce it'.[35] That is why it is vital to examine the zombie Shakespeare films in their industrial and generic contexts as well, not simply as channels of general social critique, and certainly not only as distorted forms of the Bard. As an examination of *Zombie Hamlet* and *Warm Bodies* will show, these films successfully incorporate both Shakespearean drama and the zombie theme into the dominant narrative of the zombie comedy/parody, illustrating how the adapting genre overrides the former associations any character or motif may bring with it.

First and foremost, it is worth pondering about why the combination of Shakespeare with zombie horror also typically happens within the comic versions of the genre. There are many reasons for this, some of them already implied and mostly attributable to the natural lifespan of the genre that reached its post-maturity by the twenty-first century. As A. S. Hamrah writes concerning 'Edgar Wright's 2004 *Shaun of the Dead*, the first movie zomcom', this 'goofy rethinking of the zombie movie proved how firmly zombies are entrenched in our consciousness, and how easy they are to manipulate for comedic effect'.[36] In the discussions that follow, we can also note how the canonised elements of high culture – Shakespeare and his best-known plays in particular – are at the same time contrasted and combined with these entrenched images of popular visual culture. While the zombie hype itself often seems to come in for criticism, as does Shakespeare and his cultural authority, the films do not completely discard the original socio-critical attitude of the zombie genre, they simply present their social commentary in a more light-hearted manner.

Yet the combinations of zombie horror and comedy (the 'zomcom', or 'zombedy') display significant differences from the classical horror genre, as Kyle Bishop points out in his analysis. They 'offer viewers all the shock, gore, and horror of the zombie tragedies, but their resolutions are markedly different: zombedies, true to their classical roots, end on a note of hope, promise, and stability in the form of a newly constituted family and/or marriage'.[37] This classical comic form is undoubtedly present in the zom-rom-com *Warm Bodies*, with the romantic comedy dominating the plotline and the zombie elements providing the obstacles in the course of true love. *Zombie Hamlet*, on the other hand, relies on farcical adventure-comedy elements instead of the conventions of the romantic comedy – in this sense it is more a relative of *Zombieland* (2009, dir. Ruben Fleischer) than George A. Romero's films, or even of *Warm Bodies*. As Bishop sums up, 'the key to all zombedies' success lies in what has come to be called "splatstick" comedy', which 'exploits the frailty of the human body, exploring its abjection through extreme violence, physical pratfalls, and lots and lots of blood and gore'.[38] Yet *Zombie Hamlet*, as we shall see, only imitates the realism of zombie comedies, and in its hybrid mix the most defining elements come from the mockumentary, in which a fictional event is presented using the devices and techniques of documentary filmmaking. Its criticism, however, openly targets both the commercial film industry, for its cheap and predictably formulaic conventions, and attacks perhaps even more the zombified hordes of popular culture consumers, who unthinkingly devour everything presented by the ruthlessly exploitative industry. In this way viewers can be held culpable for their own zombification, invoking the moral issues implied by the zombie genre in its more serious iterations, where victimhood and complicity are always intricately intertwined.

Low-budget undead – *Zombie Hamlet*

John Murlowski's comedy is centred around the criticism of the unimaginative and repetitive world of genre cinema, but it does not spare cultural snobbery either, pointing out how Shakespeare's cultural authority can be (ab)used in the hope of financial gains. In *Zombie Hamlet*, young director Osric Taylor's (Travis Wester) dream project is to direct Shakespeare's *Hamlet* in a spectacular big-budget production, set in the American Civil War, to add an epic dimension à la *Gone With the Wind* to the prestigious story. When the promised funding falls through, he has no choice but to accept the money he is offered by an unlikely supporter, on condition that the enterprise will include zombies. In this way, the film joins the long line of (semi-)comic works – from *Shakespeare Wallah* (1965, dir. James Ivory) to *Hamlet 2* (2008, dir. Andrew Fleming) – that lament the decline of *auteur* theatre and cinema in the face of the financially more powerful opposition of popular visual culture. The zombie film, however, combines this age-old lament with the trope of the undead, which becomes associated with the four-hundred-year-old body of Shakespeare's work, regarded as a decomposing corpse, rather than a live participant in contemporary culture. The plot abounds in the complexities characteristic of slapstick comedy, from a dead body hidden in, and then disappearing from, the freezer, to voodoo loan sharks and Southern belles, not to mention gossip-hungry small-town media presenters and more. Suffice it to say that Osric's original project ends up twisted completely out of recognition, but by an unexpected turn of events he still achieves fame and even financial success.

The whole project shares more than a few similarities with *Rosencrantz and Guildenstern are Undead*, and it features a number of surprisingly self-reflexive moments. In fact, it includes another film shot simultaneously with the *Zombie Hamlet* enterprise, as Osric is so fascinated by the idea of making a behind-the-scenes documentary that he gives his small camera to the first wannabe actor and make-up artist, local boy Lester (Brendan Michael Coughlin). This meta-cinematic interest is what makes *Zombie Hamlet* more than a 'horror mash-up', as one reviewer says: it is 'a mocking spoof of the worst things that could go into a film of that kind. Taken as the silly farce that it is, *Zombie Hamlet* can be a very funny film about what not to do in a Shakespeare adaptation',[39] and this awareness of its own failings makes it almost comparable to *A Midsummer Night's Dream*'s critique on popular entertainment. Its embeddedness in popular culture provides a number of its jokes, as the brainstorming session of the filmmaking team is full of references to previous cultic or blockbuster films, from *Gone with the Wind* to *A Clockwork Orange*, all suggesting that artistic success depends to a great extent on a successful imitation of earlier formulas (which, in essence, is what genre film production is based on). The clownish name of the director, Osric, associates him with Hamlet's foppish courtier, who 'only got the tune of the time' (5.2.186–7) and follows the direction wherever the wind blows him.

All the compulsory elements of comic failures are coded into the picture from the start; Osric's previous directorial credits comprise a single advertisement that was a resounding artistic failure and the *Hamlet* project also seems doomed from the start. It is rather telling that the undead appear to be more alive than cinemagoers' undying appreciation for the Bard, and the necessity to compromise between what one believes in and what is on demand provides the main source of amusement throughout the film. As Osric says: 'zombies are hot, and it's kind of where Shakespeare was going anyway', his serious opportunism mocking the overused phrase that 'if Shakespeare were alive today, he would be writing screenplays', a line no one can trace back to its first author, but everyone keeps quoting. (Barbara Hodgdon observes that already 'by the late 1960s and early 1970s the idea that Shakespeare wrote "cinematically" was circulating in academic culture'.[40])

The hotness of zombies, however, comes into question when it turns out that the Southern patroness of the project, Hester Beauchamp (June Lockhart), slightly mixes her post-millennial undead, since she professes to like 'all that team Edward – team Jacob stuff'. On the whole, however, she is just as much a fan of popular cinema as the younger target audience (her own fame and wealth is based on a single volume of romantic pulp fiction that is still a favourite with young women). She believes that artistic inspiration can only come from one's own life experience (another common feature with *Rosencrantz and Guildenstern are Undead*), therefore when her seemingly lifeless body is moving around the house, the zombie movie turns into uncanny (and highly ironic) reality after all. Nonetheless, the film's implication that the South is not so much the land of voodoo magic as a place of pragmatic business interests works against old-fashioned social and racist stereotypes, while it also shatters the last shreds of illusion concerning the romantic mysticism of the setting and proves that in the world of the media it is only money that matters.

It is true that *Zombie Hamlet* neither is, nor pretends to be, more than a low-budget garage project, and the zombie characters never even appear other than masked amateur actors, yet in a few cases the film does not only mock but also adopts the conventions of the serious zombie genre. Such a tongue-in-cheek scene shows the zombie-playing extras shuffling off the shooting location, exactly in the same type of undead motion as when they are in role, but with their eyes turned to their smartphone screens. It is, however, at the film's ending that the real zombification of the cinema-going population is shown. While Osric and Lester, the documentary cameraman-cum-make-up artist are in jail for fraudulently impersonating Hester in order to get access to her bank account, they edit the film (including the behind-the-scene documentary scenes). Without their knowledge, the film goes viral online, the net is full not only of admirers' comments but even children's home-made re-enactments of the scenes, and suddenly the jail is surrounded by screaming teenagers, all shouting their undying devotion to the filmmakers.

The film even goes on to poke fun at academics as well, embodied by a more-than-stereotypical, balding moustachioed scholar in an old-fashioned pinstripe suit and a red bow tie (his name and affiliation are given as 'Proff. Reginald Chester Wellington III Chair of Cambridge School of Arts and Humanities'), who interprets and evaluates the film, describing it as a masterpiece of documentary filmmaking which 'also elevated the entire form of cinema – it's extraordinary filmmaking, it's extraordinary!' The film he praises, as it turns out, is not Osric's *Zombie Hamlet* but *Bringing the Undead to Life: The Making of Zombie Hamlet*, Lester's behind-the-scene film. Lester in an interview (included in the film, which is now revealed to be a film about the making of a film about the making of a film) tells the secret of all directors: 'I was just trying to tell a story' – one of the most often heard clichés in award-ceremony speeches and interviews. In the wake of this cinematic craze, Osric's *Zombie Hamlet* seems also to have taken off, albeit enraging Shakespeare purists (aka aspiring actors who did not make the cut), who ask: 'What's next? *Taming of the Shrew*

Figure 5.4 Whatever it takes – Hulk Hogan in *Zombie Hamlet*. Directed by John Murlowski, 2012. Three Girls Running/Maple Island Films/Zombie Hamlet.

with vampires?' The reply comes from the executive producer, who earlier refused to fund Osric but now is fully on board, seeing the business opportunity in the popular Shakespeare crossovers. He promises not only *Taming of the Shrew* with vampires, but a *Romeo and Ghouliet* with ghouls and werewolves, *The Merry Stepford Wives of Windsor*, not to mention a vampire *Macbeth* project, in which Hulk Hogan himself appears for a moment (see figure 5.4), whom Osric named earlier as the worst possible choice for a Shakespeare role.

From a generic viewpoint, the film is a hybrid of several genres: its structure, camera technique and editing imitate the mockumentary, but its self-conscious digs at popular genre cinema also make its relationship to zombie horror and literary adaptations more than clear. The computer-generated imagery (CGI) titles and special effects are also characteristic of all humorous blood-and-gore films, as the creative effects often become part of the diegesis. While *Zombie Hamlet* has little to offer to Shakespeare scholarship, apart from a few moderately clever puns that work in much the same way that *Rosencrantz and Guildenstern are Undead* twists the Shakespearean language into monstrous undead references, as a parodic take on contemporary popular cultural production, artistic integrity and the consumers of such works of art it regularly hits its target. Yet the film also reveals the multiple meanings associated with Shakespeare in contemporary culture, as in a discussion with Hester's beau and attorney (John Amos), who demands that they cut 'all the talkie stuff' from the film – to Osric's protest, saying that 'it's Shakespeare', Edgar simply replies: 'Not yet, it isn't.' Shakespeare serves not only as an authenticating high cultural label and a corpse that can be freely robbed for his best sentences, but also as an excuse for the incomprehensible cultural deadwood such phrases mean for a zombie film. At the same time, the name is still a mark of quality, a sign of value that serves as a point of reference in all cultural contexts.

Zombie romance – *Warm Bodies*

The best-known, financially most successful and critically most acknowledged film discussed in the chapter is undoubtedly Jonathan Levine's *Warm Bodies* (2013). The film was based on Isaac Marion's novel, published in 2010, and it became an instant blockbuster, grossing above $116 million, which is a considerable amount not only in a market already saturated with zombie movies, but also when compared to Shakespeare adaptations overall. For its commercial and even critical success, some of the credit may undoubtedly go to Shakespeare, and the film may offer the perfect glimpse at how a conscious adaptation of Shakespearean source material into the undead genres may function best.

This consciousness, though, needs some qualification: Christy Desmet argues that 'for *Warm Bodies* … the debt to Shakespeare was articulated and elaborated only in retrospect by its readers in electronic venues, until the status of *Warm Bodies* as an appropriation of Shakespeare's love tragedy finally became institutionalized within educational circles'.[41] But whether we take issue with such retrospective identifications, audiences and reviewers have already accepted the film as a contemporary version of *Romeo and Juliet*, and debate only whether the survival of both young lovers, or the benevolent and loving (even lovable) zombie, capable of human emotions, are more unusual or subversive in the light of the film's origins. Here again, however, the zombie comedy may be the more relevant background, as *Warm Bodies* seems to adopt its rules on many levels. As Bishop argues, the 'central defining feature of the screen zombedy is *not* the cathartic sight gags resulting from the excessive slaughter of various reanimated corpses but rather the recreation of an almost utopian human society, one in which the previously ostracized hero has found purpose, stability, and social inclusion by establishing a traditional family structure'.[42]

Warm Bodies certainly chooses the romantic comedy as its predominant mode, and it does not target the hard-core horror fans, but, by toning down on the blood and gore, uses it as background motivation, in order to provide some excitement for the blossoming romance. Yet certain elements of the zombie comedy's cinematography are employed by *Warm Bodies* as well, including slow-motion photography and voiceover narration, often derided as overused techniques, here serving the purposes of ironic self-reflection. For one thing, the zombie genre, and particularly the zombie as a figure, has been analysed sufficiently to show that it can and indeed should be seen as a symbol, representing the very real problems of human society. Rob Latham's review of *Zone One* refers to the genre's tendency to turn into 'brooding meditations on cultural inertia and social collapse',[43] recalling the somewhat 'zombified' human culture of the Western world, but George A. Romero's films, the genre's classics, are also clear examples of social criticism.

In *Warm Bodies*, it is a very straightforward parallel between zombies and the brainless masses of contemporary consumer society, emphasised by the ironically nostalgic contemplation of zombie boy R (Nicholas Hoult), who lives in an abandoned airport: 'It must have been so much better before, when everyone could express themselves, communicate their feelings, and just enjoy each other's company.' What we see on screen is a crowd of people – rather like the zombies currently inhabiting the airport – shuffling around, their heads bent over their smartphones, occasionally bumping into each other, but definitely showing no signs of feelings or communication. As even the least sophisticated reviews note, such images are straight references to other films in the genre (even *Zombie Hamlet* features a similar scene), with a number of reviewers calling it another 'witty reinvention of the genre like *Shaun of the Dead* before it, drawing parallels between the apathy of youth and the zombie masses'.[44] Such brainless masses appearing in shopping malls, amusement parks and other staple locations of consumer society populate zombie films, serious and comic ones alike. In these iconic settings, suddenly emptied out of humans and filled (or threatened) with zombified crowds, the contrast between humanity as an ideal and its real-life embodiment is the most striking. The narrow line between the human and the non- (or in-)human is at the undead heart of zombie cinema, whose main intention seems to be to provide a reminder of the most important values of humanity. In this respect, *Warm Bodies* is no exception and not even unusual, as Romero's films had already shown a gradual dehumanisation of humans paralleled by an increasing humanisation of zombies, paving the way for the fully humanised monsters of the new millennium.[45]

This tendency of the endemic modern technology to zombify urban crowds is acknowledged for its severity far beyond this metaphorical manner in Hollywood films. In Germany, the word 'smombie', a combination of 'smartphone zombie', was voted the official Youth Word of the year 2015,[46] and the phenomenon of technology-obsessed crowds is well known all over the world; therefore this joke in *Warm Bodies* is easy to get – but, as with most of the film's jokes, it is also earnestly meant. Another message of zombie films that remains central in comic versions as well is targeted at the disintegration of contemporary society, the failure of the family (together with larger social units) and the consequent isolation and marginalisation that is as much cause as effect of the outbreak of the zombie apocalypse. The technical or scientific explanations that these films offer are simply implausible (even in the 'serious' zombie films, if one wants to be perfectly honest, although those are often more successful in playing on real or realistic contemporary fears of the Other, of unstoppable viral infections or brainwashed societies), but they are also presented as irrelevant. It no longer matters how or why the whole thing started, probably since the central claim is that the time in which we thought we were not yet zombies, was when society was most zombie-like. In the same vein, *Warm Bodies* simply presents a world divided between two camps: the hordes of zombies shuffling around in the open plains, set against the heavily fortified, much more inhuman, indeed prison-like settlements where humans are caught up in a seemingly endless fight for survival. In *Warm Bodies* the only remaining family tie is between Julie (Teresa Palmer) and her father (John Malkovich), but it is no longer a functioning one, and, based on a few passing references, the father's alienation from his family is not an entirely new phenomenon, therefore it cannot be fully blamed on the zombies either. This is the context in which the love plot between R and Julie is set, naturally deemed impossible from the start, but eventually blossoming into a world-saving narrative device.

A lack of explanation for the outbreak is, interestingly, not only characteristic of comic versions of the zombie genre; interpreting the successful *The Walking Dead* series of Kirkman, Kim Paffenroth also emphasises how the optimism of *The Walking Dead* comes from its representation of love and the family, both of which are 'more positive and powerful in *The Walking Dead* than they are in *Night of the Living Dead* or many other current versions of the zombie apocalypse'.[47] This love, however, points beyond the simple adherence to blood ties, which become lethal if too tight, as Shakespeare's star-crossed lovers are all too well aware. Love is only powerful when it can be extended to outsiders, and the right kind of love 'is also shown to be stronger than (un)death', since the real threat comes no longer from the zombies alone, but from the living, who threaten the newly established social units.[48]

Looking at it this way, this summary may easily fit Shakespeare's *Romeo and Juliet*, the source play for *Warm Bodies*, as the drama is fundamentally based on the concept of the family, where the unthinking adherence to familial duty turns out to be the most poisonous weapon. In fair Verona, the family (as blood tie and unquestionable duty) is the most closely guarded prison; however, the newly established family unit – the marriage between the young lovers – will be able to break the curse of the long feud between the families. What is more, the Shakespearean text takes pains not to identify the causes of the deadly enmity in any way, or to distinguish between the two opposing factions, thus leaving the feud just as unexplained as the viral outbreaks in zombie cinema. What we see in *Warm Bodies* is a sick and distorted family, which only becomes an actually functioning social unit in the end through R's self-sacrificing gesture and his subsequent revival in human form. It is also the love of R and Julie that begins to have an effect on all other zombies, and thus proves more powerful than (un)death. The dysfunctional family in *Warm Bodies*, however, must not be seen as fully interchangeable with the Montague and Capulet houses; nonetheless, the manifestations of unorthodox families that replace blood ties are indeed significant.

Longing for the past, longing for a home is there in all zombie comedies, and this general nostalgia finds expression in the films on many levels, including the technological, as we will see. But in the more optimistic variant of the zombedy, there is also a strong survival instinct at work: if the old home is no longer a viable option, then a new home will have to be created, as it is repeatedly stated in *Zombieland*, among other works. *Warm Bodies*, when Julie asks R whether he wants his old life back (including his name that seems to have been lost through his zombiehood), he simply replies: 'No, I want this one.' R's satisfaction with his lot underlines the happy union of love and the prospective future in front of the couple, which the cinematography also emphasises by the warm colours and the light of the sun flooding the landscape when the wall dividing the two worlds is torn down. The breaking down of borders could be interpreted as a recreation of the 'glooming peace' (5.3.304) and reconciliation at the end of *Romeo and Juliet* (a problematic aspect of the play, no wonder it is often absent from film versions). Yet here there is nothing glooming about the peace, because it represents a more complete restoration of the ideal and universal family home of humankind, when no group or individual is othered by gun-toting fanatics.

The issue of othering also points out that we would not do justice to the zombie and its cinematic appearances if we reduced it to a straightforward identification with the consumer masses of modern society. Sasha Cocarla lists how since the earliest manifestations of the genre, zombies have 'stood in as metaphors for deep cultural fears and tensions, including racism and enslavement of racial minorities, cannibalism, bio-terrorism and disease outbreaks, the fall of rationality and independence to instinct-motivated herd mentality, and the complete numbing of humanity, to name but a few examples'.[49] The zombie is always a symbol of contemporary anxieties, like the Cold War in the 1970s or the 'industrial military complex of the United States'[50] in the 1980s, and the most typical recent metaphorical use of the zombie is its reference to the racial Other, often visible on news screens in migrant masses. Analyses of the racial politics of traditional representations of zombies shed light on the ways, to quote James McFarland, that 'the zombie-image opens onto racism's genocidal violence in its own terms, and as powerfully as any of the anthropological concepts developed to comprehend and to combat the perverse persistence of that violence'.[51] The fence-building instinct of various governments in a move to fend off the hordes of the dispossessed is all too familiar for twenty-first-century viewers.

Warm Bodies, it must be admitted, does not enter the territory of explicit racial conflict, as characters of colour can be found on both sides of the great divide, among the zombies and also the soldiers hell-bent on exterminating them, but none are granted any specific role in the plot. What the film emphasises instead is the enemy within: as Julie's father, the Colonel, warns the young volunteers who venture out into the abandoned town to search for medical supplies: 'whether they were your mother or your best friend, they are beyond your help'. This speech, reminding viewers that appearances are deceptive and the real danger can hide behind the most familiar of faces, is a nearly verbatim quote from George A. Romero's *Dawn of the Dead*. There, in a television broadcast, 'Dr Milliard Rausch (Richard France) … exhort[s] viewers that "we must not be lulled by the concept that these are our family members or friends. They are not. … They must be destroyed on sight."'[52] But by proving this view wrong, *Warm Bodies* denies 'the assertion … in the current deluge of zombie films that the Other deserves little or no empathy, except for the occasional twitch of concern that the human killers may become desensitized to violence'.[53] The romance plotline works precisely on the condition that the Other is just as human deep inside as we are and the power of love can help it regain its full humanity.

This monstrous Other is naturally a staple element of the horror genre, yet zombie films are set apart from other types of horror, whose basic scenario is described by film critic Robin Wood as 'normality … threatened by the Monster'.[54] The zombie film, however, even Romero's trilogy, resists this simplistic structure and displays a more triangular set-up, where it turns out that the common enemy of all is not the horde of zombies but a violent and inhuman group of humans, set against both the undead and the rest of humanity. Even such a light-hearted romantic comedy as *Warm Bodies* subscribes to this interpretation, where right at the very beginning Julie observes how the way zombies are described by the central authority figure – her father, the Colonel – as 'uncaring, unfeeling, incapable of remorse' – fits her father himself best. When the Colonel signs off the video message by the emptied-out phrase 'Good luck, God speed, and God bless America', it is hard not to see the hypocrisy in the way he implies that he and the small group of leftover humans should be seen as saviours of the world. Still, being a romantic comedy, *Warm Bodies* cannot afford to dispense with any human family members (not even as many as in the source of the film, Isaac Marion's novel, where Julie's father is deemed impossible to save and is duly killed off). Here alliances shift and the not completely skeletal zombies join forces with humans to wipe out the Boneys, who are too far gone to be saved, but Julie and her father are allowed a happy reunion. The phrase 'God bless America' is actually a clear reference to another characteristic feature of zombie cinema: its patriotism. Even in its comic form, as in *Zombieland*, the viewer is given a conscious reminder that it is America, the indestructible land of opportunities, whose demise we are witnessing – and in both (as in all other zombie apocalypse narratives) America equals the world, period.

The short videocast mentioned is symptomatic of one further feature of zombie films: their consistent employment of diverse types of media. As Allan Cameron observes, 'The modern zombie is a media zombie',[55] arguing that 'the zombie film's engagement with media extends well beyond ... obvious examples of social critique and the associated notion that media are capable of "zombifying" their audiences', and that 'this engagement ... extends to the very materiality of recording and broadcast media'.[56] Indeed, while the most blatant instance of social critique in *Warm Bodies* is the described flashback scene at the airport, there are several, more subtle details that tie in nicely with Cameron's analysis. For one thing, the grainy image of broadcast media, emphasising its material qualities – and their susceptibility to decay and disembodiment – reinforces the link between the Colonel and the zombies even in the videocast at the outset of the film.

Moreover, the zombie's engagement with the past, such as R's fascination with vinyl records, is presented as a vital ability and inclination to hold onto the values of humanity, as opposed to the self-destructive race towards and beyond the apocalypse in which the rest of human (and zombie) society appears to be engaged. Ironically, R prefers vinyl to digital media because it is more 'alive', and indeed, he subsequently turns his record collection into a channel of communication with Julie. Here the hoarding of discarded objects is without the eerie qualities that appear, for instance, in the *Saw* films, whose serial killer protagonist fills his lair 'with odd detritus, including tangles of wire, rusted iron machinery, and broken dolls and mannequins'.[57] Even there we get a sense of how the rubbish of the past can be turned into some form of artistic expression, but here R's ability to see the greater value and full functionality – a form of life – in these remnants of the past, is a sign of his own, fully retained, humanity.

In the same way, the Polaroid camera R and Julie find in an abandoned house and its nearly instant materialisation of images can also be seen as fitting: instead of the intangible but instantly visible images of digital media, the slowly visualising Polaroid hangs on to the printed paper just as the slow-motion zombie hangs on to the material body. The Holmes stereoscope, one of the early viewing devices, is instrumental in the development of romantic intimacy between the central characters, where even the images viewed on the device are references to an old-fashioned courtship ritual, nostalgically viewed and desired by both protagonists. Subsequently, the conscious effort of preserving memories (rather than the instant but disappearing images transmitted by the consumption of brains) is what triggers the change in zombies and becomes the salvation of humankind. This common need of both humans and well-meaning zombies is also signalled by their shared vocabulary, for instance the word 'exhume', which Julie uses to refer to bringing back memories and things lost in the world. R repeats the word when referring to his wish to retrieve Julie herself, who has gone back to the closed military zone of humanity and is therefore seemingly dead to him.

Even though *Warm Bodies* offers a refreshingly ironic, even comic, take on not only its narrative source material but on its adopted genre, the zombie film, it does follow most of the required narrative and cinematic conventions that make the genre recognisable to its audiences, as the discussion thus far has tried to illustrate. Less obvious is the way it is indebted to Shakespeare's *Romeo and Juliet*, although a few of its references, the names R and Julie, and particularly the two star-crossed lovers from enemy camps, would ring bells even for the most ignorant of viewers. Then there is the most iconic of Shakespeare scenes: the young and besotted boy standing below the balcony on which his beloved one is declaring her love, although here there is no declaration, as R would find it hard to join in the quick repartee anyway. Digging deeper in the film script, we may also recognise a Mercutio figure (Rob Corddry), another zombie, called M, who turns out to be a Marcus in the end, and who does not get killed, but is the first to join the fight on R's side. Julie's friend, Nora (Analeigh Tipton) will also be supportive of the cross-cultural romance, and when we learn that she dreams of becoming a nurse, another Shakespearean association is ticked off. Nor does it take a giant leap of the imagination to see Julie's ex-boyfriend Perry Kelvin (Dave Franco) as Count Paris, the alternate male partner, who has, however, turned repulsive in the eyes of the girl.

The fact that R saves Julie only after finishing off Perry and devouring his brain, acquiring in this way his memories, only complicates the case a little, and this motive is thoroughly exploited in the original novel by Isaac Marion. Cocarla's analysis, based on an understanding of the novel's participation in the neoliberal discourse, offers an interesting element of potential queering within the text, in the relationship forged between R and Perry through R's consumption of Perry's brains. The film, however, consciously follows a more conventional line in terms of heteronormativity and the centrality of romance in the diegesis, emphasising the transformative power of love rather than R's independent desire to change. This desire would be 'key to a neoliberal politic, where one must see the ability to obtain social and economic privileges as resting solely on one's ability to change and adapt'.[58] But the film makes subtle changes all the way through the narrative, to signal that the originary moment of all changes in R are directly linked to his first encounter with Julie. Afterwards it is his increasing bodily proximity to her, from touching, holding hands, to kissing (the sight of which will begin to have a similar transformative effect on other zombies), rather than a mediated relationship through Perry's spectral consciousness, that complete R's transformation (see figure 5.5). Still, this evolutionary narrative may not need to be explained by a neoliberal or other political stance, but simply by a common theme in several zombie films: 'As in *28 Days Later*, the primary narratives of *Land of the Dead* and *Warm Bodies* are based in a comic and communal view of survival, rather than a tragic view that equates survival with extermination, but in *Land of the Dead* and *Warm Bodies*, ideals of community extend to include zombies and the nonhuman nature they represent.'[59] These interpretive contexts also show how the zombie film, even in its comic iteration, is created – and certainly read – as social commentary rather than literary narrative, explaining why the highly formulaic and extremely limited plot variations are rarely seen as failures.

Apart from Perry's inelegant demise into zombie food, Isaac Marion's novel also makes a few light-hearted jokes at the cost of Shakespeare

Figure 5.5 The personal touch – Nicholas Hoult and Teresa Palmer in *Warm Bodies*. Directed by Jonathan Levine, 2013. Summit Entertainment/ Make Movies/Mandeville Pictures/Quebec Film and Television Tax Credit.

and other classics, but does not include textual quotations from the play (although it relies heavily on the lyrics of romantic classics from Frank Sinatra to Paul McCartney). Interestingly, even Marion saw the Shakespearean influence as somehow sneaking into the text during the writing process, and only after the recognition of the parallels did he decide 'to run with it, so [he] named the characters accordingly, and scattered cute little references throughout'.[60] Apart from these previously listed 'cute little references' in names, characters and the balcony scene in particular, Shakespeare nonetheless haunts the film in more indirect ways. One of these is a classroom scene – a flashback memory that R gets when he consumes a chunk of Perry's brain – where we see Julie and Perry smile at each other, while in the background the teacher drones on, practically unheard. On the blackboard, however, we may glimpse the word Hamlet, together with other notes implying that the class was discussing Shakespeare's play, but apparently this did not leave lasting memories in Perry's brain (just as school Shakespeare left Owen unimpressed in *Let Me In*). This scene, a staple in the teen genre, as discussed in Chapter 4, points to the film's hybrid generic origins and supports early reviewers' identification of the film with a *Twilight*-type teen horror romance – but the diegetic focus on the post-apocalyptic events sets it apart from high school films.

The most striking difference between the Shakespearean tragedy and *Warm Bodies* is clearly the ending – for all its gruesome topic and the gory details, *Warm Bodies* can in no way be classified as a tragedy. Not only because it pokes fun at its own genre, but rather as it ends on a note of unqualified happiness, with the live reunion of no-longer-zombie R and his Julie. Funnily enough, observing the rules of the genre, the post-apocalyptic romantic comedy actually requires keeping both protagonists alive, or, more precisely, bringing the boy back from the dead. This decision is clearly justified by the genre itself, since the narrative of zombie films typically includes a 'saving humanity' scenario (and, in this instance, the remedy is, of course, true love). This rejection of medical or scientific explanations in favour of a romantic solution is not entirely alien to supernatural teen films, as many young adult romances overwrite their science-fiction or fantasy narratives for the sake of this archetypal ending, for instance in the romantic fantasy *Upside Down* (2012, dir. Juan Diego Solanas).

As we could see, while *Warm Bodies* as a Shakespeare film may not merit in-depth textual analysis, it serves as a perfect example to illustrate the claim that instead of a fidelity-based interpretation, film adaptations are best approached from the perspective of the adapting genre, which will define all significant aspects of the new product, not only its cinematography or casting, but even its textual policy and narrative development. Yet it is also important to mention that instead of textual parallels to Shakespeare, *Warm Bodies* repeatedly displays visual links to the screen history of *Romeo and Juliet*. Magdalena Cieślak emphasises the film's indebtedness to Luhrmann's *William Shakespeare's Romeo + Juliet* (1996) in the way it introduces the Romeo character in his self-inflicted solitude, but also in the centrality of the burning heart imagery, together with the pool motif as the scene of transformation, the scene where the young lovers are 'new baptis'd' (2.2.50) and awakened (here literally) to a new life.[61]

Desmet also argues that 'the Shakespeareanization of the film *Warm Bodies* depends more on cinematic than on textual evidence', and adds to the traces of Luhrmann's film the visual echoes to Zeffirelli's 1968 *Romeo and Juliet* adaptation, particularly in and around the balcony scene. She goes as far as claiming that 'Levine's balcony scene establishes a connection between Nicolas Hoult as R and not so much Shakespeare's Romeo, as Leonard Whiting's Romeo'.[62] Whether young adult audiences recognise any of these echoes is naturally open to debate, but that is the case with textual allusions and even literal quotations as well – what they exemplify is a combination of what Desmet describes as 'accidental Shakespeare' and what Douglas Lanier calls 'post-textual Shakespeare'. The latter term refers to appearances of Shakespeare in purely visual images that contain 'not a single word from Shakespeare's text ..., despite the fact that they depend for their effect on being identified as "Shakespearean"'.[63] In the balcony scene of *Warm Bodies* the effect is not entirely visual, but R's limited speech heavily downplays the role of the text; at the same time, the intricate connections in which text and screen, words and images equally participate show a lot of irreverent and accidental creative reworking.

What is, however, a rather more intriguing aspect that needs to be mentioned before coming to a conclusion is that Shakespeare and the undead as notions not only meet under the dubious contexts of popular culture but are often associated in a metaphorical way in critical literature as well. The concept of undead Shakespeare implies that vampires and zombies have become part of our literal and cultural vocabularies, but also that the afterlife of Shakespeare is in many ways comparable to a vampirical or zombie-like existence. Brian Cummings, in a 2016 article aptly entitled 'Zombie Shakespeare', discusses the celebrations of the 400th anniversary of Shakespeare's death, and argues that 'the Anniversary has produced a "Zombie Shakespeare", a twenty-first century biographical fantasy indicative of commodification rather than literary or creative imagination'.[64] This idea of the commodified revival of the dead playwright is equally relevant for a discussion of adaptations, and we may easily equate the tons of new adaptations made every year with the masses of soulless zombies, rejuvenated in form, re-embodied to resemble their origins, but lacking the soul of their source that made all the difference.

Vampire and zombie adaptations are of course no more than a fad, riding the wave of the undead genre's popularity that may not last much longer in this current form. At the same time, they effectively illustrate Leitch's theses on adaptations being parasitical creatures that feast on undead hosts, keeping the latter alive while staying alive themselves. Yet one minor element added to these may be connected to a different aspect of the contemporary mediascape: its love of sequels and ongoing narratives, dominating all types and sizes of screens, from blockbuster cinema franchises through TV series down to online memes and so on. Of course, one reason for the popularity of adapted or continued narratives is rooted purely in economic interests: the 'safe bet' of the reliable material is essential in such expensive and highly volatile industrial environments.[65] At the same time, the post-millennial anxieties of the world and humanity rushing towards an untimely demise might also explain why we are so eager to invest money and time, and emotional consideration, in characters and their conflicts that may provide at least a semblance of continuity and divert our thoughts from an impending doom. As the undead and their collaboration with Shakespeare and the film industry prove, the long-dead body of the author is alive and kicking, and let us hope it will continue to be so for another couple of centuries.

Notes

1. K. J. Wetmore, Jr, '*Titus Redux*, and: *Hamlet, Prince of Darkness*, and: *Pulp Shakespeare* (Review)', *Shakespeare Bulletin*, 30:2 (2012), 207–12, 209.
2. K. J. Wetmore, Jr, 'The Immortal Vampire of Stratford-upon-Avon', in A. Hansen and K. J. Wetmore, Jr (eds), *Shakespearean Echoes* (Basingstoke: Palgrave Macmillan, 2015), pp. 68–79, p. 70.
3. 'Treehouse of Horror III', Season 4, episode 5, of *The Simpsons*, https://simpsonswiki.com/wiki/Treehouse_of_Horror_III (accessed 15 January 2018).
4. G. Byron, '"As One Dead": Romeo and Juliet in the "Twilight" Zone', in Drakakis and Townshend (eds), *Gothic Shakespeares*, pp. 167–85.
5. S. Chaplin, *The Postmillennial Vampire: Power, Sacrifice and Simulation in True Blood, Twilight and Other Contemporary Narratives* (Cham: Palgrave Macmillan, 2017), p. 2.
6. B. H. Onishi, 'Vampires, Technology, and Racism: The Vampiric Image in *Twilight* and *Let Me In*', in M. K. Bloodsworth-Lugo and D. Flory (eds), *Race, Philosophy, and Film* (New York: Routledge, 2013), pp. 197–210, p. 197.
7. Chaplin, *The Postmillennial Vampire*, p. 2.
8. T. Leitch, 'Vampire Adaptation', *Journal of Adaptation in Film & Performance*, 4:1 (2011), 5–16, 8.
9. S. Collins, *The Hunger Games* (New York: Scholastic Press, 2008).
10. N. Hertz, 'Think Millennials Have it Tough? For "Generation K", Life is Even Harsher', *Guardian* (19 March 2016), www.theguardian.com/world/2016/mar/19/think-millennials-have-it-tough-for-generation-k-life-is-even-harsher (accessed 27 January 2020).
11. J. Hibberd, 'Sucked Dry: Is the Vampire Trend Dead?' *Entertainment Weekly* (12 February 2014), http://ew.com/article/2014/02/12/vampire-trend-dead/ (accessed 27 January 2020) (italics in original).
12. S. Jenkins, '*Underworld*: Romeo & Juliet – Vampire & Werewolf Style', *Animation World Network* (19 September 2003), www.awn.com/vfxworld/underworld-romeo-juliet-vampire-werewolf-style (accessed 27 January 2020).
13. S. Abbott, *Celluloid Vampires: Life after Death in the Modern World* (Austin: University of Texas Press, 2007), p. 197.
14. 'Selene/Trivia', *Fandom*, http://underworld.wikia.com/wiki/Selene/Trivia (accessed 27 January 2020).
15. J. G. Melton, *The Vampire Book: The Encyclopedia of the Undead* (Canton, MI: Visible Ink Press, 2011), p. 727.
16. Ibid.
17. M. Collins and E. Bond, '"Off the Page and into Your Brains!": New Millennium Zombies and the Scourge of Hopeful Apocalypses', in D. Christie and S. J. Lauro (eds), *Better Off Dead: The Evolution of the Zombie as Post-Human* (New York: Fordham University Press, 2011), pp. 187–204, p. 202.

18 S. Abbott, *Undead Apocalypse: Vampires and Zombies in the 21st Century* (Edinburgh: Edinburgh University Press, 2016), p. 128.
19 *Ibid.*, p. 131.
20 For a discussion of the Shakespearean elements in HBO's *Westworld*, see K. Földváry, 'Fragmented Shakespeare in SF TV: The Case of *Westworld*', *Foundation: The International Review of Science Fiction 134*, 48:3, Special Issue: *Winter's Tales: Shakespeare and Science Fiction* (2019), 8–18.
21 Leitch, 'Vampire Adaptation'.
22 Wetmore, 'The Immortal Vampire of Stratford-upon-Avon', p. 74.
23 G. M. C. Semenza, 'Echoes of *Romeo and Juliet* in *Let the Right One In* and *Let Me In*', in Hansen and Wetmore (eds), *Shakespearean Echoes*, pp. 56–67, p. 67.
24 *Ibid.*, p. 63.
25 Hutchings, 'Theatres of Blood', p. 161.
26 *Ibid.*
27 *Ibid.*
28 P. Gray, 'Shakespeare's Vampire: *Hubris* in *Coriolanus*, Meyer's *Twilight*, and Stoker's *Dracula*', *Shakespeare en devenir – Les Cahiers de La Licorne*, 5 (2011), §22, http://shakespeare.edel.univ-poitiers.fr/index.php?id=557 (accessed 27 January 2020).
29 See R. Reagan, 'Address to the National Association of Evangelicals ("Evil Empire Speech"), 3 March 1983', *Voices of Democracy*, https://voicesofdemocracy.umd.edu/reagan-evil-empire-speech-text/ (accessed 27 January 2020).
30 Hutchings, 'Theatres of Blood', p. 161.
31 Semenza, 'Echoes of *Romeo and Juliet*', p. 67.
32 Leitch, 'Vampire Adaptation', esp. 7–8.
33 P. Hoad, 'Zombies: The Film Genre That Won't Die', *Aljazeera* (31 October 2016), www.aljazeera.com/indepth/features/2016/10/zombies-film-genre-won-die-161017060631418.html (accessed 27 January 2020).
34 R. Kirkman, T. Moore and C. Rathburn, *The Walking Dead*, vol.1: *Days Gone By* (Berkeley, CA: Image Comics, 2004).
35 Sutherland, 'Rigor/Mortis', 76.
36 A. S. Hamrah, 'Now Streaming: The Plague Years', *The Baffler*, 28 (2015), 113–21, 118.
37 K. W. Bishop, 'Vacationing in *Zombieland*: The Classical Functions of the Modern Zombie Comedy', *Journal of the Fantastic in the Arts*, 22:1 (2011), 24–38, 29.
38 *Ibid.*, 31.
39 J. C. Macek III, 'To a Cemetery Go!', *Popmatters* (30 December 2013), www.popmatters.com/177026-zombie-hamlet-2495704599.html (accessed 27 January 2020).
40 B. Hodgdon, 'The Last Shakespeare Picture Show or Going to the Barricades', in G. B. Shand (ed.), *Teaching Shakespeare: Passing it On* (Chichester: Wiley-Blackwell, 2009), pp. 105–20, p. 108.

41 C. Desmet, 'Dramas of Recognition: *Pan's Labyrinth* and *Warm Bodies* as Accidental Shakespeare', in Desmet, Loper and Casey (eds), *Shakespeare/Not Shakespeare*, pp. 275–91, p. 282.
42 Bishop, 'Vacationing in *Zombieland*', 29 (italics in original).
43 R. Latham, 'The Zombie Zone' (Review), *American Book Review*, 34:2 (2013), 4.
44 S. Papamichael, '*Warm Bodies* Review: Nicholas Hoult Stars in Warm-Hearted Zombie Rom-Com', *Digital Spy* (8 February 2013), www.digitalspy.com/movies/review/a456467/warm-bodies-review-nicholas-hoult-stars-in-warm-hearted-zombie-rom-com/ (accessed 27 January 2020).
45 K. W. Bishop, 'Humanizing the Living Dead: The Evolution of the Zombie Protagonist', in K. Murphy (ed.), *The Zombie Reader* (Boulder: University Press of Colorado, 2019), pp. 189–204.
46 H. Butler, 'Teens Pick "Smombie" as Hippest German Word', *The Local* (14 November 2015), www.thelocal.de/20151114/are-you-a-smombie-german-youth-word-2016 (accessed 27 January 2020).
47 K. Paffenroth, 'For Love is Strong as Death', in J. Lowder (ed.), *Triumph of the Walking Dead, Robert Kirkman's Zombie Epic on Page and Screen* (Dallas, TX: BenBella Books, 2011), pp. 217–30, p. 225.
48 *Ibid.*, p. 226.
49 S. Cocarla, 'A Love Worth Un-Undying For: Neoliberalism and Queered Sexuality in *Warm Bodies*', in S. McGlotten and S. Jones (eds), *Zombies and Sexuality: Essays on Desire and the Living Dead* (Jefferson, NC: McFarland, 2014), pp. 52–72, p. 54.
50 Bishop, 'Humanizing the Living Dead', p. 198.
51 McFarland, 'Philosophy of the Living Dead', 24.
52 Bishop, 'Humanizing the Living Dead', p. 197.
53 C. Sharrett, 'The Horror Film as Social Allegory (And How it Comes Undone)', in H. M. Benshoff (ed.), *A Companion to the Horror Film* (Chichester: Wiley Blackwell, 2014), pp. 56–72, p. 64.
54 R. Wood, 'The American Nightmare: Horror in the 70s', in M. Jancovich (ed.), *Horror, The Film Reader* (London and New York: Routledge, 2002), pp. 25–32, p. 31.
55 A. Cameron, 'Zombie Media: Transmission, Reproduction, and the Digital Dead', *Cinema Journal*, 52:1 (2012), 66–89, 66.
56 *Ibid.*, 67.
57 Sharrett, 'The Horror Film as Social Allegory', p. 70.
58 Cocarla, 'A Love Worth Un-Undying For', p. 69.
59 R. L. Murray and J. K. Heumann, *Monstrous Nature: Environment and Horror on the Big Screen* (Lincoln and London: University of Nebraska Press, 2016), p. 90.
60 L. Staples, 'Are R and Julie based off *Romeo and Juliet*. Will you be bringing any other Shakespearean themes/motifs to your next book(s)?', *Goodreads*, www.goodreads.com/questions/575495-are-r-and-julie-based-off-romeo-and

(accessed 27 January 2020). Quoted in Desmet, 'Dramas of Recognition', p. 284.
61 Cf. M. Cieślak, 'Shakespeare and Zombies: *Romeo and Juliet*, Baz Luhrmann and *Warm Bodies*', unpublished conference paper, '*Romeo and Juliet* on Screen' seminar at the Shakespeare on Screen in the Digital Era Congress organised by the Université Paul-Valéry Montpellier 3 (26–28 September 2019).
62 Desmet, 'Dramas of Recognition', p. 286.
63 D. M. Lanier, 'Post-Textual Shakespeare', in P. Holland (ed.), *Shakespeare Survey*, vol. 64: *Shakespeare as Cultural Catalyst* (Cambridge: Cambridge University Press, 2011), pp. 145–62, p. 145.
64 B. Cummings, 'Zombie Shakespeare', *Palgrave Communications* (6 September 2016), 1–4, 1, http://dx.doi.org/10.1057/palcomms.2016.63 (accessed 29 June 2020).
65 See Hutcheon, *A Theory of Adaptation*, esp. pp. 4–5.

6

Will, Bill and the Earl: versions of the author in contemporary biopics

The introduction to Part II of this volume has already established that, like the teenpic or the undead horror film, the biopic is not an entirely new phenomenon in cinema history, and yet at the end of the millennium it has made a spectacular return to public awareness. Shakespeare biopics provide an eminent example: while a few films with William Shakespeare as a character had already been made in the first half of the twentieth century, it is only since the 1990s that any biopic proper can be associated with his name. Earlier films which include images of the author start with the silent short film *Shakespeare Writing Julius Caesar* (1907, dir. Georges Méliès), which is believed to be lost, although surviving catalogue descriptions and a still photograph give us a fairly accurate idea of its plot and setting.[1] Another example is *Old Bill Through the Ages* (1924, dir. Thomas Bentley), a comedy in which a First World War soldier dreams himself into various historical eras, including the Elizabethan period, where the Queen attends a performance of Shakespeare's play and meets the author himself.[2] In *The Immortal Gentleman* (1935, dir. Widgey R. Newman), Shakespeare meets fellow playwrights Ben Jonson and Michael Drayton in a tavern, where they observe patrons' resemblance to several Shakespearean characters.[3] Finally, in *Time Flies* (1944, dir. Walter Forde), three American music hall performers use a newly invented time machine to travel back to the Elizabethan era, where they meet Shakespeare – and incidentally help him to write *Romeo and Juliet*.[4] In the post-war period, however, the biopic seemed to lose interest in Shakespeare, and we can find nothing until the 1990s, when the newly returned Shakespearean author is presented in a radically changed cinematic environment. As Megan Murray-Pepper suggests: 'when the subject re-emerges on the cinema screen, it is with some evidence of the technological and theoretical revolutions of the intervening years, and with a renewed desire to foreground Shakespeare's composition as central'.[5]

As we can see from this short summary, compared to depictions of monarchs and other historical characters, and particularly compared to the number of films based on Shakespeare's texts, the list is rather scant; what is more, the earlier films can hardly be described as more than sketches of Shakespeare's imagined life. Since they do not even create an impression of biographical authenticity, they may be labelled biopics only with strong reservations.[6] The absence of any Shakespearean biopic during the post-war decades also undermines the theory put forward by Jane Kingsley-Smith, who argues that 'With each wave of popular film adaptation of Shakespeare's work comes a film in which Shakespeare is made present as an author.'[7] If this were true, we should expect to find further examples at least from the 1960s, in the wake of Franco Zeffirelli's blockbuster adaptations, but there are no traces of any. The post-1990s boom of Shakespeare adaptations was, however, accompanied by an 'explosion of interest in the life of Shakespeare: according to Anne Barton's count, at least one formal biography of Shakespeare has appeared every year since 1996'.[8] Even more interestingly, though the great Shakespearean decade of the 1990s is clearly over, popular interest in the biography and the psychology of the author has not shown any signs of abating since.

Thus, at the end of the millennium, a whole new fashion of screen Shakespeares appeared, testifying partly to the mentioned claim that the biopic as a genre experienced a spectacular revival in the 1990s, and also justifying our treatment of this group as a significant contemporary phenomenon. After a brief introduction to the narrative and cinematographic clichés of Shakespeare biopics, this chapter discusses the mainstream Hollywood features *Shakespeare in Love* (1998, dir. John Madden) and *Anonymous* (2011, dir. Roland Emmerich), a made-for-television biopic, *A Waste of Shame* (2005, dir. John McKay) and a comic musical version produced by the Horrible Histories team under the title *Bill* (2015, dir. Richard Bracewell). The chapter closes with a brief discussion of Kenneth Branagh's 2018 take on Shakespeare's final years, released under the title *All Is True*. Although it was tempting to include two television series as well, the short-lived drama *Will* (2017, created by Craig Pearce for TNT) and the more successful BBC sitcom *Upstart Crow* (2016–, created by Ben Elton), the chapter is confined to a discussion of standalone feature films.

As characteristic of contemporary cinema production, most of these biopics can be regarded as generic hybrids, displaying a variety of other genres mixed with the biopic's conventions. At the same time, they clearly employ the staple features of the biopic formula and apparently rely on a number of elements characteristic of a particularly Shakespearean variant of the biopic. One of these recurring features is the biopic's attitude to authorship, which is surprisingly old-fashioned when compared to our knowledge of early modern writing practices. For all the new discoveries in Shakespearean biography, we rarely see anything reminiscent of the scholarly understanding of contemporary authorship. Most films, although in diverse ways, still engage in the time-honoured cliché of presenting the author as a solitary Romantic genius – preferably in shirtsleeves – sitting and composing at his desk (Murray-Pepper considers the desk itself a focal point of cinematic interpretations of authorship).[9] Equally absent is any reference to literary sources and the author's readings, let alone research for ideas. As Kamilla Elliott points out concerning *Shakespeare in Love*, the film 'astonishingly omits any credit to Shakespeare's actual *written* sources'; but in a way this is no surprise, since 'the screenplay not only hides Shakespeare's written sources and Shakespeare as its own source, it also hides its other written sources', most importantly the novel *No Bed for Bacon* (1941) by Caryl Brahms and S. J. Simon.[10] Kingsley-Smith goes as far as claiming that Shakespeare biopics (she examines *The Immortal Gentleman*, *Time Flies* and *Shakespeare in Love*) 'represent a cinematic form that is inherently conservative, a by-product of the increasingly radical process of adapting Shakespeare's plays for the screen'.[11] The variations in these recurring clichés appear to depend mostly on the presence of other generic elements added to the hybrid mix of the productions.

Nonetheless, most of these films display signs of their own era, in their postmodern sensitivity to certain topical issues and their predilection for irreverent play and pastiche. Apart from the cliché of the Byronic author, most films discussed in this chapter include characters of contemporary playwrights and, even more typically, feature Queen Elizabeth. The variety of fellow dramatists making an appearance in the genre is impressive, as are their diverse involvements in providing inspiration for the struggling young author. The end result, nonetheless, as Kingsley-Smith and others agree, is always a confirmation of the Shakespearean genius who can sublimate all materials, from accidentally overheard snatches of conversation to heartfelt personal experience suppressed in the authorial unconscious. Such common features are all the more interesting as the various works tend to interpret the link between fact and fiction, life and art in rather diverse ways.

In line with the biopic's declared attention to historical and biographical research, all the works align themselves with academic advisers and theories, although these seemingly respectful nods are often no more than token gestures towards scholarship, to grant the fictional narrative an element of authenticity. *Shakespeare in Love*, as its title suggests, considers authorial inspiration as primarily romantic in nature, as opposed to the predominantly political approach exemplified by *Anonymous*, which is also famous for its representation of the Oxfordian theory of authorship. *Will*, the 2017 TNT series (not discussed here) subscribes to a religious interpretation, supporting the idea of a Catholic Shakespeare, while *A Waste of Shame* seeks to give a local habitation and a name to the fair youth and the Dark Lady of the sonnets, and relies on Katherine Duncan-Jones's theory of the syphilitic Shakespeare.[12] Finally, *All Is True* focuses on the role of family and particularly the loss of a child as the most defining aspects of the author's life and work, together with the unsung praises of women supporting every great enterprise. Yet, for all their differences, each of these films includes a number of stereotypical elements in terms of plot, characterisation, casting and visual design that appear to be compulsory for all self-respecting biopics, with some extra clichés reserved for Shakespeare's biographies.

One of the common problems that biopics of writers face is inherent in the subject itself: the fact that the writing process is notoriously undramatic, not to mention unromantic. The visual reminder of the physical nature of writing often finds expression in the graphic design of intro sequences, the font styles employed in titles and cast lists, and the reproduced manuscripts or printed materials always serve the purpose of authenticity. (In *Shakespeare in Love*, Joseph Fiennes famously produced all manuscripts himself, to add another layer of realism to his performance of authorship.[13]) To increase dramatic tension, an element of danger is essential, which is manifested either as a threat to the author's life, or even more often, a threat to the manuscript, the great work itself. While such (over)dramatised menaces are not completely absent from other biopics either, the Shakespeare biopic thrives on them more than any other, probably because the absence of authorised manuscripts is much more commonly known than in the case of other authors. The actual danger often takes the form of a writer's block (from *Shakespeare in Love* to *Bill*, the films abound in images of the author staring into space over the empty parchment), but also of the perishing of the completed work. The latter is sometimes used as a mock threat, as in *Shakespeare in Love*, when an early version of 'Romeo and Ethel, the Pirate's Daughter' is burned on a street fire by Will in a bout of romantic disappointment. In *Anonymous*, on the other hand, the narrative frame of the whole film is constructed on the excitement over the fate of the casket of manuscripts hidden in the burning theatre. *Anonymous* also relies on the thriller element of the unsolved mystery of authorship, as the film never makes it entirely clear how many unknown masterpieces may have remained unidentified in the library of the Earl of Oxford.

Blockbuster romance – *Shakespeare in Love*

Any discussion of the Shakespeare biopic must take John Madden's 1998 film *Shakespeare in Love* as its starting point, in no small part thanks to it being the financially most successful film not only among all those discussed in this chapter, but among all Shakespeare adaptations.[14] It could also be (and often is) discussed as an adaptation of *Romeo and Juliet*, and partly of *Twelfth Night*, but since the film's declared ambition is to present an image of Shakespeare as an author, its primary interpretational context is the biopic. As a result of its wide international dissemination, spectacularly assisted by the film's thirteen Oscar nominations and seven subsequent wins, *Shakespeare in Love* defined the way Shakespearean authorship, the private life of the dramatist and Elizabethan theatre (re-)entered the public imagination at the end of the millennium.

More than twenty years after its first release, in 2020 *Shakespeare in Love* still seems to be going strong, not only as a recurring feature in cable television programmes, but also through its adaptation into a stage play by Lee Hall, directed by Declan Donnellan, that opened at the West End in London in 2014. This film-to-stage adaptation then practically turned into a franchise, the performance appearing on countless stages worldwide, both in Europe and North America; based on the website of its licensing agency, it was still performed on almost twenty stages in the USA in early 2020.[15] This undiminished popularity, more than two years after the sexual abuse allegations against the film's producer, Harvey Weinstein, surfaced, also seems to prove that the story has become independent of the film's production features, and that the narrative (together with its visualisation) has not lost its appeal for audiences.

Moreover, John Madden's *Shakespeare in Love* provides a perfect example of how the Shakespeare biopic is typically mixed with other cinematic genres, in this case the romantic comedy, with the film's plotline focusing on the fictional love story between William Shakespeare (Joseph Fiennes) and Lady Viola Lesseps (Gwyneth Paltrow). At the same time, the film also uses some of the conventions of the postmodern artist's biopic, which often retells the story from the viewpoint of the (unknown or forgotten) muse.[16] *Shakespeare in Love* grants central roles to the female characters around William Shakespeare: the love interest(s) and the patroness, Queen Elizabeth I (Judi Dench) herself, in spite of the latter's very brief onscreen presence. Among the film's seven Oscars, it was the female cast that won two – Gwyneth Paltrow as Best Actress and Judi Dench as Best Supporting Actress – for the roles that the film's marketing put in the limelight. Interestingly enough, the film competed in both the Best Picture and Best Actress categories with another historical biopic about the same era: Shekhar Kapur's *Elizabeth*, with Cate Blanchett in the lead role. The 'overrepresentation' of Elizabethan culture at the 1999 Oscars was amply emphasised, even mocked by Whoopi Goldberg, the host of the award ceremony, who opened the gala dressed as Queen Elizabeth and later returned in a series of period costumes. In any case, this infusion of the romantic comedy into the biopic seems to have been one of the keys to the film's success. As Andrew Higson explains the process: 'The cranking up of the romantic comedy in *Shakespeare in Love* ... enabled the film-makers to re-energize the genre, to create something that would appeal to a wider audience.'[17] He sees this mostly a result of catering for the demands of 'a highly educated and culturally discerning middle-class audience and for a mainstream romantic comedy audience' at the same time.[18]

Looking back at the film's release from our post-#MeToo vantage point, it is also interesting to see several critics return to the aggressive Miramax marketing strategies and imply that the producer's role in the campaign was less than impeccable. Most of these critics attribute the film's success to what they call Weinstein's 'unprecedented blitzkrieg of the press', and his general tactics of effectively forcing the movie's talent into participation in the campaign.[19] The face of Gwyneth Paltrow (now a key figure in the allegations against Weinstein) was already capable of launching a thousand ships in 1998 (see figure 6.1), and the film's cinematography makes ample use of it – but now it appears that her involvement in the marketing may have been less than voluntary. At the same time, there is less agreement on Shakespeare's role in garnering critical and commercial success for the film. Deborah Cartmell refers to a contemporary review claiming that Weinstein hated the title and feared the Bard's poisonous influence over the box office, hence the aggressive campaign.[20] This, however, is somewhat contradicted by Emma French, who argues that Shakespeare was indeed a selling attraction and that Tom Stoppard's involvement as screenwriter was precisely a consequence of his 'high cultural theatrical expertise', which complemented Marc Norman's 'experience in the writing of Hollywood blockbusters' to achieve the winning combination.[21]

Michael Anderegg also describes the seemingly uphill task that the

Figure 6.1 The face that launched a genre – Gwyneth Paltrow in *Shakespeare in Love*. Directed by John Madden, 1998. Universal Pictures/Miramax/ The Bedford Falls Company.

filmmakers of *Shakespeare in Love* set themselves, in trying to please highbrow audiences as well as Hollywood producers intent on making a profit on their investments.[22] As a result (but more as a result of the film's script, replete with tongue-in-cheek references to contemporary popular and visual culture), the film indeed allows us an insight into the workings of Hollywood, although not as a focal point in either its narrative or its marketing.[23] The theme that sells the film is romance – and this romance is classic and contemporary, that is, sophisticated and relatable at the same time. This focus in turn necessitated the transformation of William Shakespeare into a loveable – and somewhat feminised – human being, to enable the film to target an audience interested in romantic comedy (apparently a much larger segment of the populace than those interested in Shakespeare's work). As a result, the central question of the biopic – authorial inspiration and the tension between the private and public personas of the celebrity character – is interpreted in a predominantly romantic (even Freudian) context.

But the mixing of genres is more than an inherited tradition, it is always a marketing strategy as well, as according to Higson, 'generic hybridity enabled it to draw in both the audience for the more genteel and romantic costume dramas of the modern past, and those audiences seeking the attractions of the historical adventure or the political thriller'.[24] On the one hand, the historicity of the film is created by the lavish beauty of the setting that perfectly exemplifies the 'spectacular space, a space of monumental architecture, a space filled with luxurious furnishings and fittings and rich costumes, a space of fabulous colour and texture' – all of which characterise recent cinematic representations of the Renaissance.[25] At the same time, as Higson also notes, the need for the biopic to combine the past with the present,[26] the facial features, including the hairstyle of the protagonists – in an interesting contrast to, but without completely disrupting, the historicity of the background – need to be as unalienating as possible (a notion of which the creators of *A Waste of Shame* or *All Is True* were sadly unaware). In this way, in spite of the nearly statuesque ceremonial dresses of the females, the most successful biopics' stylists also succeed in presenting their protagonists as celebrities who fit contemporary beauty ideals. This tendency is visible in *Anonymous*, and even more in *Will*, whose up-to-date and even anachronistic stylistic representation is a perfect match for the visuality of the contemporary mediascape.

The cinematography of *Shakespeare in Love* (in the same way as its marketing) therefore emphasises the star appeal of the most attractive body in the cast, focusing on twenty-six-year-old Gwyneth Paltrow. Even where Shakespeare and his love, Fiennes and Paltrow, are photographed together in publicity shots, the colour scheme of the costumes and the background works to leave Fiennes in the shadow, highlighting Paltrow. French, in her oft-quoted excellent monograph on the marketing of Shakespeare films,[27] describes the publicity materials in convincing detail, but one may wonder why a film, allegedly on the life of the most canonical British author, would rely on a fictional character, played by an American actress, for most of its appeal. The answer of course lies in the way romantic comedy, the primary cinematic genre informing *Shakespeare in Love*, operates, yet Cartmell also lists the many ways in which *Shakespeare in Love* remains consistently within the framework of the biopic genre. In its focus on the 'conflict between an individual and the establishment ..., a trial scene or performance in which the central figure proves their worth ..., the moral that success comes at a price ... and ... the notion that art imitates the life of the author', the film is a stereotypical biopic.[28] However, Higson and Cartmell also refer to the connection between the biopic and the theme of romance: the latter is one of the most commonly used tools within the genre to present the private life of the author, the human side that enhances greater audience identification.

Unsurprisingly, this staple element is characteristic of the biopic genre as a whole, not only its Shakespearean iteration. Royal biopics in particular tend to 'reflect the conflict suffered by the main characters between being true to themselves and fulfilling the duties expected of a king or queen', but this contrast is at the heart of all biographies.[29] The focus on the inner sphere is of particular interest to biopics of writers, as their subject, the invisible, inner working of the creative mind is almost entirely unfilmable. But what appears to be a new element is the artist's attitude to the tension between private and public, the creative urge and social demands. As Julie F. Codell argues, 'Artists in post-1990 biopics aggressively resist the social demands of the art world or domestic life, and are unwilling to appease social protocol', as opposed to previous depictions.[30] This point is easily confirmed by all Shakespeare biopics' representation of the marital failings of the artist, his predilection to find creative inspiration in extramarital romantic relationships and the narratives' tendency to attribute his artistic success to his refusal to make compromises.

The hybridity mentioned may not only refer to the mixture of genres, but can also take the form of blending high and low cultural elements, 'in order to maintain the balance of hybridity between veneration and irreverence' that French claims to have been one of the keys to the commercial success of *Shakespeare in Love*.[31] This high/low blend is one of the most important aspects by which the contemporary biopic can be distinguished from its generic forerunners. Hila Shachar offers further arguments in support of this postmodern connection, claiming that

> *Shakespeare in Love* utilizes the postmodern strategies of quotation and parody. The representation of Shakespeare in the film is not a realistic one, but rather a pastiche of various cultural stereotypes and historical time periods, presented in an amusingly self-conscious guise. The film does not aim to make us believe that this is what Shakespeare was really like; it rather reveals the manner in which history is itself a construction.[32]

Paul Franssen confirms this when he refers to the strategy of scriptwriters, who keep reminding the audience that 'this is not meant to be a historical reconstruction'; although 'knowledgeable about the Elizabethan era, they pack the film with deliberate anachronisms'.[33] Yet the role anachronisms play in the genre is curiously complex; on the one hand, the rules of the biopic dictate that no major divergences from the historically recorded plotline are allowed. On the other hand, postmodern biopics, among them *Shakespeare in Love*, revel in using anachronisms, which provide 'the audience with a sense of familiarity' and supply 'viewers with a system of cultural referents that transform *Shakespeare in Love*'s otherwise alien Elizabethan locale into an immediately recognizable urban landscape'.[34]

As has been mentioned, the genre tends to respect better-known historical dates and plots, but one typical strategy to circumvent this requirement is for the biopic to 'open just before the moment when the subject begins to make his/her impact on the world', which gives the narrative a flexibility that later better-documented periods would not allow.[35] That is why the majority of Shakespeare biopics claim to provide a version of history concerning the so-called 'lost years' of Shakespeare's life, which also heavily featured in the marketing of *Shakespeare in Love*.[36] In actual fact, however, Shakespeare biopics rarely concern themselves with the years between 1585 and 1592, which critical literature most often defines as the 'lost' or 'dark' ones, and neither does *Shakespeare in Love*.[37] Its interest lies with the birth of the greatest love story of all times, *Romeo and Juliet*, created most probably between 1591 and 1595, and the film itself begins by specifying its setting as 'London 1593'.[38] Interestingly, this liberal attitude to history is a regular feature both within the genre, and in the type of expertise apparently required of filmmakers venturing into the period, who tend to be experts at filmmaking – whether in the genre of costume drama, period drama or even television series – but rarely scholars of history.[39] This is all the more striking as they tend to announce their desire to present a 'true' retelling of the author's life, always authenticating their version with the involvement of well-known Shakespeare scholars as expert advisers and typically subscribing to some academic hypothesis supported by a minority of scholars, to combine this sense of authenticity with the power of novelty.

The fact that filmmakers still feel the need to refer to the 'lost' years nevertheless emphasises a convention of the biopic: while openly declaring that their account of Shakespeare's life is fictional, they are aware that the genre demands that the fictional version be at least nominally rooted in the commonly accepted version of history. Similar compromises are present all throughout the film, as social history is treated with the utmost flexibility but certain boundaries are still respected. For the sake of the comedy, we may allow a woman to appear on the stage, and even Queen Elizabeth to appear in disguise in a public playhouse, but the Queen herself as an authenticating character is practically compulsory. Also, since it is commonly known that William Shakespeare was married to Anne Hathaway – the one with the cottage, Stratford-upon-Avon's favourite tourist attraction – the plausibility of even such a fictionalised account of Shakespeare's life would suffer by allowing him to be united with any other woman in matrimony. Besides, based on the logic of the romantic comedy (and our knowledge of history), we are aware that class differences may only be resolved at a price, either of Shakespeare's art and livelihood of being a dramatist, or the aristocratic woman's position. Since neither of these sacrifices can be imagined to bring about a happy ending in this glittering context of the Elizabethan court, not even the fictional Viola de Lesseps is allowed to marry the man she loves.

Within the confines of recorded history, the romantic comedy, in its struggle with the biopic, can only reach the best compromise: focusing on the courtship and love of the couple until the romantic union, their love evidenced not only by their words and actions, but also by the keen eyes of Queen Elizabeth. Even the Queen declares the limited power of individual desire over recorded history: 'Those whom God has joined in marriage, not even I can put asunder.'[40] After the ending credits, however, audiences are allowed to dream on, and that is what the romantic plot implies that our heroes would do, come hell or high water ('tears and a journey').[41] High water is indeed what comes, liberating Viola from the confines of a despised union, and even if that is as far as liberation goes, this already points in the direction of a blossoming career for the playwright. 'As a postmodern meta-narrative in which linear notions of history and culture become elastic, ... *Shakespeare in Love* eschews chronological facticity in order to highlight the indeterminacy of language and the multivocality of authorship.'[42] As Todd F. Davis and Kenneth Womack conclude, so can we: this film makes no pretence of caring about documented history, but, under the guise of the romantic comedy, it does offer a truly contemporary combination of early modern and postmodern sensibilities, just like the best of biopics.

An unpleasant author – *A Waste of Shame*

Created six years after *Shakespeare in Love*, John McKay's made-for-television account of the lost years of Shakespeare, based on William Boyd's screenplay, appeared as a supporting programme for the 2005 BBC ShakespeaRe-Told series, co-produced by the Open University and the BBC. It was first broadcast in November 2005, during the same month when the four dramatised plays were shown on the BBC, but from the outset it remained a marginal item within the series. The twenty-first century saw a significant shift in audience attention (and creative efforts in production) from the cinema to the television, which could have worked in its advantage – Higson notes that 'there have been rather more television productions [than feature films] in the 2000s, both dramas and documentaries, that touched on the Renaissance period'.[43] Nonetheless, *A Waste of Shame* did not make much of a stir either at the time of its original broadcast or even after its subsequent release on DVD.

The Open University on the BBC review describes the film as 'partly a chamber-piece that captures the solitary nature of writing, but also conversely identifies the key figures in Shakespeare's personal and professional life'.[44] Yet this focus on the solitary nature of creative work reveals a fundamentally conservative, even clichéd, attitude to what the biopic can and should do. Shachar refers to this pattern as follows: 'What we typically expect to see in a film about an author is the stereotypical imagery of the author at work, in a removed setting: that is, the idea of the distanced solitary genius, creating within private confines, and being admired by the camera and his diegetic supporters.'[45] *A Waste of Shame* indeed presents us with the isolated figure of William Shakespeare (Rupert Graves), as the film focuses on the private inspiration for the sonnets, but the admiration, either by the camera or other characters, is limited. Both plot construction and cinematography support the essentially Romantic belief in the genius sublimating his life experiences into words, but the close-ups are directed at the unappealing carnal side and subsequent bodily disintegration of the ageing author (see figure 6.2). Inspiration comes from love, as in *Shakespeare in Love*, but this film 'presents a dark vision of love as a disease' and a source of subsequent shame.[46] In one sense, of course, the film stands out from the group by virtue of its focus on the decline, rather than the making, of the genius (the only film entirely concerned with the dying poet is Branagh's *All Is True*). Yet a closer look at *A Waste of Shame* confirms that it still follows the majority of generic clichés, only presenting them in a less spectacular (and consequently less successful) combination.

Figure 6.2 Dirty work – Indira Varma and Rupert Graves in *A Waste of Shame*. Directed by John McKay, 2005. British Broadcasting Corporation.

The film can be described as conservative not simply in its attitude to authorship, but its whole narrative and cinematography resemble the televisual biopics that were the dominant manifestations of the genre in Britain between the 1970s and the 1990s. Created for the small screen, and lamentably lacking in the postmodern playfulness of its contemporaries discussed here, the most unique quality of *A Waste of Shame* is a somewhat disingenuous self-seriousness. As Franssen claims, this is noticeable precisely in the way the film presents 'itself as historically correct', an impression assisted by the BBC and Open University's endorsement of it as suitable for course material.[47] Yet, in Franssen's words, its historical accuracy is 'an overstatement, of course: the background may be historically based, but the plot is pure fiction'.[48] Graham Holderness explains this with reference to a gender bias, claiming that 'female biographers prefer the tradition that Shakespeare died of tertiary syphilis, contracted in his youth from prostitutes', a view shared by Duncan-Jones and Germaine Greer as well.[49] Nonetheless, Holderness claims, just like the identification of the fair youth of the sonnets with Shakespeare's 'gay lover ... Henry Wriothsley', 'None of this colourful material has any firm basis in history'[50] – thus the film's liberal treatment of historical facts is not fundamentally different from that of other Shakespeare biopics.

As all other representatives of the genre, *A Waste of Shame* also relies on academic advice for its vision, in this case the theory of Oxford University Professor Duncan-Jones, and the film's timeline of the sonnets' creation is clearly indebted to her work.[51] The film's narrative frame begins in 1609, the year of the publication of the *Sonnets*, but the embedded plot returns to 1596, flashback-style, and continues to show the poet at work on his sonnets until 1609, the closing frame of the narrative, when Shakespeare passes on the manuscript collection to the printer Thomas Thorpe. These cinematic devices – embedded narratives, using title cards to identify time and place, even conflict – are not unique within the genre, although here they often reach a slightly didactic level, even at the start when specifying the film's quest by asking 'Who was the fair youth that inspired such passion? Who was Shakespeare's dark lady?' as if the film would finally offer an answer to these age-old unsolved mysteries.

The cast names in the introductory sequence alternate with the other staple icon of literary biopics: the quill on paper, practically the same image as that which precedes our first glimpse at the author in *Shakespeare in Love*. Over the music, we also hear the deep sighs and murmured words that signal the genius at work – rather hard labour – before the camera moves on to explore the surroundings, an untidy room furnished with period detail, an almost completely burnt candle, fireplace with the fire nearly out (implying a long night of work? or the poverty of the author who cannot afford to pile it up again? or possibly both?), and a desk covered in paper, drafts with nearly illegible, often crossed-out, writing, gradually buried under more and more fair copies that show how the flow is gathering momentum towards a composition of the masterpiece. These 'material properties encoded with frustration', such as 'the screwed-up papers and inked-slashed false starts at *Shakespeare in Love*'s opening'[52] are visual clichés that cannot be absent from any representation of the author at work, but here they take centre stage to such an extent that no other diegetic interest can compete with them.

The potential rival for our attention, the poet's private life, is even more desolate, as the film only allows us to see the author in the most unspectacular moments of his existence. When Shakespeare is not arguing with his shrewish wife in Stratford, we see him rarely eating but constantly drinking, urinating in the pub yard, and even vigorously and ungently making love to Lucy Negro (Indira Varma), the dark-skinned half-breed French prostitute, who will turn out to be the inspiration for the Dark Lady sonnets (see figure 6.2). In presenting the early modern world as dominated by dirt and squalor, with a strong emphasis on physicality, the viewer is denied the belief in the poet's ability to transcend the experience and sublimate it into poetry. The environment in which he creates his work is shown in all its variations, from the shabby inns, plenty of brothel scenes and solitary bachelor rooms to the materially well-endowed, but spiritually even more desolate, room of the final sequence.

The reminders of mortality abound on the screen, from the plague victims' corpses to Shakespeare's rush home to visit his dying son, Hamnet. Interestingly, the inclusion of this personal tragedy again connects *A Waste of Shame* to Branagh's *All Is True*, where the poet's guilt over his absence at Hamnet's bedside is centralised by the narrative as the most significant source of inspiration. None of the other biopics includes even a passing reference to the death of Shakespeare's son, probably because such a general atmosphere of death, 'all chaos and misery', as John Shakespeare admits to his son here, would certainly dampen any comic, let alone romantic, bliss. This may be one of the reasons why the film was no critical success (commercial success is hard to measure on a publicly funded television channel): the presentation of a thoroughly miserable man with the 'warts-and-all' approach, where psychological realism is provided by showing the downside of celebrity life, is hardly conducive to exciting televisual entertainment.

As opposed to *Shakespeare in Love*, and to a certain extent even *Anonymous*, *A Waste of Shame* is no star vehicle, even if its cast includes several well-known names of British stage and screen acting, and it is described by Paul Edmondson and Stanley Wells as 'a polished piece of work with high production values, very well cast and performed by a fine group of actors'.[53] Yet these modest adjectives also suggest a lack of star attraction, either in name or appearance, and the visualisation of the author aims at authenticity by approximating the few available pictorial representations, which does no favours to the otherwise handsome actor in the lead role. Indeed, it is not Shakespeare's beauty but that of young William Herbert, the Earl of Pembroke (Tom Sturridge), that we are supposed to admire for its fairness, and his face is brought into view regularly in flashbacks of earlier scenes. Yet the fact remains that the face most often occupying centre screen is a less than desirable one, an image with which contemporary viewers may find it hard to identify; in this way the film fails to establish an important aspect of biopics, which are supposed to be 'films about the present as much as they are about the past. They are certainly very much commodities produced at a particular moment in the development of the contemporary media economy.'[54] Hairstyles may be a small detail, but in this film the rather unfortunate decision to strive for authenticity at all costs only resulted in making the central protagonist look out of place as much in the past as in the present.

It is true, poetry is not drama – and therefore the dramatisation of poetry may be a particular challenge for filmmakers – but *A Waste of Shame* does not even wish to please the popular audiences of multiplex cinemas. A down-to-earth representation of human failings, bodily corruption and decay rarely glues viewers to the screen, even if such grim details as the beating of prostitutes and the sweating tubs of the mercury bath add to the historical authenticity. Indeed, Edmondson and Wells find it problematic that the film 'no doubt will be seriously considered by not a few Open University students', even though the direct connection, for example, between the 'seething bath' in Sonnet 153 (line 7) and Shakespeare undergoing treatment for venereal disease, is mostly conjectural.[55] Yet the film's cinematography and interpretation of its poetic material are equally unspectacular; the regular use of voiceover narration cannot make the creative process appear any more dramatic, and the interpretation of the Dark Lady as a dark-skinned prostitute, although an exotic beauty, lacks any other interpretive complexities of darkness that characterise the sonnets. Her portrayal, of course, could be seen as a 'politically correct response to gender and stereotyping', but her victimised nobility functions as a contradiction to the narrative.[56] She is an elegant, intelligent and sensitive woman, who does not 'tread on the ground' as Sonnet 130 (line 12) would suggest (which the film quotes), therefore her darkness is identified in the venereal disease – the French pox – that Shakespeare contracts in his frequent visits to the brothel. Close-ups on pustulent sores on the poet's skin are repeatedly shown, and later even the blackening flesh in his mouth is granted an unwanted image. What it all adds up to is that the quotation selected from Sonnet 129 for the film's title, 'a waste of shame' (line 1), is interpreted in the most straightforward physical sense, referring to Shakespeare's biography as a wasteful – and even wasted – life, full of shameful details that one would prefer not to know.

Interestingly enough, even the physical reality of writing is shown in the least romantic light; when the compulsory pen and paper are in the focus, we are distracted by the scratching sound of the quill, accompanied by grunts emanating from the artist. True, the film intends to display the multifaceted work of poetic composition as hard labour in a physical as well as a mental-spiritual sense, but poetry cannot transcend this down-to-earth physicality. Absent is the postmodern parody of authorship that we have seen in *Shakespeare in Love*, or the complex multisensory universe of Peter Greenaway's *Prospero's Books*, where 'The film's opening is marked by the regular visual and aural interpolation of a vivid ink droplet falling. Linking a naked Prospero in the bathhouse with the scratching of quill on paper, the frame expands shot by shot to gradually reveal the complete image of Prospero as author scripting the operation of the scene.'[57] There the water imagery, combined with the image of the bare essence of the naked author creating drama all explain why the scratching sound does not come across as a disturbance but rather as evidence for the physical process of creation. Here, however, there is nothing but the scratches – compared to the evenly spaced, aesthetically beautiful script in *Prospero's Books*, *A Waste of Shame* offers us close-ups of nearly illegible scratches that are anything but aesthetically pleasing or suggestive of an orderly mind.

A direct correspondence between the bodily reality of love and poetic creation is established by the theme of the love triangle explored by the narrative, providing almost too literal scenes of inspiration for a wide range of the sonnets. One montage sequence, though, which appears to go beyond the self-evident, shows Shakespeare and Herbert lying next to each other on the riverbank, the young man on his back, his eyes closed, while the poet's hand is hovering over the body of the boy, desiring but also afraid to touch him. Interweaved with these shots we can see the quill hovering above the paper, moving closer, only to jump fearfully back, until the moment when the hand touches the skin in the second the young man wakes up. This touch, in a hardly visible second, functions like a spark, energising the pen that begins to run on the paper, with poetry in free flow – yet in a way even this moving scene ties poetic inspiration to a tangible bodily reality, pointing to the erotic touch as essential for love poetry.

But for all its centralisation of suffering, physical struggle and deprivation, *A Waste of Shame* eventually presents authorship just like *Shakespeare in Love*, or even *Bill*, implying that the author is no different from his fellow human beings (he may even be morally inferior to some). The only exception is his ability to sublimate the mundane world and his everyday experiences into the treasury of his work. There is no reference to literary sources, not even in the case of the last two sonnets which are commonly accepted as indebted to a Greek epigram,[58] and certainly no implication that early modern authorship, even of lyric poetry, was dependent on a 'collective publishing enterprise' and thus should be interpreted within 'the collaborative context of the book trade – the material circumstances of textual production'.[59] In the same way, the presence of contemporaries, primarily Ben Jonson, is limited in *A Waste of Shame* to an identification with the sonnets' rival poet, the film translating the fictional character into biographical inspiration, rather than acknowledging the complex processes of early modern authorship.

Forgotten royal bastards – *Anonymous*

The film that takes the most adventurous leap in offering an alternative version of Shakespearean authorship is obviously *Anonymous* (2011, dir. Roland Emmerich), which tells an Oxfordian story, although on close inspection, we may realise this anti-Stratfordian fiction also subscribes to the single genius theory. The biographical details of the genius may differ from the Stratford-born William Shakespeare, but *Anonymous* still argues for a single creative mind behind all the masterpieces that bring the world to its knees. At the same time, *Anonymous* is also the only Shakespeare biopic that presents a nearly complete biography of the author, telling the life story of the 17th Earl of Oxford practically from the cradle (his illegitimate birth) to the grave. Understandably, the conspiracy theory that inspired the script needs a complete and complex presentation, to pre-empt as many potential issues of contention as possible.

However, neither the excitement of a historical thriller, nor the presence of Shakespeare as a character, were sufficient to sell Emmerich's film, which ended up failing rather spectacularly at the box office. It is true that in this particular case, marketing the film by focusing on the director's previous association with the action-horror-disaster genres may have been counter-productive. Already the previews hinted at the dangers of contradictory expectations: 'instead of destroying the world, director Roland Emmerich is setting his sights on destroying William Shakespeare with period thriller *Anonymous*. The movie has actually been receiving solid reviews out of a few festivals, though a period piece with no big names (and few, if any natural disasters) seems like a tough sell.'[60] The marketing of this film as in some way a sequel to Emmerich's earlier work may have destroyed its chances of success and alienated potential viewers who would have been interested in a fictional reconstruction of the life of the man who was (not) Shakespeare, a theory surprisingly well known among non-academics.

What is also surprising in this summary is the reference to the lack of big names, when even a superficial knowledge in the world of British theatre acting and Shakespearean performance in particular would suggest to the reviewer that the cast was practically star-studded, with Vanessa Redgrave, Derek Jacobi, Mark Rylance and Rhys Ifans among the performers. Nonetheless, their apparent lack of credits in popular Hollywood cinema may have been a contributing factor to the lack of blockbuster success, although no one could deny that the popular critical response to the veracity of the film's content (or lack thereof) can still be regarded as considerable. Even Roger Ebert spends approximately half of his enthusiastic review discussing Shakespeare's authorship, not only Emmerich's version as manifested in the film, but also his own (i.e. Ebert's), supported by the scholarly opinion of James Shapiro.[61]

Anonymous, although subverting one commonly accepted theory concerning the authorship of Shakespeare's *oeuvre*, is in many other ways still a traditional literary biopic, offering an account and an explanation for the creation and lasting success of this most canonical *oeuvre*. The film is a period piece, employing the spectacular details of (CGI-created) locations, props and costumes, and it relies on as many historical facts as possible, to create the sense of authenticity for the central, essentially fictional, story. These facts include not only the names of peers, members and courtiers of the royal family, or the theatrical world, but also minor events preserved in documents. Such an event is the murder of a servant by the young Edward de Vere, 17th Earl of Oxford, transformed by the film into an inspiration for the murder of Polonius in *Hamlet*. As fitting the genre of the biopic, *Anonymous* also focuses on the early part of the story: the creation of the artistic persona of William Shakespeare (Rhys Ifans), even though it goes against the trend by implying that most of the plays had been written previously and were waiting their turn on the shelves of the Earl of Oxford's library. It is not the lost years this time, but the lost truth about Shakespearean authorship that the film offers to uncover, otherwise sharing with other biopics the popular assumption that the amount of information available on the life of William Shakespeare, the Stratford-born actor, is not only insufficient but suspiciously unconvincing not to invite further elaboration.

Douglas Lanier also points out how '*Anonymous* is actually quite conventional in its conceptualization of authorship and shares with recent fictional treatments of Shakespeare a body of crucial assumptions'.[62] This relatively conservative attitude is tangible in the film's adherence to the conventions of the genre, including its characteristic iconography. The author – not the illiterate actor Shakespeare (Rafe Spall) but the Earl of Oxford – is repeatedly shown in his study in shirtsleeves, creating drama, with quill in hand, scribbling line after line on paper, with an impressive collection of earlier work on his bookshelves, awaiting its fate, either anonymity or destruction (see figure 6.3). This threat of destruction, just like the almost-but-not-quite burning of the known manuscripts, is another biopic cliché, employed to induce tension into an otherwise less than action-packed genre.

The evidence of Shakespeare's various attempts to sign his own name is also included – based on another staple item of popular trivia that there are various spelling variants of the name, making such scenes practically compulsory. While in *Shakespeare in Love* we see Will Shakespeare

Figure 6.3 Endangered species – authors and their masterpieces – Sebastian Armesto and Rhys Ifans in *Anonymous*. Directed by Roland Emmerich, 2011. Columbia Pictures/Relativity Media/Centropolis Entertainment/Studio Babelsberg.

experimenting with spelling variants, evidence of his budding but as yet hesitant professional identity, in *Anonymous* this scene is transformed into a sign of a consciously created artistic persona. Since his aristocratic background does not allow him to be associated with public playhouses, the Earl of Oxford is forced to use a mediator for his work to reach an audience. As a result, the diverse signatures are shown to be produced by Oxford as he is getting acquainted with the new *nom de plume* under which his plays can see the light of day. The material proof of his authorship is hard to hide – the fingers on his right hand are always covered in ink (parallel images abound in *Shakespeare in Love* as well, although there the ink stains are found on the authorial fingernails only – Lanier cites this as one of many elements *Anonymous* owes to the earlier film).[63] In *Anonymous*, the opportunistic and illiterate drunken actor William Shakespeare recognises the power of ink, too, and decides to authenticate his claim for the authorship of *Henry V* after the resounding success of the play, by putting his finger into the inkhorn, in imitation of this common proof of creativity.

Authorial inspiration in *Anonymous* is presented as predominantly internal, coming from the lived experiences of the author, but not the result of some streetwalking commoner's power of observation, as in *Shakespeare in Love*, nor the emotional upheaval of illicit attractions, as in *A Waste of Shame*. *Anonymous* subscribes to a conservative view of authorship, the Romantic ideal of the solitary author, whose 'works express their author's life experience, and on that basis it creates a biographical tale retrofitted to those works', as Lanier argues.[64] Yet I believe there is a significant element distinguishing it from other biopics, including *Shakespeare in Love*: the Earl of Oxford writes because he hears 'voices' speaking to him, voices of people from all classes and walks of life, wishing to find embodiment through his pen. Apparently it is only when their words are put to parchment that these voices are 'cast loose, freed', and only then can the author's mind find peace. In this scene we can find the necessary motivation required by the literary biopic for the birth of the great work, complemented by the usual psychological element that informs the whole genre. The wisdom of everyday psychology argues that the borderline between madness and inspiration is a hazy one, and genius has often been regarded as a more or less dangerous form of 'possession'. The Earl's fears of madness explain his insistence on continuing to write despite all obstacles, as well as the daunting amount of his output, but it also reinforces contemporary stereotypes regarding the emotional imbalance of artists. At the same time, as Donovan Sherman notes, this insistence on the non-bodily source of intellectual production 'results from the film painting itself into a performative corner:

the audience must witness the act of writing while the film maintains, somehow, a clear separation of body and text', all of which is intricately tied up in the fundamentally elitist argument powering the Oxford theory and *Anonymous*.[65]

Besides the inner voices, we can also witness how external circumstances play a role in the creation of one masterpiece after another: the mentioned accidental murder of a servant finding its way into *Hamlet*, or the hunchback Robert Cecil becoming *Richard III*, which was – in this version of history – written to incite rebellion against the Secretary of State, rather than as part of Tudor propaganda. Yet, as the film avoids the self-mocking tone of postmodern parody and pastiche that characterises *Shakespeare in Love*, one is not tempted to question the historical veracity of the cause-and-effect implications or even some of the factual details. (The death of Thomas Brincknell, servant of the Cecil household is reported to have happened during fencing practice, rather than behind an arras;[66] and *Richard III* is one of the earliest plays in the canon, as opposed to *Richard II*, which is well known to have been performed on the eve of the Essex uprising – this exchange of the two plays is what Lanier calls 'one of the film's more glaring historical errors'.[67])

At the same time, the emphasis is rather on the intellectual's ability to use his talent, based on his understanding of popular psychology, even if the film is somewhat inconsistent in its presentation of authorial inspiration. For one thing, the majority of the plays appear to have been produced previously, some – *A Midsummer Night's Dream* in particular – as early as in the childhood of the author; therefore, here we have no way of knowing when and in what order most of the dramatic works were written. After the initial success of *Henry V*, Oxford searches through his library to find what should come next, allowing us to witness that *Julius Caesar*, *Macbeth* and *Romeo and Juliet* have all been waiting on the shelf, with *Twelfth Night* just having been finished (see figure 6.3). What is more, the utilisation of lived events, whenever included in the narrative, is always shown as a consciously chosen means to an end, even in the case of *Hamlet*, in which the youthful memory of the accidental murder is included. The performance, however, appears to be a test case for the author's ability to manipulate the theatrical crowd, which promptly identifies Polonius as a representation of the Cecils, and this manipulative skill and intent is even more evident in the case of *Richard III*, which Oxford produces when the Earl of Essex needs an angry mob. Playwriting may be an instinctive activity for the Romantic genius, able to sublimate experience into the work, but its application on the stage is an overly political act according to the

Earl of Oxford (and to Emmerich). What matters here is not so much the poetic skill (although that is also acknowledged as considerable, writing a whole play in iambic pentameters being child's play for him, while all other contemporary playwrights find it practically impossible) but the ability to use it to achieve one's own goals.

All these – relatively minor and certainly not intrusive – hypothetical connections or distortions of history are embedded in a generally accurate and fact-based historical environment, as expected of any biopic. In line with the rules of the genre, *Anonymous* also contains the somewhat didactic summaries of factual information on the age and the world of the Elizabethan theatre. Just as *Shakespeare in Love* begins with a scene in which Fennyman, the moneylender, discusses the monetary aspects of the theatre business with Henslowe, the theatre owner with burning money problems (and boots), in *Anonymous* we are granted a similar overview of numbers and structure in the discussion in the tennis court when the Earl of Oxford is beginning to grasp the political potential of the public playhouse. Equally important in providing authenticity for the fictitious account of the birth of the Shakespearean *oeuvre* are the historical figures, both the names of Elizabethan nobility and the theatrical names, of Ben Jonson, Thomas Dekker, Thomas Nashe and Christopher Marlowe. The cast list also includes Shakespeare's fellow actors Richard Burbage and Spencer, who both get passing references in the dialogue, without enabling the viewer to identify them as characters. In the credits we can find a number of completely unidentified contemporaries, including Heminge, Condell, Pope and Sly, members of the Lord Chamberlain's Men, but like the CGI-created setting, they remain entirely superfluous in the plot. Their role in the setting, however, is more tangible: Peter Kirwan argues convincingly that both *Shakespeare in Love* and *Anonymous* 'are involved in work of authorial construction, and both situate their author in relation to the surrounding intellectual, creative, and professional contexts of the early modern London theatre scene'.[68] As I have already mentioned it in passing, and will discuss further later in this chapter, this strategy of authenticating Shakespearean authorship through contemporary dramatists is characteristic of the whole subgenre.

Marlowe's death, one of the few popularly known incidents from the age, features here again (as in *Shakespeare in Love* and *Bill* as well). But in *Anonymous*, Marlowe has to die obviously in service of the Oxfordian theory, meaning that he knew too much – not of court politics, but of theatre politics – and thus must have suspected the conspiracy behind the birth of a new genius. Sherman also notes more subtle 'glimpses at identifiably

Shakespearean tokens of authenticity – even if misplaced entirely from their proper context', such as the personal badge of Richard II, the white hart in one frame, or the similarity of the actor playing Thomas Nashe to the historical portrait of Ben Jonson.[69] Although I am not at all certain that these hardly noticeable visual jokes succeed in 'rewarding the audience' in any way, it is true that they add to the film's '"palimpsestic" quality that Linda Hutcheon identifies as the marker of an adaptation'.[70] Nonetheless, public recognition of these 'traces from the previous version of reality',[71] as indeed traces of anything, rather than accidental or purely decorative elements, is slightly doubtful.

On the whole, *Anonymous* is not without humour or even irony, and besides its long list of inter-cinematic references it is also willing to engage in self-mockery, as when self-appointed author Will Shakespeare thanks his colleagues on stage, offering a less than laudatory comment on contemporary celebrity culture.[72] Yet the postmodern qualities of the film are rather found in its subversive intent, and even more in its cinematic blending of old and new, then and now. The appearance of Derek Jacobi, a veteran Shakespearean actor and avid believer in the Oxford theory at the introduction is all the more interesting as it illustrates another trend in postmodern biopics: their self-reflexivity regarding history as fiction, a story that is being told, or in this case, presented and performed. (Mark Rylance, who plays here Henry Condell, a member of the King's Men and one of the editors of the First Folio, is incidentally another avid anti-Stratfordian in real life. Together with Derek Jacobi, he is among the signatories of the so-called *Declaration of Reasonable Doubt*, advocating the academic research of the authorship controversy.[73]) The story that is presented by *Anonymous* intends to be an alternative version that may have just as good a claim to the truth as the official one, at least that is what the theatrical introduction implies, as Jacobi lists a number of reasons why disbelief in the Stratford theory seems justified. The implication is, naturally, that what we get in the film is the true story – or at least a more plausible hypothesis – although most of the problems Jacobi lists (no manuscript, nothing book-related in Shakespeare's will, and so on) are just as relevant for the Oxford theory, which works on an equally noticeable absence of documentary evidence. The fact that Edward de Vere, 17th Earl of Oxford, died in 1604, more than a decade before William Shakespeare, and quite a few years before the first references to the last plays attributed to Shakespeare, is easily accounted for by conspiracy theories, and *Anonymous* solves this problem by simply claiming that the plays had all been written previously.

The film's introduction shows the filmmakers' approach to the blurred line between fact and fiction: while the first titles appear against a black background, we hear very contemporary urban street noises and the screen opens to an aerial view of New York's Times Square. Here we move along with the evening bustle of inner-city traffic, until arriving with Jacobi at a building that can be recognised as the Broadhurst Theatre in West 44th Street, opposite St James Theatre, whose sign even appears on screen. We are thus situated in the here and now, in the very much physical reality of twenty-first-century New York, with the tangible material details of the theatre surrounding us – and we are left to wonder about the role of Jacobi, or the man played by Jacobi. He needs no costume change or make-up – has he arrived already in role for the performance? Or is he playing himself? Is it his own story he offers to tell or is he simply a narrator in a show? (Knowing Jacobi's personal dedication to the Oxford cause, one is forced to wonder even more about these questions.) The neon lights at the theatre's entrance advertise a performance of *Anonymous*, and the poster above it is the same as that of the movie itself – self-referentiality as a theme is thus introduced early on, but its power or earnestness is dependent upon an unusually broad spectrum of audience awareness.

The story is thus set up as that of an actor, a stage presentation in which acting, indeed playing a part, will become real, and in which actors have just as much claim to the truth as scholars or politicians. This reflection of the film on itself – the meta-cinematic self-reference, and the interpretation of the whole genre of the biopic as a fictional recreation, a re-presentation acted out for an audience – informs the whole text, supporting Shachar's view on postmodern biopics already discussed. At the same time, it also implies that despite all the elements borrowed from the thriller, *Anonymous* can and indeed should be interpreted as a biopic, whose requirements it fulfils easily and even conventionally. But measured against either the previous disaster movies of its director, or other period thrillers and historical conspiracy theories, such as *The Da Vinci Code* (2006, dir. Ron Howard) or even *The Three Musketeers* (2011, dir. Paul W. S. Anderson) released only a week previously, *Anonymous* has too thin a romantic thread for the female viewer, too convoluted a plotline for the thrill-seeker and too unimpressive static visuals for the action-adventure lover. The convoluted plot itself undermines its plausibility for the historical biopic fan, who would have been happy to accept Shakespeare's royal power on the Elizabethan stage without having to make him a royal bastard (and a father of another royal bastard to boot). As Edel Semple noted, the film's version of Elizabeth as a sex-crazed theatre lover with multiple illegitimate children but without any interest in her kingdom also goes against the commonly accepted view of the powerful ruler.[74] If, however, one approaches *Anonymous* as another, thematically untraditional, but otherwise mostly conservative biopic, the film may prove worthy of attention, and the discerning viewer can attest to its place as a curiosity among other cinematic accounts of Shakespeare's life and authorship.

Shakespeare in edutainment – *Bill*

At first sight, the musical comedy *Bill* stands at the other end of the scale of historical authenticity from *A Waste of Shame*, in its openly parodic tone and self-mockery with which it appears to laugh not only at itself but the whole genre of the biopic as well. *Bill* was released in 2015, when the continued celebrations of Shakespeare's 450th birth (2014) and 400th death (2016) anniversaries gave rise to cultural events and Shakespeare-related works on a global scale. The film was jointly produced by Cowboy Films and Punk Cinema for BBC Films, but even more importantly, *Bill* is the first feature film of the popular franchise *Horrible Histories*, which has produced over a hundred books and magazines, several television series and all types of related merchandise, popularising history for young and old alike since the early 1990s.

Implying another stylistic association, in the press release announcing the film the BBC media centre refers to the way the six lead actors of the cast of the *Horrible Histories* television series 'will play multiple roles ..., in the style of the Python films'.[75] As a result, *Bill*'s generic hybridity associates it not so much with romantic comedy, as is the case with *Shakespeare in Love*, or the thriller genre that underpins *Anonymous*, but implies a combination of educational television (edutainment) and farcical, slapstick British television comedy instead. The film has remained mostly unknown outside the United Kingdom, as the only other country where it was released was Australia, and there only for a period of three weeks, in no more than two theatres at the same time. Its financial success is therefore not comparable to Hollywood productions, but critical response to the film was generally favourable, with most critics emphasising the entertaining qualities of the film and happily recommending it to their readers.

Although the elements of edutainment and slapstick are significant in the generic mixture of *Bill*, it is still defined by its main theme as a biopic, a fictionalised cinematic account of the life and times of young William Shakespeare (Mathew Baynton), following his struggles until his first public success. As typical of the genre, the development depicted somehow implies an achievement of the author's true self, that he becomes himself contrary to all obstacles that try to repress not only his talent but his whole identity. Thus it is symbolic that the final line in the film's dialogue is the rhetorical question: 'Is the world ready for Shakespeare?' – as if earlier it had been the world, rather than his work, that showed signs of immaturity.

Following the time-honoured tradition of Shakespeare biopics, *Bill* also focuses on the 'lost years' of the Bard's life, as the BBC website sums up its plot: '*Bill* tells the story of what really happened during Shakespeare's "Lost Years" – how hopeless lute player Bill Shakespeare leaves his family and home to follow his dream. It's a tale of murderous kings, spies, lost loves, and a plot to blow up Queen Elizabeth!'[76] But however free and low-budget a version of Elizabethan history it presents, already this short summary implies that the film does not completely differ from its more serious relatives, as this sentence could be used almost without alteration to sum up the plot of *Anonymous* as well. *Bill* does not fully discount the facts either, but rather uses them in the same way as *Horrible Histories* founder Terry Deary describes the creation of his first *Horrible Histories* books: what the publishers had in mind was 'a joke book with a history theme', but after some initial research, he found the facts 'much more interesting than the jokes. So we ended up with a fact book with jokes. We created a new genre.'[77] By the time the film *Bill* came along, the successful recipe seems to have become a staple of not only the British but even the global edutainment industry, as some of the book series and television shows reached the USA, Australia, Brazil and Russia as well. Yet the marketing of similar programmes that combine historical education with slapstick comedy, the best-known example being *Blackadder*, has typically focused on Europe, rather than the United States. It is no wonder therefore that *Bill*'s release was also mostly restricted to the mother country, where a positive reception by generations brought up on *Horrible Histories* could be reasonably expected.

The *Horrible Histories* book series are marketed with particular emphasis on their irreverent attitude; in the words of Jerome de Groot, they 'play on children's fascination with goriness, selling themselves as "history with the nasty bits left in". The books are mischievous, irreverent and iconoclastic, appealing to a child audience's desire for silly jokes, presenting history as something tactile and simple.'[78] Yet there is more to this style of mixing the serious with the silly than a childish enjoyment of bodily humour, as the unceasing popularity of such products testifies. In the same vein, *Bill*, although on one level clearly suitable for presentation to children, includes allusions and references that can fully be appreciated only by someone well versed in Elizabethan history and Shakespeare's plays, often on the textual

Figure 6.4 Elizabethan parody – Helen McCrory in *Bill*. Directed by Richard Bracewell, 2015. BBC Films/Cowboy Films/Punk Cinema.

level as well. As de Groot says, '*Horrible Histories* illustrates a popular iconoclasm, a challenge to standard narratives, and a pedagogical desire to present information in complex and dynamic ways'[79] – and in a sense, a more daring acknowledgement of what most Shakespeare films intend to do: spice up the canonical source material in a commercially viable way, sugar-coating the educational element with laughter.

As regards historical authenticity, *Bill*'s plot is naturally full of outrageously fictitious ideas, but through an association with commonly known historical names, from Queen Elizabeth I (Helen McCrory), presented in an absurdly comic version (see figure 6.4), through King Philip II of Spain (Ben Willbond) and Sir Francis Walsingham (Laurence Rickard), the comic fiction still gains an element of realism. For instance, Walsingham, Queen Elizabeth's principal secretary and spymaster, who actually died in 1590, three years before the plot begins, is greeted every time he makes an unexpected appearance with the sentence 'I thought you were dead!' as a standing joke that is meaningful only for the initiate. Another well-known character is Anne Hathaway (Martha Howe-Douglas), Shakespeare's long-suffering wife, who steps out of the shadows and shows her true talents here, anticipating Branagh's *All Is True* in its gender politics, although in a more comical version, suggesting that not only common sense but also mastery of language are female qualities. Foregrounding women, both as the brains in the family enterprise and as unacknowledged heroes of everyday life, is almost a compulsory element in recent biopics about artists (the BBC sitcom series *Upstart Crow* also makes ample use of this attitude). As Shachar claims: the 'strategy of focusing on the muse's role in the creation of "great men" and "great authors" has now become common amongst contemporary literary biopics',[80] and even within the comic world of *Bill* Anne Hathaway's character is treated with the most sympathy.

As already mentioned, *Bill* is interested in the so-called 'lost years', but it interprets the term with exactly the same flexibility as all other films do: it begins with a handwritten parchment-style title specifying 1593, the very year used as the setting of *Shakespeare in Love* (and exactly one year after the period usually described as 'lost' in Shakespeare biographies). The title cards give further details, pointing out that the historical background, particularly England's conflict with Spain, is of special significance for the plot about to unfold, as Bill and his wife, Anne Hathaway, both get involved in the conspiracy of Philip II, King of Spain, against Queen Elizabeth. Naturally, Bill and Anne manage to thwart the plot in the end, while also securing Shakespeare's reputation as a playwright, and at the same time even repairing their own relationship (whose greatest tribulations have been caused precisely by Bill's daydreaming and artistic aspirations).

The film's attitude to authorship is not very different from that of the rest of the group, emphasising that Shakespeare has talent and vision from the start, but that he needs to work on his writing skills – and, most of all, that the best inspiration comes from the life experiences of the author himself. At the same time, the film grants a significant role to Christopher Marlowe as well, acknowledging that Shakespeare's contemporary had already achieved fame and success by the time the Stratford-born country bumpkin stepped on the London scene. This is another shared element between all Shakespeare biopics, but *Bill* goes further in representing the two dramatists as actual collaborators (rather than Marlowe offering just a few prompts, as in *Shakespeare in Love*).[81] Here it is Marlowe who provides the best ideas that will make Shakespeare's play a success (Bill's early stuff truly needs more work), but also the encouragement he needs to be able to continue.

When their first collaborative effort is lost, and Bill is forced to present a play – literally to save his life and his wife, in time-honoured biopic tradition, as both text and author are regularly in mortal danger – it is the ghost of the already dead Marlowe who wakes him up from his lethargy, pointing him towards their shared adventures. Marlowe's command: 'Write what you know' is clearly not a novel idea, as this notion was well known, even mocked already in the Renaissance, expressed most famously in Sir Philip Sidney's *Astrophil and Stella* 1 as '"Fool", said my Muse to me, "look in thy heart and write"' (line 14).[82] Thus, after the collaborative start, we arrive at Shakespeare as the actual physical writer – one with quill in hand, crossing out and rewriting lines on piles of paper, sometimes scrunching pages up and throwing them at the wall, as usual. Collaboration, therefore, just as Kingsley-Smith suggested, here again gives way to a re-establishment of Shakespeare's originality and pre-eminence among his contemporaries.[83]

Bill makes much of Marlowe's lack of talent for comedy, which echoes the other biopics' authenticating references to the literary and theatrical context of early modern London. In *Shakespeare in Love* we meet Marlowe, but also a young John Webster, who prefers beheadings and mutilations to romance and comedy; in *Anonymous*, Ben Jonson is one of the central characters, together with several other contemporaries, but Christopher Marlowe is also present, a sly traitor and spy, who openly dislikes comedy, like his embodiment in *Bill*. More importantly, *Bill* also presents Marlowe in the most famous – or rather infamous – scene of his life: stabbed to death in the Bull's Inn in Deptford (which he earlier assures Shakespeare is 'quite safe'). Although the filmmakers spare the viewer the gory sight of Marlowe being stabbed through the eye (as in *Anonymous*, where the eyes of the corpse are nice and intact), the commonly known, and even more commonly disputed, cause of his death – disagreement over the bill – provides occasion for another joke, linking *Bill* and its tongue-in-cheek verbality to the postmodern textual strategies of *Shakespeare in Love*. In *Shakespeare in Love*, on hearing that Marlowe was killed after a dispute over the bill, Henslowe exclaims, saying 'The bill! Oh, vanity!' – misunderstanding the payment slip for the billing, the order of listing actors' names on the playbill. Here in *Bill*, the nickname of the future Bard provides the obvious joke: when Marlowe is stabbed by Philip II of Spain, he groans for his friend 'Bill', and appropriately gets the bill for his consumption.

Bill's strategy as regards authorship and the use of recognisable historical and literary material is much the same as that of *Shakespeare in Love*: the text is full of cleverly dispersed textual puns that those in the know may be able to recognise and enjoy. Even in the first scene, still in Stratford, Shakespeare is a member of a band called Mortal Coil, who kick him out after yet another performance when he cannot stick to the band's style and improvises mid-gig on his lute like a jazz player. The clearly anachronistic introduction of contemporary popular music into an early modern cultural-visual environment is not unusual in biopics or other mock-historical films, as evident in *A Knight's Tale* (2001, dir. Brian Helgeland), or particularly the TNT series *Will*. When Mortal Coil finally moves on without Bill, they signal their farewell by saying 'We'd better shuffle off', adding another twist to the *Hamlet* pun. The scene also shows how the humour of the film comes from a combination of textual fragments and quotations from the broadest spectrum of Shakespearean work, with allusions to contemporary popular culture, including inter-cinematic or inter-medial cultural references. The final court performance that ends up saving, rather than killing, Queen Elizabeth, is a mixture of several Shakespearean plays, including *Macbeth*, *Romeo and Juliet*, *Hamlet*, *As You Like It*, *The Tempest* and even the *Sonnets*, winking at the extremely popular late twentieth-century show *The Complete Works of William Shakespeare (Abridged)*, first produced by the Reduced Shakespeare Company in 1981.[84] Queen Elizabeth, when inviting Shakespeare to develop his ideas into further plays (recalling the finale of *Shakespeare in Love*) also remarks on this hybrid mix: 'Though maybe one at a time, eh? 'Cos that was a bit dense.'

The dialogue of the film is equally full of more or less easily recognisable references, again reminding the viewer of *Shakespeare in Love*, with no attempt made at reconstructing a chronological biography. In line with postmodernism's inclination towards the parodic and the pastiche, diluted with the pure fun of comic entertainment and a childish enjoyment of the gross and gory, the result is a surprisingly respectful treatment of the theme. It is not as if the figure of Shakespeare is presented in a respectful light, or documented history taken seriously, but the sheer fact of making a film about Shakespeare's journey to fame and stardom, with quotations from his work spicing up the comedy, presupposes both his status as a canonical author and a star, whose lines are recognisable and, as such, offer intellectual entertainment for audiences. Whether these attitudes gear the film towards a high-class audience or are meant to elevate a lower-class audience whose aspirations for erudition can be served, even if sugar-coated through such comic compositions (much like the original *Horrible Histories* series, which was consciously created for a youthful market, with the Horatian mission to 'teach and delight'), is anyone's guess. What is clear, however, is that *Bill* intends and manages to entertain its viewers, in familiar British comic fashion, and, similarly to other postmodern works, succeeds in doing so on a broad and democratic basis, offering something for all comers and therefore finding its rightful position in this group of Shakespearean biopics.

Autumnal farewells – *All Is True*

Released after much audience anticipation, Branagh's most recent instalment of his Shakespearean series received a mixed reaction from critics and general audiences alike. *All Is True* might seem an exception within

Figure 6.5 Autumnal author – Kenneth Branagh in *All is True*. Directed by Kenneth Branagh, 2018. TKBC.

this chapter, but not because it turns to the final years of the author's life; after all, the dying artist is an existing subgroup within the biopic genre, and not only *A Waste of Shame*, but even *Anonymous*, have tackled the representation of the failing body that housed the famous mind. What comes as more of a surprise is the nearly complete suppression of the literary for the sake of the mundane; in the words of one reviewer, the film 'bypasses the worthy immortal regard earned by the writer's works and lets us see the humanity – and the drama – beneath that surface'.[85] A focus on the human side of the great artist is, of course, a central concern of the genre, as this chapter has also discussed in connection with most other films. At the same time, Branagh's autumnal story (see figure 6.5) relies on a number of generic clichés that feel as tired as the viewer by the end of the film, from the ghost of young Hamnet haunting his father, asking him to finish his story, to the very contemporary (i.e. twenty-first-century) foregrounding of the disempowered position of females inhabiting the early modern era and the Shakespeare household.

True, as we have seen with *Bill* already, the contemporary biopic no longer allows the artist's muse or female companion to be silenced, and the topicality of this dominance of female characters has not escaped reviewers' attention, but it was rarely considered a sufficient saving grace. As Peter Debruge laments, the film's incorporation of '21st-century gender politics, suggesting that Shakespeare unfairly pressured his daughters to bear him a grandson so that the family name might continue while overlooking that either of them might also have been capable of carrying on his poetic legacy' never loses its artificiality. As a result, 'It all feels incongruous for its time, far too conveniently reimagined for 2018, in which artists of the past are being torn down by contemporary moral standards'.[86] Sarah Hatchuel even referred to the film as a 'post-MeToo' production, which may be somewhat misleading in the sense that it is not concerned with harassment or abuse in any way, although the phrase is very apt in its reference to the way the film consciously tackles contemporary gender anxieties.[87]

Even though an episodic structure is common in biopics, particularly ones that set out to represent a more or less complete biography, this approach seems rather distracting in *All Is True*. The relatively short chronological span (three years) does not justify this structureless mosaic of a plot, and what the fragmented narrative reveals is simply a lack of focus: there is no momentous event here, only recollections and reflections, relationships and, most of all, regrets. The almost complete absence of textual references to Shakespeare's work is explained by the narrative's starting point with the burning down of the Globe Theatre, after which – a title card argues – he never wrote again. (In this, Branagh and his scriptwriter Ben Elton display a similar attitude to all other biopic authors: a complete disregard for available scholarship, with all reference to later collaborative works, such as *The Two Noble Kinsmen*, glossed over in favour of a fictional storyline.) Instead of the writer at work, what we witness is the end of his career, culminating in his death and his uplifting funeral ceremony, which almost literally follows the description by Codell: 'Death in artist biopics often frames the narrative, appearing at the beginning and the end to foretell the cleansing of abjection as art's first step on its trajectory toward timelessness. Only in death does the artist attain symbolization, or rather his art does. In life he is emasculated.'[88] At the same time, it must be acknowledged that Branagh presents this emasculation in an aesthetically pleasing manner, not only with the help of the beautiful landscape as background to the drama, but also via carefully arranged shots that allow us to see the great man as diminished by his surroundings.

What the film is concerned with is the author's legacy, both in the sense of his family and his poetry. On the whole, however, *All Is True* is more interested in offering an explanation for the tourist attractions in Stratford-upon-Avon (why we should care about the garden of New Place or Hall's Croft), the famous reference in the will to 'the second best bed' and, most importantly, the lack of descendants of the author, than the literary legacy. For all the (scant) references to his living fame and work, the film does not visualise practically any of it (except for an invocation of Aaron's angry spirit from *Titus Andronicus* as imaginary bouncer, employed to scare off an accuser of Shakespeare's daughter Susanna). As a result, the film makes it rather hard to understand why we are supposed to care about a man who no longer writes, and who only tries to create a garden for which he admittedly and visibly has no talent whatsoever.

Still, even in this odd biographic lament, we can find the staples of the biopic, not only the visual signifiers of the period setting (some of them markedly at odds with historical Stratford-upon-Avon and its medieval architectural heritage), but also the presence of contemporaries. Apart from Ben Jonson (Gerard Horan), who makes an appearance only to highlight how much more successful Shakespeare is considered already in his age, the most spectacular short cameo is Ian McKellen's embodiment of the Earl of Southampton. Shakespeare's old flame denies any possibility of a requited affection, but he nonetheless remembers the poetic praise dedicated to him. As both Branagh's Shakespeare and McKellen's Southampton recite Sonnet 29, one after another, it is hard to disagree with Odie Henderson: 'As far as acting battle royales go, this is one for the books.'[89]

Yet this remains a short-lived spark in an otherwise extremely slow-paced narrative, which does not appear entirely meaningful. The tediousness of rural life is not contrasted to a faster pace of London's theatrical life or the author's youth – it simply creates an autumnal atmosphere, which, albeit shot in breathtaking cinematography, feels artificially metaphorical at times, preparing the viewer for the author's death even when the narrative does not. But neither is this death presented as snatching the poet away in the prime of his life – the psychological justification of having come to terms with his son's death is just not powerful enough to explain why he has been digging in a dying garden from the outset. Eventually, mourning for the only son is overtaken by a sense of achievement and pride in the intelligent women in the family, who eventually all learn to read and write, including Anne Hathaway (Judi Dench) – their greatest feat is their ability to read out Shakespeare's poem 'Fear no more' at the funeral.[90] The usual (and admittedly overused) connection between the death of Hamnet and the writing of *Hamlet* is not even hinted at, and the psychological explanation and cure for the delayed grief is simple acceptance: others have also lost children and others have also had ordinary children.

In a sense, the return to 'the lives and loves of the genius' is not without precedent in the post-1990-era biopics, but what is nearly unprecedented (and rather lamentable) in Branagh's latest enterprise is the complete absence of irony, or even a sense of humour, whether self-deprecating or directed at the local backwater of Stratford society. The moment when the film becomes a bit of an 'underdog' story – when Shakespeare finally talks back at Sir Thomas Lucy (Alex Macqueen), showing how he is also the little man who makes it in the world, contrary to his humble origins and the envy and enmity by which he is surrounded – entices a spark of laughter, but it remains an isolated incident.

Whether the Shakespeare biopic's return to the dying author variant signals the decline (and fall) of the genre as such, or simply its diminishing interest in canonical authors, giving way to future films on recent contemporaries, political and media celebrities, criminals and other, more controversial, figures, is hard to say at this point. In one sense, *All Is True* is certainly a culmination and an arrival: it has crowned the career of Kenneth Branagh, whose long-term engagement with Shakespeare's *oeuvre* has now allowed him to finally become the Bard himself. Yet when one observes how his own, extremely diverse and prolific, but critically surprisingly underappreciated, in many ways Wellesian career has begun to move away from Shakespeare, we may also expect the enthusiastic cinematic dalliance with Shakespeare's character since the 1990s to come to a slow conclusion.[91]

Notes

1 Original title *La Rêve de Shakespeare*; for more details, see J. Buchanan, *Shakespeare on Silent Film: An Excellent Dumb Discourse* (Cambridge: Cambridge University Press, 2009), esp. pp. 105–6; and J. Buchanan, 'Introduction: Image, Story, Desire: The Writer on Film', in J. Buchanan (ed.), *The Writer on Film: Screening Literary Authorship* (Basingstoke and New York: Palgrave Macmillan, 2013), pp. 3–32, esp. pp. 7–8.
2 Lanier, 'Film Spin-Offs and Citations', p. 337.
3 *Ibid.*
4 *Ibid.*, pp. 269–70.
5 M. Murray-Pepper, 'The "Tables of Memory": Shakespeare, Cinema and the Writing Desk', in Buchanan (ed.), *The Writer on Film*, pp. 92–105, p. 99.
6 Douglas Lanier lists several other titles in which Shakespeare as character or icon appears, including short and lost films; cf. 'Film Spin-Offs and Citations', pp. 337–9, and some studies, e.g. Megan Murray-Pepper's chapter cited in note 5, include Peter Greenaway's *Prospero's Books* (1991) in their discussions of screen versions of Shakespeare as author. Nonetheless, in spite of the various authorial figures appearing in the films, these works can hardly be regarded as biopics in the commonly used meaning of the term.
7 J. E. Kingsley-Smith, 'Shakespearean Authorship in Popular British Cinema', *Literature/Film Quarterly*, 30:3 (2002), 158–65, 163, n. 1.
8 K. Scheil and G. Holderness, 'Introduction: Shakespeare and "the Personal Story"', *Critical Survey*, 21:3 (2009), 1–5, 2–3.

9 See Murray-Pepper, 'The "Tables of Memory"'.
10 K. Elliott, 'Screened Writers', in Cartmell (ed.), *A Companion to Literature, Film, and Adaptation*, pp. 179–97, p. 193 (italics in original).
11 Kingsley-Smith, 'Shakespearean Authorship in Popular British Cinema', 205.
12 K. Duncan-Jones, *Ungentle Shakespeare: Scenes from His Life* (London: The Arden Shakespeare, 2001), esp. pp. 224–6.
13 Cf. Kingsley-Smith, 'Shakespearean Authorship in Popular British Cinema', 163, n. 5.
14 Based on available box-office data, as of January 2020.
15 '*Shakespeare in Love*', *Concord Theatricals*, www.concordtheatricals.com/p/56914/shakespeare-in-love (accessed 27 January 2020).
16 Shachar, 'Authorial Histories', p. 205.
17 A. Higson, 'Private Lives and Public Conflicts: The English Renaissance on Film, 1998–2010', in M. T. Burnett and A. Streete (eds), *Filming and Performing Renaissance History* (Basingstoke: Palgrave Macmillan, 2011), pp. 178–92, p. 182.
18 *Ibid.*, p. 183.
19 R. Keegan and N. Sperling, '*Shakespeare in Love* and Harvey Weinstein's Dark Oscar Victory', *Vanity Fair* (8 December 2017), www.vanityfair.com/hollywood/2017/12/shakespeare-in-love-and-harvey-weinsteins-dark-oscar-victory (accessed 27 January 2020).
20 Cartmell, 'Marketing Shakespeare Films', p. 18.
21 French, *Selling Shakespeare to Hollywood*, p. 138.
22 M. Anderegg, 'James Dean Meets the Pirate's Daughter: Passion and Parody in *William Shakespeare's Romeo + Juliet* and *Shakespeare in Love*', in R. Burt and L. E. Boose (eds), *Shakespeare, the Movie, II: Popularizing the Plays on Film, TV, Video, and DVD* (London and New York: Routledge, 2003), pp. 56–71, p. 70.
23 Cf. R. Burt, '*Shakespeare in Love* and the End of the Shakespearean: Academic and Mass Culture Constructions of Literary Authorship', in M. T. Burnett and R. Wray (eds), *Shakespeare, Film, Fin de Siècle* (Basingstoke: Macmillan, 2000), pp. 203–31, esp. p. 206.
24 Higson, 'Private Lives and Public Conflicts', p. 183.
25 *Ibid.*, p. 190.
26 *Ibid.*, p. 188.
27 French, *Selling Shakespeare to Hollywood*.
28 Cartmell, 'Marketing Shakespeare Films', p. 70.
29 M. Frago and E. Alfonso, '2008–2013 Political Biopics: Adapting Leaders for a Time of Crisis', *Javnost: The Public*, 24:1 (2017), 1–14, 7.
30 J. F. Codell, 'Gender, Genius, and Abjection in Artist Biopics', in T. Brown and B. Vidal (eds), *The Biopic in Contemporary Film Culture* (New York: Routledge, 2014), pp. 159–75, p. 173.
31 French, *Selling Shakespeare to Hollywood*, p. 145.

32 Shachar, 'Authorial Histories', p. 202.
33 P. J. C. M. Franssen, 'Shakespeare's Life on Film and Television: *Shakespeare in Love* and *A Waste of Shame*', in M. Minier and M. Pennacchia (eds), *Adaptation, Intermediality and the British Celebrity Biopic* (Abingdon and New York: Ashgate, 2014), pp. 101–13, p. 103.
34 T. F. Davis and K. Womack, 'Reading (and Writing) the Ethics of Authorship: *Shakespeare in Love* as Postmodern Metanarrative', *Literature/Film Quarterly*, 32:2 (2004), 153–62, 156.
35 Bingham, 'The Lives and Times of the Biopic', p. 236.
36 See e.g. R. Burt, '*Shakespeare in Love* and the End of the Shakespearean', p. 203.
37 Cf. R. E. Burkhart, 'Finding Shakespeare's "Lost Years"', *Shakespeare Quarterly*, 29:1 (1978), 77–9; E. A. J. Honigmann, *Shakespeare: The 'Lost Years'* (Manchester and New York: Manchester University Press, 1985).
38 The screenplay indicates an even more specific setting: 'SKY. Over which a title "LONDON—SUMMER 1593" appears.' M. Norman and T. Stoppard, *Shakespeare in Love: A Screenplay* (New York: Hyperion, 1998), p. 1.
39 Higson, 'Private Lives and Public Conflicts', pp. 184–5.
40 Norman and Stoppard, *Shakespeare in Love: A Screenplay*, p. 150.
41 *Ibid.*
42 Davis and Womack, 'Reading (and Writing) the Ethics of Authorship', 161, n. 9.
43 Higson, 'Private Lives and Public Conflicts', p. 180.
44 The OpenLearn Team, 'OU on the BBC: Shakespeare Re-Told – *A Waste of Shame*', *OpenLearn* (27 October 2005), www.open.edu/openlearn/body-mind/ou-on-the-bbc-shakespeare-re-told-waste-shame (accessed 27 January 2020).
45 Shachar, 'Authorial Histories', p. 207.
46 Franssen, 'Shakespeare's Life on Film and Television', p. 107.
47 *Ibid.*
48 *Ibid.*
49 G. Holderness, *Nine Lives of William Shakespeare* (London and New York: Continuum, 2011), p. 11.
50 *Ibid.*, p. 96.
51 Cf. K. Duncan-Jones (ed.), *Shakespeare's Sonnets*, The Arden Shakespeare, Third Series (London: Thomas Nelson & Sons, 1997). All parenthetical references to the Sonnets are to this edition.
52 Murray-Pepper, 'The "Tables of Memory"', p. 94.
53 P. Edmondson and S. Wells, 'Interrogating the *Sonnets*', *Actes des congrès de la Société français Shakespeare*, 24 (2007), online 30 March 2011, https://doi.org/10.4000/shakespeare.1021, §7 (accessed 27 January 2020).
54 Higson, 'Private Lives and Public Conflicts', p. 181.
55 Edmondson and Wells, 'Interrogating the *Sonnets*', §7.
56 Franssen, 'Shakespeare's Life on Film and Television', p. 107.

57 Murray-Pepper, 'The "Tables of Memory"', p. 100.
58 Cf. Duncan-Jones (ed.), *Shakespeare's Sonnets*, p. 422.
59 S. B. Dobranski, 'Renaissance Authorship: Practice versus Attribution', in C. Bates (ed.), *A Companion to Renaissance Poetry* (Hoboken, NJ: Wiley-Blackwell, 2018), pp. 115–27, p. 124.
60 R. Subers, 'October Preview', *Box Office Mojo* (28 October 2011), www.boxofficemojo.com/news/?id=3284&p=.htm (accessed 27 January 2020).
61 R. Ebert, 'We All Think Somebody Wrote the Plays, Right?', *Rogerebert.com* (26 October 2011), www.rogerebert.com/reviews/anonymous-2011 (accessed 27 January 2020).
62 D. M. Lanier, '"There Won't Be Puppets, Will There?": "Heroic" Authorship and the Cultural Politics of *Anonymous*', in P. Edmondson and S. Wells (eds), *Shakespeare Beyond Doubt: Evidence, Argument, Controversy* (Cambridge: Cambridge University Press, 2013), pp. 215–24, p. 215.
63 *Ibid.*, p. 216.
64 *Ibid.*, p. 223.
65 D. Sherman, 'Stages of Revision: Textuality, Performance, and History in *Anonymous*', *Literature/Film Quarterly*, 41:2 (2013), 129–42, 132.
66 See e.g. M. Wainwright, *The Rational Shakespeare: Peter Ramus, Edward de Vere, and the Question of Authorship* (Cham: Palgrave Macmillan, 2018), pp. 43–4.
67 Lanier, '"There Won't Be Puppets, Will There?"', p. 219.
68 P. Kirwan, '"You Have No Voice!" Constructing Reputation through Contemporaries in the Shakespeare Biopic', *Shakespeare Bulletin* 32:1 (2014), 11–26, 12.
69 Sherman, 'Stages of Revision', 138.
70 *Ibid.*
71 *Ibid.*
72 See Lanier, '"There Won't Be Puppets, Will There?"', esp. pp. 215–16.
73 The Shakespeare Authorship Coalition, 'Declaration of Reasonable Doubt About the Identity of William Shakespeare', https://doubtaboutwill.org/declaration (accessed 27 January 2020).
74 Oral communication in the 'Shakespeare as Character on Screen in the Digital Era' seminar at the Shakespeare on Screen in the Digital Era Congress.
75 'Stars of BBC's *Horrible Histories* to Make Shakespeare Comedy Film', *BBC Media Centre* (13 May 2013), www.bbc.co.uk/mediacentre/latestnews/2013/bbc-films-bill-press-release.html (accessed 27 January 2020).
76 'Bill', *BBC Films*, www.bbc.com/bbcfilms/films/bill (accessed 22 July 2020).
77 S. McKay, 'Horrible Histories', *Telegraph* (1 September 2009), www.telegraph.co.uk/culture/books/6120942/Horrible-Histories.html (accessed 27 January 2020).
78 De Groot, *Consuming History*, p. 39.
79 *Ibid.*, p. 42.

80 See e.g. H. Shachar, 'The Muse's Tale: Rewriting the English Author in *The Invisible Woman*', in Pettey and Palmer (eds), *Rule, Britannia!*, pp. 145–62, p. 149.
81 Cf. Kirwan, '"You Have No Voice!"'
82 P. Sidney, 'Astrophil and Stella 1', in G. Braden (ed.), *Sixteenth-Century Poetry: An Annotated Anthology* (Oxford and Malden, MA: Blackwell Publishing, 2005), p. 348.
83 Kingsley-Smith, 'Shakespearean Authorship in Popular British Cinema'.
84 *Reduced Shakespeare Company*, www.reducedshakespeare.com/ (accessed 27 January 2020).
85 O. Henderson, 'All is True', *Rogerebert.com* (10 May 2019), www.rogerebert.com/reviews/all-is-true-2019 (accessed 27 January 2020).
86 P. Debruge, 'Film Review: *All Is True*', *Variety* (20 December 2019), https://variety.com/2018/film/reviews/all-is-true-review-kenneth-branagh-shakespeare-1203094669/ (accessed 27 January 2020).
87 Introduction to the film's special screening in Montpellier's Cinéma Utopia, 27 September 2019.
88 Codell, 'Gender, Genius, and Abjection in Artist Biopics', p. 172.
89 Henderson, 'All is True'.
90 W. Shakespeare, *Cymbeline*, The Arden Shakespeare, Second Series, ed. J. M. Nosworthy (London and New York: Routledge, 1994), Act 4, Scene 2, line 258.
91 I am indebted for this argument to Samuel Crowl, presented in his plenary lecture entitled 'Citizen Ken: Branagh, Shakespeare, and the Movies' at the Shakespeare on Screen in the Digital Era Congress.

Conclusion

From *Men Are Not Gods* to *All Is True*, the journey this volume undertook to search for traces of the Shakespearean in genre cinema spanned nearly the entire history of sound film – fourscore and upward years – and yet it can only leave the reader now with the acknowledgement of its incompleteness. Not that I deluded myself I would ever even come close to a complete account – I have always been aware of the temporal and spatial constraints that forced me to limit the number of genres and, within each generic group, to select only the most representative examples. Moreover, it is also a fact that with each passing moment, the list of films not included in the investigation keeps growing, as new films are released or the association of earlier works with Shakespeare is identified by fans, critics or scholars in faraway corners of the globe. Whether we like it or not (I for one certainly do), Shakespeare continues to inspire creators to try their hands at a combination of the inherited source material and a newly emerging screen format, which results in a constantly changing pool of works, contesting previously accepted notions about the workings of the field.

Yet in many ways this has always been one of the goals of the whole enterprise: to encourage the reader to continue where this volume leaves off, and to follow these lines of thought to other genres, even other media forms, which have all but taken over the previously unchallenged dominance of the cinematic feature film. As I have already suggested in the Introduction, both theoretical and more pragmatic branches of adaptation studies have lately been turning towards new media, trying to gauge the impacts of a fundamentally changed consumer environment, the appearance of users and prosumers on the market, and a whole line of such research fields that require our attention. Still, I am convinced that even in the light of these new investigations, the continued relevance of genre as an analytical category remains unchallenged. Not only do viewers still rely on generic labels in defining or describing the products they encounter as recipients, but creators and critics also fall back on these categories as reference points, even if the categories themselves have undergone significant change over the decades. Moreover, if we accept that we live in the aftermath of an algorithmic turn in visual culture,[1] and contemplate the new processes of selection or organisation of various products as achieved by various types of algorithms, we keep coming back to genre as a crucial element. Based on our previous viewing patterns, streaming providers offer us new films that we may enjoy; online video sellers suggest additional films we should buy; the Internet Movie Database mentions further examples of what we might be interested in – and if we look carefully at these recommendations, it is easy to see the elements of genre that are running through them. Observations such as these can be directly connected to the findings of this volume, confirming that investing our energies in genre studies has pragmatic benefits even in the twenty-first century. A deeper understanding of how many elements of a work of art may be connected to its genre will hopefully also enable us to develop new approaches and research methodologies when it comes to archiving, digitising, labelling and trying to make sense of the vast amounts of material at our disposal.

Looking back at the previous chapters, it is worthwhile once again to take stock of how many ways those seemingly disparate entities, the individual films, have turned out to be intricately connected to each other through what we call, for want of a better term, their common genre. Regarding these films as adaptations of Shakespearean drama would not in itself explain, for instance, the increased (or decreased) role of certain characters, and gender roles provide a particularly interesting case in point. In the western and in the gangster-*noir* groups, females have often been reduced to one of two types: the innocent, passive, patient and loving wife material, confined to the domestic environment; or its opposite, the alluring and passionate, active and often dangerous, but socially isolated, lover, *femme fatale* or prostitute with a heart of gold. Depending on which era we are talking about, these films may allow us to sympathise even with the marginalised woman, but the narrative will not include her in the happy ending. Even the Native American wife of the patriarch in *Broken Lance* is forced to return to her people by the end of the narrative, as the future of the protagonist, and by extension, that of American civilisation, is in the hand of the Eastern-educated blonde bourgeois girl, who encourages the young man to move away from his painful past. The melodrama, on the other hand, expands on female roles and often grants women a chance to tell their own side of the story as focalisers or even narrators, both in the early woman's film and in the late twentieth-century television melodrama. What is more, by placing Anglo-American melodramas side by side with their counterparts rooted in the Eastern cinematic tradition, we may note the correspondences between the underlying narrative patterns, characterisation and stylistic features of these classical genres. Each of these genres, aware of their broad embeddedness in the social imaginary, also play a dual role in reinforcing the finite number of choices within social interactions: on the one hand, representing the stereotypical plotlines, but also confirming these as idealised or feared resolutions of conflicts, their power based on precisely the fact of their broad dissemination.

The industrial background that led to the creation of generic cycles in the Hollywood studio era is well known and extensively discussed in historical film studies. The social and economic factors of the 1990s, however, were equally significant in bringing about a cinematic boom worldwide, and creating a new wave of screen Shakespeares along the way. Yet what Part II of the book argued is that beside this shared industrial background, certain aesthetic features characterising post-1990s adaptations in the revived new genres allow us to see them as a coherent group, which systematically reflect on their own era of creation. One of these features is a desire to reinterpret the inherited stories through an in-depth psychological identification with characters and conflicts. This is what we can observe in the way Shakespeare is approached by high school students, who tend to apply the plays' words directly to their own everyday trials and tribulations. This need for identification also explains the rise of the humanised undead, who are no longer the monstrous Others of civilisation, but are represented as victims of an oppressive and inhuman society, whose institutions are most likely to betray their citizens. In these narratives, Shakespeare regularly appears to provide guidance on how to embrace one's victimhood, but more importantly, how to find the inner strength for fighting back against the real monsters and proving that humanity can be found in the unlikeliest forms if one looks close enough. Neither do contemporary biopics emphasise greatness or canonical status in the authors they bring to life on the screen, but focus on the pains and losses, shortcomings and failures of their subject, who turns out to be just as much of a human being as the average viewer the films wish to educate and entertain at the same time.

Another common feature of films made since the 1990s – it is the reign of the postmodern, after all – directly concerns a central challenge of adaptation studies: how the written text is transmitted into the visual format. The era's artistic production subscribes to the postmodern tendency to embrace the irreverent and playful, revelling in decontextualised and recontextualised textual fragments. This, on the one hand, challenges the pessimistic visions of the loss of the text, since the text is clearly here to stay. At the same time, the seemingly random and piecemeal insertion of classical quotations into new texts is a conscious strategy, which clearly illustrates how readily contemporary popular and visual culture absorbs and repurposes inherited materials according to its momentary needs.

Yet, for all their irreverence and superficial engagement with their canonical source, these films also illustrate a continued interest in the authorship debate, not so much in the biographical reality of the person who wrote what we call the Shakespearean *oeuvre*, but more in terms of the power and glory of creation itself. In the age of fifteen-minute fame, when creating or destroying reputations can happen at a viral speed, the Shakespeare phenomenon and its survival in education, elite and mass culture, and particularly in scholarship, provides us with an intriguing and enduring challenge but also endless fascination. In terms of a contemporary understanding of authorship and the creative process, this consistent link between Shakespeare and lived experience is an inherently conservative one, which nonetheless fits our own cultural context. Even if the Romantic image of the author – working in shirtsleeves in the privacy of his home – survives in visual representations, the notion of such a singularly powerful imagination whose output would be based on his own inner talent finds less acceptance than the image of an ordinary human being whose life resembles our very own. As a compromise, contemporary representations tend to emphasise his position as a channel, a mediator, who relies on an interpretive community. This meta-cinematic message in turn is what all genre films appear to convey: Shakespeare may no longer be our idol, and he is certainly no superhero, but his stories continue to help us tell our own stories, fight our own battles, find our own voices.

These voices are naturally diverse and colourful, and this in itself may make the reader feel slightly confused by the endlessly multiplying variations on a few old themes. But, as I said at the beginning, this is precisely why Shakespeare-inspired genre cinema never loses its fascination for me, and why I feel that it supports a fundamentally optimistic message about human creativity. In this diversity I find hope that Shakespeare will continue to play a part in the future of our culture, although no doubt this role will hardly resemble the parts he has been cast in during the past four centuries. Whether he will at one point ride off into the sunset, all alone, like a cowboy, and leave us behind to cultivate our petty affairs, or return from the dead even though no natural law can explain how he is still alive – these are some of the questions that I conclude with, in the hope that the reader may find at least as much enjoyment in their contemplation as I did spending my time with Shakespeares, cowboys and zombies.

Note

1 Cf. W. Uricchio, 'The Algorithmic Turn: Photosynth, Augmented Reality and the Changing Implications of the Image', *Visual Studies*, 26:1 (2011), 25–35.

Bibliography

Abbott, S. *Celluloid Vampires: Life after Death in the Modern World* (Austin: University of Texas Press, 2007).
—. *Undead Apocalypse: Vampires and Zombies in the 21st Century* (Edinburgh: Edinburgh University Press, 2016).
Aebischer, P. *Screening Early Modern Drama: Beyond Shakespeare* (Cambridge: Cambridge University Press, 2013).
— and S. Greenhalgh, 'Introduction: Shakespeare and the "Live" Theatre Broadcast Experience', in P. Aebischer, S. Greenhalgh and L. Osborne (eds), *Shakespeare and the 'Live' Theatre Broadcast Experience* (London: The Arden Shakespeare, 2018), pp. 1–16.
Aftab, K. 'Brown: The New Black! Bollywood in Britain', *Critical Quarterly*, 44:3 (2002), 88–98.
Altman, R. 'Cinema and Genre', in G. Nowell-Smith (ed.), *The Oxford History of World Cinema* (Oxford: Oxford University Press, 1996), pp. 276–85.
—. *Film/Genre* (London: British Film Institute, 1999).
—. 'A Semantic/Syntactic Approach to Film Genre', *Cinema Journal*, 23:3 (1984), 6–18.
Anderegg, M. 'James Dean Meets the Pirate's Daughter: Passion and Parody in *William Shakespeare's Romeo + Juliet* and *Shakespeare in Love*', in R. Burt and L. E. Boose (eds), *Shakespeare, the Movie, II: Popularizing the Plays on Film, TV, Video, and DVD* (London and New York: Routledge, 2003), pp. 56–71.
Arthur, P. 'How the West Was Spun: *McCabe & Mrs. Miller* and Genre Revisionism', *Cinéaste*, 28:3 (2003), 18–20.
Bailey, S. and J. Hay, 'Cinema and the Premises of Youth: "Teen Films" and Their Sites in the 1980s and 1990s', in S. Neale (ed.), *Genre and Contemporary Hollywood* (London: BFI Publishing, 2002), pp. 218–35.
Balizet, A. M. 'Just Say Yes: Shakespeare, Sex, and Girl Culture', *Women's Studies*, 44:6 (2015), 815–41.

—. 'Teen Scenes: Recognizing Shakespeare in Teen Film', in Keller and Stratyner (eds), *Almost Shakespeare*, pp. 122–36.

Bandy, M. L. and K. Stoehr, *Ride, Boldly Ride: The Evolution of the American Western* (Berkeley, Los Angeles and London: University of California Press, 2012).

Baron, C. 'Film Noir: Gesture under Pressure', in Cornea (ed.), *Genre and Performance*, pp. 18–37.

Bazin, A. 'The Western: Or The American Film Par Excellence', in A. Bazin, *What is Cinema? Essays Selected and Translated by Hugh Gray*, vol. 2 (1971; Berkeley, Los Angeles and London: University of California Press, 2005), pp. 140–8.

Beckett, S. L. *Crossover Fiction: Global and Historical Perspectives* (New York and London: Routledge, 2009).

Berry-Flint, S. 'Genre', in T. Miller and R. Stam (eds), *A Companion to Film Theory* (Oxford: Blackwell, 2004), pp. 25–44.

Biesen, S. C. 'Psychology in American Film Noir and Hitchcock's Gothic Thrillers', *Americana: The Journal of American Popular Culture (1900–Present)*, 13:1 (2014), www.americanpopularculture.com/journal/articles/spring_2014/biesen.htm (accessed 26 January 2020).

'Bill', *BBC Films*, www.bbc.com/bbcfilms/films/bill (accessed 22 July 2020).

Bingham, D. 'The Lives and Times of the Biopic', in Rosenstone and Parvulescu (eds), *A Companion to the Historical Film*, pp. 233–54.

—. 'Living Stories: Performance in the Contemporary Biopic', in Cornea (ed.), *Genre and Performance*, pp. 76–95.

Bishop, K. 'Dead Man *Still* Walking: Explaining the Zombie Renaissance', *Journal of Popular Film and Television*, 37:1 (2009), 16–25.

—. 'Humanizing the Living Dead: The Evolution of the Zombie Protagonist', in K. Murphy (ed.), *The Zombie Reader* (Boulder: University Press of Colorado, 2019), pp. 189–204.

—. 'Vacationing in *Zombieland*: The Classical Functions of the Modern Zombie Comedy', *Journal of the Fantastic in the Arts*, 22:1 (2011), 24–38.

Bladen, V., S. Hatchuel and N. Vienne-Guerrin (eds), *Shakespeare on Screen: King Lear* (Cambridge: Cambridge University Press, 2019).

Borde, R. and É. Chaumeton, 'Towards a Definition of *Film Noir*', in A. Silver and J. Ursini (eds), *Film Noir Reader* (New York: Limelight, 1996), pp. 17–26.

Bradley, L. '*Zombieland: Double Tap* Proves the Zombie Craze Will Never Die', *Vanity Fair* (16 October 2019), www.vanityfair.com/hollywood/2019/10/zombieland-double-tap-zombie-movies-trend-history (accessed 5 January 2020).

Brooke, M. '*Men Are Not Gods* (1936)', *Screenonline*, www.screenonline.org.uk/film/id/439260/index.html (accessed 26 January 2020).

Brown, E. C. 'The Bard Comes to *Yellow Sky*: Shakespeare's Tempestuous Western', in E. C. Brown and E. Rivier (eds), *Shakespeare in Performance* (Newcastle-upon-Tyne: Cambridge Scholars Publishing, 2013), pp. 138–54.

—. 'Cinema in the Round: Self-Reflexivity in Tim Blake Nelson's O', in Keller and Stratyner (eds), *Almost Shakespeare*, pp. 73–85.
Brown, S. A., R. I. Lublin and L. McCulloch (eds), *Reinventing the Renaissance: Shakespeare and His Contemporaries in Adaptation and Performance* (Basingstoke: Palgrave Macmillan, 2013).
Browning Erwin, S. and C. Dickens, *Grave Expectations* (New York: Simon & Schuster, 2011).
Buchanan, J. 'Introduction: Image, Story, Desire: The Writer on Film', in Buchanan (ed.), *The Writer on Film*, pp. 3–32.
—. *Shakespeare on Film* (Harlow: Pearson Education Limited, 2005).
—. *Shakespeare on Silent Film: An Excellent Dumb Discourse* (Cambridge: Cambridge University Press, 2009).
— (ed.), *The Writer on Film: Screening Literary Authorship* (Basingstoke and New York: Palgrave Macmillan, 2013).
Burkhart, R. E. 'Finding Shakespeare's "Lost Years"', *Shakespeare Quarterly*, 29:1 (1978), 77–9.
Burnett, W. R. *Stretch Dawson* (New York: Fawcett Gold Medal, 1950).
Burt, R. 'Afterword: T(e)en Things I Hate about Girlene Shakesploitation Flicks in the Late 1990s, or, Not-So-Fast Times at Shakespeare High', in Lehmann and Starks (eds), *Spectacular Shakespeare*, pp. 205–32.
—. '*Shakespeare in Love* and the End of the Shakespearean: Academic and Mass Culture Constructions of Literary Authorship', in M. T. Burnett and R. Wray (eds), *Shakespeare, Film, Fin de Siècle* (Basingstoke: Macmillan, 2000), pp. 203–31.
—. *Unspeakable ShaXXXspeares* (New York: St. Martin's Press, 1998).
Burton, A. and T. O'Sullivan, *The Cinema of Basil Dearden and Michael Relph* (Edinburgh: Edinburgh University Press, 2009).
Buscombe, E. 'The Idea of Genre in the American Cinema', *Screen*, 11:2 (1970), 33–45.
—. *'Injuns!' Native Americans in the Movies* (London: Reaktion Books, 2006).
Butler, H. 'Teens Pick "Smombie" as Hippest German Word', *The Local* (14 November 2015), www.thelocal.de/20151114/are-you-a-smombie-german-youth-word-2016 (accessed 27 January 2020).
Byron, G. '"As One Dead": Romeo and Juliet in the "Twilight" Zone', in Drakakis and Townshend (eds), *Gothic Shakespeares*, pp. 167–85.
Cameron, A. 'Zombie Media: Transmission, Reproduction, and the Digital Dead', *Cinema Journal*, 52:1 (2012), 66–89.
Carney, R. (ed.), *Cassavetes on Cassavetes* (London: Faber and Faber, 2001).
Cartelli, T. and K. Rowe, *New Wave Shakespeare on Screen* (Cambridge and Malden, MA: Polity, 2007).
Cartmell, D. 'Marketing Shakespeare Films: From Tragedy to Biopic', in D. Shellard and S. Keenan (eds), *Shakespeare's Cultural Capital: His Economic Impact from the Sixteenth to the Twenty-First Century* (Basingstoke: Palgrave Macmillan, 2016), pp. 57–76.

— (ed.), *A Companion to Literature, Film, and Adaptation* (Chichester: Wiley-Blackwell, 2012).
Casillo, R. *Gangster Priest: The Italian American Cinema of Martin Scorsese* (Toronto, Buffalo, NY, and London: University of Toronto Press, 2006).
Cavell, S. *Pursuits of Happiness: The Hollywood Comedy of Remarriage* (Cambridge, MA: Harvard University Press, 1981).
Cawelti, J. G. *Adventure, Mystery, and Romance: Formula Stories as Art and Popular Culture* (Chicago and London: University of Chicago Press, 1976).
—. 'The Question of Popular Genres', *Journal of Popular Film and Television*, 13:2 (1985), 55–61.
—. *The Six-Gun Mystique Sequel* (Bowling Green, OH: Bowling Green State University Popular Press, 1999).
Ceplair, L. *The Marxist and the Movies: A Biography of Paul Jarrico* (Lexington: University Press of Kentucky, 2007).
Chaplin, S. *The Postmillennial Vampire: Power, Sacrifice and Simulation in* True Blood, Twilight *and Other Contemporary Narratives* (Cham: Palgrave Macmillan, 2017).
Charry, B. and G. Shahani, 'The Global as Local/Othello as Omkara', in C. Dionne and P. Kapadia (eds), *Bollywood Shakespeares* (New York: Palgrave Macmillan, 2014), pp. 107–23.
Cieślak, M. 'Shakespeare and Zombies: *Romeo and Juliet*, Baz Luhrmann and *Warm Bodies*', unpublished conference paper presented at the '*Romeo and Juliet* on Screen' seminar at the Shakespeare on Screen in the Digital Era Congress organised by the Université Paul-Valéry Montpellier 3 (26–28 September 2019).
'classic', in *English Oxford Living Dictionaries* (Oxford: Oxford University Press, 2017), https://en.oxforddictionaries.com/definition/classic (accessed 1 December 2017).
Clover, C. J. 'Her Body, Himself: Gender in the Slasher Film', *Representations*, 20 (1987), 187–228.
Clover, J. 'Based on Actual Events', *Film Quarterly*, 62:3 (2009), 8–9.
Cocarla, S. 'A Love Worth Un-Undying For: Neoliberalism and Queered Sexuality in *Warm Bodies*', in S. McGlotten and S. Jones (eds), *Zombies and Sexuality: Essays on Desire and the Living Dead* (Jefferson, NC: McFarland, 2014), pp. 52–72.
Codell, J. F. 'Gender, Genius, and Abjection in Artist Biopics', in T. Brown and B. Vidal (eds), *The Biopic in Contemporary Film Culture* (New York: Routledge, 2014), pp. 159–75.
Collins, M. and E. Bond, '"Off the Page and into Your Brains!": New Millennium Zombies and the Scourge of Hopeful Apocalypses', in D. Christie and S. J. Lauro (eds), *Better Off Dead: The Evolution of the Zombie as Post-Human* (New York: Fordham University Press, 2011), pp. 187–204.
Collins, S. *The Hunger Games* (New York: Scholastic Press, 2008).

Comolli, J.-L. 'Historical Fiction: A Body Too Much', trans. B. Brewster, *Screen*, 19:2 (1978), 41–54.

Corkin, S. *Cowboys as Cold Warriors: The Western and U.S. History* (Philadelphia, PA: Temple University Press, 2004).

Cornea, C. (ed.), *Genre and Performance: Film and Television* (Manchester and New York: Manchester University Press, 2010).

Corredera, V. 'Far More Black than Black: Stereotypes, Black Masculinity, and Americanization in Tim Blake Nelson's *O*', *Literature/Film Quarterly*, 45:3 (2017), https://lfq.salisbury.edu/_issues/45_3/far_more_black_than_black.html (accessed 26 January 2020).

Coursen, H. R. *Shakespeare Translated: Derivatives on Film and TV* (New York: Peter Lang, 2005).

Cowie, E. '*Film Noir* and Women', in J. Copjec (ed.), *Shades of Noir* (London and New York: Verso, 1993), pp. 121–65.

Croteau, M. 'Kat and Bianca Avenged: Or, Things to Love about *10 Things I Hate About You*', in L. Wilson (ed.), *Americana: Readings in Popular Culture* (Los Angeles, CA: Press Americana, 2006), pp. 65–9.

Crowl, S. 'Flamboyant Realist: Kenneth Branagh', in Jackson (ed.), *The Cambridge Companion to Shakespeare on Film*, pp. 226–42.

—. *Shakespeare at the Cineplex: The Kenneth Branagh Era* (Athens: Ohio University Press, 2003).

Crowther, B. 'Screen: Lust Out West; *Jubal* Tells Tale of Cowboy and Female', *New York Times* (25 April 1956), www.nytimes.com/1956/04/25/archives/screen-lust-out-west-jubal-tells-tale-of-cowboy-and-female.html (accessed 26 January 2020).

Cummings, B. 'Zombie Shakespeare', *Palgrave Communications* (6 September 2016), 1–4, http://dx.doi.org/10.1057/palcomms.2016.63 (accessed 30 June 2020).

Dash, I. G. *Shakespeare and the American Musical* (Bloomington and Indianapolis: Indiana University Press, 2010).

Davis, H. H. 'I Was a Teenage Classic: Literary Adaptation in Turn-of-the-Millennium Teen Films', *Journal of American Culture*, 29:1 (2006), 52–60.

Davis, T. F. and K. Womack, 'Reading (and Writing) the Ethics of Authorship: *Shakespeare in Love* as Postmodern Metanarrative', *Literature/Film Quarterly*, 32:2 (2004), 153–62.

De Groot, J. *Consuming History: Historians and Heritage in Contemporary Popular Culture* (London and New York: Routledge, 2009).

Debruge, P. 'Film Review: *All Is True*', *Variety* (20 December 2019), https://variety.com/2018/film/reviews/all-is-true-review-kenneth-branagh-shakespeare-1203094669/ (accessed 27 January 2020).

Deitchman, E. A. 'Shakespeare Stiles Style: Shakespeare, Julia Stiles, and American Girl Culture', in B. Hodgdon and W. B. Worthen (eds), *A Companion to Shakespeare and Performance* (Oxford: Blackwell, 2005), pp. 478–93.

Deleuze, G. and F. Guattari, *A Thousand Plateaus: Capitalism and Schizophrenia*, trans. Brian Massumi (Minneapolis: University of Minnesota Press, 1987).
Derrida, J. 'The Law of Genre', trans. A. Ronell, *Critical Inquiry*, 7:1, Special Issue: *On Narrative* (1980), 55–81.
Desmet, C. 'Dramas of Recognition: *Pan's Labyrinth* and *Warm Bodies* as Accidental Shakespeare', in Desmet, Loper and Casey (eds), *Shakespeare/Not Shakespeare*, pp. 275–91.
—, N. Loper and J. Casey, 'Introduction', in Desmet, Loper and Casey (eds), *Shakespeare/Not Shakespeare* (Cham: Palgrave Macmillan, 2017), pp. 1–22.
—, N. Loper and J. Casey (eds), *Shakespeare/Not Shakespeare* (Cham: Palgrave Macmillan, 2017).
DeWitt, J. 'Cars and Culture: The Cars of *American Graffiti*', *American Poetry Review*, 39:5 (2010), 47–50.
Dick, B. F. *Radical Innocence: A Critical Study of the Hollywood Ten* (Lexington: University Press of Kentucky, 1989).
Dickinson, P. *Screening Gender, Framing Genre: Canadian Literature into Film* (Toronto, Buffalo, NY, and London: University of Toronto Press, 2007).
Dixon, W. W. '"Fighting and Violence and Everything, That's Always Cool": Teen Films in the 1990s', in W. W. Dixon (ed.), *Film Genre 2000* (New York: State University of New York Press, 2000), pp. 125–41.
Dobranski, S. B. 'Renaissance Authorship: Practice versus Attribution', in C. Bates (ed.), *A Companion to Renaissance Poetry* (Hoboken, NJ: Wiley-Blackwell, 2018), pp. 115–27.
Doherty, T. *Teenagers and Teenpics: The Juvenilization of American Movies in the 1950s* (Philadelphia, PA: Temple University Press, rev. edn, 2002).
Dowell, P. 'The Mythology of the Western: Hollywood Perspectives on Race and Gender in the Nineties', *Cinéaste*, 21:1–2 (1995), 6–10.
Drakakis, J. and D. Townshend (eds), *Gothic Shakespeares* (Abingdon: Routledge, 2008).
Driver, S. 'Girls Looking at Girls Looking for Girls: The Visual Pleasures and Social Empowerment of Queer Teen Romance Flicks', in T. Shary and A. Seibel (eds), *Youth Culture in Global Cinema* (Austin: University of Texas Press, 2007), pp. 241–55.
Duncan-Jones, K. *Ungentle Shakespeare: Scenes from His Life* (London: The Arden Shakespeare, 2001).
— (ed.), *Shakespeare Sonnets*, The Arden Shakespeare, Third Series (London: Thomas Nelson & Sons, 1997).
Durham, P. and E. L. Jones, *The Negro Cowboys* (Lincoln: University of Nebraska Press/Bison Books, 1983).
Dwyer, R. 'Planet Bollywood', in N. Ali, V. Kalra and S. Sayyid (eds), *A Postcolonial People: South Asians in Britain* (London: Hurst & Company, 2006), pp. 361–9.
Ebert, R. *I Hated, Hated, Hated This Movie* (Kansas City: Andrews McMeel Publishing, 2000).

—. 'We All Think Somebody Wrote the Plays, Right?', *Rogerebert.com* (26 October 2011), www.rogerebert.com/reviews/anonymous-2011 (accessed 27 January 2020).

Edmondson, P. and S. Wells, 'Interrogating the *Sonnets*', *Actes des congrès de la Société français Shakespeare*, 24 (2007), online 30 March 2011, https://doi.org/10.4000/shakespeare.1021, §7 (accessed 27 January 2020).

Elam, K. 'Introduction', in Shakespeare, *Twelfth Night*, pp. 1–154.

Elliott, K. 'Screened Writers', in Cartmell (ed.), *A Companion to Literature, Film, and Adaptation*, pp. 179–97.

Ellis, J. 'The Literary Adaptation', *Screen*, 23:1 (1982), 3–5.

Elsaesser, T. 'Tales of Sound and Fury: Observations on the Family Melodrama', in Grant (ed.), *Film Genre Reader IV*, pp. 433–62.

Fagen, H. *The Encyclopedia of Westerns* (New York: Facts on File, 2003).

Falconer, R. *The Crossover Novel: Contemporary Children's Fiction and Its Adult Readership* (New York and London: Routledge, 2009).

Farrell, S. E. *Jane Smiley's* A Thousand Acres: *A Reader's Guide* (New York and London: Continuum, 2001).

Fay, J. and J. Nieland, *Film Noir: Hard-Boiled Modernity and the Cultures of Globalization* (London and New York: Routledge, 2010).

Fazel, V. M. and L. Geddes, 'Introduction: The Shakespeare User', in V. M. Fazel and L. Geddes (eds), *The Shakespeare User: Critical and Creative Appropriations in a Networked Culture* (Cham: Palgrave Macmillan, 2017), pp. 1–22.

Flamming, D. 'African Americans in the Twentieth-Century West', in W. Deverell (ed.), *A Companion to the American West* (Malden, MA, and Oxford: Blackwell, 2007), pp. 221–39.

Földváry, K. '"Brush Up Your Shakespeare": Genre-Shift from Shakespeare to the Screen', in Brown, Lublin and McCulloch (eds), *Reinventing the Renaissance*, pp. 47–62.

—. 'Fragmented Shakespeare in SF TV: The Case of *Westworld*', *Foundation: The International Review of Science Fiction 134*, 48:3, Special Issue: *Winter's Tales: Shakespeare and Science Fiction* (2019), 8–18.

—. 'Trendy or Topical? Sexual Politics and Panopticism in the 2016 BBC *Midsummer Night's Dream*', *Cahiers Élisabéthains: A Journal of English Renaissance Studies*, 99:1 (2019), 137–46.

Frago, M. and E. Alfonso, '2008–2013 Political Biopics: Adapting Leaders for a Time of Crisis', *Javnost: The Public*, 24:1 (2017), 1–14.

Frank, N. 'Un nouveau genre "policier": L'aventure criminelle', *L'Ecran français*, 61 (28 August 1946), 8–9, 14.

Franssen, P. J. C. M. 'Shakespeare's Life on Film and Television: *Shakespeare in Love* and *A Waste of Shame*', in M. Minier and M. Pennacchia (eds), *Adaptation, Intermediality and the British Celebrity Biopic* (Abingdon and New York: Ashgate, 2014), pp. 101–13.

French, E. *Selling Shakespeare to Hollywood: The Marketing of Filmed Shakespeare Adaptations from 1989 into the New Millennium* (Hatfield: University of Hertfordshire Press, 2006).
Gano, G. and W. Dixon, 'Gone Daddy Gone', *Metrolyrics*, www.metrolyrics.com/gone-daddy-gone-lyrics-violent-femmes.html (accessed 26 January 2020).
Gardaphé, F. L. 'The Gangster Figure in American Film and Literature', in G. Muscio, J. Sciorra, G. Spagnoletti and A. J. Tamburri (eds), *Mediated Ethnicity: New Italian-American Cinema* (New York: John D. Calandra Italian American Institute, 2010), pp. 55–63.
Gledhill, C. 'Prologue: The Reach of Melodrama', in C. Gledhill and L. Williams (eds), *Melodrama Unbound: Across History, Media and National Cultures* (New York: Columbia University Press, 2018), pp. ix–xxv.
Golden, D. 'Pasta or Paradigm: The Place of Italian-American Women in Popular Film', *Explorations in Ethnic Studies*, 2:1 (1979), 3–10.
Grahame-Smith, S. and J. Austen, *Pride and Prejudice and Zombies* (Philadelphia, PA: Quirk Books, 2009).
Grant, B. K. *Film Genre Reader IV* (Austin: University of Texas Press, 2012).
Grant Ferguson, A. *Shakespeare, Cinema, Counter-Culture: Appropriation and Inversion* (New York and London: Routledge, 2016).
Gray, B. 'Matrix Weekend Two', *Box Office Mojo* (12 April 1999), www.boxofficemojo.com/news/?id=1030&p=.htm (accessed 26 January 2020).
Gray, P. 'Shakespeare's Vampire: *Hubris* in *Coriolanus*, Meyer's *Twilight*, and Stoker's *Dracula*', *Shakespeare en devenir – Les Cahiers de La Licorne*, 5 (2011), http://shakespeare.edel.univ-poitiers.fr/index.php?id=557 (accessed 27 January 2020).
Green, R. 'Educating for Pleasure: The Textual Relations of *She's the Man*', in Brown, Lublin and McCulloch (eds), *Reinventing the Renaissance*, pp. 32–46.
Greven, D. 'Contemporary Hollywood Masculinity and the Double-Protagonist Film', *Cinema Journal*, 48:4 (2009), 22–43.
Griggs, Y. '"All Our Lives We'd Looked Out for Each Other in the Way That Motherless Children Tend to Do": *King Lear* as Melodrama', *Literature/Film Quarterly*, 35:2 (2007), 101–7.
—. '"Humanity Must Perforce Prey Upon Itself Like Monsters of the Deep": *King Lear* and the Urban Gangster Movie', *Adaptation*, 1:2 (2008), 121–39.
—. '*King Lear* as Western Elegy', *Literature/Film Quarterly*, 35:2 (2007), 92–100.
—. *Screen Adaptations: Shakespeare's* King Lear: *The Relationship between Text and Film* (London: Methuen Drama, 2009).
Hakola, O. *Rhetoric of Modern Death in American Living Dead Films* (Bristol and Chicago, IL: Intellect, 2015).
Hamrah, A. S. 'Now Streaming: The Plague Years', *The Baffler*, 28 (2015), 113–21.
Handeland, L. *Shakespeare Undead* (London: St Martin's Press, 2010).

—. *Zombie Island* (London: St Martin's Press, 2012).

Hansen, A. and K. J. Wetmore, Jr (eds), *Shakespearean Echoes* (Basingstoke: Palgrave Macmillan, 2015).

Henderson, D. E. 'Romancing *King Lear*: *Hobson's Choice*, *Life Goes On* and Beyond', in Bladen, Hatchuel and Vienne-Guerrin (eds), *Shakespeare on Screen: King Lear*, pp. 125–39.

Henderson, O. 'All is True', *Rogerebert.com* (10 May 2019), www.rogerebert.com/reviews/all-is-true-2019 (accessed 27 January 2020).

Hertz, N. 'Think Millennials Have it Tough? For "Generation K", Life is Even Harsher', *Guardian* (19 March 2016), www.theguardian.com/world/2016/mar/19/think-millennials-have-it-tough-for-generation-k-life-is-even-harsher (accessed 27 January 2020).

Hibberd, J. 'Sucked Dry: Is the Vampire Trend Dead?' *Entertainment Weekly* (12 February 2014), http://ew.com/article/2014/02/12/vampire-trend-dead/ (accessed 27 January 2020).

Higson, A. 'Private Lives and Public Conflicts: The English Renaissance on Film, 1998–2010', in M. T. Burnett and A. Streete (eds), *Filming and Performing Renaissance History* (Basingstoke: Palgrave Macmillan, 2011), pp. 178–92.

Hoad, P. 'Zombies: The Film Genre That Won't Die', *Aljazeera* (31 October 2016), www.aljazeera.com/indepth/features/2016/10/zombies-film-genre-wondie-161017060631418.html (accessed 27 January 2020).

Hodgdon, B. 'The Last Shakespeare Picture Show or Going to the Barricades', in G. B. Shand (ed.), *Teaching Shakespeare: Passing it On* (Chichester: Wiley-Blackwell, 2009), pp. 105–20.

Hoffmann, H. *Western Film Highlights: The Best of the West, 1914–2001* (Jefferson, NC: McFarland, 2003).

Holderness, G. *Nine Lives of William Shakespeare* (London and New York: Continuum, 2011).

Honigmann, E. A. J. *Shakespeare: The 'Lost Years'* (Manchester and New York: Manchester University Press, 1985).

Howard, T. 'Shakespeare's Cinematic Offshoots', in Jackson (ed.), *The Cambridge Companion to Shakespeare on Film*, pp. 295–313.

Hubner, L., M. Leaning and P. Manning (eds), *The Zombie Renaissance in Popular Culture* (Basingstoke: Palgrave Macmillan, 2015).

Hutcheon, L. *A Theory of Adaptation* (Abingdon and New York: Routledge, 2006).

Hutchings, P. 'Theatres of Blood: Shakespeare and the Horror Film', in Drakakis and Townshend (eds), *Gothic Shakespeares*, pp. 153–66.

Innes, C. L. *The Cambridge Introduction to Postcolonial Literatures in English* (Cambridge: Cambridge University Press, 2007).

Jackson, R. (ed.), *The Cambridge Companion to Shakespeare on Film* (Cambridge: Cambridge University Press, 2nd edn, 2007).

Jacobson, G. 'The Myth of the American Frontier', *New Statesman* (26 June 2019), www.newstatesman.com/end-myth-frontier-america-greg-grandin-empire-greater-united-states (accessed 10 January 2020).

Jameson, F. *Postmodernism, or, The Cultural Logic of Late Capitalism* (London and New York: Verso, 1991).

Jenkins, H. *Textual Poachers: Television Fans and Participatory Culture* (London and New York: Routledge, 1992).

Jenkins, S. '*Underworld*: Romeo & Juliet – Vampire & Werewolf Style', *Animation World Network* (19 September 2003), www.awn.com/vfxworld/underworld-romeo-juliet-vampire-werewolf-style (accessed 27 January 2020).

Jess-Cooke, C. 'Screening the McShakespeare in Post-Millennial Shakespeare Cinema', in M. T. Burnett and R. Wray (eds), *Screening Shakespeare in the Twenty-First Century* (Edinburgh: Edinburgh University Press, 2006), pp. 163–84.

Johnson, M. K. 'Introduction: Television and the Depiction of the American West', *Western American Literature*, 47:2 (2012), 123–31.

Keegan, R. and N. Sperling, '*Shakespeare in Love* and Harvey Weinstein's Dark Oscar Victory', *Vanity Fair* (8 December 2017), www.vanityfair.com/hollywood/2017/12/shakespeare-in-love-and-harvey-weinsteins-dark-oscar-victory (accessed 27 January 2020).

Keller, J. R. *Food, Film and Culture: A Genre Study* (Jefferson, NC: McFarland, 2006).

— and L. Stratyner (eds), *Almost Shakespeare: Reinventing His Works for Cinema and Television* (Jefferson, NC: McFarland & Company, 2004).

Kempley, R. 'In *A Thousand Acres*, A Tired Feminist Plot', *Washington Post* (19 September 1997), www.washingtonpost.com/wp-srv/style/longterm/movies/review97/thousandacreskemp.htm (accessed 26 January 2020).

Keyishian, H. 'Shakespeare and Movie Genre: The Case of *Hamlet*', in Jackson (ed.), *The Cambridge Companion to Shakespeare on Film*, pp. 72–84.

Kingsley-Smith, J. E. 'Shakespearean Authorship in Popular British Cinema', *Literature/Film Quarterly*, 30:3 (2002), 158–65.

Kirkman, R., T. Moore and C. Rathburn, *The Walking Dead*, vol. 1: *Days Gone By* (Berkeley, CA: Image Comics, 2004).

Kirwan, P. '"You Have No Voice!" Constructing Reputation through Contemporaries in the Shakespeare Biopic', *Shakespeare Bulletin*, 32:1 (2014), 11–26.

Klett, E. 'Reviving Viola: Comic and Tragic Teen Film Adaptations of *Twelfth Night*', *Shakespeare Bulletin*, 26:2 (2008), 69–87.

[Kliman, B. W.], '*Broken Lance* is Not *Lear*', *Shakespeare on Film Newsletter*, 2:1 (1977), 3.

Knapp, W. 'The War on Drugs', *Federal Sentencing Reporter*, 5:5 (1993), 294–7.

Kozusko, M. 'Shakesqueer, the Movie: *Were the World Mine* and *A Midsummer Night's Dream*', in P. Holland (ed.), *Shakespeare Survey*, vol. 65: *A Midsummer Night's Dream* (Cambridge: Cambridge University Press, 2012), pp. 168–80.

Lam, A. 'Gangsters and Genre', in *Oxford Research Encyclopedia of Criminology*, 22 November 2016, http://dx.doi.org/10.1093/acrefore/9780190264079.013.149 (accessed 26 January 2020).

Landy, M. *British Genres: Cinema and Society, 1930–1960* (Princeton, NJ: Princeton University Press, 1991).

—. 'Introduction', in M. Landy (ed.), *Imitations of Life: A Reader on Film and Television Melodrama* (Detroit, MI: Wayne State University Press, 1991), pp. 13–30.

Langford, B. 'Revisiting the "Revisionist" Western', *Film & History: An Interdisciplinary Journal of Film and Television Studies*, 33:2 (2003), 26–35.

Lanier, D. M. '"Easy Lear": *Harry and Tonto* and the American Road Movie', in Bladen, Hatchuel and Vienne-Guerrin (eds), *Shakespeare on Screen: King Lear*, pp. 140–54.

—. 'Film Spin-Offs and Citations', in R. Burt (ed.), *Shakespeares after Shakespeare: An Encyclopedia of the Bard in Mass Media and Popular Culture*, vol. 1 (Westport, CT, and London: Greenwood Press, 2007), pp. 132–365.

—. 'Murdering *Othello*', in Cartmell (ed.), *A Companion to Literature, Film, and Adaptation*, pp. 198–215.

—. 'Post-Textual Shakespeare', in P. Holland (ed.), *Shakespeare Survey*, vol. 64: *Shakespeare as Cultural Catalyst* (Cambridge: Cambridge University Press, 2011), pp. 145–62.

—. *Shakespeare and Modern Popular Culture* (Oxford: Oxford University Press, 2002).

—. 'Shakespeare and the Indie Auteur: Michael Almereyda and James Gray', *Shakespeare Bulletin* 34:3 (2016), 451–68.

—. 'Shakespearean Rhizomatics: Adaptation, Ethics, Value', in A. Huang and E. Rivlin (eds), *Shakespeare and the Ethics of Appropriation* (New York: Palgrave Macmillan, 2014), pp. 21–40.

—. '"There Won't Be Puppets, Will There?": "Heroic" Authorship and the Cultural Politics of *Anonymous*', in P. Edmondson and S. Wells (eds), *Shakespeare Beyond Doubt: Evidence, Argument, Controversy* (Cambridge: Cambridge University Press, 2013), pp. 215–24.

—. 'Will of the People: Recent Shakespeare Film Parody and the Politics of Popularization', in D. E. Henderson (ed.), *A Concise Companion to Shakespeare on Screen* (Oxford: Blackwell, 2006), pp. 176–96.

Latham, R. 'The Zombie Zone' (Review), *American Book Review*, 34:2 (2013), 4.

Leach, J. 'A Matter of Life and Art: Artist Biopics in Post-Thatcher Britain', in Pettey and Palmer (eds), *Rule, Britannia!*, pp. 163–82.

Lee, A. R. 'Western Sightings: John G. Cawelti in Conversation with A. Robert Lee', *Weber: The Contemporary West*, 19:1 (2001), http://weberjournal.weber.edu/archive/archive%20C%20Vol.%2016.2-18.1/Vol.%2019.1/Lee.htm (accessed 26 January 2020).

Lehmann, C. 'Film Adaptations', in R. Burt (ed.), *Shakespeares after Shakespeare: An Encyclopedia of the Bard in Mass Media and Popular Culture*, vol. 1 (Westport, CT, and London: Greenwood Press, 2007), pp. 74–131.

— and L. S. Starks (eds), *Spectacular Shakespeare: Critical Theory and Popular Cinema* (Madison and Teaneck, NJ: Fairleigh Dickinson University Press; London: Associated University Presses, 2002).

Leibowitz, F. 'Apt Feelings, or Why "Women's Films" Aren't Trivial', in D. Bordwell and N. Carroll (eds), *Post-Theory: Reconstructing Film Studies* (Madison: University of Wisconsin Press, 1996), pp. 219–29.

Leitch, T. 'Vampire Adaptation', *Journal of Adaptation in Film & Performance*, 4:1 (2011), 5–16.

Lim, D. 'An Auteur for a Neglected New York City', *New York Times* (9 September 2007), www.nytimes.com/2007/09/09/movies/moviesspecial/09lim.html (accessed 30 January 2020).

Loacker, A. and M. Prucha, 'Österreichisch-deutsche Filmbeziehungen und die unabhängige Spielfilmproduktion 1933–1937', *Modern Austrian Literature*, 32:4, Special Issue: *Austria in Film* (1999), 87–117.

Lott, E. 'The Whiteness of Film Noir', *American Literary History*, 9:3 (1997), 542–66.

Loy, R. P. 'The Frontier and the West', in Rollins (ed.), *The Columbia Companion to American History on Film*, pp. 578–82.

Lynch, T. '"We Own the Night": Amadou Diallo's Deadly Encounter with New York City's Street Crime Unit', *Cato Institute Briefing Papers*, 56 (31 March 2000), www.cato.org/sites/cato.org/files/pubs/pdf/bp56.pdf (accessed 30 January 2020).

Macek III, J. C. 'To a Cemetery Go!', *Popmatters* (30 December 2013), www.popmatters.com/177026-zombie-hamlet-2495704599.html (accessed 27 January 2020).

McFarland, J. 'Philosophy of the Living Dead: At the Origin of the Zombie Image', *Cultural Critique*, 90 (2015), 22–63.

McFarlane, B. 'It Wasn't Like That in the Book', in J. M. Welsh and P. Lev (eds), *The Literature/Film Reader: Issues of Adaptation* (Lanham, MD: Scarecrow Press, 2007), pp. 3–14.

McKay, S. 'Horrible Histories', *Telegraph* (1 September 2009), www.telegraph.co.uk/culture/books/6120942/Horrible-Histories.html (accessed 27 January 2020).

Mallin, E. S. *Reading Shakespeare in the Movies: Non-Adaptations and Their Meaning* (Cham: Palgrave Macmillan, 2019).

Manheim, M. 'The English History Play on Screen', in A. Davies and S. Wells (eds), *Shakespeare and the Moving Image* (Cambridge: Cambridge University Press, 1994), pp. 121–45.

Manning, P. 'Zombies, Zomedies, Digital Fan Cultures and the Politics of Taste', in Hubner, Leaning and Manning (eds), *The Zombie Renaissance in Popular Culture*, pp. 160–73.

Marquardt, A.-K. 'Unlearning Tradition: William Shakespeare's *King Lear*, Jane Smiley's and Jocelyn Moorhouse's *A Thousand Acres*', in M. Dobson and E. Rivier-Arnaud (eds), *Rewriting Shakespeare's Plays for and by the Contemporary Stage* (Newcastle-upon-Tyne: Cambridge Scholars Publishing, 2017), pp. 11–30.

Martin, S. 'From Book to Screen: A Story in Three Acts', *Globe and Mail* (7 July 2001), www.theglobeandmail.com/arts/from-book-to-screen-a-story-in-three-acts/article1032156/ (accessed 6 January 2020).

Mason, F. *American Gangster Cinema from Little Caesar to Pulp Fiction* (Basingstoke and New York: Palgrave Macmillan, 2002).

Matheson, S. 'Introduction', in S. Matheson (ed.), *Love in Western Film and Television: Lonely Hearts and Happy Trails* (New York: Palgrave Macmillan, 2013), pp. 1–5.

Melton, J. G. *The Vampire Book: The Encyclopedia of the Undead* (Canton, MI: Visible Ink Press, 2011).

Mintz, S. 'The Family', in Rollins (ed.), *The Columbia Companion to American History on Film*, pp. 352–62.

Mitchell, E. 'Apes and Essences: Some Sources of Significance in the American Gangster Film', in Grant (ed.), *Film Genre Reader IV*, pp. 255–64.

Mizejewski, L. 'Movies and the Off-White Gangster', in C. Holmlund (ed.), *American Cinema of the 1990s: Themes and Variations* (New Brunswick, NJ, and London: Rutgers University Press, 2008), pp. 24–44.

Modenessi, A. M. '(Un)doing the Book "Without Verona Walls": A View from the Receiving End of Baz Luhrmann's *William Shakespeare's Romeo + Juliet*', in Lehmann and Starks (eds), *Spectacular Shakespeare*, pp. 62–85.

Moraru, C. 'Zombie Pedagogy: Rigor Mortis and the U.S. Body Politic', *Studies in Popular Culture*, 34:2 (2012), 105–27.

Murray, R. L. and J. K. Heumann, *Monstrous Nature: Environment and Horror on the Big Screen* (Lincoln and London: University of Nebraska Press, 2016).

Murray-Pepper, M. 'The "Tables of Memory": Shakespeare, Cinema and the Writing Desk', in Buchanan (ed.), *The Writer on Film*, pp. 92–105.

Naremore, J. *More than Night: Film Noir in Its Contexts* (Berkeley, Los Angeles and London: University of California Press, 2008).

Neale, S. *Genre* (London: British Film Institute, 1980).

—. *Genre and Hollywood* (London and New York: Routledge, 2000).

Negra, D. *Off-White Hollywood: American Culture and Ethnic Female Stardom* (London and New York: Routledge, 2001).

Newell, K. *Expanding Adaptation Networks: From Illustration to Novelization* (London: Palgrave Macmillan, 2017).

Nicholls, M. 'From Divestment to Due Resolution: *King Lear* and the New York Fabulists, 1989–92', *Journal of Film and Video*, 65:3 (2013), 3–13.

Norman, M. and T. Stoppard, *Shakespeare in Love: A Screenplay* (New York: Hyperion, 1998).

Nowell-Smith, G. 'Minnelli and Melodrama', *Screen*, 18:2 (1977), 113–18.

Nystrom, D. 'The New Hollywood', in C. Lucia, R. Grundmann and A. Simon (eds), *The Wiley-Blackwell History of American Cinema Vol. III: 1946–1975* (Oxford: Blackwell, 2012), pp. 409–34.

O'Neill, S. *Shakespeare and YouTube: New Media Forms of the Bard* (London and New York: Bloomsbury Publishing, 2014).

— (ed.), *Broadcast Your Shakespeare: Continuity and Change Across Media* (London and New York: The Arden Shakespeare, 2018).

Onishi, B. H. 'Vampires, Technology, and Racism: The Vampiric Image in *Twilight* and *Let Me In*', in M. K. Bloodsworth-Lugo and D. Flory (eds), *Race, Philosophy, and Film* (New York: Routledge, 2013), pp. 197–210.

OpenLearn Team, 'OU on the BBC: Shakespeare Re-Told: A Waste of Shame', *OpenLearn* (27 October 2005), www.open.edu/openlearn/body-mind/ou-on-the-bbc-shakespeare-re-told-waste-shame (accessed 27 January 2020).

Osborne, L. E. '*Twelfth Night*'s Cinematic Adolescents: One Play, One Plot, One Setting, and Three Teen Films', *Shakespeare Bulletin*, 26:2 (2008), 9–36.

Ottoson, R. *A Reference Guide to the American Film Noir: 1940–1958* (Metuchen, NJ, and London: Scarecrow Press, 1981).

Paffenroth, K. 'For Love is Strong as Death', in J. Lowder (ed.), *Triumph of the Walking Dead, Robert Kirkman's Zombie Epic on Page and Screen* (Dallas, TX: BenBella Books, 2011), pp. 217–30.

Papamichael, S. '*Warm Bodies* Review: Nicholas Hoult Stars in Warm-Hearted Zombie Rom-Com', *Digital Spy* (8 February 2013), www.digitalspy.com/movies/review/a456467/warm-bodies-review-nicholas-hoult-stars-in-warm-hearted-zombie-rom-com/ (accessed 27 January 2020).

Paterson, R. 'Box Office Poison?', *Shakespeare in Southern Africa*, 25:1 (2013), 13–29.

Patricia, A. G. *Queering the Shakespeare Film: Gender Trouble, Gay Spectatorship and Male Homoeroticism* (London and New York: Bloomsbury Arden Shakespeare, 2017).

Pettey, H. B. 'Elizabeth I and the Life of Visual Culture', in Pettey and Palmer (eds), *Rule, Britannia!*, pp. 41–66.

— and R. B. Palmer (eds), *Rule, Britannia! The Biopic and British National Identity* (Albany: State University of New York Press, 2018).

Pittman, L. M. *Authorizing Shakespeare on Film and Television* (New York: Peter Lang Publishing, 2011).

—. 'Dressing the Girl/Playing the Boy: *Twelfth Night* Learns Soccer on the Set of *She's the Man*', *Literature/Film Quarterly*, 36:1 (2008), 122–36.

—. 'Taming *10 Things I Hate About You*: Shakespeare and the Teenage Film Audience', *Literature/Film Quarterly*, 32:2 (2004), 144–52.

Power, T. *Shakespeare and Gender in Practice* (London: Palgrave, 2016).

Quinsland, K. 'The Sport of Asses: *A Midsummer Night's Dream*', in G. Stanivukovic (ed.), *Queer Shakespeare: Desire and Sexuality* (London and New York: Bloomsbury Arden Shakespeare, 2017), pp. 69–85.

Rambuss, R. '*A Midsummer Night's Dream*: Shakespeare's Ass Play', in M. Menon (ed.), *ShakesQueer: A Queer Companion to the Complete Works of Shakespeare* (Durham, NC, and London: Duke University Press, 2011), pp. 234–44.

Reagan, R. 'Address to the National Association of Evangelicals ("Evil Empire Speech"), 3 March 1983', *Voices of Democracy*, https://voicesofdemocracy.umd.edu/reagan-evil-empire-speech-text/ (accessed 27 January 2020).

Reduced Shakespeare Company, http://reducedshakespeare.com/ (accessed 27 January 2020).

Richards, J. 'Gender and Authority in the Queen Victoria Films', in Pettey and Palmer (eds), *Rule, Britannia!*, pp. 67–84.

Richter, S. '*A Thousand Acres*', *Tucson Weekly* (29 September, 1997), www.filmvault.com/filmvault/tw/t/thousandacresa1.html (accessed 26 January 2020).

Rieupeyrout, J.-L. 'The Western: A Historical Genre', *Quarterly of Film Radio and Television*, 7:2 (1952), 116–28.

Rippy, M. H. 'All Our *Othellos*: Black Monsters and White Masks on the American Screen', in Lehmann and Starks (eds), *Spectacular Shakespeare*, pp. 25–46.

Roan Group, Edgar Ulmar's *Strange Illusion* [DVD cover], 2000.

Rollins, P. C. (ed.), *The Columbia Companion to American History on Film: How the Movies Have Portrayed the American Past* (New York: Columbia University Press, 2003).

Rosenstone, R. A. and C. Parvulescu (eds), *A Companion to the Historical Film* (Chichester: John Wiley & Sons, 2003).

Rosenthal, D. 'The Bard on Screen', *Guardian* (7 April 2007), www.theguardian.com/film/2007/apr/07/stage.shakespeare (accessed 26 January 2020).

—. *Shakespeare on Screen* (London: Hamlyn, 2000).

Rothwell, K. *A History of Shakespeare on Screen: A Century of Film and Television* (Cambridge: Cambridge University Press, 2004).

Ruberto, L. E. 'Where Did the Goodfellas Learn How to Cook? Gender, Labor, and the Italian American Experience', *Italian Americana*, 21:2 (2003), 164–76.

San Filippo, M. *The B Word: Bisexuality in Contemporary Film and Television* (Bloomington and Indianapolis: Indiana University Press, 2013).

Sanders, J. *Adaptation and Appropriation* (Abingdon and New York: Routledge, 2006).

Santoro, G. *Myself When I Am Real: The Life and Music of Charles Mingus* (New York: Oxford University Press, 2000).

Schatz, T. *Hollywood Genres: Formulas, Filmmaking, and the Studio System* (New York: Random House, 1981).

Scheil, K. and G. Holderness, 'Introduction: Shakespeare and "the Personal Story"', *Critical Survey*, 21:3 (2009), 1–5.

Selby, S. *Dark City: The Film Noir* (Jefferson, NC, and London: McFarland Publishing, 1984).

'Selene/Trivia', *Fandom*, http://underworld.wikia.com/wiki/Selene/Trivia (accessed 27 January 2020).

Semenza, G. M. C. 'Echoes of *Romeo and Juliet* in *Let the Right One In* and *Let Me In*', in Hansen and Wetmore (eds), *Shakespearean Echoes*, pp. 56–67.

—. 'Teens, Shakespeare, and the Dumbing Down Cliché: The Case of the Animated Tales', *Shakespeare Bulletin*, 26:2 (2008), 37–68.

Serra, I. 'Italian American Cinema: Between Blood Family and Bloody Family', in G. Muscio, J. Sciorra, G. Spagnoletti and A. J. Tamburri (eds), *Mediated Ethnicity: New Italian-American Cinema* (New York: John D. Calandra Italian American Institute, 2010), pp. 189–99.

Shachar, H. 'Authorial Histories: The Historical Film and the Literary Biopic', in Rosenstone and Parvulescu (eds), *A Companion to the Historical Film*, pp. 199–218.

—. 'The Muse's Tale: Rewriting the English Author in *The Invisible Woman*', in Pettey and Palmer (eds), *Rule, Britannia!*, pp. 145–62.

Shadoian, J. *Dreams and Dead Ends: The American Gangster Film* (Oxford and New York: Oxford University Press, 2003).

'*Shakespeare in Love*', Concord Theatricals, www.concordtheatricals.com/p/56914/shakespeare-in-love (accessed 27 January 2020).

Shakespeare, W. *Cymbeline*, The Arden Shakespeare, Second Series, ed. J. M. Nosworthy (London and New York: Routledge, 1994).

—. *Hamlet*, The Arden Shakespeare, Second Series, ed. H. Jenkins (London and New York: Methuen, 1982).

—. *King Lear*, The Arden Shakespeare, Third Series, ed. R. A. Foakes (Walton-on-Thames: Thomas Nelson & Sons, 1997).

—. *Macbeth*, The Arden Shakespeare, Second Series, ed. K. Muir (Walton-on-Thames: Thomas Nelson & Sons, 1999).

—. *The Merchant of Venice*, The Arden Shakespeare, Second Series, ed. J. R. Brown (London and New York: Routledge, 1993).

—. *Othello*, The Arden Shakespeare, Third Series, ed. E. A. J. Honigmann (Walton-on-Thames: Thomas Nelson & Sons, 1997).

—. *Romeo and Juliet*, The Arden Shakespeare, Second Series, ed. B. Gibbons (Walton-on-Thames: Thomas Nelson & Sons, 1997).

—. *Shakespeare's Sonnets*, ed. K. Duncan-Jones, The Arden Shakespeare, Third Series (London: Thomas Nelson & Sons, 1997).

—. *The Taming of the Shrew*, The Arden Shakespeare, Second Series, ed. B. Morris (London and New York: Routledge, 1994).

—. *The Tempest*, The Arden Shakespeare, Third Series, ed. V. M. Vaughan and A. T. Vaughan (London: The Arden Shakespeare, 1999).

—. *Twelfth Night*, The Arden Shakespeare, Second Series, ed. J. M. Lothian and T. W. Craik (London and New York: Routledge, 1975).

The Shakespeare Authorship Coalition, 'Declaration of Reasonable Doubt about the Identity of William Shakespeare', https://doubtaboutwill.org/declaration (accessed 27 January 2020).

Sharma, S. 'Teaching British South Asian Cinema: Towards a "Materialist" Reading Practice', *South Asian Popular Culture*, 7:1 (2009), 21–35.

Sharrett, C. 'The Horror Film as Social Allegory (And How it Comes Undone)', in H. M. Benshoff (ed.), *A Companion to the Horror Film* (Chichester: Wiley-Blackwell, 2014), pp. 56–72.

Shary, T. *Generation Multiplex: The Image of Youth in Contemporary American Cinema* (Austin: University of Texas Press, 2002).

—. 'Teen Films: The Cinematic Image of Youth', in Grant (ed.), *Film Genre Reader IV*, pp. 576–601.

Sherman, D. 'Stages of Revision: Textuality, Performance, and History in *Anonymous*', *Literature/Film Quarterly*, 41:2 (2013), 129–42.

Shults, S. *The Taming of the Werewolf* (Hertford, NC: Crossroad Press, 2011).

Sidney, P. 'Astrophil and Stella 1', in G. Braden (ed.), *Sixteenth-Century Poetry: An Annotated Anthology* (Oxford and Malden, MA: Blackwell Publishing, 2005), p. 348.

Siegel, R. 'The Lone Ranger: Justice from Outside the Law', *NPR* (14 January 2008), www.npr.org/templates/story/story.php?storyId=18073741 (accessed 26 January 2020).

Silver, A. 'The Gangster and Film Noir: Themes and Style', in Silver and Ursini (eds), *Gangster Film Reader*, pp. 290–322.

— and J. Ursini (eds), *Gangster Film Reader* (Pompton Plains, NJ: Limelight, 2007).

Silverstone, C. 'Shakespeare, Cinema and Queer Adolescents: Unhappy Endings and Heartfelt Conclusions', *Shakespeare*, 10:3 (2014), 309–27.

Simmon, S. 'Concerning the Weary Legs of Wyatt Earp: The Classic Western According to Shakespeare', *Literature/Film Quarterly*, 24:2 (1996), 114–27.

Skrebels, P. '*All Night Long*: Jazzing Around with *Othello*', *Literature/Film Quarterly*, 36:2 (2008), 147–56.

Slotkin, R. *Regeneration Through Violence: The Mythology of the American Frontier, 1600–1860* (Norman: University of Oklahoma Press, 2000).

Smiley, J. 'Shakespeare in Iceland', in J. Bate, J. L. Levenson and D. Mehl (eds), *Shakespeare and the Twentieth Century: The Selected Proceedings of the International Shakespeare Association World Congress Los Angeles, 1996* (Newark: University of Delaware Press, London: Associated University Presses, 1998), pp. 41–59.

—. *A Thousand Acres* (New York: Alfred A. Knopf, 1992).

Smith, F. *Rethinking the Hollywood Teen Movie: Gender, Genre and Identity* (Edinburgh: Edinburgh University Press, 2017).

Smith, H. N. *Virgin Land: The American West as Symbol and Myth* (Cambridge, MA: Harvard University Press, 1950).

Smith, J. L. *Melodrama*, The Critical Idiom 28 (London: Methuen, 1973).

Smith, R. 'A Thousand Acres', *Austin Chronicle* (19 September 1997), www.austinchronicle.com/calendar/film/1997-09-19/a-thousand-acres/ (accessed 26 January 2020).

Speed, L. 'Tuesday's Gone: The Nostalgic Teen Film', *Journal of Popular Film and Television*, 26:1 (1998), 24–32.
Staples, L. 'Are R and Julie based off *Romeo and Juliet*. Will you be bringing any other Shakespearean themes/motifs to your next book(s)?', *Goodreads*, www.goodreads.com/questions/575495-are-r-and-julie-based-off-romeo-and (accessed 27 January 2020).
'Stars of BBC's *Horrible Histories* to Make Shakespeare Comedy Film', *BBC Media Centre* (13 May 2013), www.bbc.co.uk/mediacentre/latestnews/2013/bbc-films-bill-press-release.html (accessed 27 January 2020).
Steiger, J. 'Hybrid or Inbred: The Purity Hypothesis and Hollywood Genre History', in Grant (ed.), *Film Genre Reader IV*, pp. 203–17.
Stephen, '*Men Are Not Gods* Review', *Letterboxd* (8 October 2016), https://letterboxd.com/film/men-are-not-gods/ (accessed 26 January 2020).
'Stormglass Productions', *Mandy.com*, https://crew.mandy.com/uk/company/3975/stormglass-productions (accessed 26 January 2020).
Stróbl, E. 'The Tilbury Speech and Queen Elizabeth: Iconic Moments of English History on Film', in É. Antal, Cs. Czeglédi and E. Krakkó (eds), *Contemporary Perspectives on Language, Culture and Identity in Anglo-American Contexts* (Newcastle upon Tyne: Cambridge Scholars Publishing, 2019), pp. 251–67.
Subers, R. 'October Preview', *Box Office Mojo* (28 October 2011), www.boxofficemojo.com/news/?id=3284&p=.htm (accessed 27 January 2020).
Sutherland, M. 'Rigor/Mortis: The Industrial Life of Style in American Zombie Cinema', *Framework: The Journal of Cinema and Media*, 48:1 (2007), 64–78.
Swan, S. *The Wives of Bath* (New York: Knopf, 1993).
Taylor, Q. *In Search of the Racial Frontier* (New York and London: W.W. Norton, 1999).
Teague, F. *Shakespeare and the American Popular Stage* (Cambridge: Cambridge University Press, 2006).
Tempera, M. '"Whose Grave's This?": References to *Hamlet* V.1 in Italian Cinema', in C. Dente and S. Soncini (eds), *Crossing Time and Space: Shakespeare Translations in Present-Day Europe* (Pisa: PLUS – Pisa University Press, 2008), pp. 79–87.
Tibbets, J. C. 'The Machine in the Garden', in Rollins (ed.), *The Columbia Companion to American History on Film*, pp. 590–5.
'Treehouse of Horror III', *The Simpsons*, season 4, episode 5, https://simpsonswiki.com/wiki/Treehouse_of_Horror_III (accessed 15 January 2018).
Turner, F. J. *The Frontier in American History* (New York: Henry Holt & Company, 1920).
Turner, M. R. 'Cowboys and Comedy: The Simultaneous Deconstruction and Reinforcement of Generic Conventions in the Western Parody', in P. C. Rollins and J. E. O'Connor (eds), *Hollywood's West: The American Frontier in Film, Television, and History* (Lexington: University of Kentucky Press, 2005), pp. 218–35.

Uricchio, W. 'The Algorithmic Turn: Photosynth, Augmented Reality and the Changing Implications of the Image', *Visual Studies*, 26:1 (2011), 25–35.

Vaughan, V. M. and A. T. Vaughan, 'Introduction', in Shakespeare, *The Tempest*, pp. 1–138.

Wainwright, M. *The Rational Shakespeare: Peter Ramus, Edward de Vere, and the Question of Authorship* (Cham: Palgrave Macmillan, 2018).

Walker, E. 'Getting Back to Shakespeare: Whose Film is it Anyway?', in D. E. Henderson (ed.), *A Concise Companion to Shakespeare on Screen* (Oxford: Blackwell, 2006), pp. 8–30.

Walker, I. 'Family Values and Feudal Codes: The Social Politics of America's Fin-de-Siècle Gangster', in Silver and Ursini (eds), *Gangster Film Reader*, pp. 381–405.

Warren, K. J. 'Taking Empirical Data Seriously: An Ecofeminist Philosophical Perspective', in K. J. Warren (ed.), *Ecofeminism: Women, Culture, Nature* (Bloomington and Indianapolis: Indiana University Press, 1997), pp. 3–20.

Warshow, R. 'The Gangster as Tragic Hero', in J. Gross (ed.), *The Oxford Book of Essays* (Oxford: Oxford University Press, 2008), pp. 581–6.

Weierman, K. W. *One Nation, One Blood: Interracial Marriage in American Fiction, Scandal, and Law, 1820–1870* (Amherst and Boston: University of Massachusetts Press, 2005).

Welsch, T. 'Yoked Together by Violence: *Prizzi's Honor* as a Generic Hybrid', *Film Criticism*, 22:1, Special Issue: Genre (1997), 62–73.

Westrup, L. 'Merchandising Gen X: The *Singles* Soundtrack Album (1992/2017)', *Film Criticism*, 42:2, Special issue: Film and Merchandise (2018), https://doi.org/10.3998/fc.13761232.0042.204 (accessed 21 July 2020).

Wetmore, K. J., Jr. 'The Immortal Vampire of Stratford-upon-Avon', in Hansen and Wetmore (eds), *Shakespearean Echoes*, pp. 68–79.

—. 'Shakespeare and Teenagers', in M. T. Burnett, A. Streete and R. Wray (eds), *The Edinburgh Companion to Shakespeare and the Arts* (Edinburgh: Edinburgh University Press, 2011), pp. 377–87.

—. '*Titus Redux*, and: *Hamlet, Prince of Darkness*, and: *Pulp Shakespeare* (Review)', *Shakespeare Bulletin*, 30:2 (2012), 207–12.

White, R. S. 'Sex, Lies, Videotape – and Othello', in Keller and Stratyner (eds), *Almost Shakespeare*, pp. 86–98.

Whitney, J. S. 'A Filmography of Film Noir', *Journal of Popular Film*, 5:3–4 (1976), 321–71.

Wildermuth, M. E. *Feminism and the Western in Film and Television* (Cham: Palgrave Macmillan, 2018).

Williams, L. 'Film Bodies: Gender, Genre, and Excess', in Grant (ed.), *Film Genre Reader IV*, pp. 159–77.

—. 'Melodrama Revised', in N. Browne (ed.), *Refiguring American Film Genres: History and Theory* (Berkeley, Los Angeles and London: University of California Press, 1998), pp. 42–88.

Willson, R. F. Jr. 'The Selling of *Joe Macbeth*', *Shakespeare on Film Newsletter*, 7:1 (1982), 1, 4.
—. *Shakespeare in Hollywood, 1929–1956* (Cranbury, NJ, and London: Associated University Presses, 2002).
Winters, B. H. *Android Karenina* (Philadelphia, PA: Quirk Classics, 2010).
Wood, R. 'The American Nightmare: Horror in the 70s', in M. Jancovich (ed.), *Horror, The Film Reader* (London and New York: Routledge, 2002), pp. 25–32.
—. 'Ideology, Genre, Auteur', in Grant (ed.), *Film Genre Reader IV*, pp. 78–92.
Wray, R. '*King Lear*: Performative Traditions/Interpretative Positions', in A. Hiscock and L. Hopkins (eds), *King Lear: A Critical Guide* (London and New York: Continuum, 2011), pp. 56–77.
Young, P. 'Film Genre Theory and Contemporary Media: Description, Interpretation, Intermediality', in R. Kolker (ed.), *The Oxford Handbook of Film and Media Studies* (New York: Oxford University Press, 2008), pp. 224–59.

Filmography

10 Things I Hate About You (1999, dir. Gil Junger. Touchstone Pictures/Mad Chance/Jaret Entertainment)
28 Days Later (2002, dir. Danny Boyle. DNA Films/British Film Council)
30 Days of Night (2007, dir. David Slade. Columbia Pictures/Ghost House Pictures/Dark Horse Entertainment)
All Is True (2018, dir. Kenneth Branagh. TKBC)
All Night Long (1962, dir. Basil Dearden. The Rank Organisation)
Anonymous (2011, dir. Roland Emmerich. Columbia Pictures/Relativity Media/Centropolis Entertainment/Studio Babelsberg)
As You Like It (1992, dir. Christine Edzard. Sands Films)
Behind Locked Doors (1948, dir. Budd Boetticher. Aro Productions Inc.)
Bend It Like Beckham (2002, dir. Gurinder Chadha. Kintop Productions/Film Council/Filmförderung Hamburg/British Sky Association/British Screen Productions/Helkon Media/The Works/Scion Films/Bend It Films/Roc Media/Road Movies Filmproduktion/Future Films/Redbus Pictures)
Bill (2015, dir. Richard Bracewell. BBC Films/Cowboy Films/Punk Cinema)
Blade (1998, dir. Stephen Norrington. Amen Ra Films/Imaginary Forces/Marvel Enterprises/New Line Cinema)
Bollywood Queen (2002, dir. Jeremy Wooding. Dream Fish Productions/Enterprise Films/Great British Films/Spice Factory/Stretch Limo Productions)
Bram Stoker's Dracula (1992, dir. Francis Ford Coppola. American Zoetrope/Columbia Pictures/Osiris Films)
Broken Arrow (1950, dir. Delmer Daves. Twentieth Century Fox)
Broken Lance (1954, dir. Edward Dmytryk. Twentieth Century Fox)
A Bunch of Amateurs (2008, dir. Andy Cadiff. Isle of Man Film/CinemaNX/Limelight/Lipsync Productions/Trademark Films)
Caligari, original title: *Das Cabinet des Dr. Caligari* (1920, dir. Robert Wiene. Decla-Bioscop AG)

A Clockwork Orange (1971, dir. Stanley Kubrick. Warner Bros/Polaris Productions/ Hawk Films/Max L. Raab Productions/Si Litvinoff Film Production)
Clueless (1995, dir. Amy Heckerling. Paramount Pictures)
The Da Vinci Code (2006, dir. Ron Howard. Columbia Pictures/Imagine Entertainment/Skylark Productions/Government of Malta)
Dawn of the Dead (1978, dir. George A. Romero. Dawn Associates/Laurel Groups)
Daybreakers (2009, dir. Michael and Peter Spierig. Lionsgate/Australian Film Finance Corporation/Pictures in Paradise/Pacific Film and Television Commission/ Furst Films/Mandate Pictures International)
Dazed and Confused (1993, dir. Richard Linklater. Gramercy Pictures/Alphaville Films/Detour Filmproduction)
A Double Life (1947, dir. George Cukor. Kanin Productions/Universal)
Dracula (1931, dir. Tod Browning. Universal Pictures)
East is East (1999, dir. Damien O'Donnell. Film4/British Broadcasting Corporation/ Assassin Films)
Eastern Promises (2007, dir. David Cronenberg. Kudos Film and Television/BBC Films/Serendipity Point Films/Corus Entertainment/Scion Films/Shine Pictures/ Astral Media/Téléfilm Canada/Focus Features)
A Fistful of Dollars (1964, dir. Sergio Leone. Jolly Film/Constantin Film/Ocean Films)
The Flesh and Blood Show (1972, dir. Pete Walker. Peter Walker (Heritage) Ltd.)
For a Few Dollars More (1965, dir. Sergio Leone. Produzioni Europee Associate/ Arturo González Producciones Cinematográficas/Constantin Film)
Gaslight (1944, dir. George Cukor. Metro-Goldwyn-Mayer)
Get Over It (2001, dir. Tommy O'Haver. Miramax/Ignite Entertainment/Keshan/ Morpheus)
Gnomeo & Juliet (2011, dir. Kelly Asbury. Touchstone Pictures/Rocket Pictures/ Arc Productions/Miramax/Starz Animation)
The Godfather (1972, dir. Francis Ford Coppola. Paramount Pictures/Alfran Productions)
The Godfather: Part II (1974, dir. Francis Ford Coppola. Paramount Pictures/The Coppola Company/American Zoetrope)
The Godfather: Part III (1990, dir. Francis Ford Coppola. Paramount Pictures/ Zoetrope Studios)
Gone with the Wind (1939, dir. Victor Fleming. Selznick International Pictures/ Metro-Goldwyn-Mayer)
The Good, the Bad and the Ugly (1966, dir. Sergio Leone. Produzioni Europee Associate/Arturo González Producciones Cinematográficas/Constantin Film)
GoodFellas (1990, dir. Martin Scorsese. Warner Bros.)
Hamlet (1948, dir. Laurence Olivier. Two Cities Films)
Hamlet (1990, dir. Franco Zeffirelli. Icon Productions/Carolco Pictures/Canal+/ Nelson Entertainment/Sovereign Pictures)

Hamlet (1996, dir. Kenneth Branagh. Castle Rock Entertainment/Turner Pictures/ Fishmonger Films)
Hamlet 2 (2008, dir. Andrew Fleming. Bona Fide Productions/ContentFilm International/L+E Pictures)
Harry and Tonto (1974, dir. Paul Mazursky. Twentieth Century Fox)
Henry V (1944, dir. Laurence Olivier. Two Cities Films)
High Noon (1952, dir. Fred Zinnemann. Stanley Kramer Productions)
House of Strangers (1949, dir. Joseph L. Mankiewicz. Twentieth Century Fox)
The Immortal Gentleman (1935, dir. Widgey R. Newman. Bernard Smith Productions)
Innocent Blood (1992, dir. John Landis. Warner Bros.)
Interview with the Vampire (1994, dir. Neil Jordan. Geffen Pictures)
Iris (2001, dir. Richard Eyre. British Broadcasting Corporation/Fox Iris Productions/ Intermedia Films/Mirage Enterprises/Miramax)
The Iron Lady (2011, dir. Phyllida Lloyd. DJ Films/Pathé/Film4/Canal+/Goldcrest Pictures/UK Film Council/CinéCinéma)
Joe Macbeth (1955, dir. Ken Hughes. Columbia Pictures/Film Locations)
Johnny Hamlet, original title: *Quella sporca storia nel West*, US title: *The Wild and the Dirty* (1968, dir. Enzo G. Castellari. Daiano Film/Leone Film)
Jubal (1956, dir. Delmer Daves. Columbia Pictures)
Julius Caesar (1953, dir. Joseph L. Mankiewicz. Metro-Goldwyn-Mayer)
Just One of the Guys (1985, dir. Lisa Gottlieb. Columbia Pictures/Summa Entertainment Group/Triton)
Killer's Kiss (1955, dir. Stanley Kubrick. Minotaur Productions)
The Killers (1946, dir. Robert Siodmak. Mark Hellinger Productions)
King of New York (1990, dir. Abel Ferrara. Reteitalia/Scena International/Augusto Caminito)
Kiss Me Deadly (1955, dir. Robert Aldrich. Parklane Pictures Inc.)
Kiss Me Kate (1953, dir. George Sidney. Metro-Goldwyn-Mayer)
Kiss of Death (1947, dir. Henry Hathaway. Twentieth Century Fox)
A Knight's Tale (2001, dir. Brian Helgeland. Columbia Pictures/Escape Artists/ Finestkind/Black and Blu Entertainment)
Land of the Dead (2005, dir. George A. Romero. Universal Pictures/Atmosphere Entertainment MM/Romero-Grunwald Productions/Wild Bunch/Rangerkim/ Ontario Media Development Corporation/Exception Wild Bunch)
The Last Movie (1971, dir. Dennis Hopper. Alta-Light)
The Last Patriarch (1956, dir. Lewis Allen. 20th Century Fox Television)
Let Me In (2010, dir. Matt Reeves. Overture Films/Exclusive Media Group/ Hammer Films/EFTI)
Let the Right One In, original title: *Låt den Rätte Komma In* (2008, dir. Tomas Alfredson. EFTI/Sandrew Metronome Distribution Sverige AB/Filmpool Nord/ Sveriges Television/WAG/Canal+/Fido Film AB/Ljudligan/The Chimney Pot)
Life Goes On (2009, dir. Sangeeta Datta. SD Films/Stormglass Productions)

Little Caesar (1931, dir. Mervyn LeRoy. First National Pictures)
The Lone Ranger (1938, dir. John English, William Witney. Republic Pictures)
Lost and Delirious (2001, dir. Léa Pool. Cité-Amérique/Dummett Films)
The Lost Boys (1987, dir. Joel Schumacher. Warner Bros.)
The Magnificent Seven (1960, dir. John Sturges. The Mirisch Company/Alpha Productions/Alpha)
The Man Who Shot Liberty Valance (1962, dir. John Ford. John Ford Productions)
McLintock! (1963, dir. Andrew V. McLaglen. Batjac Productions)
Mean Girls (2004, dir. Mark Waters. Paramount Pictures/M. G. Films/Broadway Video)
Men Are Not Gods (1936, dir. Walter Reisch. London Film Productions)
Men of Respect (1990, dir. William Reilly. Arthur Goldblatt Productions/Central City Films/Grandview Avenue Pictures)
The Merchant of Venice (2004, dir. Michael Radford. Movision/Avenue Pictures/UK Film Council/Film Fund Luxembourg/Delux Productions/Immagine e Cinema/Dania Film/Istituto Luce/Navidi-Wilde Productions Ltd./39 McLaren St. Sydney/LSG Productions/Rough Diamond Productions/Spice Factory)
A Midsummer Night's Dream (1999, dir. Michael Hoffman. Fox Searchlight Pictures/Regency Enterprises/Taurus Film/Panoramica)
Miller's Crossing (1990, dir. Joel and Ethan Coen. Circle Films/Twentieth Century Fox)
Motocrossed (2001, dir. Steve Boyum. Film Roman Productions/Stu Segall Productions)
Much Ado About Nothing (1993, dir. Kenneth Branagh. Renaissance Films/American Playhouse Theatrical Films/BBC Films)
My Kingdom (2001, dir. Don Boyd. Close Grip Films Ltd./Primary Pictures/Sky Pictures)
Never Been Kissed (1999, dir. Raja Gosnell. Fox 2000 Pictures/Bushwood Pictures/Flower Films/Never Been Kissed Productions)
Night of the Living Dead (1968, dir. George A. Romero. Image Ten)
Ninotchka (1939, dir. Ernst Lubitsch. Metro-Goldwyn-Mayer)
Nosferatu (1922, dir. Friedrich Wilhelm Murnau. Jofa-Atelier Berlin-Johannisthal/Prana-Film GmbH)
Not Another Teen Movie (2001, dir. Joel Gallen. Columbia Pictures/Original Film/Neal H. Moritz Productions)
O (2001, dir. Tim Blake Nelson. Chickie the Cop/Daniel Fried Productions/Dimension Films/FilmEngine/Rhulen Entertainment)
Old Bill Through the Ages (1924, dir. Thomas Bentley. Ideal)
Omkara (2006, dir. Vishal Bhardwaj. Shemaroo Video Pvt. Ltd./Big Screen Entertainment/Panorama Studios)
Once Upon a Time in the West (1968, dir. Sergio Leone. Rafran Cinematografica/San Marco/Paramount Pictures/Euro International Film)
Pretty in Pink (1986, dir. Howard Deutch. Paramount Pictures)

Pride and Prejudice and Zombies (2016, dir. Burr Steers. Cross Creek Pictures/MadRiver Pictures/QC Entertainment/Allison Shearmur Productions/Handsomecharlie Films/Head Gear Films/PPZ Holdings/Screen Gems/Sierra/Affinity/Stage 6 Films)
Private Romeo (2011, dir. Alan Brown. Wolfe Video)
Prizzi's Honor (1985, dir. John Houston. ABC Motion Pictures)
Prospero's Books (1991, dir. Peter Greenaway. Allarts/Cinéa/Caméra One/Penta Film/Elsevier-Vendex Film Beheer/Channel 4 International/Vrijzinnig Protestantse Radio Omroep/Canal+/NHK/Pierson, Heldring & Pierson N.V./Palace Pictures)
Public Enemy (1931, dir. William A. Wellman. Warner Bros.)
The Quiet Man (1952, dir. John Ford. Republic Pictures/Argosy Pictures)
Rio Grande (1950, dir. John Ford. Republic Pictures/Argosy Pictures)
Risky Business (1983, dir. Paul Brickman. The Geffen Company)
Romeo and Juliet (1936, dir. George Cukor. Metro-Goldwyn-Mayer)
Romeo and Juliet (1968, dir. Franco Zeffirelli. BHE Films/Verona Produzione/Dino de Laurentiis Cinematografica)
Rosencrantz and Guildenstern are Undead (2009, dir. Jordan Galland. C Plus Pictures/Off Hollywood Pictures/Offhollywood Digital)
Scarface (1932, dir. Howard Hawks. The Caddo Company)
Scotland, PA (1994, dir. Billy Morrissette. Abandon Pictures/Veto Chip Productions/Paddy Wagon Productions/Nova Scotia Film Development Corporation/Canadian Film or Video Production Tax Credit)
Shadows (1959, dir. John Cassavetes. Lion International)
Shakespeare in Love (1998, dir. John Madden. Universal Pictures/Miramax/The Bedford Falls Company)
Shakespeare Wallah (1965, dir. James Ivory. Merchant Ivory Productions)
Shakespeare Writing Julius Caesar, original title *La Rêve de Shakespeare* or *La mort de Jules César* (1907, dir. Georges Méliès. Star-Film)
Shane (1953, dir. George Stevens. Paramount Pictures)
Shaun of the Dead (2004, dir. Edgar Wright. Rogue Pictures/StudioCanal/Working Title Films/WT2 Productions/Big Talk Productions/Inside Track 2/Film4)
She's All That (1999, dir. Robert Iscove. Miramax/Tapestry Films/FilmColony/All That Productions)
She's the Man (2006, dir. Andy Fickman. DreamWorks/Lakeshore Entertainment/Donners' Company)
Show Me Love, original title *Fucking Åmål* (1998, dir. Lukas Moodysson. Memfis Film/Det Danske Filminstitut/Film i Väst/SVT Drama, Göteborg/Svenska Filminstitutet/Sveriges Television/Trollywood AB/Zentropa Entertainments)
Stage Beauty (2004, dir. Richard Eyre. Lions Gate Films/Qwerty Films/Tribeca Productions/N1 European Film Produktions GmbH & Co. KG)
Stagecoach (1939, dir. John Ford. Walter Wanger Productions)

State of Grace (1990, dir. Phil Joanou. Cinehaus/Orion Pictures/The Rank Organisation)
Strange Illusion (1945, dir. Edgar G. Ulmer. Producers Releasing Corporation)
Street King, original title *King Rikki* (2002, dir. James Gavin Bedford. Mistral Pictures LLC)
A Thousand Acres (1997, dir. Jocelyn Moorhouse. Touchstone Pictures/Propaganda Films/Prairie Films/Beacon Pictures/Via Rosa Productions)
The Three Musketeers (2011, dir. Paul W. S. Anderson. Summit Entertainment/Constantin Film/Impact Pictures/Nouvelles Éditions de Films/New Legacy/Studio Babelsberg)
Time Flies (1944, dir. Walter Forde. Gainsborough Pictures)
Underworld (2003, dir. Len Wiseman. Lakeshore Entertainment/Subterranean Productions/Underworld Produktions GmbH/Laurinfilm)
Upside Down (2012, dir. Juan Diego Solanas. Upside Down Films/Les Films Upside Down/Onyx Films/Transfilm/Studio 37/Kinologic Films/Jouror Productions/France 2 Cinéma/MELS)
Upstart Crow (2016, creator Ben Elton. BBC Comedy)
Van Helsing (2004, dir. Stephen Sommers. Universal Pictures/The Sommers Company/Stillking Films/Carpathian Pictures)
The Vanishing American (1925, dir. George B. Seitz. Paramount Pictures)
Wagon Master (1950, dir. John Ford. Argosy Pictures)
Warm Bodies (2013, dir. Jonathan Levine. Summit Entertainment/Make Movies/Mandeville Pictures/Quebec Film and Television Tax Credit)
A Waste of Shame (2005, dir. John McKay. British Broadcasting Corporation)
We Own the Night (2007, dir. James Gray. Columbia Pictures/2929 Productions/Industry Entertainment)
Were the World Mine (2008, dir. Tom Gustafson. SPEAKproductions/The Group Entertainment)
West Side Story (1961, dir. Jerome Robbins and Robert Wise. The Mirisch Corporation/Seven Arts Productions)
Whirlpool (1949, dir. Otto Preminger. Twentieth Century Fox)
The Wild Bunch (1969, dir. Sam Peckinpah. Warner Bros./Seven Arts)
Will (2017, creator Craig Pearce. TNT)
William Shakespeare's Romeo + Juliet (1996, dir. Baz Luhrmann. Bazmark Films/Estudios Churubusco Azteca S.A./Twentieth Century Fox)
Yellow Sky (1948, dir. William A. Wellman. Twentieth Century Fox)
Zombie Hamlet (2012, dir. John Murlowski. Three Girls Running/Maple Island Films/Zombie Hamlet)
Zombieland (2009, dir. Ruben Fleischer. Columbia Pictures/Relativity Media/Pariah)

Index

References to Shakespeare's plays are listed under the author's name; film adaptations with identical titles are listed alphabetically, followed by the director's name in parentheses.

Titles in bold are the films discussed extensively in the volume.

10 Things I Hate About You 7, 170–8, 182, 183, 187, 188, 192, 195
28 Days Later 239
30 Days of Night 214

algorithms 11, 286
All Is True 164, 165, 248, 250, 254, 258, 260, 273, 276–80, 285
All Night Long 24, 72, 80–6
American Graffiti 182
Anonymous 161, 166, 248, 250–1, 254, 261, 263–71, 272, 275, 277
As You Like It (Edzard) 3
auteur theory 4
authorship 249–51, 257, 259, 262–6, 268, 271, 274–5, 288
  controversy 269
  Oxfordian theory of 250–1, 263, 268

Behind Locked Doors 107
Bend It Like Beckham 94, 184
Bill 166, 248, 250, 263, 268, 271–6, 277
biopic 8, 13, 147–9, 161–6, 247–80, 287
Blade 214, 216
Bollywood 26–7, 32n.28, 93–6, 99
  see also British-Asian films

Bollywood Queen 93, 98–9
Bram Stoker's Dracula 159
Broken Arrow 46
Broken Lance 21, 35, 42–8, 64, 119, 141n.14, 286
British-Asian films 26, 72, 93–100
Buffy the Vampire Slayer 158, 212
Bunch of Amateurs, A 3
Burbage, Richard 268

Cabinet of Dr. Caligari, The 107
Cecil, Robert 267
Clockwork Orange, A 229
Clueless 149, 172, 178

Dark Lady 250, 259–61
Da Vinci Code, The 270
Dawn of the Dead 236
Daybreakers 214
Dazed and Confused 196
Dekker, Thomas 268
Double Life, A 28, 30, 76, 105, 108, 112–18, 124
Dracula 157
Drayton, Michael 247
dumbing down 149, 153–5
dystopia 26, 214, 215

East is East 94
Eastern Promises 139
Elizabeth I *see* Queen Elizabeth

femme fatale 114, 115, 124, 132, 137, 286
film noir (also *noir*) 3, 4, 6, 12, 20, 27–30, 42, 76, 104–20, 122–38, 151, 215, 286
  see also neo-*noir*
Fistful of Dollars, A 59, 61
Flesh and Blood Show, The 117
For a Few Dollars More 59, 61
frontier 20–2, 36, 38, 39, 44, 46, 64

gangster 3, 6, 12, 20, 27–30, 104–5, 111, 116, 118–39, 286
Gaslight 73
genre theory 4, 6, 7, 128
Get Over It 201
Gnomeo & Juliet 3, 162
Godfather, The (trilogy) 119, 127, 139
Godfather Part III, The 132
Gone with the Wind 228, 229
Good, the Bad and the Ugly, The 59, 61
GoodFellas 127, 139
Gothic 123, 159, 213, 214, 223

Hamlet (Almereyda) 195
Hamlet (Branagh) 157
Hamlet (Olivier) 104, 120, 141n.27
Hamlet (Zeffirelli) 147
Hamlet 2 228
Hamnet (Shakespeare's son) 260, 277, 279
Harry and Tonto 22, 35, 62–7
Hathaway, Anne 256, 273–4, 279
Henry V (Olivier) 34
Henslowe, Philip 268, 275
Herbert, William, Earl of Pembroke 261–2
High Noon 46, 68n.8
horror 6, 8, 13, 25, 117, 147, 148, 156–60, 166, 191, 211–42
  see also undead; vampire; zombie
House of Strangers 42–3, 119
hybridity (of genres) 7, 26, 93, 148, 161, 165, 253, 255, 271

Immortal Gentleman, The 247, 249
Innocent Blood 159

Interview with the Vampire 158, 159
Iron Lady, The 164

Joe Macbeth 29, 105, 118–30, 132
Johnny Hamlet 7, 22, 35, 58–62
Jonson, Ben 247, 263, 268–9, 275, 279
Jubal 21, 35, 42, 46, 48–53
Julius Caesar (Mankiewicz) 42
Just One of the Guys 183

Killer's Kiss 117
Killers, The 131
King of New York 127
Kiss Me Deadly 116
Kiss Me Kate 54, 55
Kiss of Death 116
Knight's Tale, A 275

Land of the Dead 239
Last Movie, The 63, 64
Last Patriarch, The 119
Let Me In 212–15, 222–6, 240
Let the Right One In 214, 222
Life Goes On 26, 72, 93–100
Little Caesar 121, 122, 128, 131
Lone Ranger, The 65, 66
Lost and Delirious 4, 152, 156, 170–2, 176, 182, 191, 195–9, 200
Lost Boys, The 159
'lost years' 256–7, 272, 274
Lucy Negro *see* Dark Lady
Lucy, Sir Thomas 279

Macbeth (Polański) 130, 157
McCarthy era 53, 81
McLintock! 22, 35, 54–8
Magnificent Seven, The 34
Man Who Shot Liberty Valance, The 34, 65, 66
Marlowe, Christopher 268, 274–5
Mean Girls 183
melodrama 3, 6, 12, 20, 23–7, 42, 72–100, 108, 111, 112, 134, 215, 286–7
Men Are Not Gods 24, 72, 73–80, 115, 285
Men of Respect 29, 105, 119, 126, 127–34
Merchant of Venice, The (Radford) 3
Midsummer Night's Dream, A (Hoffman) 147

Miller's Crossing 127
monsters *see* undead; vampire; zombie
Motocrossed 183
Much Ado About Nothing (Branagh) 34
My Kingdom 119

Nashe, Thomas 268, 269
neo-*noir* 27–9, 105, 127, 134–5
Never Been Kissed 170, 173, 176–84, 188
new media 1, 8, 10, 285
Night of the Living Dead 157, 234
Ninotchka 73
noir see film noir
Nosferatu 156, 167n.24
Not Another Teen Movie 190

O 152, 153, 156, 170, 176, 189–95, 198
Old Bill Through the Ages 247
Omkara 34
Once Upon a Time in the West 60
Othello (Verdi) 194
Othello (Welles) 104
Oxford, Earl of 251, 263–9
  see also Vere, Edward de
Oxfordian theory 250, 263, 268

parody 8, 54, 56, 149, 158, 163, 166, 198, 203, 208n.64, 210–13, 218, 220–2, 227, 255, 262, 267, 273
pastiche 8, 149, 166, 222, 249, 255, 267, 276
Philip II, King of Spain 273, 274, 275
postmodern 8, 140, 148–9, 161–2, 164, 212, 218, 220, 249, 251, 255, 257, 259, 262, 267, 269, 270, 275–6, 287–8
Pretty in Pink 174
Pride and Prejudice and Zombies 160
Private Romeo 172, 200, 205n.2
Prizzi's Honor 124
Prospero's Books 262, 280n.6
Public Enemy 122

Queen Elizabeth 165, 169n.63, 247, 249, 252, 256–7, 272–4 *passim*, 276
Quella sporca storia nel West see Johnny Hamlet
queer film 152, 171–2, 177, 195–205
Quiet Man, The 54–5

rhizome 7–9
Rio Grande 54–5
Risky Business 180
Romeo and Juliet (Cukor) 72
Romeo and Juliet (Zeffirelli) 225, 241
Rosencrantz and Guildenstern are Undead 212, 218–22, 228, 230, 231

Scarface 128
science fiction 3, 26, 160, 241
Scotland, PA 123, 126, 198
Shakespeare, William
  Antony and Cleopatra 176, 197
  As You Like It 176–80 *passim*, 183, 276
  contemporaries of 263, 268, 275, 279
    see also individual names
  Hamlet 5, 34, 40, 58–62 *passim*, 104–12 *passim*, 210–12 *passim*, 218–22, 228–9, 264, 267, 275, 276, 279
  Henry IV 119, 135–7
  Henry V 34, 266–7
  Julius Caesar 10, 267
  King Lear 1–3 *passim*, 35, 42–4, 46, 64–65, 72, 86–8, 91, 93–7, 100, 102n.32, 119, 121, 122, 128
  lost years of *see* 'lost years'
  Macbeth 56, 104–5, 119–30, 134, 175, 176, 191, 197, 208n.64, 212, 231, 267, 276
  Merchant of Venice, The 179, 211
  Midsummer Night's Dream, A 171, 176, 199–201, 203, 229, 267
  Othello 3, 30, 35, 42, 46, 48–9, 51–2, 72–83, 104, 112–17, 152, 189, 191–2, 198, 211
  Richard II 267
  Richard III 119, 121, 267
  Romeo and Juliet 3, 93, 98, 127, 171, 211–12, 216–17, 222–3, 225–6, 232, 234–5, 238, 241, 247, 251, 256, 267, 276
  Sonnets 176, 250, 258–63, 276
  Taming of the Shrew, The 54–56, 173, 175, 177, 192, 230–1
  Tempest, The 35–7, 39, 41, 210, 211, 276
  Troilus and Cressida 34

Twelfth Night 4, 171, 176, 183–4, 188, 195, 197–8, 251, 267
Two Noble Kinsmen, The 278
Shakespeare in Love 161–3, 166, 169n.53, 248–63, 265–8, 271, 274–6
Shakespeare Wallah 228
Shakespeare Writing Julius Caesar 247
Shane 51–2
Shaun of the Dead 227, 233
She's All That 178
She's the Man 153, 170, 171, 173, 177, 182–90
Show Me Love 205
Southampton, Earl of 279
Spencer, Gabriel 268
sports film 152, 184, 190
Stage Beauty 3
Stagecoach 37
State of Grace 127
Strange Illusion 28, 105–12, 117
Street King 119

teen film (*also* teenpic; teen flick) 5, 7, 8, 13, 147–56, 159, 170–205, 241, 247
textual poaching 8, 15n.17, 188, 220
Thousand Acres, A 25, 72, 86–93, 100
Three Musketeers, The 270
thriller 6, 115–16, 136, 166, 224, 251, 253, 263–4, 270–1
Time Flies 247, 249
True Blood 158

undead 8, 13, 147–9, 156–61, 210–42, 247, 287
Underworld 212, 214, 215–18, 223
Upside Down 241
Upstart Crow 248, 273

vampire 13, 148, 156–60, 210–26, 231, 242
Van Helsing 216
Vanishing American, The 22
Vere, Edward de, 17th Earl of Oxford 264, 269
see also Oxford, Earl of

Wagon Master 52–3
Walsingham, Sir Francis 273
Warm Bodies 210, 212, 227, 232–42
Waste of Shame, A 165, 248, 250, 254, 257–63, 266, 271, 277
We Own the Night 30, 105, 119, 134–40
Were the World Mine 171–2, 176, 182, 199–205
West Side Story 225
western 3, 4, 6, 7, 12, 20–3, 30, 34–67, 122, 136, 151, 215, 286
revisionist 22, 35, 54, 57–8, 62–3, 65, spaghetti 22, 34, 35, 58–62
Whirlpool 108
Wild and the Dirty, The see Johnny Hamlet
Wild Bunch, The 65
Will 248, 250, 254, 275
William Shakespeare's Romeo + Juliet 34, 147, 150, 154, 155, 162, 171, 173, 194, 225, 241
woman's film 23–6, 72–3, 79, 87, 287
see also melodrama
Wriothsley, Henry 259

Yellow Sky 21, 35, 36–42, 45, 68n.11

zombie 1, 13, 148, 156–60, 210–14, 217–18, 226–42, 289
Zombie Hamlet 212, 227, 228–32, 233
Zombieland 227, 235, 237

www.ingramcontent.com/pod-product-compliance
Lightning Source LLC
Chambersburg PA
CBHW050202240426
4367ICB00013B/2216

EU authorised representative for GPSR:
Easy Access System Europe, Mustamäe tee 50,
10621 Tallinn, Estonia
gpsr.requests@easproject.com